Windows 7
FOR
DUMMIES®

by Andy Rathbone

John Wiley & Sons, Inc.

Windows® 7 For Dummies®

Published by
John Wiley & Sons, Inc.
111 River Street
Hoboken, NJ 07030-5774

www.wiley.com

Copyright © 2009 by John Wiley & Sons, Inc., Hoboken, New Jersey

Published by John Wiley & Sons, Inc., Hoboken, New Jersey

Published simultaneously in Canada

About the Author

Andy Rathbone started geeking around with computers in 1985 when he bought a 26-pound portable CP/M Kaypro 2X. Like other nerds of the day, he soon began playing with null-modem adapters, dialing computer bulletin boards, and working part-time at Radio Shack.

He wrote articles for various techie publications before moving to computer books in 1992. He's written the *Windows For Dummies* series, *Upgrading and Fixing PCs For Dummies*, *TiVo For Dummies*, *PCs: The Missing Manual*, and many other computer books.

Today, he has more than 15 million copies of his books in print, and they've been translated into more than 30 languages. You can reach Andy at his Web site, www.andyrathbone.com.

Author's Acknowledgments

Special thanks to Dan Gookin, Matt Wagner, Tina Rathbone, Steve Hayes, Nicole Sholly, Virginia Sanders, and James Kelly.

Thanks also to all the folks I never meet in editorial, sales, marketing, proofreading, layout, graphics, and manufacturing who work hard to bring you this book.

Publisher's Acknowledgments

We're proud of this book; please send us your comments at http://dummies.custhelp.com. For other comments, please contact our Customer Care Department within the U.S. at 877-762-2974, outside the U.S. at 317-572-3993, or fax 317-572-4002.

Some of the people who helped bring this book to market include the following:

Acquisitions and Editorial

Project Editor: Nicole Sholly

Executive Editor: Steve Hayes

Copy Editor: Virginia Sanders

Technical Editor: James F. Kelly

Editorial Manager: Kevin Kirschner

Sr. Editorial Assistant: Cherie Case

Cartoons: Rich Tennant
(www.the5thwave.com)

Composition Services

Project Coordinator: Katherine Crocker

Layout and Graphics: Christin Swinford, Ronald Terry

Proofreaders: Laura L. Bowman, John Greenough

Indexer: Potomac Indexing, LLC

Publishing and Editorial for Technology Dummies

    Richard Swadley, Vice President and Executive Group Publisher

    Andy Cummings, Vice President and Publisher

    Mary Bednarek, Executive Acquisitions Director

    Mary C. Corder, Editorial Director

Publishing for Consumer Dummies

    Kathleen Nebenhaus, Vice President and Executive Publisher

Composition Services

    Debbie Stailey, Director of Composition Services

Contents at a Glance

Table of Contents

Introduction

Welcome to *Windows 7 For Dummies,* the world's best-selling book about Windows 7!

This book's popularity probably boils down to this simple fact: Some people want to be Windows whizzes. They love interacting with dialog boxes. Some randomly press keys in the hope of discovering hidden, undocumented features. A few memorize long strings of computer commands while washing their hair.

And you? Well, you're no dummy, that's for sure. But when it comes to Windows and computers, the fascination just isn't there. You want to get your work done, stop, and move on to something more important. You have no intention of changing, and there's nothing wrong with that.

That's where this book comes in handy. Instead of making you a whiz at Windows, it merely dishes out chunks of useful computing information when you need them. Instead of becoming a Windows 7 expert, you'll know just enough to get by quickly, cleanly, and with a minimum of pain so that you can move on to the more pleasant things in life.

About This Book

Don't try to read this book in one sitting; there's no need. Instead, treat this book like a dictionary or an encyclopedia. Turn to the page with the information you need and say, "Ah, so that's what they're talking about." Then put down the book and move on.

Don't bother trying to memorize all the Windows 7 jargon, such as Select the Menu Item from the Drop-Down List Box. Leave that stuff for the computer enthusiasts. In fact, if anything technical comes up in a chapter, a road sign warns you well in advance. Depending on your mood, you can either slow down to read it or speed on around it.

Instead of fancy computer jargon, this book covers subjects like these, all discussed in plain English:

- ✔ Keeping your computer safe and secure
- ✔ Finding, starting, and closing programs
- ✔ Locating the file you saved or downloaded yesterday

 ✒ Setting up a computer for the whole family to use

 ✒ Copying information to and from a CD or DVD

 ✒ Working with your digital camera's photos and making slide shows

 ✒ Printing your work

 ✒ Creating a network between PCs to share an Internet connection or printer

 ✒ Fixing Windows 7 when it's misbehaving

There's nothing to memorize and nothing to learn. Just turn to the right page, read the brief explanation, and get back to work. Unlike other books, this one enables you to bypass the technical hoopla and still get your work done.

How to Use This Book

Something in Windows 7 will eventually leave you scratching your head. No other program brings so many buttons, bars, and babble to the screen. When something in Windows 7 leaves you stumped, use this book as a reference. Look for the troublesome topic in this book's table of contents or index. The table of contents lists chapter and section titles and page numbers. The index lists topics and page numbers. Page through the table of contents or index to the spot that deals with that particular bit of computer obscurity, read only what you have to, close the book, and apply what you've read.

If you're feeling spunky and want to find out more, read a little further in the bulleted items below each section. You can find a few completely voluntary extra details, tips, or cross-references to check out. There's no pressure, though. You aren't forced to discover anything that you don't want to or that you simply don't have time for.

If you have to type something into the computer, you'll see easy-to-follow bold text like this:

Type **Media Player** into the Search box.

In the preceding example, you type the words *Media Player* and then press the keyboard's Enter key. Typing words into a computer can be confusing, so a description follows that explains what you should be seeing on the screen.

This book doesn't wimp out by saying, "For further information, consult your manual." Windows 7 doesn't even *come* with a manual. This book also doesn't contain information about running specific Windows software packages, such as Microsoft Office. Windows 7 is complicated enough on its own! Luckily, other *For Dummies* books mercifully explain most popular software packages.

Don't feel abandoned, though. This book covers Windows in plenty of detail for you to get the job done. Plus, if you have questions or comments about *Windows 7 For Dummies,* feel free to drop me a line on my Web site at www. andyrathbone.com.

Finally, keep in mind that this book is a *reference*. It's not designed to teach you how to use Windows 7 like an expert, heaven forbid. Instead, this book dishes out enough bite-sized chunks of information so that you don't *have* to learn Windows.

And What about You?

Chances are good that you already own Windows 7 or are thinking about upgrading. You know what *you* want to do with your computer. The problem lies in making the *computer* do what you want it to do. You've gotten by one way or another, perhaps with the help of a computer guru — either a friend at the office, somebody down the street, or your fourth-grader.

But when your computer guru isn't around, this book can be a substitute during your times of need. (Keep a doughnut nearby in case you need a quick bribe.)

How This Book Is Organized

The information in this book has been well sifted. This book contains seven parts, and I divide each part into chapters relating to the part's theme. With an even finer knife, I divide each chapter into short sections to help you figure out a bit of Windows 7 weirdness. Sometimes, you may find what you're looking for in a small, boxed sidebar. Other times, you may need to cruise through an entire section or chapter. It's up to you and the particular task at hand.

Here are the categories (the envelope, please).

Part 1: Windows 7 Stuff Everybody Thinks You Already Know

This part dissects Windows 7's backbone: its opening screen and username buttons, the mammoth Start button menu that fetches all your important stuff, and your computer's desktop — the background where all your programs live. It explains how to move windows around, for example, and click the right buttons at the right time. It explains the Windows 7 stuff that everybody thinks that you already know.

Part II: Working with Programs and Files

Windows 7 comes with bunches of free programs. Finding and starting the programs, however, often proves to be a chore. This part of the book shows you how to prod programs into action. If an important file or program has vanished from the radar, you discover how to make Windows 7 dredge your computer's crowded cupboards and bring it back.

Part III: Getting Things Done on the Internet

Turn here for a crash course in today's computing playground, the Internet. This part explains how to send e-mail and globetrot across Web sites. Best yet, an entire chapter explains how to do it all safely, without viruses, spyware, and annoying pop-up ads.

A section explains Internet Explorer's built-in security tools. They stop evil phishing sites from tricking you and keep Web parasites from attaching themselves to your board as you Web surf.

Part IV: Customizing and Upgrading Windows 7

When Windows 7 needs a jolt, fix it by flipping one of the switches hidden in its Control Panel, described here. Another chapter explains computer maintenance you can easily perform yourself, reducing your repair bills. You discover how to share your computer with several people in your family or in a shared apartment — without letting anybody peek into anybody else's information.

And when you're ready to add a second computer, head to the networking chapter for quick instructions on linking computers to share an Internet connection, files, and a printer, as well.

Part V: Music, Movies, Memories (And Photos, Too)

Turn here for information on playing music CDs, DVDs, digital music, and movies. Buy some cheap CDs and create your own greatest hits CDs from your favorite tunes. (Or just copy a CD so that your favorite one doesn't get scratched in the car.)

Digital camera owners should visit the chapter on transferring pictures from your camera to your computer, organizing the pictures, and e-mailing them to friends. Bought a camcorder? Head to the section that explains how to edit out the dopey parts with the Windows Live Movie Maker program and save your completed masterwork onto a DVD the relatives will *enjoy* for a change.

Part VI: Help!

Although glass doesn't shatter when Windows crashes, it still hurts. In this part, you find some soothing salves for the most painful irritations. Plus, you find ways to unleash the Windows 7 program's team of troubleshooters.

Stuck with the problem of moving your files from an old computer to a new one? You can find help here, as well. (If you're ready to upgrade your Windows XP or Vista computer to Windows 7, check out the appendix, too, which holds complete instructions.)

Part VII: The Part of Tens

Everybody loves lists (except during tax time). This part contains lists of Windows-related trivia, such as ten aggravating things about Windows 7 (and how to fix them). As a bonus for the laptoppers, I've collected Windows 7's most useful laptop tips and placed them into one chapter, complete with step-by-step instructions for the most frequently used laptopping tasks.

Icons Used in This Book

It just takes a glance at Windows 7 to notice its *icons*, which are little push-button pictures for starting various programs. The icons in this book fit right in. They're even a little easier to figure out.

Watch out! This signpost warns you that pointless technical information is coming around the bend. Swerve away from this icon to stay safe from awful technical drivel.

This icon alerts you about juicy information that makes computing easier: a tried-and-true method for keeping the cat from sleeping on top of the monitor, for example.

Don't forget to remember these important points. (Or at least dog-ear the pages so that you can look them up again a few days later.)

The computer won't explode while you're performing the delicate operations associated with this icon. Still, wearing gloves and proceeding with caution is a good idea.

Are you moving to Windows 7 from Windows Vista? This icon alerts you to areas where 7 works significantly differently from its predecessor.

More than a few folks skipped Windows Vista altogether. If you're a Vista skipper, this XP icon alerts you to the many places where Windows 7 works significantly differently from Windows XP. (Keep an eye out for the New in Windows 7 icon, too, because you've missed quite a few changes.)

Where to Go from Here

Now, you're ready for action. Give the pages a quick flip and scan a section or two that you know you'll need later. Please remember, this is *your* book — your weapon against the computer nerds who've inflicted this whole complicated computer concept on you. Please circle any paragraphs you find useful, highlight key concepts, add your own sticky notes, and doodle in the margins next to the complicated stuff.

The more you mark up your book, the easier it will be for you to find all the good stuff again.

Part I

Windows 7 Stuff Everybody Thinks You Already Know

The 5th Wave   By Rich Tennant

"We're much better prepared for this upgrade than before. We're giving users additional training, better manuals, and a morphine drip."

In this part . . .

Most people are dragged into Windows 7 without a choice. Their new computers probably came with Windows 7 already installed. Or maybe the office switched to Windows 7, and everyone has to learn it except for the boss, who still doesn't have a computer. Or maybe Microsoft's marketing hype pushed you into it.

Whatever your situation, this part gives a refresher on Windows basics and buzzwords like dragging and dropping, cutting and pasting, and tugging at vanishing toolbars.

This part explains how Windows 7 has changed things for the better, and it warns you when Windows 7 has messed things up completely.

Chapter 1

What Is Windows 7?

Chances are good that you've heard about Windows: the boxes and windows and mouse pointer that greet you whenever you turn on your computer. In fact, millions of people all over the world are puzzling over it as you read this book. Almost every new computer sold today comes with a copy of Windows preinstalled — cheerfully greeting you when first turned on.

This chapter helps you understand why Windows lives inside your computer and introduces Microsoft's latest Windows version, called *Windows 7*. I explain how Windows 7 differs from previous Windows versions, whether you should upgrade to Windows 7, and how well your faithful old PC will weather the upgrade.

What Is Windows 7, and Why Are You Using It?

Created and sold by a company called Microsoft, Windows isn't like your usual software that lets you write term papers or send angry e-mails to mail-order companies. No, Windows is an *operating system,* meaning it controls the way you work with your computer. It's been around for more than 20 years, and the latest whiz-bang version is called *Windows 7,* shown in Figure 1-1.

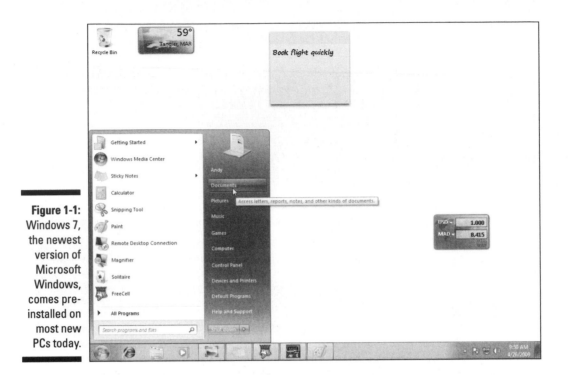

Figure 1-1:
Windows 7,
the newest
version of
Microsoft
Windows,
comes pre-
installed on
most new
PCs today.

Windows gets its name from all the cute little windows it places on your monitor. Each window shows information, such as a picture, a program that you're running, or a baffling technical reprimand. You can put several windows on-screen at the same time and jump from window to window, visiting different programs. You can also enlarge a window to fill the entire screen.

Like the mother with the whistle in the lunch court, Windows controls every window and each part of your computer. When you turn on your computer, Windows jumps onto the screen and supervises any running programs. Throughout all this action, Windows keeps things running smoothly, even if the programs start throwing food at each other.

In addition to controlling your computer and bossing around your programs, Windows 7 comes with a bunch of free programs. Although your computer can run without these programs, they're nice to have. These programs let you do different things, like write and print letters, browse the Internet, play music, and even create a slide show from your vacation photos and burn it to a DVD — automatically.

And why are you using Windows 7? If you're like most people, you didn't have much choice. Nearly every computer sold since October 22, 2009 comes with Windows 7 preinstalled. A few people escaped Windows by buying Apple computers (those nicer-looking computers that cost a lot more). But chances are good that you, your neighbors, your boss, your kids at school, and millions of other people around the world are using Windows.

✔ Microsoft took pains (and several years of work) to make Windows 7 the most secure version of Windows yet. (Just ask people who upgraded from previous versions.)

✔ Windows makes it easy for several people to share a single computer. Each person receives his or her own user account. When users click their name at the Windows opening screen, they see their *own* work — just the way they left it. Windows 7 includes controls for parents to limit the time their kids spend on the PC, as well as what programs they can open.

✔ Windows includes a new backup program that makes it easier to do what you should have been doing all along: Make copies of your important files every night, a task I describe in Chapter 12.

✔ The powerful new search program and library system in Windows 7 mean that you can forget about where you've stored your files. To find a missing file, just click the Start menu and type what that file contained: a few words in a document, the name of the band singing the song, or even the year your favorite jazz albums were released.

Should I Bother Switching to Windows 7?

Microsoft hopes *everybody* will immediately switch to Windows 7. Because people buying new PCs automatically already receive Windows 7 preinstalled on their PC, Microsoft is targeting two other groups: people using Windows XP and people using Windows Vista.

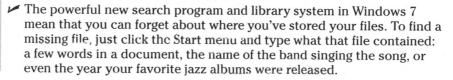

Separating the ads from the features

Microsoft may tout Windows as your helpful computing companion, always keeping your best interests in mind, but that's not really true. Windows always keeps *Microsoft's* interests in mind. You'll find that out as soon as you call Microsoft for help with making Windows work right. They charge more than $50 per call.

Microsoft also uses Windows to plug its own products and services. For example, Internet Explorer's Favorites area, a place for you to add your favorite Web destinations, comes stuffed with Microsoft's Web sites.

Simply put, Windows not only controls your computer, but also serves as a huge Microsoft advertising vehicle. Treat the built-in advertising flyers as a salesperson's knock on your door.

The next two sections describe what Windows 7 offers to Windows Vista owners, and to those holdouts still running Windows XP.

Why Vista owners will like Windows 7

Vista owners will rejoice at Windows 7, with many folks calling the new operating system "What Windows Vista should have been." Windows 7 certainly isn't perfect, but it's a welcome relief for Windows Vista owners. Here's why:

- **Easy upgrade path:** As a perk for suffering through Vista, you can upgrade to Windows 7 simply by slipping in a Windows 7 Upgrade DVD. Your programs, printer, and nearly everything else that worked with Vista work fine with Windows 7. Windows XP owners face a dirty chore: They must erase their hard drives and install Windows 7 from scratch.

- **No more nag screens:** Easily the most loudly cursed feature of Windows Vista, User Account Control (UAC) perpetually popped up messages asking if you're *sure* you want to do something. Windows 7 comes with a toned-down version that merely warns you if something drastic might happen. You can even adjust UAC's warning level to match your comfort level, from paranoid to relaxed.

- **Streamlined controls:** Vista demanded many keystrokes and clicks to accomplish what Windows 7 does in a few. In Vista, for example, trying to turn off a PC brought up two shortcut icons and an arrow that fetches a seven-option menu. Windows 7's single-click "Shut Down" key does what most folks want: Saves work, closes programs, and turns off the PC.

- **Better backup:** In an effort to simplify backing up your PC, Vista made backup copies of *everything,* even if you wanted to back up only a few files or folders. Windows 7, by contrast, lets you back up everything, but it also offers an option for selecting only a few things to back up.

- **Runs better on laptops:** Vista's sloth-like performance upset many laptop owners. Many new netbooks — ultralight laptops built for on-the-road Internet access and word processing — couldn't even run Vista, forcing Microsoft to extend the Windows XP expiration deadline twice.

Why Windows XP owners should switch to Windows 7

Microsoft releases a new version of Windows every few years. If you bought your PC between 2001 and 2006, you've probably grown accustomed to the mechanics of Windows XP. That leaves the nagging question, why bother upgrading to Windows 7 when Windows XP works just fine?

So, what *doesn't* Windows 7 have for Vista upgraders?

With all the nifty new items stuffed into Windows 7, what *doesn't* it include? Plenty. Microsoft axed the following programs from Windows Vista when creating Windows 7:

✔ **Free programs:** Windows Mail, Windows Photo Gallery, Windows Movie Maker, and Windows Calendar no longer come with Windows 7. That's right — Windows 7 doesn't come with an e-mail program. Instead, Microsoft wants you to download replacement programs from the Web. I cover e-mail replacements in Chapter 9 (e-mail), and I cover photos and moviemaking replacements in Chapter 16. (I'm afraid I don't have space to cover the calendar replacement.)

✔ **Quick Launch toolbar:** This handy repository for favorite programs no longer lives on the taskbar beneath the Start menu. Instead, Microsoft redesigned the taskbar to hold icons of favorite programs *and* currently running programs. I cover the taskbar in Chapter 2.

✔ **InkBall:** Although axing this game isn't as inconvenient as ditching an e-mail program, many will miss this little "drop the ball in the hole" timewaster.

✔ **Sidebar:** Windows Vista's Sidebar clung to the side of the desktop, housing gadgets to track the stock market, activities of friends, and even the weather. The Sidebar's gone, but the gadgets remain, now sprinkled freely upon your desktop.

Actually, if Windows XP is running just fine, you may not need Windows 7. But because your PC could be almost six years old — an antique in the tech world — Microsoft hopes the following improvements in Windows 7 will push your hand toward your credit card:

✔ **DVD burning:** More than five years after DVD burners hit the market, Windows can finally take advantage of them without third-party software. Windows 7 can copy files and movies to DVDs as well as to CDs. Its DVD Maker program gathers your vacation photos and burns a slick slide show onto a DVD, ready for passing out to every yoga retreat attendee.

✔ **Easier file searches:** Windows XP really drags its feet when searching for files. Searching for a filename takes several minutes on a crowded hard drive, and if you're searching your files for a particular word or phrase, you're in for a long weekend. Windows 7, by contrast, spends its idle time fine-tuning an index of every word on your hard drive. Type a word from a file's name or contents into the Start menu's Search box, and Windows 7 quickly finds the goods.

✔ **New Internet Explorer:** Windows 7's new Internet Explorer 8 lets you surf the Web more easily and securely. It has the old standbys — tabbed browsing, RSS feeds, and a filter alerting you to potential fraudulent Web sites — and other new features I cover in Chapter 8.

✔ **Media Center:** This entertainment center not only plays DVDs and music but also lets you watch TV on your PC and even record shows onto your hard drive for later viewing. Recording TV shows requires a PC with a TV Tuner in your PC, an upgrade I cover in one of my other books, *Upgrading and Fixing PCs For Dummies,* published by Wiley Publishing, Inc.

✔ **Taskbar:** Microsoft spent some time building on Vista's three-dimensional look. The new taskbar in Windows 7 adds pop-up thumbnails, shown in Figure 1-2, that help you find a lost window. Or, right-click a taskbar icon to see more information about it — your recent history of browsed Web sites, for example, is shown in Figure 1-3.

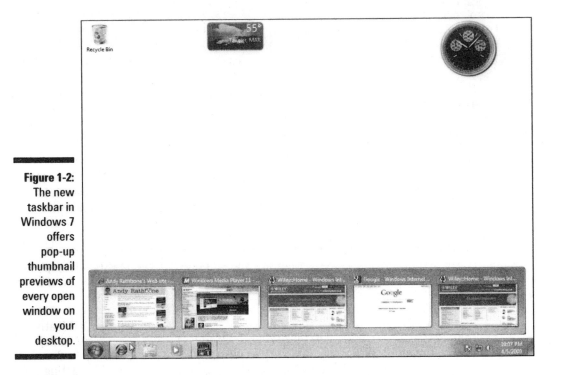

Figure 1-2:
The new taskbar in Windows 7 offers pop-up thumbnail previews of every open window on your desktop.

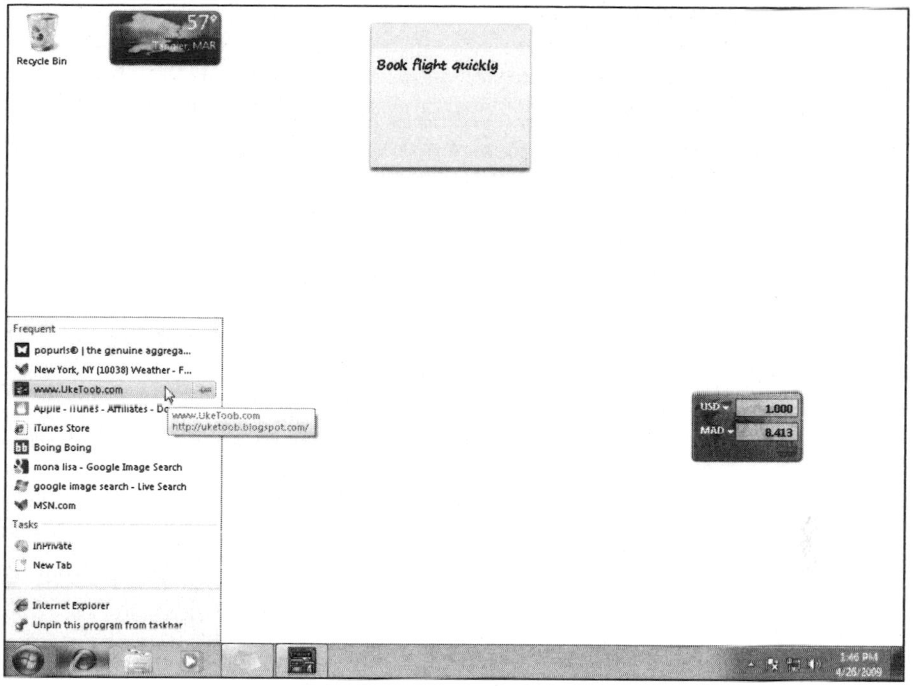

Figure 1-3:
Right-click
an icon on
Windows 7's
new taskbar
to see more
information,
including
a list of
recently
viewed
Web sites
in Internet
Explorer.

Can My PC Still Run Windows 7?

If your PC already runs Windows Vista, it will probably run Windows 7. In fact, Windows 7 runs better on some PCs, mostly laptops, than Windows Vista does.

If your PC already runs Windows XP well, it will probably run Windows 7, but perhaps not at its best. Upgrading your PC with a few things will help Windows 7 run better, a job I tackle in *Upgrading and Fixing PCs For Dummies,* 8th Edition. Here's the shopping list:

✔ **Video:** Windows 7 requires powerful graphics for its fanciest 3-D features. Upgraded video cards cost around $50, and they're not available for laptops. But if your PC's video lacks the muscle and your wallet lacks the cash, don't despair. Windows 7 simply slips into more casual clothes, letting your PC run without the 3-D views.

✔ **Memory:** Windows 7 loves memory. For best results, your PC should have 1GB of memory or more. Memory's easy to install and relatively cheap, so don't skimp here.

✔ **DVD drive:** Unlike Windows XP, which comes on a CD, Windows 7 (like Windows Vista) comes on a *DVD*. That means your PC needs a working DVD drive to install it. That probably won't rule out many PCs these days, but it may rule out some older laptops and netbooks.

Windows 7 can run nearly any program that runs on Windows Vista, and it can run a great number of Windows XP programs. Some older programs, however, won't work, including most security-based programs, such as antivirus, firewall, and security programs. You'll need to contact the program's manufacturer to see whether it'll give you a free upgrade.

Shopping for a new PC to run Windows 7? To see how well a particular showroom PC will handle Windows 7, click the PC's Start button, choose Control Panel, and open the System and Security category. In the System area, choose Check the Windows Experience Index. Windows tests the PC and gives it a grade ranging from 1 (terrible) to 7.9 (extraordinary).

Not sure what version of Windows your PC has? Right-click Computer from the Start menu and choose Properties. The screen that appears states your Windows version.

Speeding up Windows 7 on a laptop or an old PC

Both Windows Vista and Windows 7 love slick graphics, but all those smooth edges and fancy colors can bog down a laptop or an old PC. Follow these steps to strip away the eye-candy and make Windows 7 run as quickly as possible:

1. **Click the Start button, right-click the Computer icon, and choose Properties.**

   The Computer icon lives on the Start menu's right side.

2. **Click Advanced System Settings, found in the window's left pane.**

You may need to type in a password from an Administrator account to enter this mysterious settings area.

3. **In the Performance area, click the Settings button, click the Adjust For Best Performance button, and click OK.**

These steps revert your system to the look of previous Windows versions that didn't rely on fancy graphics. To return to Windows 7's normal look, repeat the steps, but in Step 3, click the button called Let Windows Choose What's Best For My Computer.

The Flavors of Windows 7

Windows XP came in two easy-to-understand versions: one for home and one for business. Windows Vista split into five different versions, each with a different price tag, and a confusing array of features. Windows 7 ups the confusion level with six versions, but the versions are much easier to figure out.

The vast majority of consumers will choose Windows 7 Home Premium, and most businesses will choose Windows 7 Professional. Still, to clear up the confusion, I describe all six versions in Table 1-1.

Table 1-1	The Flavors of Windows 7
The Version of Windows 7	*What It Does*
Windows 7 Starter	This stripped-down version of Windows 7 runs mostly on netbooks — tiny PCs that lack the power for much more than Web browsing and simple word processing.
Windows 7 Home Basic	Designed for developing countries, this version contains everything from the Starter edition and tosses in better graphics, Internet connection sharing, and settings for more powerful laptops.
Windows 7 Home Premium	Built to fill most consumers' needs, this version includes programs to let people watch and record TV on their PC, as well as create DVDs from their camcorder footage.
Windows 7 Professional	Aimed at the business market, this features everything from Home Premium, as well as tools used by small businesses: extra networking features, for example, and similar business tools.
Windows 7 Enterprise	Microsoft sells this large business version in bulk to large businesses.
Windows 7 Ultimate	This version aims at the wallets of information technology specialists who spend much of their lives in front of their keyboards. If you're reading this book, you don't need this version.

Although six versions may seem complicated, choosing the one you need isn't that difficult. And because Microsoft stuffed all the versions on your Windows 7 DVD, you can upgrade at any time simply by whipping out the credit card and unlocking the features in a different version.

Unlike with Vista, each version contains all the features of the version below it. Windows 7 Professional contains everything found in Windows 7 Home Premium.

Here are some guidelines for choosing the version you need:

- ✔ If you'll be using your PC at home, pick up **Windows 7 Home Premium.**

- ✔ If you need to connect to a domain through a work network — and you'll know if you're doing it — you want **Windows 7 Professional.**

- ✔ If you're a computer industry professional, you should get your hands on **Windows 7 Ultimate** because it includes *everything* found in the other versions.

- ✔ If you're a computer tech who works for businesses, go ahead and argue with your boss over whether you need **Windows 7 Professional** or **Windows 7 Enterprise**. The boss will make the decision based on whether its a small company (Windows Professional) or a large company (Windows Enterprise).

If you own a netbook — a tiny laptop — that runs Windows 7, you can upgrade to a more powerful version right from the Start menu.

That inexpensive Windows 7 Home Basic version isn't sold in the United States. It's sold at reduced prices in developing nations like Malaysia. (It's not really a goodwill gesture as much as it's an attempt to reduce software piracy.)

Windows 7 around the world

Because of legal issues in Europe, Microsoft considered releasing a special "E" version of Windows 7 in Europe that wouldn't include Internet Explorer. The company changed its mind, however, and now Europeans will receive the same version of Windows 7 sold around the world. When Europeans first install Windows 7 or turn on a new Windows 7 PC, they'll see a ballot screen letting them choose their preferred browser, be it Internet Explorer, Firefox, or another browser. Choose the browser, and Windows 7 automatically installs it, if necessary, and begins using it.

Chapter 2

The Desktop, Start Menu, Taskbar, Gadgets, and Other Windows 7 Mysteries

. . . .

In This Chapter

▶ Starting Windows 7

▶ Entering a password

▶ Logging on to Windows 7

▶ Using the desktop and other Windows 7 features

▶ Logging off of Windows 7

▶ Turning off your computer

. . . .

This chapter provides a drive-by tour of Windows 7. You turn on your computer, start Windows, and spend a few minutes gawking at Windows 7's various neighborhoods: the desktop, the taskbar, the Start menu, and the environmentally correct (and compassionate) Recycle Bin.

The programs you're using hang out on the Windows *desktop* (a fancy word for the Windows background). The taskbar serves as a head turner, letting you move from one program to another. To invite yet more programs onto the desktop, drop by the Start menu: It's full of push buttons that let you add programs to your mix.

Want to get rid of something? Dump it into the Recycle Bin, where it either fades away with time or, if necessary, can be safely revived.

If you're installing or upgrading your PC to Windows 7, I give the complete step-by-step instructions in this book's appendix.

Being Welcomed to the World of Windows 7

Starting Windows 7 is as easy as turning on your computer — Windows 7 leaps onto the screen automatically with a futuristic flourish. But before you can start working, Windows 7 may throw you a fastball with its first screen: Windows wants you to *log on*, as shown in Figure 2-1, by clicking your name.

I've customized my Welcome screen. Yours will look different. If you don't see a username listed for you on the Welcome screen, you have three options:

 ✔ **If you just bought the computer, use the account named Administrator.** Designed to give the owner full power over the computer, the Administrator account user can set up new accounts for other people, install programs, start an Internet connection, and access *all* the files on the computer — even those belonging to other people. Windows 7 needs at least one person to act as administrator. Hit Chapter 13 if you care about this stuff.

Figure 2-1: Windows 7 wants all users to log on so that it knows who's using the computer at all times.

✔ **Use the Guest account.** Designed for household visitors, this account lets guests, such as the babysitter or visiting relatives, use the computer temporarily. (It's turned on or off in the Add or Remove User Accounts area, described in Chapter 13.)

✔ **No Guest account *and* no user?** Then find out who owns the computer and beg that person to set up a username for you. (If the owner doesn't know how, show her Chapter 13, where I explain how to set up a user account.)

Don't *want* to log on at the Welcome screen? These hidden Welcome screen buttons control other options:

✔ The little blue button in the screen's bottom-left corner, shown in Figure 2-1 and the margin, customizes Windows 7 for people with physical challenges in hearing, sight, or manual dexterity, all covered in Chapter 11. If you push this button by mistake, press Cancel to remove the option menu from your screen without changing any settings.

✔ The little red button in the screen's bottom-right corner, shown in Figure 2-1 and the margin, lets you turn off your PC. (If you've accidentally clicked it and turned off your PC, don't panic. Press your PC's power button, and your PC will return to this screen.)

✔ Click the little arrow next to the red button, and Windows 7 will end your session by either hibernating, turning off your PC, or restarting — options all explained at this chapter's end.

Want Windows 7 to revert automatically to this safe, password-protected logon screen whenever you leave your desk for a few minutes? After you enter your username and password, right-click on the desktop and choose Personalize. Choose the Screen Saver option in the lower-right corner and select the On Resume, Display Logon Screen check box. Feel free to adjust the number of minutes before the logon screen kicks in. Then click OK to save your settings and close the window.

Fiddling around with user accounts

Windows 7 allows several people to work on the same computer, yet it keeps everybody's work separate. To do that, it needs to know who's currently sitting in front of the keyboard. When you *log on* — introduce yourself — by clicking your *username,* as shown in Figure 2-1, Windows 7 presents your personalized desktop, ready for you to make your own personalized mess.

When you're through working or just feel like taking a break, log off (explained at this chapter's end) so that somebody else can use the computer. Later, when you log back on, your messy desktop will be waiting for you.

Running Windows 7 for the first time

If you've just installed Windows 7 or you're turning on your computer for the first time, click the Start button and click Getting Started to visit the Welcome Center. The Welcome Center presents the following buttons customized to your particular PC:

✔ **Go Online to Find Out What's New in Windows 7:** Handy for those upgrading from Windows XP or Windows Vista, this button takes you online and introduces you to new features in Windows 7.

✔ **Personalize Windows:** Head here to splash a new photo across your desktop, change colors, or tweak your monitor (all covered in Chapter 11).

✔ **Transfer Files and Settings from Another Computer:** Just turned on your *new* Windows 7 PC? This helpful area lets you lug all your old PC's files and settings to your new one, a chore I walk you through in Chapter 19.

✔ **Use a Homegroup to Share with Other Computers in Your Home:** In Windows 7, the new *Homegroups* offer a simpler way to share information with other PCs in a home (covered in Chapter 14).

✔ **Choose When to Be Notified about Changes to Your Computer:** Windows Vista owners should drop by here. It lets you adjust how much your PC should nag you when potentially unsafe situations arise, which I describe in Chapter 10.

✔ **Go Online to Get Windows Live Essentials:** Surprise! Windows 7 no longer includes an e-mail program. (Nor does it have Vista's Calendar, photo-editing tools, or movie-editing program.) Instead, Microsoft wants you to download its new Windows Live suite of replacement programs. Or, you can sign up for an e-mail account with Microsoft's two biggest competitors, Google's Gmail (www.gmail.com) and Yahoo! (www.mail.yahoo.com). I cover e-mail in Chapter 9 and the Windows Live photo- and movie-editing programs in Chapter 16.

✔ **Back Up Your Files:** Computers can trash your work faster than you can create it, so I describe how to back up your files in Chapter 10.

✔ **Add New Users to Your Computer:** Ignore this one unless other people will be sharing your PC. If that's the case, click here to set up accounts for them on your PC. This area also lets you control what your kids (or roommates) can do on your PC, covered in Chapter 13.

✔ **Change the Size of the Text on Your Screen:** A boon for the baby boomers, this quick fix helps avoid eyestrain from tiny text.

To see more information about any of these tasks, click the button once. Or double-click a button to move directly to that particular chore.

Although you may turn your desktop into a mess, it's your *own* mess. When you return to the computer, your letters will be just as you saved them. Jerry hasn't accidentally deleted your files or folders while playing Widget Squash. Tina's desktop contains links to her favorite Web sites. And all of Steve's Miles Davis MP3s stay in his own personalized Music folder.

Of course, the first big question boils down to this: How do you customize the picture next to your username, like my face in Figure 2-1? After you've logged on, open the Start menu and click the little picture at the top of the Start menu. Windows conveniently opens a menu where you can choose Change Your Picture. (For ideas, click Browse for More Pictures and look through the digital photos you've saved in your Pictures folder. I explain how to crop photos to a nice head shot in Chapter 16.)

Keeping your account private with a password

Because Windows 7 lets bunches of people use the same computer, how do you stop Rob from reading Diane's love letters to Henry Rollins? How can Josh keep Grace from deleting his *Star Wars* movie trailers? Windows 7's optional *password* solves some of those problems.

By typing a secret password when logging on, as shown in Figure 2-2, you enable your computer to recognize *you* and nobody else. If you protect your username with a password, nobody can access your files (except for the computer's administrator, who can peek anywhere — and even delete your account).

To set up or change your password, follow these steps:

1. **Click the Start button and then click Control Panel.**

2. **In the Control Panel, click User Accounts and Family Safety and then choose Change Your Windows Password.**

   If your Control Panel contains dozens of icons (*way* more than the usual eight), choose the User Accounts icon.

3. **Choose Create a Password for Your Account or Change Your Password.**

   The wording that you see depends on whether you're creating a new password or changing an old one.

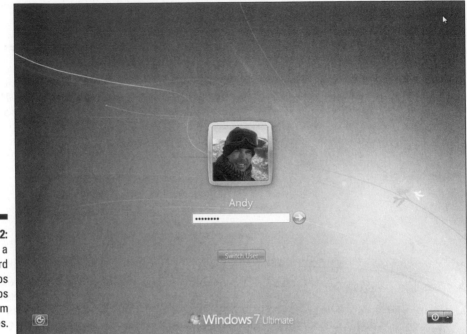

Figure 2-2:
Creating a
password
keeps
snoops
away from
your files.

4. **Type a password that will be easy for you — and nobody else — to remember.**

Keep your password short and sweet: the name of your favorite vegetable, for example, or your dental floss brand. To beef up its security level, embed a number in the password, like **3carrots** or **Ski2Alps**. (Don't use these exact two examples, though, because they've probably been added to every password cracker's arsenal by now.)

5. **If asked, retype that same password in the Confirm New Password box, so Windows knows you're not making a typo.**

6. **Type a hint that reminds you — and only you — of your password.**

7. **Click the Create Password button.**

8. **When the User Accounts screen returns, choose Create a Password Reset Disk from along the screen's left side.**

Windows 7 walks you through the process of creating a Password Reset Disk from a floppy disk, memory card, or USB flash drive. (Head to Chapter 17 if you need to reset your password with the disk.)

Once you've created the password, Windows 7 begins asking for your password whenever you log on.

- ✔ Passwords are *case-sensitive*. The words *Caviar* and *caviar* are considered two different passwords.

- ✔ Forgotten your password *already?* When you type a password that doesn't work, Windows 7 automatically displays your hint, which should help to remind you of your password. Careful, though — anybody can read your hint, so make sure that it's something that makes sense only to you. As a last resort, insert your Password Reset Disk, a job I cover in Chapter 17.

I explain lots more about user accounts in Chapter 13.

Working on the Desktop

Normally, people want their desktops to be flat, not vertical. Keeping pencils from rolling off a normal desk is hard enough. In Windows 7, your monitor's screen is known as the Windows *desktop,* and that's where all your work takes place. You can create files and folders right on your new electronic desktop and arrange them all across the screen. Each program runs in its own little *window* on top of the desktop.

Make Windows stop asking me for a password!

Windows asks for your name and password only when it needs to know who's tapping on its keys. And it needs that information for any of these three reasons:

- ✔ Your computer is part of a network, and your identity determines what goodies you can access.

- ✔ The computer's owner wants to limit what you can do on the computer.

- ✔ You share your computer with other people and want to keep others from logging on with your name and changing your files and settings.

If these concerns don't apply to you, purge the password by following the first two steps in the section "Keeping your account private with a password," but choose Remove Your Password instead of Change Your Windows Password.

Without that password, anybody can now log on, using your user account, and view (or destroy) your files. If you're working in an office setting, this setup can be serious trouble. If you've been assigned a password, it's better to simply get used to it.

Windows 7 starts with a freshly scrubbed, nearly empty desktop. After you've been working for a while, your desktop will fill up with *icons* — little push buttons that load your files with a quick double-click of the mouse. Some people leave their desktops strewn with icons for easy access. Others organize their work: When they finish working on something, they store it in a *folder,* a task covered in Chapter 4.

The desktop boasts four main parts, shown in Figure 2-3.

- ✔ **Start menu:** Seen at the taskbar's left edge, the Start menu works like the restaurant's waiter: It presents menus at your bidding, letting you choose what program to run.

- ✔ **Taskbar:** Resting lazily along the desktop's bottom edge, the taskbar lists the programs and files you currently have open, as well as icons for a few favored programs. (Point at a program's icon on the taskbar to see the program's name or perhaps a thumbnail photo of that program in action.)

- ✔ **Recycle Bin:** The desktop's *Recycle Bin,* that little wastebasket-shaped icon, stores your recently deleted files for easy retrieval. Whew!

- ✔ **Gadgets:** Windows 7 includes small programs that stick to your desktop like magnets on a refrigerator. (They're identical to the ones Windows Vista runs in its Sidebar.) Feel free to clutter your desktop with weather forecasters, Sudoku games, and instant messages.

I cover each of the desktop's four sections more thoroughly throughout this chapter; the following tips will help you anywhere on the desktop:

- ✔ You can start new projects directly from your desktop: Right-click the desktop, choose New, and select the project of your dreams from the pop-up menu, be it loading a favorite program or creating a folder to store new files. (The New menu lists most of your computer's programs for quick 'n' easy access.)

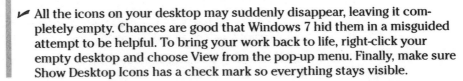

- ✔ Are you befuddled about some object's reason for being? Timidly rest the pointer over the mysterious doodad, and Windows pops up a little box explaining what that thing is or does. Right-click the object, and ever helpful Windows 7 usually tosses up a menu listing nearly everything you can do with that particular object. This trick works on most icons found on your desktop and throughout your programs.

- ✔ All the icons on your desktop may suddenly disappear, leaving it completely empty. Chances are good that Windows 7 hid them in a misguided attempt to be helpful. To bring your work back to life, right-click your empty desktop and choose View from the pop-up menu. Finally, make sure Show Desktop Icons has a check mark so everything stays visible.

Recycle Bin   Gadgets

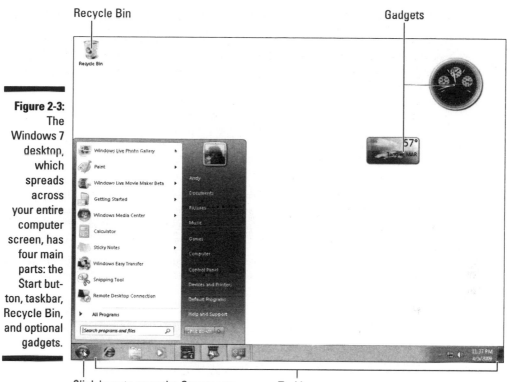

Figure 2-3:
The
Windows 7
desktop,
which
spreads
across
your entire
computer
screen, has
four main
parts: the
Start but-
ton, taskbar,
Recycle Bin,
and optional
gadgets.

Click here to open the Start menu   Taskbar

Cleaning up a messy desktop

When icons cover your desktop like a year's worth of sticky notes, Windows 7 offers several ways to clean up the mess. If you just want your desktop clutter to look more organized, right-click the desktop, choose Sort By from the pop-up menu, and choose any of these choices:

- **Name:** Arrange all icons in alphabetical order using neat, vertical rows.

- **Size:** Arrange icons according to their size, placing the smallest ones at the top of the rows.

- **Item Type:** This lines up icons by their *type*. All Word files are grouped together, for example, as are all links to Web sites.

- **Date Modified:** Arrange icons by the date you or your PC last changed them.

Right-clicking the desktop and choosing the View option lets you change the icons' size, as well as play with these desk-organizing options:

- ✔ **Auto Arrange Icons:** Automatically arrange everything in vertical rows — even newly positioned icons are swept into tidy rows.

- ✔ **Align Icons to Grid:** This option places an invisible grid on the screen and aligns all icons within the grid's borders to keep them nice and tidy — no matter how hard you try to mess them up.

- ✔ **Show Desktop Icons:** Always keep this option turned on. When turned off, Windows hides every icon on your desktop. If you can remember in your frustration, click this option again to toggle your icons back on.

Most View options are also available for any of your folders, and you can find these options by clicking the folder's View menu or icon.

Jazzing up the desktop's background

To jazz up your desktop, Windows 7 covers it with pretty pictures known as a *background*. (Most people refer to the background as *wallpaper*.)

When you tire of the normal scenic garb, choose your own background — any picture stored on your computer:

1. **Right-click a blank part of the desktop, choose Personalize, and click the Desktop Background option along the window's bottom left corner.**

2. **Click any one of the pictures, shown in Figure 2-4, and Windows 7 quickly places it onto your desktop's background.**

Figure 2-4:
Try different backgrounds by clicking them; click the Browse button to see pictures from different folders.

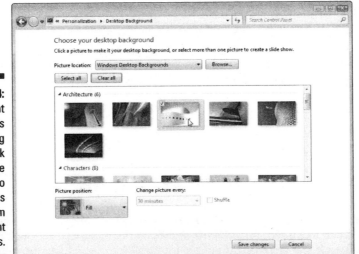

Found a keeper? Click the Save button to keep it on your desktop. Click the Picture Location menu to see more pictures. Or, if you're still searching, move to the next step.

3. **Click the Browse button and click a file from inside your Pictures folder.**

   Most people store their digital photos in their Pictures folder or library. (I explain browsing folders and libraries in Chapter 4.)

4. **Found a good picture?**

   Exit the program, and your chosen photo stays stuck to your desktop as the background.

Here are some tips for sprucing up your desktop:

✔ As you browse through different pictures, you can decide whether the image should be *tiled* repeatedly across the screen, *centered* directly in the middle, or *stretched* to fill the entire screen by selecting your preference from the Picture Position option. Windows 7's new *Fill* and *Fit* options enlarge small photos, like those taken with cell phones, to fit the screen's borders.

✔ You can easily borrow any picture found on the Internet for a background. Right-click on the Web site's picture and select Set as Background from the pop-up menu. Microsoft sneakily copies the image onto your desktop as its new background. (You can also right-click any photo in your Pictures folder and choose Set as Desktop Background — handy for quick wallpaper changes.)

✔ If a background photograph makes your desktop icons too difficult to find, splash your desktop with a single color instead: In Step 2 of the preceding list, click the Picture Location box's down arrow. When the drop-down list appears, choose Solid Colors. Choose one of the offered colors, and that color fills your desktop.

✔ To change the entire *look* of Windows 7, right-click on the desktop, choose Personalize, and select a Theme. Aimed at heavy-duty procrastinators, different themes splash different colors across Windows' various buttons, borders, and boxes. I explain more about Themes in Chapter 11. (If you download any Themes offered on the Internet, check them with antivirus software, covered in Chapter 10.)

Dumpster diving in the Recycle Bin

The Recycle Bin, that little wastebasket icon in the corner of your desktop, works much like a *real* recycle bin. Shown in the margin, it lets you retrieve Sunday's paper when somebody has pitched the comics section before you had a chance to read it.

You can dump something — a file or folder, for example — into the Windows 7 Recycle Bin in either of these ways:

- Simply right-click on it and choose Delete from the menu. Windows 7 asks cautiously if you're *sure* that you want to delete the item. Click Yes, and Windows 7 dumps it into the Recycle Bin, just as if you'd dragged it there. Whoosh!

- For a quick deletion rush, click the unwanted object and poke your Delete key.

Want something back? Double-click the Recycle Bin icon to see your recently deleted items. Right-click the item you want and choose Restore. The handy little Recycle Bin returns your precious item to the same spot where you deleted it. (You can also resuscitate deleted items by dragging them to your desktop or any other folder; drag 'em back into the Recycle Bin to delete them again.)

 The Recycle Bin can get pretty crowded. If you're searching frantically for a recently deleted file, tell the Recycle Bin to sort everything by the date and time you deleted it: Right-click an empty area inside the Recycle Bin, choose Sort By, and select Date Deleted from the pop-up menu.

To delete something *permanently,* just delete it from inside the Recycle Bin: Click it and press the Delete key. To delete *everything* in the Recycle Bin, right-click the Recycle Bin icon and choose Empty Recycle Bin.

 To bypass the Recycle Bin completely when deleting files, hold down Shift while pressing Delete. Poof! The deleted object disappears, ne'er to be seen again — a handy trick when dealing with sensitive items, such as credit-card numbers or late-night love letters meant for a nearby cubicle dweller.

- The Recycle Bin icon changes from an empty wastepaper basket to a full one as soon as it's holding a deleted file.

- How long does the Recycle Bin hold onto deleted files? It waits until the garbage consumes about 5 percent of your hard drive space. Then it begins purging your oldest deleted files to make room for the new. If you're low on hard drive space, shrink the bin's size by right-clicking the Recycle Bin and choosing Properties. Decrease the Custom Size number to automatically delete files more quickly; increase the number, and the Recycle Bin hangs onto files a little longer.

 The Recycle Bin saves only items deleted from your *own* computer's drives. That means it won't save anything deleted from a CD, memory card, MP3 player, flash drive, or digital camera.

✔ If you delete something from somebody else's computer over a network, it can't be retrieved. The Recycle Bin holds only items deleted from your *own* computer, not somebody else's computer. (For some awful reason, the Recycle Bin on the other person's computer doesn't save the item, either.) Be careful.

The Start Button's Reason to Live

The bright-blue Start button lives in the bottom-left corner of the desktop, where it's always ready for action. By clicking the Start button, you can start programs, adjust Windows settings, find help for sticky situations, or, thankfully, shut down Windows and get away from the computer for a while.

Click the Start button once, and a stack of menus pops out, as shown in Figure 2-5.

Your Start menu will change as you add more programs to your computer. That's why the Start menu on your friend's computer is probably arranged differently than the Start menu on your computer.

✔ Your Documents, Pictures, and Music folders are always one click away on the Start menu. These folders are specially designed for their contents. The Pictures folder, for example, displays little thumbnails of your digital photos. The biggest perk to these three folders? Keeping your files in these folders helps you remember where you stored them and makes backing up your files even easier. I cover file organization in Chapter 4.

✔ Windows thoughtfully places your most frequently used programs along the left side of the Start menu for easy point-'n'-click action. And see the arrows to the right of some programs listed in Figure 2-5? Click any of those arrows to see a list of the last few files you worked on in those programs.

✔ See the words *All Programs* near the Start menu's bottom left? Click there, and yet another menu opens to offer more options. (That new menu covers up the first, though; to bring back the first, click the word *Back.*)

✔ Spot something confusing on the Start menu's right side? Hover your mouse pointer over the mysterious icon. Windows responds with a helpful explanatory message.

✔ Strangely enough, you also click the Start button when you want to *stop* using Windows. (You click the Shut Down button along the Start menu's bottom right, described at this chapter's end.)

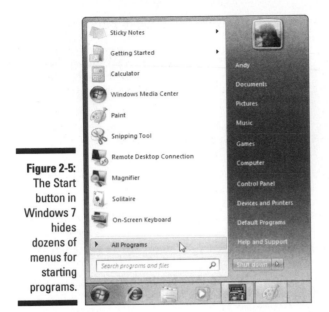

Figure 2-5:
The Start
button in
Windows 7
hides
dozens of
menus for
starting
programs.

The Start menu's buttons

The Start menu (shown in Figure 2-5) comes conveniently split into two sides: one filled with icons, the other with words. The left side constantly changes, always listing the icons of your most frequently used programs. Your most oft-accessed program eventually resides atop the stack.

The Start menu's right side, by contrast, never changes. Instead, it lists these places, each one leading to a special spot in Windows:

If you find Start menus exciting, you'll love the upcoming "Customizing the Start menu" section, which explains how to rearrange your entire Start menu.

  ✔ **Your Name:** The name of your user account appears at the Start menu's top-right corner. Click here to see a folder containing your most commonly opened folders: Downloads, My Documents, Favorites, Links, My Pictures, My Music, and My Videos.

  ✔ **Documents:** This command quickly shows the contents of your Documents library, stressing the importance of storing your work here.

  ✔ **Pictures:** Click here to see your stored digital photos and images. Each picture's icon is a thumbnail image of your photo. Not seeing images of your photos? Press the Alt key, click the View menu, and choose Large Icons.

- ✔ **Music:** Store your digital music here so that Media Player can find and play it more easily.

- ✔ **Games:** Windows 7 offers many of the same games as Windows Vista, including a decent chess game. Microsoft left out InkBall but brought back Internet Checkers and Internet Backgammon, which let you compete with other players worldwide.

- ✔ **Computer:** This option displays your computer's storage areas: folders, disk drives, CD drives, digital cameras, flash drives, networked PCs, and other places that hide your Most Wanted items.

- ✔ **Control Panel:** This bundle of switches lets you adjust your computer's oodles of confusing settings, all described in Chapter 11.

- ✔ **Devices and Printers:** This lists your printer, monitor, mouse, and other attached gadgets to make sure they're working properly. The ones with a yellow exclamation point icon need some fixing, so right-click them and choose Troubleshoot.

- ✔ **Default Programs:** Click here to control which program steps in when you open a file. Here's where you tell Windows to let iTunes handle your music instead of Media Player, for example.

- ✔ **Help and Support:** Befuddled? Click here for an answer. (Chapter 20 explains the stoic Windows Help system.)

Shut Down ▸

- ✔ **Shut Down:** Clicking here turns off your PC. Or, click the icon's little arrow for Switch User, Log Off, Lock, Restart, Sleep, and Hibernate options, explained in this chapter's last section.

- ✔ **Search box:** Conveniently placed directly above the Start button, this area lets you find files by typing a bit of their name or contents — a few words in an e-mail or a document, the name of a program or song, or nearly anything else. Press Enter, and Windows 7 quickly dredges it up for you. I cover Search more thoroughly in Chapter 6.

Both Windows Vista and XP listed icons for Internet Explorer and Outlook Express atop the Start menu's left edge. Windows 7 dumps Outlook Express completely (Chapter 9) and drops Internet Explorer's icon to the taskbar. To reattach Internet Explorer atop the Start menu, click the Start button, choose All Programs, right-click the Internet Explorer icon, and choose Pin to Start Menu.

Technically, the Start menu's Documents, Pictures, and Music options don't take you to those folders but to their *libraries* instead — a Windows 7 term for a "super" folder that shows contents of several folders. The Documents library, for example, displays files in your My Documents folder as well as the Public Documents folder. I explain more about libraries and folders in Chapter 4.

Starting a program from the Start menu

This task is easy. Click the Start button, and the Start menu pops out of the button's head. If you see an icon for your desired program, click it, and Windows loads the program.

If your program isn't listed, though, click All Programs, located near the bottom of the Start menu. Yet another menu pops up, this one listing the names of programs and folders full of programs. Spot your program? Click the name, and Windows kicks that program to the front of the screen.

If you *still* don't see your program listed, try pointing at the tiny folders listed on the All Programs menu. The menu fills with that folder's programs. Don't spot it? Click a different folder and watch as its contents spill out onto the Start menu.

When you finally spot your program's name, just click it. That program hops onto the desktop in a window, ready for action.

- ✔ If you don't spot a program listed, type the program's name into the Start menu's Search box. Type **Chess**, for example, press Enter, and Windows' Chess Titans program pops onto the screen, ready to crush you.

- ✔ Still don't see your program? Then head for Chapter 6 and find the section on finding lost items. Windows 7 can track down your missing program.

- ✔ There's another way to load a lost program — if you can find something you created or edited with that program. For example, if you wrote letters to the tax collector using Microsoft Word, double-click one of your tax letters to bring Microsoft Word to the screen from its hiding place.

- ✔ No program yet? Try right-clicking a blank part of your desktop, choosing New, and choosing your program's name from the pop-up menu. Your program will appear, ready to create your new masterpiece.

- ✔ If you don't know how to navigate through *folders,* visit Chapter 4. That chapter helps you move gracefully from folder to folder, decreasing the time it takes to stumble across your file.

Customizing the Start menu

The Windows 7 Start menu works great — until you're hankering for something that's not listed on the menu, or something you rarely use is just getting in the way.

✔ **To add a favorite program's icon to the Start button's menu,** right-click the program's icon and choose Pin to Start Menu from the pop-up menu. Windows copies that icon to your Start menu's top left column. (From there, you may drag it to the All Programs area.)

✔ **To purge unwanted icons from the Start menu's left column,** right-click them and choose either Unpin from Start Menu or Remove from This List. (Removing an icon from the Start menu doesn't remove the actual program from your computer; it just removes one of many push buttons that launch it.)

When you install a program, as described in Chapter 11, the program almost always adds itself to the Start menu *automatically*. Then the program boldly announces its presence, as shown in Figure 2-6, by displaying its name with a different background color.

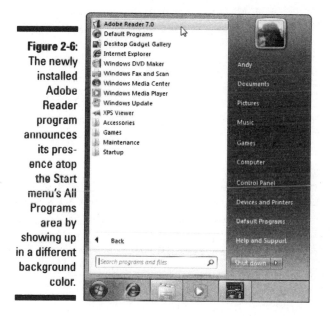

Figure 2-6: The newly installed Adobe Reader program announces its presence atop the Start menu's All Programs area by showing up in a different background color.

You can customize the Start menu even more by changing its properties. To start playing, right-click the Start button, choose Properties, and click the Start menu's Customize button. Select the check boxes next to the options you want or deselect check boxes to remove the options. Messed up your Start menu somehow? Click the Use Default Settings button, click OK, and click OK again to start from scratch.

Making Windows start programs automatically

Many people sit down at a computer, turn it on, and go through the same mechanical process of loading their oft-used programs. Believe it or not, Windows 7 can automate this task. The solution is the Startup folder, found lurking in the Start button's All Programs menu. When Windows 7 wakes up, it peeks inside that Startup folder. If it finds a program lurking inside, it immediately tosses that program onto the screen.

To make your favorite programs wake up along with Windows 7, follow these steps:

1. **Click the Start button and choose All Programs.**

2. **Right-click the Start menu's Startup icon and choose Open.**

The Startup icon, which lives in the Start menu's All Programs area, opens as a folder.

3. **While holding down the right mouse button, drag and drop any of your favorite programs or files into the Startup folder, then choose Create Shortcuts Here.**

Windows 7 automatically places shortcuts to those items inside the Startup folder.

4. **Close the Startup folder.**

Now, whenever you turn on your PC and log on to your user account, Windows 7 automatically loads those programs or files so that they'll be waiting for you.

Bellying Up to the Taskbar

The biggest new trick in Windows 7 could be its redesigned taskbar, so pull in your chair a little closer. Whenever you run more than one window on the desktop, there's a big problem: Programs and windows tend to cover up each other, making them difficult to locate. To make matters worse, programs like Internet Explorer and Microsoft Word can each display several windows apiece. How do you keep track of all the windows?

Windows 7's solution is the *taskbar* — a special area that keeps track of all your running programs and their windows. Shown in Figure 2-7, the taskbar lives along the bottom of your screen, constantly updating itself to show an icon for every currently running program. It also serves as a dock for your favorite programs that you want to have one click away.

Rest your mouse pointer over any of the taskbar's programs to see either the program's name or a thumbnail image of the program's contents, as shown in Figure 2-7. In that figure, Internet Explorer is currently showing two Web pages.

Figure 2-7:
Click
buttons for
currently
running
programs on
the taskbar.

From the taskbar, you can perform powerful magic on your open windows, as described in the following list:

✓ To play with a program listed on the taskbar, click its icon. The window rises to the surface and rests atop any other open windows, ready for action.

✓ Whenever you load a program, its name automatically appears on the taskbar. If one of your open windows ever gets lost on your desktop, click its name on the taskbar to bring it to the forefront.

✓ To close a window listed on the taskbar, *right-click* its icon and choose Close from the pop-up menu. The program quits, just as if you'd chosen its Exit command from within its own window. (The departing program gives you a chance to save your work before it quits and walks off the screen.)

✓ Traditionally, the taskbar lives along your desktop's bottom edge, but you can move it to any edge you want. (***Hint:*** Just drag it from edge to edge. If it doesn't move, right-click the taskbar and click Lock the Taskbar to remove the check mark by its name.)

✓ If the taskbar keeps hiding below the screen's bottom edge, point the mouse at the screen's bottom edge until the taskbar surfaces. Then right-click the taskbar, choose Properties, and remove the check mark from Auto-hide the Taskbar.

✓ The new taskbar has ditched the Quick Launch toolbar — a small strip near the Start button that contained icons for your favorite programs. Instead, you can add your favorite programs directly to the taskbar: Right-click the favored program's icon and choose Pin to Taskbar. The program's icon then lives on the Taskbar for easy access, just as if it were running. Tired of the program hogging space on your taskbar? Right-click it and choose Unpin This Program from Taskbar.

Shrinking windows to the taskbar and retrieving them

Windows spawn windows. You start with one window to write a letter of praise to the your local taco shop. You open another window to check an address, for example, and then yet another to ogle online reviews. Before you know it, four more windows are crowded across the desktop.

To combat the clutter, Windows 7 provides a simple means of window control: You can transform a window from a screen-cluttering square into a tiny button on the *taskbar,* which sits along the bottom of the screen. The solution is the Minimize button.

See the three buttons lurking in just about every window's top-right corner? Click the *Minimize button* — the button with the little line in it, shown in the margin. Whoosh! The window disappears, represented by its little button on the taskbar at your screen's bottom.

To make a minimized program on the taskbar revert to a regular, on-screen window, just click its name on the taskbar. Pretty simple, huh?

✔ Can't find the taskbar icon for the window you want to minimize or maximize? Each taskbar button shows the name of the program it represents. And if you hover your mouse pointer over the taskbar button, Windows 7 displays a thumbnail photo of that program or the program's name.

✔ When you minimize a window, you neither destroy its contents nor close the program. And when you click the window's name on the taskbar, it reopens to the same size you left it, showing its same contents.

Switching to different tasks from the taskbar's Jump Lists

The new, improved taskbar in Windows 7 doesn't limit you to opening programs and switching between windows. You can jump to other tasks, as well, by right-clicking the taskbar's icons.

As shown in Figure 2-8, right-clicking the Internet Explorer icon brings up a quick list of your recently visited Web sites. Click any site on the list to make a quick return visit.

Called Jump Lists, these right-click menus add a new trick to the taskbar: They let you jump quickly between tasks as well as between open windows.

Figure 2-8:
Jump Lists,
from left
to right:
Windows
Explorer's
recently
visited
folders,
Media
Player's
recently
played
items, and
Internet
Explorer's
recently
visited Web
sites.

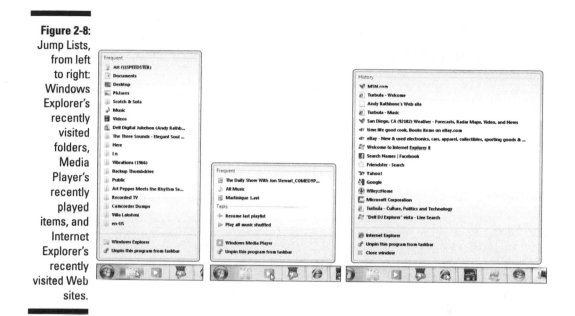

 In earlier versions of Windows, right-clicking a taskbar item brought up an austere menu with three options: Restore, Close, or Maximize. You can still call up that menu for nostalgia's sake by holding down Shift as you right-click the taskbar icon.

Clicking the taskbar's sensitive areas

Like a crafty card player, the taskbar comes with a few tips and tricks. For example, here's the lowdown on the icons near the taskbar's right edge, shown in Figure 2-9, known as the *notification area*. Different items appear in the Notification area depending on your own PC and programs, but you'll probably encounter some of these:

- ✔ **Minimize Windows:** Always in view, this small strip instantly minimizes all open windows when you click it. (Click it again to put the windows back in place.)

- ✔ **Time/Date:** Click the time and date to fetch a handy monthly calendar and clock. If you want to change the time or date, or even add a second time zone, click the Time/Date area and choose Change Date and Time Settings, a task I cover in Chapter 11.

- ✔ **Media Center Recording:** The glowing red circle means Media Center is currently recording something off the television.

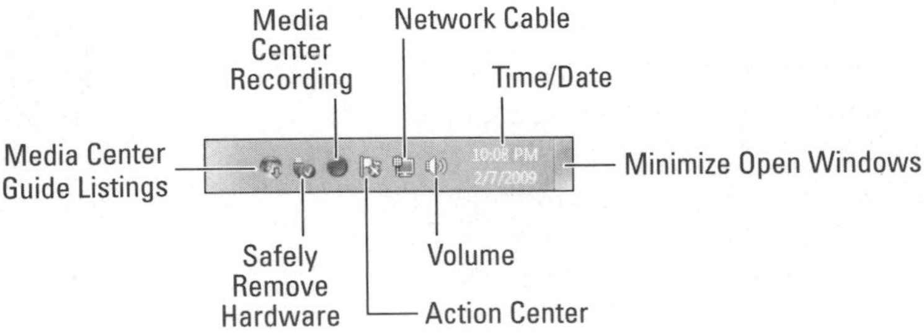

Figure 2-9:
The task-bar's tiny icons along the right edge mostly show items running in the back-ground on your PC.

Media Center Recording

Network Cable

Time/Date

Media Center Guide Listings

Minimize Open Windows

Safely Remove Hardware

Volume

Action Center

✔ **Media Center Guide Listings:** Media Center is downloading new TV listings automatically.

✔ **Safely Remove Hardware:** Before unplugging a storage device, be it a tiny flash drive, a portable music player, or a portable hard drive, click here. That tells Windows to prepare the gadget for unplugging.

✔ **Action Center:** Windows wants you to need to do something, be it to click a permission window or install or turn on an antivirus program.

✔ **Network:** This appears when you're connected to the Internet or other PCs through a network. Not connected? A red X appears over the icon.

✔ **Volume:** Click this ever-so-handy little speaker icon to adjust your PC's volume, as shown in Figure 2-10. (Or double-click the word Mixer to bring up a mixing panel. *Mixers* let you adjust separate volume levels for each program, letting you keep Media Player's volume louder than your other programs' annoying beeps.)

✔ **Windows Problem Reporting:** When Windows runs into trouble, this icon appears; click it to see possible solutions.

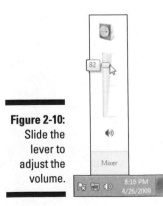

Figure 2-10:
Slide the lever to adjust the volume.

- **Windows Automatic Updates:** This icon appears when Windows downloads *updates,* usually small programs designed to fix your PC, from Microsoft's Web site at Windows Update.

- **Task Manager:** Coveted by computer technicians, this little program can end misbehaving programs, monitor background tasks, monitor performance, and do other stuff of techie dreams.

- **Windows Host Process:** This dismally named icon delivers an even worse message: Your newly plugged-in gadget won't work, be it your printer, scanner, music player, or other item. Try unplugging the device, running its installation software again, and plugging it back in.

- **Explorer:** Most PCs come with two types of USB ports: fast and slow. This icon means you've plugged a speedy gadget into your slow port. Try unplugging it and plugging it into a different port. (The USB ports on a desktop computer's back side are often the faster ones.)

- **Power, Outlet:** This shows that your laptop is plugged into an electrical outlet and is charging its battery.

- **Power, Battery:** Your laptop is running on batteries only. (Rest your mouse pointer over the icon to see how much power remains.)

- **Wireless:** Your PC is wirelessly connected to the Internet or a network.

- **Arrow:** Sometimes the taskbar hides things. If you see a tiny upward-pointing arrow on the far left, click it to see a few hidden icons slide out. (Check out the "Customizing the taskbar" section for tips and tricks on whether icons should hide.)

Customizing the taskbar

Windows 7 brings a whirlwind of options for the lowly taskbar, letting you play with it in more ways than a strand of spaghetti and a fork.

First, the taskbar comes preloaded with three icons next to the Start menu: Internet Explorer (your Web browser), Windows Explorer (your file browser), and Media Player (your media browser). Like all your taskbar icons, they're movable, so feel free to drag them to any order you want.

To add more programs to the taskbar, drag and drop a program's icon directly onto the taskbar. Or, if you spot a favored program's icon on your Start menu, right-click the icon and choose Pin to Taskbar from the pop-up menu.

For even more customization, right-click a blank part of the taskbar, and choose Properties. The Taskbar and Start Menu Properties window appears, as shown in Figure 2-11.

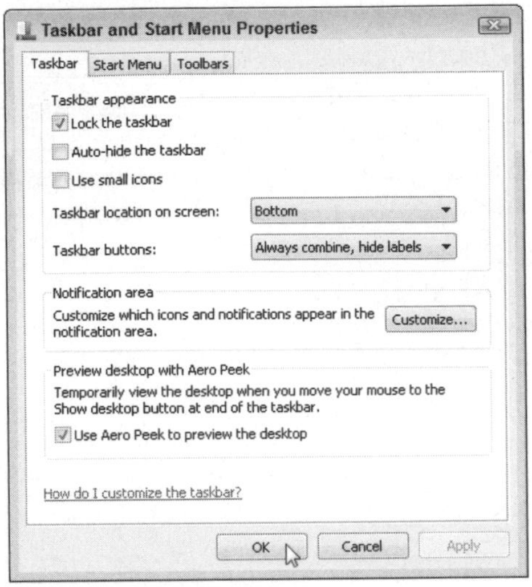

Figure 2-11:
Click the
Taskbar tab
to customize
the taskbar's
appearance
and
behavior.

Table 2-1 explains the window's options, as well as my recommendations for them. (You need to remove the check mark by Lock the Taskbar before some of these options will work.)

Table 2-1	Customizing the Taskbar
Setting	*My Recommendations*
Lock the Taskbar	Clicking here locks the taskbar in place, keeping you from changing its appearance. You can't drag it upward to make room for more icons, for example. Lock it, but only after you've set up the taskbar to suit your needs.
Auto-Hide the Taskbar	Selecting this option makes the taskbar *automatically* hide itself when you're not near it. (Point your cursor at the taskbar to bring it back up.) I leave this option unchecked to keep the taskbar always in view.
Use Small Icons	This shrinks the taskbar to half-height, letting you pack in a few extra tiny icons.
Taskbar Location On Screen	Your taskbar can live on any edge of your desktop, not just the bottom. Choose any of the four edges here.
Taskbar Buttons	When you open lots of windows and programs, Windows accommodates the crowd by grouping similar windows under one button: All open Microsoft Word documents stack atop one Microsoft Word button, for example. Choose the option called Always Combine, Hide Labels. That protects the taskbar from overcrowding.

Setting	My Recommendations
Notification Area	This section's Customize button lets you decide which icons should appear in the notification area. I choose Always Show All Icons and Notifications On the Taskbar.
Preview Desktop with Aero Peek	Normally, pointing at the strip on the taskbar's far right edge lets you behind all open windows. Selecting this check box deactivates that strip.

Feel free to experiment with the taskbar until it looks right for you. After you've changed an option, see the changes immediately by clicking the Apply button. Don't like the change? Reverse your decision, and click Apply to return to normal.

After you set up the taskbar just the way you want it, select the Lock the Taskbar check box, described in Table 2-1.

The taskbar's crazy toolbars

Your taskbar won't always be a steadfast, unchanging friend. Microsoft lets you customize it even further, often beyond the point of recognition. Some people enjoy adding *toolbars,* which tack extra buttons and menus onto their taskbar. Others accidentally turn on a toolbar and can't figure out how to get rid of the darn thing.

To turn a toolbar on or off, right-click on a blank part of the taskbar (even the clock will do) and choose Toolbars from the pop-up menu. A menu leaps out, offering these five toolbar options:

✔ **Address:** Choose this toolbar, and part of your taskbar becomes a place for typing Web sites to visit. It's convenient, but so is Internet Explorer, which does the same thing.

✔ **Links:** This toolbar adds quick access to your favorite Web sites. Click it to visit any Web site listed in Internet Explorer's Favorites menu.

✔ **Tablet PC Input Panel:** Meant only for Tablet PC owners, this translates pad scribblings into text.

✔ **Desktop:** Techies who find the Start menu burdensome add this toolbar for quick access to all their PC's resources. It lets you browse through files, folders, network locations, the Recycle Bin, and Control Panel menus by snaking your way through all the menus.

✔ **New Toolbar:** Click here to choose *any* folder to add as a toolbar. For example, choose your Documents folder for quick browsable access to all its files and folders.

Toolbars fall into the love-'em-or-hate-'em category. Some people find toolbars to be timesavers; others feel they consume too much real estate to be worth the effort. The Tablet PC Input Panel works only when you attach an expensive, touch-sensitive pad to your PC.

Toolbars are *supposed* to be dragged around with the mouse. When the taskbar is unlocked, grab the toolbar by its *handle,* a vertical line by the toolbar's name. Drag the handle to the left or right to change a toolbar's size.

A Gaggle of Gadgets

Windows Vista owners may remember the Sidebar — a strip along the desktop's right edge that housed little programs called gadgets. The little programs displayed weather updates, instant message programs, and other tasks that required a watchful eye.

Windows 7 ditches the Sidebar but keeps the gadgets, letting them roam freely on the desktop. To add a gadget to your desktop, right-click a blank part of the desktop and choose Gadgets. The window in Figure 2-12 appears, displaying Windows 7's stock gadgets: A calendar, clock, currency exchange rate tally, puzzle, and other items.

Figure 2-12: Right-click your desktop and choose Gadgets to see the available *gadgets,* minuscule programs that snap on and off the desktop.

Drag a gadget from the Gadget window onto your desktop, and it sticks, ready for viewing. Don't spot a suitable gadget? Click Get More Gadgets Online to visit gadget nirvana: A Web site packed with thousands of free gadgets, ready for the picking. Unlike the built-in gadgets, which slide onto your desktop, the ones on the Web must be downloaded and installed like any other program. (I cover installing programs in Chapter 11.)

✔ Feel free to position your gadgets anywhere you'd like on your desktop. Or don't use them at all — they're optional.

✔ To change a gadget's settings — to choose which photos appear in your Slide Show Gadget, for example — point at the gadget and click the tiny wrench icon that appears along its right edge. To remove a gadget completely, click the little X, instead.

Logging Off from Windows

Ah! The most pleasant thing you'll do with Windows 7 all day could very well be to stop using it. And you do that the same way you started: by using the Start button, that friendly little helper you've been using all along. (And if the Start menu is hiding, hold down Ctrl and press Esc to bring it back from behind the trees.) You want the button resting at the bottom of the Start menu.

Shut Down ▶   Click the Shut Down button when nobody else will be using the computer until the next morning. Windows 7 saves everything and turns off your computer.

When you're not ready to shut down, though, click the little arrow next to the Shut Down button to choose from alternatives:

✔ **Switch User:** Choose this option if somebody else just wants to borrow the computer for a few minutes. The Welcome screen appears, but Windows keeps your open programs waiting in the background. When you switch back, everything's just as you left it.

✔ **Log Off:** When you're through working at the PC and somebody else wants a go at it, choose Log Off instead of Switch User. Windows saves your work and your settings and returns to the Welcome screen, ready for the next user to log on.

✔ **Lock:** Meant for whenever you take short trips to the water cooler, this option locks your PC and places your user account picture on the screen. When you return, type your password, and Windows 7 instantly displays your desktop, just as you left it.

✔ **Restart:** Choose this option when Windows 7 screws something up (for instance, a program crashes, or Windows seems to be acting awfully weird). Windows 7 turns off and reloads itself, hopefully feeling refreshed. Some programs ask you to restart your PC after you've installed them.

NEW IN WINDOWS 7

Which task programs are actually running?

In previous versions of Windows, the taskbar's programs were always separated like boys and girls at a school dance. On the left side lived the Quick Launch toolbar with programs waiting to be launched; on the right lived the running programs, which always had a window open on the desktop.

The Windows 7 taskbar breaks the walls and lets icons for both running and closed programs to sit side by side. The big difference? Running programs have a faint gray box around them; closed programs don't.

After a while, you'll grow used to the change. And you can always see which programs are actually running by holding down your Windows key and tapping the Tab key a few times. Windows displays a three-dimensional view of your currently running programs, bringing another window to the forefront with each press of the Tab key.

✔ **Sleep:** This option saves your work in your PC's memory *and* its hard drive, and then lets your PC slumber in a low-power state. When you return to your PC, Windows 7 quickly presents your desktop, programs, and windows as if you'd never left. (On a laptop, Sleep saves your work only to memory; should the battery life grow threateningly low, Sleep dumps it onto the hard drive and turns off your laptop.)

✔ **Hibernate:** Found on some laptops, this option copies your work to your hard drive and then turns off your PC — a process requiring less battery power than Sleep mode. Hibernate is slower than Sleep at redisplaying your work where you left off.

When you tell Windows 7 that you want to quit, it searches through all your open windows to see whether you've saved all your work. If it finds any work you've forgotten to save, it lets you know so that you can click the OK button to save it. Whew!

You don't *have* to shut down Windows 7. In fact, some experts leave their computers turned on all the time, saying it's better for their computer's health. Other experts say that their computers are healthier if they're turned *off* each day. Still others say the Sleep mode in Windows 7 gives them the best of both worlds. However, *everybody* says to turn off your monitor when you're done working. Monitors definitely enjoy cooling down when not in use.

Don't just press your PC's Off button to turn off your PC. Instead, be sure to shut down Windows 7 through one of its official Off options: Sleep, Hibernate, or Shut Down. Otherwise, Windows 7 can't properly prepare your computer for the dramatic event, leading to future troubles.

Chapter 3

Basic Windows Mechanics

*T*his chapter is for curious Windows anatomy students. You know who you are — you're the one who sees all those new buttons, borders, and balloons scattered throughout Windows 7 and wonders what would happen if you just clicked that little thing over there.

This rather gruesome chapter tosses an ordinary window (your oft-used Documents folder, to be precise) onto the dissection table. I've yanked out each part for thorough labeling and explanation. You'll find the theory behind each one and the required procedures for making each piece do your bidding.

A standard field guide follows, identifying and explaining the buttons, boxes, windows, bars, lists, and other oddities you may encounter when you're trying to make Windows 7 do something useful.

Feel free to don any protective gear you may have lying about, use the margins to scribble notes, and tread forcefully into the world of Windows.

Dissecting a Typical Window

Figure 3-1 places a typical window on the slab, with all its parts labeled. You might recognize the window as your Documents library, that storage tank for most of your work.

Menu bar

Address Bar

Title bar

Backward

Forward

Folder history

Minimize

Change icon view

Maximize

Search box

Close

Toggle Preview Pane

Help

Scroll box

Preview Pane

Vertical scroll bar

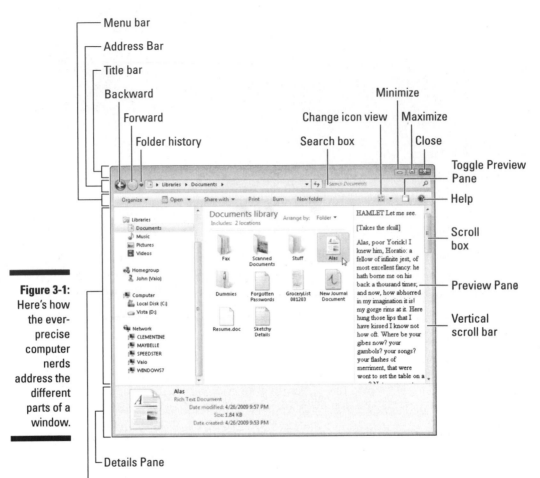

Figure 3-1: Here's how the ever-precise computer nerds address the different parts of a window.

Details Pane

Navigation Pane

Just as boxers grimace differently depending on where they've been punched, windows behave differently depending on where they've been clicked. The next few sections describe the main parts of the Documents library window in Figure 3-1, how to click them, and how Windows jerks in response.

✔ Windows XP veterans remember their My Documents folder, that stash for all their files. Windows Vista dropped the word *My* to create the Documents folder, and Windows 7 puts the word *My* back in place. (No matter what it's called, you're still supposed to stash your files inside it.)

✔ Windows 7 places your My Documents folder inside your Documents *library* — a new type of super folder described in Chapter 4. The Documents library displays both your My Documents folder and the Public Documents folder. (Everybody who uses your PC sees the same Public Documents folder, making it a handy folder for sharing files.)

✔ Windows 7 is full of little weird-shaped buttons, borders, and boxes. You don't need to remember all their names, although it would give you a leg up on figuring out Windows' scholarly Help menus. When you spot an odd portion of a window, just return to this chapter, look up its name in Figure 3-1, and read its explanation.

✔ You can deal with most things in Windows by simply clicking, double-clicking, or right-clicking. *Hint:* When in doubt, always right-click.

✔ After you click a few windows a few times, you realize how easy it is to boss them around. The hard part is finding the right controls for the *first* time, like figuring out the buttons on that new cell phone.

Tugging on a window's title bar

Found atop nearly every window (see examples in Figure 3-2), the title bar usually lists the program name and the file it's currently working on. For example, Figure 3-2 shows the title bars from Windows 7's WordPad (top) and Notepad (bottom) programs. The WordPad title bar lists the file's name as Document because you haven't had a chance to save and name the file yet.

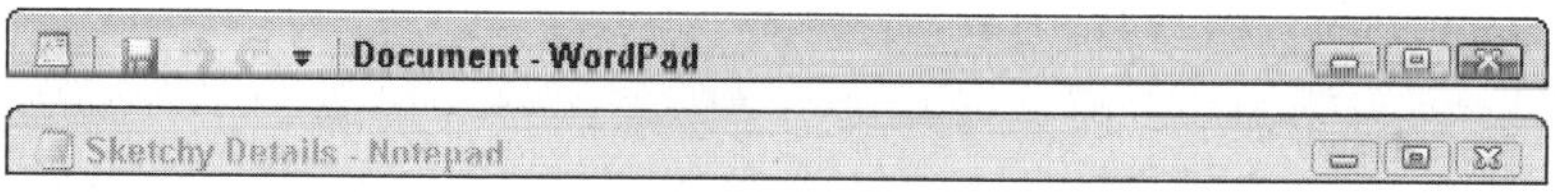

Figure 3-2:
A title bar from WordPad (top) and Notepad (bottom).

Document - WordPad

Sketchy Details - Notepad

Although mild-mannered, the mundane title bar holds hidden powers, described in the following tips:

✔ Title bars make convenient handles for moving windows around your desktop. Point at a blank part of the title bar, hold down the mouse button, and move the mouse around: The window follows along as you move your mouse. Found the right location? Let go of the mouse button, and the window sets up camp in its new spot.

✔ Double-click a blank portion of the title bar, and the window leaps to fill the entire screen. Double-click it again, and the window retreats to its original size.

- ✔ See the cluster of little icons in the WordPad program's top-left corner? New to Windows 7, those icons form the Quick Access Toolbar, and it's part of what Microsoft calls a *Ribbon interface*. Don't like the Quick Access Toolbar up there? Right-click one of the Quick Access Toolbar's icons and choose Show Quick Access Toolbar below the Ribbon.

- ✔ In Windows XP, every title bar carried a, uh, title of what you were viewing. Windows Vista and Windows 7, however, leave their folders' names *off* their title bars, preferring an empty strip (refer to Figure 3-1). But although many of the Windows 7 title bars lack titles, they work like regular title bars: Feel free to drag them around your desktop, just as you did in Windows XP.

- ✔ The right end of the title bar contains three square buttons. From left to right, they let you Minimize, Restore (or Maximize), or Close a window, topics all covered in the "Maneuvering Windows Around the Desktop" section, later in this chapter.

- ✔ To find the window you're currently working on, look for a darker title bar sporting a red Close button in its top-right corner (Figure 3-2, top). Those colors distinguish that window from windows you *aren't* working on (Figure 3-2, bottom). By glancing at all the title bars on the screen, you can tell which window is awake and accepting anything you type. (Unlike in Windows Vista, Windows 7 darkens the entire title bar of the currently active window.)

Navigating folders with a window's Address Bar

Directly beneath every folder's title bar lives the *Address Bar,* shown atop the Documents folder in Figure 3-3. Internet Explorer veterans will experience déjà vu: The Windows 7 Address Bar is lifted straight from the top of Internet Explorer and glued atop every folder.

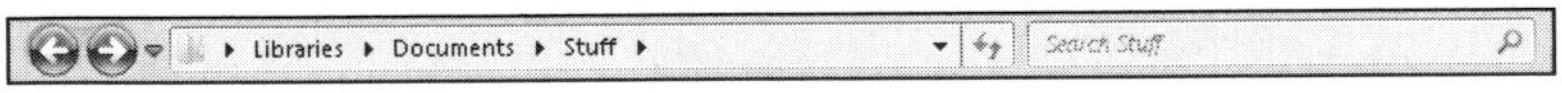

Figure 3-3:
An Address
Bar.

| ← → ▾ ↕ | ▸ Libraries ▸ Documents ▸ Stuff ▸ | ▾ | ✦ | Search Stuff | 🔎 |

The Address Bar's three main parts, described from left to right in the following list, perform three different duties:

✔ **Backward and Forward buttons:** These two arrows keep track as you forage through your PC's folders. The Backward button backtracks to the folder you just visited. The Forward button brings you back. (Click the miniscule arrow to the right of the Forward arrow to see a list of places you've visited previously; click any entry to zoom right there.)

✔ **Address Bar:** Just as the Internet Explorer Address Bar lists a Web site's address, the Windows 7 Address Bar displays your current folder's address — its location inside your PC. For example, the Address Bar shown in Figure 3-3 shows three words: *Libraries, Documents,* and *Stuff.* Those words tell you that you're looking inside the *Stuff* folder inside the *Documents* folder of *Andy's* User account. Yes, folder addresses are complicated enough to warrant an entire chapter: Chapter 4.

✔ **Search box:** In another rip-off from Internet Explorer, every Windows 7 folder sports a Search box. Instead of searching the Internet, though, it rummages through your folder's contents. For example, type the word **carrot** into a folder's Search box: Windows 7 digs through that folder's contents and retrieves every file or folder mentioning *carrot.*

In the Address Bar, notice the little arrows between the words *Libraries, Documents,* and *Stuff.* The arrows offer quick trips to other folders. Click any arrow — the one to the right of the word *Documents,* for example. A little menu drops down from the arrow, letting you jump to any other folder inside your Documents folder.

Finding the hidden menu bar

Windows 7 has more menu items than an Asian restaurant. To keep everybody's minds on computer commands instead of seaweed salad, Windows hides its menus inside the *menu bar* (see Figure 3-4).

Figure 3-4:
The menu
bar.

| File   Edit   Format   View   Help |

The menu bar sports different options for each menu. To reveal the secret options, click any word — Edit, for example. A menu tumbles down, as shown in Figure 3-5, presenting options related to editing a file.

Dragging, dropping, and running

Although the phrase *drag and drop* sounds as if it's straight out of a Mafia guidebook, it's really a nonviolent mouse trick used throughout Windows. Dragging and dropping is a way of moving something — say, an icon on your desktop — from one place to another.

To *drag,* put the mouse pointer over the icon and *hold down* the left or right mouse button. (I prefer the right mouse button.) As you move the mouse across your desk, the pointer drags the icon across the screen. Place the pointer/icon where you want it and release the mouse button. The icon *drops,* unharmed.

Holding down the *right* mouse button while dragging and dropping makes Windows 7 toss up a helpful little menu, asking whether you want to *copy* or *move* the icon.

Helpful Tip Department: Did you start dragging something and realize midstream that you're dragging the wrong item? Don't let go of the mouse button — instead, press Esc to cancel the action. Whew! (If you've dragged with your right mouse button and already let go of the button, there's another exit: Choose Cancel from the pop-up menu.)

Just as restaurants sometimes run out of specials, a window sometimes isn't capable of offering all its menu items. Any unavailable options are *grayed out,* like the Cut, Copy, Delete, and Go To options in Figure 3-5.

If you accidentally click the wrong word in a menu bar, causing the wrong menu to jump down, simply click the word you *really* wanted. A forgiving soul, Windows retracts the mistaken menu and displays your newly chosen one.

To back out of Menu Land completely, click the mouse pointer in the window's *workspace* — the area where you're supposed to be working.

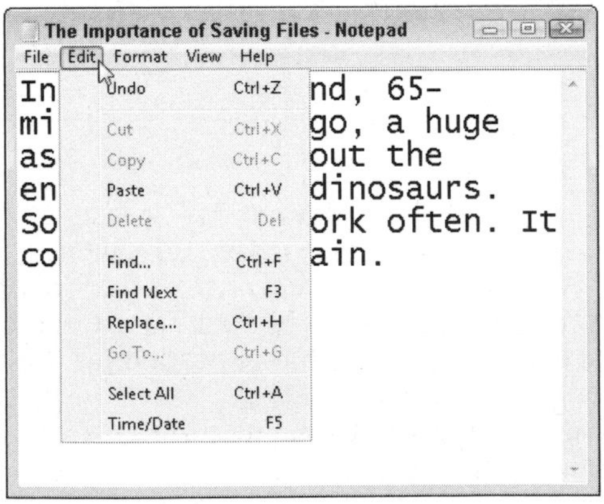

Figure 3-5:
Click any menu to see its associated commands.

Where are the folder menus?

If you're migrating from Windows XP, you may notice something missing from atop your folders: That familiar row of words reading File, Edit, View, and other commands has disappeared. Microsoft trimmed those menu commands with Windows Vista, and they're still AWOL in Windows 7. But there's a quick way to bring them back on duty: Press Alt, and the menu bar reappears in most programs, awaiting your click.

For the convenience of keyboard lovers, Windows 7 still underlines one letter on those hidden menu items. Mouse haters can press the Alt key followed by an underlined letter — the F in File, for example — to make Windows display the File menu. (Pressing Alt, then F, and then X closes a window.) To make the menu bar stay put, click Organize, choose Layout, and select Menu Bar.

Choosing the right button for the job

Many Windows XP veterans fondly remember the *task pane*, a handy strip along a folder's left side that displayed handy buttons for common chores. Windows 7 strips away the task pane, instead, handing those common chores to a thin strip of buttons called the *command bar*. The Documents library's command bar, for example, appears in Figure 3-6.

Figure 3-6:
The Documents library's command bar.

| Organize ▾ | Share with ▾ | Burn | New folder | | ▦ ▾ | ☐ | ⊚ |

You don't need to know much about the command bar, because Windows 7 automatically places the correct buttons atop the folder that needs them. Open your Music library, for example, and the command bar quickly sprouts a Play All button for marathon listening sessions. Open the Pictures library, and the friendly command bar serves up a Slide Show button.

If a button's meaning isn't immediately obvious, hover your mouse pointer over it; a little message explains the button's *raison d'être*. My own translations for the most common buttons are in the following list:

Organize: Found on every folder's command bar, the Organize button lets you cut, copy, or paste a folder's selected items. The button's Layout menu lets you change a folder's appearance by toggling those thick informational strips along the window's edges. You can turn on or off the *Navigation Pane,* that strip of shortcuts along the left edge, for example. You can also turn off the *Details Pane,* that strip along every folder's bottom that displays information about the selected file.

See the little blue stripes along each icon's edge on the Layout menu? Those stripes show on which edge of your folder the extra pane will appear.

New Folder: Need another storage spot for your current window? Clicking here tosses a new folder into your window, leaving you to type the newcomer's name.

Include in Library: New to Windows 7 and covered in Chapter 4, *libraries* work as collections of files pulled from several different folders. Click any folder's Include in Library button to see a pop-up menu offering to add that folder's contents to any of your four main libraries: Documents, Music, Pictures, or Videos. It's a handy trick when you stumble across a forgotten folder of photos that you're not sure you'll locate again.

Share With: Click here to share the selected file or files with somebody on another computer, provided they already have a User account and password on your PC. You won't see or need this button until you set up a network (which I describe in Chapter 14) to link this PC with others.

Burn: Click here to copy your selected items to a blank CD or DVD. If you haven't yet clicked on anything in the folder, this copies the entire folder's contents to your CD — a handy way to make quick backups.

View: This unlabeled icon in every folder's upper-right corner lets you choose how the folder should show off its contents. Keep clicking the View icon to cycle through different icon sizes; stop clicking when one looks good. To jump to a favorite view, click the button's adjacent arrow to see a list of every available view. Choose Details, for example, to view everything you want to know about a file: its size, creation date, and other minutia. (Photos look best when shown in Large or Extra Large Icons view.)

Are your folder's icons too big or small? Hold down the Ctrl key and spin your mouse wheel. Spin one direction to enlarge them, and spin the reverse direction to shrink them.

Preview: Also unlabeled, this icon toggles the Preview Pane: a strip along a folder's right edge that displays a selected file's contents. Handy for peeking into files without taking the time to open them, the Preview Pane works especially well with text files and photos.

Help: Click the little blue question mark icon in any folder's top-right corner for help with the item you happen to be viewing at the time.

Quick shortcuts with the Navigation Pane

Look at most "real" desktops, and you'll see the most-used items sitting within arm's reach: the coffee cup, the stapler, and perhaps a few crumbs from the coffee room snacks. Similarly, Windows 7 gathers up your PC's most frequently used items and places them in the new Navigation Pane, shown in Figure 3-7.

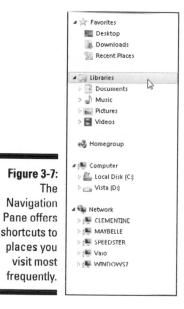

Figure 3-7: The Navigation Pane offers shortcuts to places you visit most frequently.

Found along the left edge of every folder, the Navigation Pane contains five main sections: Favorites, Libraries, Homegroup, Computer, and Network. Click any of those sections — Favorites, for example — and the window's right side shows you the contents of what you've clicked on.

Here's a more detailed description of each part of the Navigation Pane:

✔ **Favorites:** Not to be confused with your favorite Web sites in Internet Explorer (Chapter 8), the Favorites in the Navigation Pane are words serving as clickable shortcuts to your most frequently accessed locations in Windows:

 • **Desktop:** Your Windows desktop, believe it or not, is actually a folder that's always spread open across your monitor. Clicking Desktop under Favorites shows you the contents of your desktop. (Windows 7 tosses in a few extra icons for other handy spots, including the Recycle Bin, Control Panel, and your user account folder.)

- **Downloads:** Click this shortcut to find the files you've downloaded with Internet Explorer while browsing the Internet. Ah, that's where they ended up!

- **Recent Places:** You guessed it: Clicking this shortcut lists every folder or setting you've recently visited.

✔ **Libraries:** Unlike normal folders, libraries show you the contents of several folders, all collected in one place for easy viewing. Windows' libraries begin by showing the contents of two folders: your *own* folder and its *public* equivalent, which is available to anyone with an account on your PC. (I explain Public folders in Chapter 13.)

- **Documents:** This opens the Documents library, which immediately displays your My Documents and Public Documents folders.

- **Music:** Yep, this shortcut jumps straight to your Music library, where a double-click on a song starts it playing through your PC's speaker.

- **Pictures:** This shortcut opens your Pictures library, the living quarters for all your digital photos.

- **Videos:** Yep, this shortcut jumps straight to your Video library, where a double-click on a video sends the film to Media Player for immediate viewing.

✔ **Homegroup:** New to Windows 7, Homegroups are two or more PCs that share information through a simple network. Click Homegroup in the Navigation Pane to see folders shared by other networked PCs in your Homegroup. (I cover Homegroups and other networks in Chapter 14.)

✔ **Computer:** Opened mainly by PC techies, this button lets you browse through your PC's folders and disks. Other than a quick click to see what lives on a recently inserted flash drive or portable hard drive, you probably won't visit here much.

✔ **Network:** Although Homegroups are the rage in Windows 7, full-blown networks still work, and any networked PCs — including your Homegroup buddies — appear here.

Here are a few tips for making the most of your Navigation Pane:

✔ Feel free to add your own favorite places to the Navigation Pane's Favorites area: Drag and drop folders onto the word Favorites, and they turn into clickable shortcuts.

✔ Don't care for the Navigation Pane? Turn it off by clicking Organize at its top, choosing Layout, and choosing Navigation Pane from the pop-up menu.

✔ Unlike most parts of Windows, the Navigation Pane can't be sorted very much. Favorites, Libraries, Homegroups, Computer, and Network always list their entries in alphabetical order, for example.

✔ Messed up your Favorites or Libraries area? Tell Windows 7 to repair the damage by right-clicking either one and choosing Restore.

Working with the Details Pane

The Windows 7 *Details Pane,* shown in Figure 3-8, hovers like a low-lying cloud along the bottom of every folder. Just as the Details Pane's name implies, the little strip lists arcane details about the item you've currently opened or selected, a treat drooled over by techies.

Figure 3-8:
The Details Pane lists details about the folder or file you've just clicked.

Open a folder, for example, and its Details Pane dutifully lists the number of files that folder contains. It even says whether the files live on your own PC or on a network.

The real information comes when you click a file. For example, click a music file, and the Details Pane shows a thumbnail of the album cover, the song's title, artist, length, and size, and even any rating you've given it through Media Player. Click a photo file to see a thumbnail preview, the date you pressed your camera's shutter button, the photo's size, the camera model, and, on some cameras, the geographic location where you snapped the shot.

✔ The Details Pane knows much more than it first reveals. Because it's resizable, drag its top border up a bit. As the Details Pane grows larger, it starts to reveal more information about your highlighted file: its size, creation date, the date it was last changed, and similar tidbits. Drag the pane back down when you're through viewing.

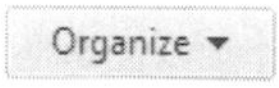

Organize ▼

✔ If you think the Details Pane consumes too much screen space, drag its top border down a bit. Or, turn it off: Click the Organize button on the Command bar's leftmost corner, click Layout from the drop-down menu, and click Details Pane. (Repeat those steps to revive a missing Details Pane.)

TECHNICAL STUFF

✔ While editing a file's properties, feel free to add a *tag* — a keyword that lets you relocate that particular file more quickly. (I cover tags in Chapter 6.)

Moving inside a window with its scroll bar

The scroll bar, which resembles a cutaway of an elevator shaft (see Figure 3-9), rests along the edge of all overstuffed windows. Inside the shaft, a little elevator (technically, the *scroll box*) rides up and down as you page through your work. In fact, by glancing at the elevator's position in the shaft, you can tell whether you're viewing the top, middle, or bottom of a window's contents.

Figure 3-9:
A scroll bar.

You can watch the little box travel up or down as you press the Page Up or Page Down key. (Yes, it's easy to get distracted in Windows 7.) But nudging the elevator around with the mouse is more fun. By clicking in various places on the scroll bar, you can quickly move around inside a document. Here's the dirt:

- ✔ Clicking in the shaft *above* the elevator shifts your view up one page, just as if you'd pressed the Page Up key. Similarly, clicking *below* the elevator shifts the view down one page. The larger your monitor, the more information you can see on each page.

- ✔ To move up your view line by line, click the little arrow (the *scroll arrow*) at the top of the scroll bar. Similarly, clicking the little arrow at the bottom moves your view down one line with each click.

- ✔ Scroll bars occasionally hang out along a window's bottom edge. Handy for viewing spreadsheets and other wide documents, scroll bars let you move your view sideways for peeking at the totals in the spreadsheet's last column.

- ✔ No little scroll box in the bar? Then you're already seeing all that the window has to offer.

- ✔ To move around in a hurry, drag the scroll box up or down the bar. As you drag, you see the window's contents race past. When you see the spot you want, let go of the mouse button to stay at that viewing position.

✔ Using a mouse that has a little wheel embedded in the poor critter's back? Spin the wheel, and the list moves up or down, just as if you were playing with the scroll bar.

Boring borders

A *border* is that thin edge surrounding a window. Compared with a bar, it's really tiny.

To change a window's size, drag the border in or out. (Dragging by a corner gives the best results.)

Some windows, oddly enough, don't have borders. Stuck in limbo, their size can't be changed — even if they're an awkward size.

Except for tugging on them with the mouse, you won't be using borders much.

Filling Out Bothersome Dialog Boxes

Sooner or later, Windows 7 will lapse into surly clerk mode, forcing you to fill out a bothersome form before carrying out your request. To handle this computerized paperwork, Windows 7 uses a *dialog box.*

A dialog box is a window displaying a little form or checklist for you to fill out. These forms can have bunches of different parts, all discussed in the following sections. Don't bother trying to remember each part's name. It's much more important to remember how they work.

Poking the correct command button

Command buttons may be the simplest part of a form to figure out — Microsoft labeled them! Command buttons usually require poking after you've filled out a form. Based on the command button you click, Windows either carries out your bidding (rare) or sends you to another form (most likely).

Table 3-1 identifies the command buttons you'll likely come across.

Table 3-1	Common Windows 7 Command Buttons
Command Button	**Description**
OK	A click on the OK button says, "I've finished the form, and I'm ready to move on." Windows 7 reads what you've typed and processes your request.
Cancel	If you've somehow loused things up when filling out a form, click the Cancel button. Windows whisks away the form, and everything returns to normal. Whew! (**Tip:** The little red X in a window's top corner makes pesky windows go away, as well.)
Next	Click the Next button to move to the next question. (Change your mind on the last question? Back up by clicking the Back arrow near the window's top left.)
Add...	If you encounter a button with dots (. . .) after the word, brace yourself: Clicking that button brings yet *another* form to the screen. From there, you must choose even more settings, options, or toppings.
Restore Defaults	When you change a form or setting for the worse, click the Restore Defaults button with full force. That brings back Windows 7's original settings.

✔ The OK button often has a slightly darker border than the others, meaning it's *highlighted*. Just pressing Enter automatically chooses the form's highlighted button, sparing you the inconvenience of clicking it. (I usually click it anyway, just to make sure.)

✔ If you've clicked the wrong button but *haven't yet lifted your finger from the mouse button,* stop! Command buttons don't take effect until you release your finger from the mouse button. Keep holding down the mouse, but scoot the pointer away from the wrong button. Move safely away and then lift your finger.

✔ Did you stumble across a box that contains a confusing option? Click the question mark in the box's upper-right corner. (It looks like the one in the margin.) Then click the confusing command button to see a short explanation of that button's function in life. Sometimes merely resting your mouse pointer over a confusing button makes Windows take pity, sending a helpful caption to explain matters.

Choosing between option buttons

Sometimes, Windows 7 gets ornery and forces you to select a single option. For example, you can play some games at either a beginner or intermediate level. You can't do *both,* so Windows 7 doesn't let you select both of the options.

Windows 7 handles this situation with an *option button.* When you select one option, the little dot hops over to it. Select the other option, and the little dot hops over to it instead. You find option buttons in many dialog boxes, such as the one in Figure 3-10.

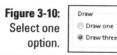

Figure 3-10:
Select one
option.

If you *can* select more than one option, Windows 7 won't present you with option buttons. Instead, it offers the more liberal *check boxes,* which are described in the "Check boxes" section, later in this chapter.

Some programs refer to option buttons as *radio buttons,* named after push buttons on car radios that switch from one station to another.

Typing into text boxes

A *text box* works like a fill-in-the-blanks test in history class. You can type anything you want into a text box — words, numbers, passwords, or epithets. For example, Figure 3-11 shows a dialog box that pops up when you want to search for words or characters in some programs. The text box is where you type the words you want to search for.

- When a text box is *active* (that is, ready for you to start typing stuff into it), either the box's current information is highlighted or a cursor is blinking inside it.

- If the text box *isn't* highlighted or there *isn't* a blinking cursor inside it, it's not ready for you to start typing. To announce your presence, click inside it before typing.

- If you need to use a text box that already contains words, delete any text you don't want before you start typing new information. (Or you can double-click the old information to highlight it; that way, the incoming text automatically replaces the old text.)

- Yes, text boxes have way too many rules.

Choosing options from list boxes

Some boxes don't let you type *anything* into them. They simply display lists of things, letting you pluck the items you want. Boxes of lists are called, appropriately enough, *list boxes*. For example, some word processors bring up a list box if you're inspired enough to want to change the *font* — the style of the letters (see Figure 3-12).

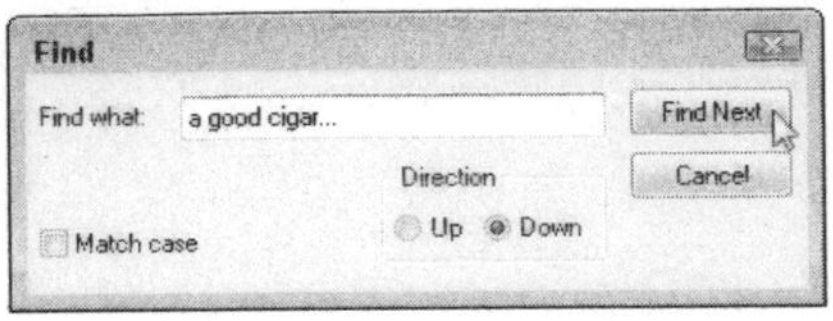

Find

Find what: a good cigar...   Find Next

                    Direction   Cancel

☐ Match case   ○ Up ◉ Down

✔ See how the Lucida Console font is highlighted in Figure 3-12? It's the currently selected item in the list box. Press Enter (or click the OK button), and your program begins using that font when you start typing.

✔ See the scroll bar along the side of the list box? It works just as it does anywhere else: Click the little scroll arrows (or press the up or down arrow) to move the list up or down, and you can see any names that don't fit in the box.

✔ Some list boxes have a text box above them. When you click a name in the list box, that name hops into the text box. Sure, you could type the name into the text box yourself, but it wouldn't be nearly as much fun.

✔ When confronted with zillions of names in a list box or folder, type the first letter of the name you're after. Windows 7 immediately hops down the list to the first name beginning with that letter.

Figure 3-12:
Select a font from the list box.

Font:

Lucida Console

Lucida Console
Lucida Sans Unicode
Microsoft Sans Serif
Palatino Linotype
Segoe Print
Segoe Script

Drop-down list boxes

List boxes are convenient, but they take up a great deal of room. So, Windows 7 sometimes hides list boxes, just as it hides pull-down menus. When you click in the right place, the list box appears, ready for your perusal.

So, where's the right place? It's that downward-pointing arrow button, just like the one shown next to the box beside the True Color (32-bit) option in Figure 3-13. (The mouse pointer is pointing to it.)

Figure 3-13:
Click the
arrow within
the Colors
box to make
a drop-
down list
box display
available
colors.

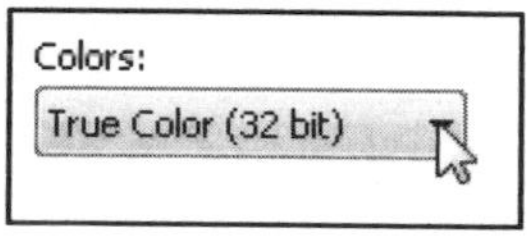

Colors:
True Color (32 bit)

Figure 3-14 shows the drop-down list box after it's been clicked by the mouse. To make your choice, click the option you want from the drop-down list.

Figure 3-14:
A list box
drops down
to display
the
available
colors.

Colors:
True Color (32 bit)
High Color (16 bit)
True Color (32 bit)

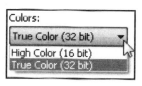

✔ To scoot around quickly in a long drop-down list box, press the first letter of the item you're after. The first item beginning with that letter is instantly highlighted. You can press the up- or down-arrow key to see nearby words and phrases.

✔ Another way to scoot around quickly in a long drop-down list box is to click the scroll bar to its right. (I cover scroll bars earlier in this chapter, if you need a refresher.)

✔ You can choose only *one* item from the list in a drop-down list box.

Check boxes

Sometimes you can choose several options in a dialog box simply by clicking in the little square boxes next to their names. For example, the check boxes shown in Figure 3-15 let you pick and choose options in the game FreeCell.

Clicking in an empty square chooses that option. If the square already has a check mark inside, a click turns off that option, removing the check mark.

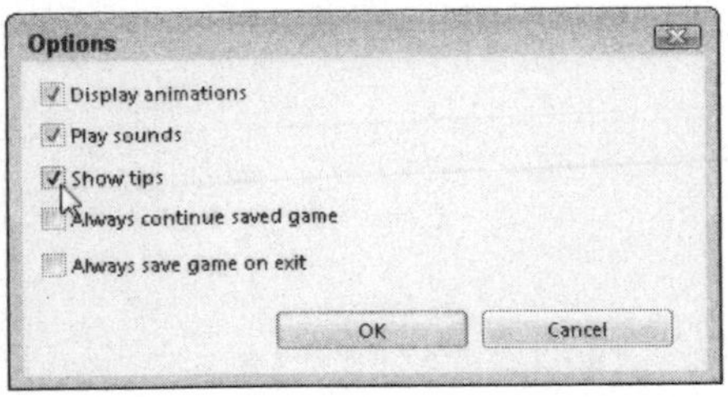

Figure 3-15: Click to check a box.

You can click next to as many check boxes as you want. Option buttons (those similar-looking but round buttons) restrict you to one option from the pack.

Sliding controls

Rich Microsoft programmers, impressed by track lights and sliding light switches in their luxurious new homes, use sliding controls in Windows 7. These virtual light switches are easy to use and don't wear out nearly as quickly as the real ones do.

Some levers slide to the left and right; others move up and down. None of them move diagonally — yet. To slide a control in Windows 7 — to adjust the volume level, for example — just drag and drop the sliding lever, like the one shown in Figure 3-16.

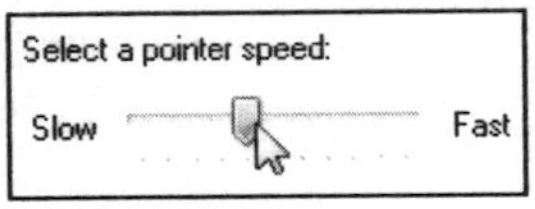

Figure 3-16: A sliding lever.

Sliding works like this: Point at the lever with the mouse and, while holding down the mouse button, move the mouse in the direction you want the sliding lever to move. As you move the mouse, the lever moves, too. When you've moved the lever to a comfortable spot, let go of the mouse button, and Windows 7 leaves the lever at its new position.

Maneuvering Windows Around the Desktop

A terrible dealer at the poker table, Windows 7 tosses windows around your desktop in a seemingly random way. Programs cover each other or sometimes dangle off the desktop. This section shows you how to gather all your windows into a neat pile, placing your favorite window on the top of the stack. If you prefer, lay them all down like a poker hand. As an added bonus, you can change their size, making them open to any size you want, automatically.

Moving a window to the top of the pile

Windows 7 says the window at the top of the pile getting all the attention is called the *active* window. The active window is also the one that receives any keystrokes you or your cat happen to type.

You can move a window to the top of the pile so that it's active in any of several ways:

✔ Move the mouse pointer until it hovers over any portion of your desired window, and then click the mouse button. Windows 7 immediately brings the window to the top of the pile.

✔ On the taskbar, click the button for the window you want. Chapter 2 explains what the taskbar can do in more detail.

✔ Hold down the Alt key and keep tapping the Tab key. A small window pops up, displaying a thumbnail of each open window on your desktop. When your press of the Tab key highlights your favorite window, let go of the Alt key: Your window leaps to the forefront.

✔ On newer PCs, hold down the Windows key (the one with the Windows symbol) and keep tapping the Tab key. A 3-D view of your open windows appears. When your tap o' the Tab key brings your window to the forefront, let go of the Windows key.

Repeat the process when necessary to bring other windows to the front. (And if you want to put two windows on the screen at the same time, read the "Placing two windows side by side" section, later in this chapter.)

Is your desktop too cluttered for you to work comfortably in your current window? Then drag the window's title bar to the left and right, giving it a few quick shakes; Windows 7 drops the other windows down to the taskbar, leaving your main window in place.

Moving a window from here to there

Sometimes you want to move a window to a different place on the desktop. Perhaps part of the window hangs off the edge, and you want it centered. Or maybe you want one window closer to another.

When one just isn't enough

Normally, you can select only one thing at a time in Windows. When you click on another item, Windows deselects the first in order to select the second. When you want to select several things simultaneously, try these tricks:

✔ To select more than one item, hold down the Ctrl key and click each item you want. Each item stays highlighted.

✔ To select a bunch of adjacent items from a list box, click the first item you want. Then hold down Shift and click the last item you want. Windows 7 immediately highlights the first item, last item, and every item in between. Pretty sneaky, huh? (To weed out a few unwanted items from the middle, hold down Ctrl and click them; Windows unhighlights them, leaving the rest highlighted.)

✔ Finally, when grabbing bunches of items, try using the "lasso" trick: Point at an area of the screen next to one item, and, while holding down the mouse button, move the mouse until you've drawn a lasso around all the items. After you've highlighted the items you want, let go of the mouse button, and they remain highlighted.

In either case, you can move a window by dragging and dropping its *title bar*, that thick bar along its top. (If you're not sure how dragging and dropping works, see the sidebar "Dragging, dropping, and running," earlier in this chapter.) When you *drop* the window in place, the window not only remains where you've dragged and dropped it, but it also stays on top of the pile.

Making a window fill the whole screen

Sooner or later, you'll grow tired of all this multiwindow mumbo jumbo. Why can't you just put one huge window on-screen? Well, you can.

To make any window grow as big as it can get, double-click its *title bar,* that topmost bar along the window's top edge. The window leaps up to fill the screen, covering up all the other windows.

To bring the pumped-up window back to its former size, double-click its title bar once again. The window quickly shrinks to its former size, and you can see things that it covered.

✔ If you're morally opposed to double-clicking a window's title bar to expand it, you can click the little Maximize button. Shown in the margin, it's the middle of the three buttons in the upper-right corner of every window.

✔ When a window is maximized to fill the screen, the Maximize button turns into a Restore button, shown in the margin. Click the Restore button, and the window returns to its smaller size.

✔ Windows 7 offers a new way to maximize a window: Drag a window's top edge until it butts against the top edge of your desktop. The shadow of the window's borders will expand to fill the monitor; let go of the mouse button, and the window's borders fill the screen. (Yes, simply double-clicking the title bar is faster, but this method looks cool.)

✔ Too busy to reach for the mouse? Maximize the current window by holding down the Windows key and pressing the Up Arrow key.

Closing a window

When you're through working in a window, close it: Click the little X in its upper-right corner. Zap: You're back to an empty desktop.

If you try to close your window before finishing your work, be it a game of Solitaire or a report for the boss, Windows cautiously asks whether you'd like to save your work. Take it up on its offer by clicking Yes and, if necessary, entering a filename so that you can find your work later.

Making a window bigger or smaller

Like big, lazy dogs, windows tend to flop on top of one another. To space your windows more evenly, you can resize them by *dragging and dropping* their edges inward or outward. It works like this:

1. **Point at any corner with the mouse arrow. When the arrow turns into a two-headed arrow, pointing in the two directions, you can hold down the mouse button and drag the corner in or out to change the window's size.**

2. **When you're happy with the window's new size, release the mouse button.**

   As the yoga master says, the window assumes the new position.

Placing two windows side by side

The longer you use Windows, the more likely you are to want to see two windows side by side. For example, you may want to copy and paste text from one document into another document. By spending a few hours with the mouse, you can drag and drop the windows' corners until they're in perfect juxtaposition.

Or you can simply right-click on a blank part of the taskbar (even the clock will do) and choose Show Windows Side by Side to place the windows next to each other, like pillars. Choose Show Windows Stacked to align them in horizontal rows. (If you have more than three open windows, Show Windows Stacked tiles them across your screen, handy for seeing just a bit of each one.)

If you have more than two windows open, click the Minimize button (shown in the margin) to minimize the ones you *don't* want tiled. Then use the Show Windows Side by Side command to align the two remaining windows.

Windows 7 offers a new way to place two windows side by side. Drag a window against one edge of your desktop; when your mouse pointer touches the desktop's edge and the window's shaded edges fill that side, let go of the mouse button. Repeat these same steps with the second window, dragging it to the opposite side of the monitor.

To make the current window fill the screen's right half, hold the ⊞ key and press the → key. To fill the screen's left half, hold the ⊞ key and press the ← key.

Making windows open to the same darn size

Sometimes a window opens to a small square; other times, it opens to fill the entire screen. But windows rarely open to the exact size you want. Until you discover this trick, that is: When you *manually* adjust the size and placement of a window, Windows memorizes that size and always reopens the window to that same size. Follow these three steps to see how it works:

1. **Open your window.**

   The window opens to its usual, unwanted size.

2. **Drag the window's corners until the window is the exact size and in the exact location you want. Let go of the mouse to drop the corner into its new position.**

   Be sure to resize the window *manually* by dragging its corners or edges with the mouse. Simply clicking the Maximize button won't work.

3. **Immediately close the window.**

   Windows memorizes the size and placement of a window at the time it was last closed. When you open that window again, it should open to the same size you last left it. But the changes you make apply only to the program you made them in. For example, changes made to the Internet Explorer window will only be remembered for *Internet Explorer,* not for other programs you open.

Most windows follow these sizing rules, but a few renegades from other programs may misbehave. Feel free to complain to the manufacturers.

Chapter 4

Flipping Through Files, Folders, Flash Drives, Libraries, and CDs

*T*he Computer program is what causes people to wake up from Windows' easy-to-use computing dream, clutching a pillow in horror. These people bought a computer to simplify their work — to banish that awful filing cabinet with squeaky drawers.

But click the little Computer icon on the Start menu, start poking around inside your new PC, and that old filing cabinet reappears. Folders, with even more folders stuffed inside of them, still rule the world. And unless you grasp Windows' folder metaphor, you may not find your information very easily.

Plus, Windows 7 complicates folders by introducing a new super folder called a *library:* a single folder that simultaneously shows the contents of several other folders.

This chapter explains how to use the Windows 7 filing program, called *Computer.* (Windows XP called the program My Computer.) Along the way, you ingest a big enough dose of Windows file management for you to get your work done. Windows may bring back your dreaded file cabinet, but at least the drawers don't squeak, and files never fall behind the cabinet.

Browsing Your Computer's File Cabinets

To keep your programs and files neatly arranged, Windows cleaned up the convenient file cabinet metaphor with light and airy Windows icons. You can see your new, computerized file cabinets in the Start menu's Computer program. Computer displays all the storage areas inside your computer, allowing you to copy, move, rename, or delete your files before the investigators arrive.

To see your own computer's file cabinets — called *drives* or *disks,* in computer lingo — click the Start menu and choose Computer. Although your PC's Computer window will look slightly different from the one shown in Figure 4-1, it has the same basic sections, each described in the upcoming list.

 Windows can display its Computer window in many ways. To make your Computer window look more like the one in Figure 4-1, click the little arrow to the right of the Views icon from the menu bar (shown in the margin). Then choose Tiles from the menu that squirts out. Finally, right-click a blank part of the Computer window, choose Group By, and select Type.

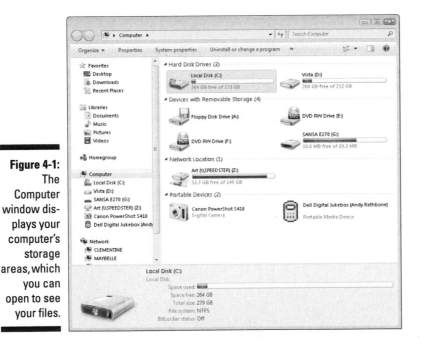

Figure 4-1:
The Computer window displays your computer's storage areas, which you can open to see your files.

These are the basic sections of the Computer window:

✔ **Navigation Pane:** That strip along the left side of most windows, the handy Navigation Pane lists shortcuts to folders carrying your most valuable computerized possessions: your Documents, Pictures, and Music. (It tosses in a few other convenient items, covered in Chapter 3.)

 ✔ **Hard Disk Drives: Shown** in Figure 4-1, this area lists your PC's *hard drives* — your biggest storage areas. Every computer has at least one hard drive, and this PC has two. Double-clicking a hard drive icon displays its files and folders, but you'll rarely find much useful information. Instead of probing your hard drive, open your Start menu to find and start programs.

Notice the hard drive bearing the little Windows icon (shown in the margin)? That means Windows lives on that drive. And see the colored lines beside the two hard drives' icons in Figure 4-1? The more colored space you see in the line, the more files you've stuffed onto your drive. When the line turns red, your drive's almost full, and you should think about upgrading to a larger drive.

✔ **Devices with Removable Storage:** This area shows detachable storage gadgetry attached to your computer. Here are some of the more common ones:

 • **Floppy Drive:** A dying breed, these drives still appear on some older PCs. But because these 20-year-old disks don't hold many files, most people now store files on CDs, DVDs, or flash drives, instead.

 • **CD and DVD drives:** As shown in Figure 4-1, Windows 7 places a short description after each drive's icon to say whether it can only *read* discs or *write* to discs, as well. For example, a DVD burner (shown in the margin) is labeled *DVD-RW,* meaning that it can both read and write to DVDs, as well as to CDs. A drive that can burn CDs but not DVDs is labeled *CD-RW.*

Writing information to a CD or DVD is called *burning.*

 • **Memory card reader and flash drives:** Memory card readers add a little slot to your PC for inserting memory cards from your camera, MP3 player, or similar gadget. Their icons, shown in the margin, look like an empty slot — even after you insert the card to see your files.

 Unlike Vista and XP, Windows 7 doesn't display icons for memory card readers until you've inserted a card into them. To see icons for the empty card readers, open Computer, click Organize, choose Folder and Search options, click the View tab, and click to remove the check mark next to the Hide Empty Drives in the Computer Folder option.

Portable hard drives and *flash drives* — little storage nubs that plug into your PC through a cable or directly into a port — also bear this icon.

- **MP3 players:** Although Windows 7 displays an icon like this for a few MP3 players, it coughs up a generic thumbdrive or hard drive icon for the ultra-popular iPod. (I cover MP3 players in Chapter 15.)

- **Cameras:** Digital cameras usually appear as icons in the Computer window. Be sure to turn on the camera and set it to View Photos mode rather than Take Photos. To grab the camera's pictures, double-click the camera's icon. After Windows 7 walks you through the process of extracting the images (Chapter 16), it places the photos in your Pictures folder.

- ✓ **Network Location:** This icon in the margin, seen only by people who've linked groups of PCs into a *network* (see Chapter 14), represents a folder living on another PC.

If you plug a digital camcorder, cell phone, or other gadget into your PC, the Computer window will often sprout a new icon representing your gadget. If Windows neglects to ask what you'd like to do with your newly plugged-in gadget, right-click the icon; you see a list of everything you can do with that item. No icon? Then you need to install a *driver* for your gadget, a journey detailed in Chapter 12.

Click almost any icon in Computer, and the Preview Pane along the screen's bottom automatically displays information about that object, ranging from its size or the date it was created, for example, or how much space a folder or drive can hold. To see even more information, enlarge the Preview Pane by dragging its top edge upward. The more room you give the pane, the more info it dishes out.

Getting the Lowdown on Folders and Libraries

This stuff is dreadfully boring, but if you don't read it, you'll be just as lost as your files.

A *folder* is a storage area on a drive, just like a real folder in a file cabinet. Windows 7 divides your computer's hard drives into many folders to separate your many projects. For example, you store all your music in your Music folder and your pictures in your Pictures folder. That lets both you and your programs find them easily.

A *library,* by contrast, is a super folder, if you will. Instead of showing the contents of a single folder, it shows the contents of *several* folders. For example, your Music library shows both the tunes living in your *My Music* folder, as well as the tunes in your *Public Music* folder. (The Public Music folder contains music available to everyone who uses your PC.)

Windows 7 created four libraries for you to store your files and folders. For easy access, they live in the Navigation Pane along the left side of every folder. Figure 4-2 shows your libraries: Documents, Music, Pictures, and Videos.

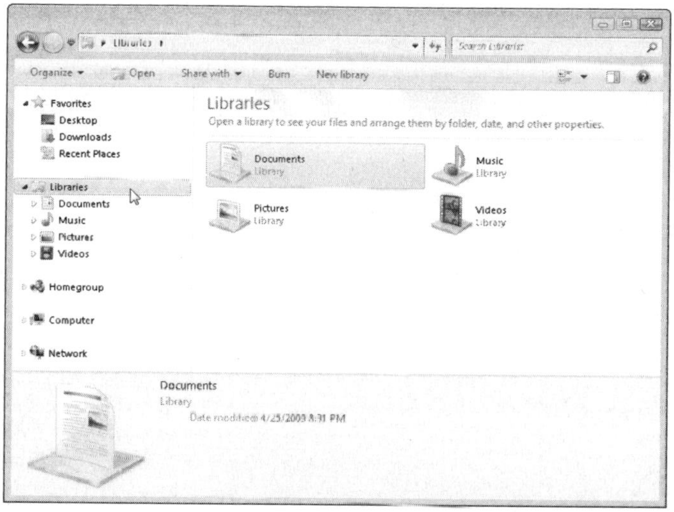

Figure 4-2: Windows 7 provides every person with these same four folders, but it keeps everybody's folders separate.

Keep these folder facts in mind when shuffling files in Windows 7:

- You can ignore folders and dump all your files onto the Windows 7 desktop. But that's like tossing everything into the back seat of the car and pawing around to find your T-shirt a month later. Organized stuff is much easier to find.

- If you're eager to create a folder or two (and it's pretty easy), page ahead to this chapter's "Creating a New Folder" section.

- Computer folders use a *tree metaphor* as they branch out from one main folder (a disk drive) to smaller folders (see Figure 4-3) to more folders stuffed inside those folders.

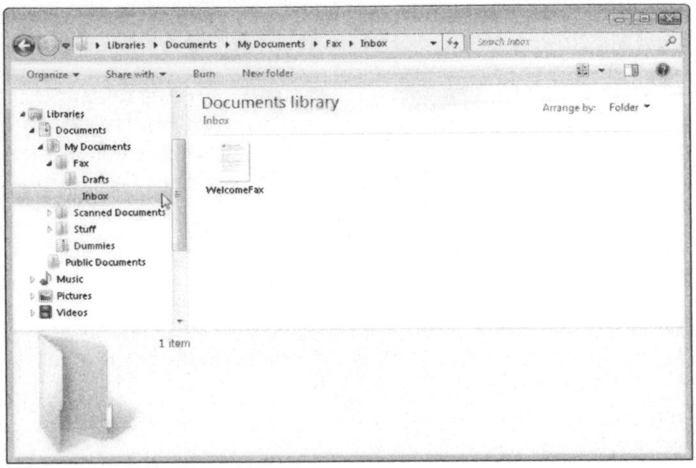

Figure 4-3: Windows' folders use a treelike structure, with main folders branching out to smaller folders.

Peering into Your Drives, Folders, and Libraries

Knowing all this folder stuff not only impresses computer store employees, but also helps you find the files you want. (See the preceding section for a lowdown on which folder holds what.) Put on your hard hat; go spelunking among your computer's drives, folders, and libraries; and use this section as your guide.

Uh, where are the folders I had in Vista?

In Windows Vista, a click on your user account's name atop the Start menu opened your User Account folder, home to your familiar folders: Contacts, Desktop, Documents, Downloads, Favorites, Links, Music, Pictures, Saved Games, Searches, and Videos.

In an effort to distance itself from the unpopular Vista, Windows 7 dumps that organizational strategy in favor of the Navigation Pane, which I cover in Chapter 3. But those old Windows Vista folders haven't disappeared — they're just tucked away. To find them, click the Start button, and double-click your user account name atop the Start menu's right column; your old folders will appear.

Seeing the files on a disk drive

Like everything else in Windows 7, disk drives are represented by buttons, or icons. The Computer program also shows information stored in other areas, such as MP3 players, digital cameras, or scanners. (I explain these icons in the section "Browsing Your Computer's File Cabinets," earlier in this chapter.)

Opening these icons usually lets you access their contents and move files back and forth, just as with any other folders in Windows 7.

When you double-click an icon in Computer, Windows 7 guesses what you want to do with that icon and takes action. Double-click a hard drive, for example, and Windows 7 promptly opens the drive to show you the folders packed inside.

Double-click your CD drive after inserting a music CD, by contrast, and Windows 7 doesn't always open it to show the files. Instead, it usually loads Media Player and begins playing the music. To change Windows 7's guess-work as to how Windows 7 treats an inserted CD, DVD, or USB drive, right-click that inserted item's icon and open AutoPlay. Windows 7 lists everything it can do with that drive and asks you to plot the course.

Adjusting the AutoPlay settings comes in particularly handy for USB thumb-drives. If your thumbdrive carries a few songs, Windows 7 wants to call up Media Center to play them, slowing your access to your thumbdrive's other files.

✔ When in doubt as to what you can do with an icon in Computer, right-click it. Windows 7 presents a menu of all the things you can do to that object. (You can choose Open, for example, to see the files on a CD that Windows 7 wants to play in Media Player.)

✔ If you click an icon for a CD, DVD, or floppy drive when no disk is in the drive, Windows 7 stops you, gently suggesting that you insert a disk before proceeding further.

✔ Spot an icon under the heading Network Location? That's a little door-way for peering into other computers linked to your computer — if there are any. You find more network stuff in Chapter 14.

Seeing what's inside folders

Because folders are really little storage compartments, Windows 7 uses a picture of a little folder to represent a place for storing files.

What's all this path stuff?

A *path* is merely the file's address, similar to your own. When a letter is mailed to your house, for example, it travels to your country, state, city, street, and finally, hopefully, your apartment or house number. A computer path does the same thing. It starts with the letter of the disk drive and ends with the file's name. In between, the path lists all the folders the computer must travel through to reach the file.

For example, look at your Downloads folder. For Windows 7 to find a file stored there, it starts from the computer's C: drive, travels through the Users folder, and then goes through the Andy folder. From there, it goes into the Andy folder's Downloads folder. (Internet Explorer follows that path when saving your downloaded files.)

Take a deep breath and exhale slowly. Now add in the computer's ugly grammar: In a path, a disk drive letter is referred to as **C:** The disk drive letter and colon make up the first part of the path. All the other folders are inside the big C: folder, so they're listed after the C: part. Windows separates these nested folders with something called a *backslash*, or \ The downloaded file's name — *Tax Form 3890*, for example — comes last.

Put it all together, and you get C:\Users\ Andy\Downloads\Tax Form 3890. That's your computer's official path to the Tax Form 3890 file in Andy's Downloads folder.

This stuff can be tricky, so here it is again: The letter for the drive comes first, followed by a colon and a backslash. Then come the names of all the folders leading to the file, separated by backslashes. Last comes the name of the file itself.

Windows 7 automatically puts together the path for you when you click folders — thankfully. But whenever you click the Browse button to look for a file, you're navigating through folders and traversing along the path leading to the file.

To see what's inside a folder, either in Computer or on the Windows 7 desktop, just double-click that folder's picture. A new window pops up, showing that folder's contents. Spot another folder inside that folder? Double-click that one to see what's inside. Keep clicking until you find what you want or reach a dead end.

Reached a dead end? If you mistakenly end up in the wrong folder, back your way out as if you're browsing the Web. Click the Back arrow at the window's top-left corner. (It's the same arrow that appears in the margin.) That closes the wrong folder and shows you the folder you just left. If you keep clicking the Back arrow, you end up right where you started.

The Address Bar provides another quick way to jump to different places in your PC. As you move from folder to folder, the folder's Address Bar — that little word-filled box at the folder's top — constantly keeps track of your trek. For example, Figure 4-4 shows the Address Bar as you peruse the Inbox folder in your Fax folder.

Figure 4-4:
The arrows
offer
shortcuts
between
folders.

Notice the little arrows between the folder names. Those little arrows provide quick shortcuts to other folders and windows. Try clicking any of the arrows; menus appear, listing the places you can jump to from that point. For example, click the arrow after Libraries, shown in Figure 4-5, to jump quickly to your Music library.

Here are some more tips for finding your way in and out of folders:

- ✔ Sometimes, a folder contains too many files or folders to fit in the window. To see more files, click that window's scroll bars. What's a scroll bar? Time to whip out your field guide, Chapter 3.

- ✔ While burrowing deeply into folders, the Forward arrow (shown in the margin) provides yet another quick way to jump immediately to any folder you've plowed through: Click the little downward-pointing arrow next to the Forward arrow in the window's top-left corner. A menu drops down, listing the folders you've plowed through on your journey. Click any name to jump quickly to that folder.

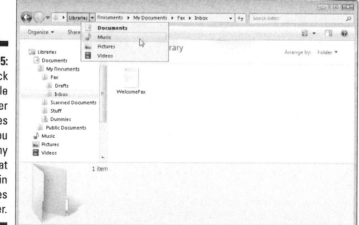

Figure 4-5:
Here, a click
on the little
arrow after
Libraries
lets you
jump to any
place that
appears in
the Libraries
folder.

- Can't find a particular file or folder? Instead of aimlessly rummaging through folders, check out the Start button's Search command, which I describe in Chapter 6. Windows can automatically find your lost files and folders.

- When faced with a long list of alphabetically sorted files, click anywhere on the list. Then quickly type the first letter or two of the file's name. Windows immediately jumps up or down the list to the first name beginning with those letters.

Managing a library's folders

The new library system in Windows 7 may seem confusing, but you can safely ignore the mechanics behind them. Just treat a library like any other folder: a handy spot to store and grab similar types of files. But if you want to know the inner workings behind a library, hang around for this section.

Libraries constantly monitor several folders, displaying all the folders' content in one window. That leads to a nagging question: How do you know *which* folders are appearing in a library? You can find out by double-clicking the library's name.

For example, double-click on the Navigation Pane's Documents library, and you'll see that library's two folders: My Documents and Public Documents, as shown in Figure 4-6.

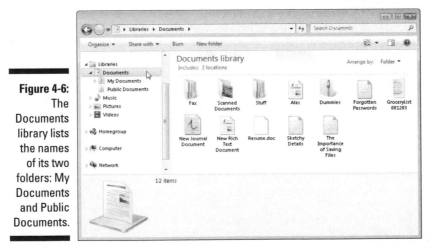

Figure 4-6: The Documents library lists the names of its two folders: My Documents and Public Documents.

If you keep files in another location, perhaps a portable hard drive or even a networked PC, feel free to add them to the library of your choice by following these steps:

2 locations

1. **Click the word Locations in the window's upper-left corner.**

   The number shown in front of the word Locations, shown in the margin, changes depending on how many folders that library currently monitors. When you click Locations, the Documents Library Locations window appears, as shown in Figure 4-7.

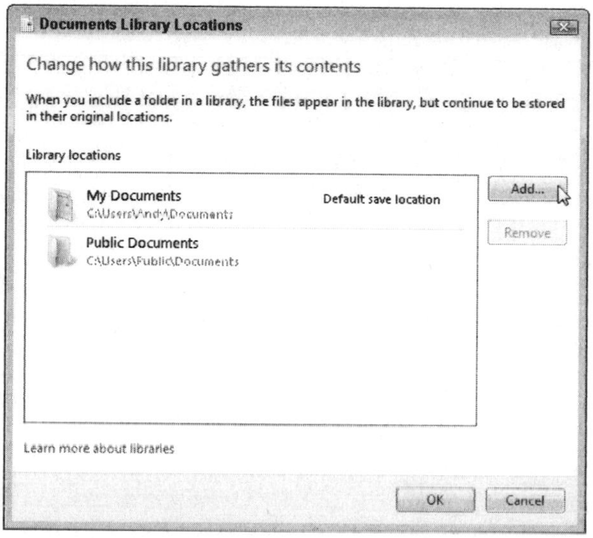

Figure 4-7: The Documents Library Locations window lists the folders visible inside a library.

> **Documents Library Locations**
>
> Change how this library gathers its contents
>
> When you include a folder in a library, the files appear in the library, but continue to be stored in their original locations.
>
> Library locations
>
> | | | | |
> |---|---|---|---|
> | 📁 | **My Documents**
C:\Users\And\Documents | Default save location | Add... |
> | 📁 | **Public Documents**
C:\Users\Public\Documents | | Remove |
>
> Learn more about libraries
>
> OK   Cancel

2. **Click the Add button.**

   The Include Folder in Documents window appears.

3. **Navigate to the folder you want to add, click the folder, and then click the Include Folder button.**

   The library automatically updates itself to display that folder's contents along with the others.

   ✔ You may add as many folders to a library as you want, which is handy when your music files are spread out across many places. The library automatically updates to show the folders' latest contents.

   ✔ To remove a folder from a library, follow the first step but click the folder to be removed and click the Remove button.

✔ So, when you drop a file into a library, which folder does that file *really* live in? It lives in the folder known as the *Default Save Location* — the folder that currently holds the honor of receiving incoming files. For example, when you drop a music file into your Music library, the file goes into your *My Music* folder. Similarly, documents end up in your *My Documents* folder, videos go into *My Videos,* and Pictures go into *My Pictures*.

And what if you want a *different* folder to receive a library's incoming files? To change the receiving folder, click the word Locations. The words Default Save Location appear next to one folder, shown earlier in Figure 4-7. To assign that noble task to a different folder, right-click the different folder and choose Set As Default Save Location.

✔ You can create additional libraries to meet your own needs: Right-click Libraries in the Navigation Pane, choose New, and choose Library from the pop-up menu. A new Library icon appears, ready for you to type in a name. Then begin stocking your new library with folders by following Steps 1–3 in the preceding step list.

✔ Find Windows 7's new libraries to be a colossal headache? Then get rid of them: Right-click any library listed in the Navigation Pane's Libraries section and choose Delete. (Your files remain safe; you're only deleting the library, not its contents.) To put the libraries back in place, right-click the word Libraries in the Navigation Pane and choose Restore Default Libraries.

Creating a New Folder

To store new information in a file cabinet, you grab a manila folder, scrawl a name across the top, and start stuffing it with information. To store new information in Windows 7 — a new batch of letters to the hospital's billing department, for example — you create a new folder, think up a name for the new folder, and start stuffing it with files.

To create a new folder quickly, click Organize from the folder's toolbar buttons and choose New Folder when the little menu drops down. If you don't spot a toolbar, here's a quick and foolproof method:

1. **Right-click inside your folder (or on the desktop) and choose New.**

   The all-powerful right-click shoots a menu out the side.

2. **Select Folder.**

   Choose Folder, as shown in Figure 4-8, and a new folder appears, waiting for you to type a new name.

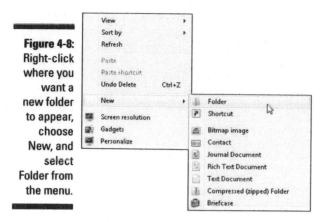

Figure 4-8:
Right-click
where you
want a
new folder
to appear,
choose
New, and
select
Folder from
the menu.

3. **Type a new name for the folder.**

A newly created folder bears the boring name of New Folder. When you begin typing, Windows 7 quickly erases the old name and fills in your new name. Done? Save the new name by either pressing Enter or clicking somewhere away from the name you've just typed.

If you mess up the name and want to try again, right-click on the folder, choose Rename, and start over.

✔ Certain symbols are banned from folder (and file) names. The "Using legal folder names and filenames" sidebar spells out the details, but you never have trouble when using plain old letters and numbers for names.

✔ Shrewd observers notice that in Figure 4-8 Windows offers to create many more things than just a folder when you click the New button. Right-click inside a folder anytime you want to create a new shortcut or other common items.

✔ Cautious observers may remark that their right-click menu looks different than the one shown in Figure 4-8. There's nothing wrong; installed programs often add their own items to the right-click list, making the list look different on different PCs.

Renaming a File or Folder

Sick of a file or folder's name? Then change it. Just right-click the offending icon and choose Rename from the menu that pops up.

Windows highlights the file's old name, which disappears as you begin typing the new one. Press Enter or click the desktop when you're through, and you're off.

Using legal folder names and filenames

Windows is pretty picky about what you can and can't name a file or folder. If you stick to plain old letters and numbers, you're fine. But don't try to stick any of the following characters in there:

```
:  /  \  *  |  <  >  ?  "
```

If you try to use any of those characters, Windows 7 bounces an error message to the screen, and you have to try again. Here are some illegal filenames:

```
1/2 of my Homework
JOB:2
ONE<TWO
He's no "Gentleman"
```

These names are legal:

```
Half of my Term Paper
JOB=2
Two is Bigger than One
A #@$%) Scoundrel
```

Or you can click the file or folder's name to select it, wait a second, and click the file's name again to change it. Some people click the name and press F2; Windows automatically lets you rename the file or folder.

- ✔ When you rename a file, only its name changes. The contents are still the same, the file is still the same size, and the file is still in the same place.

- ✔ To rename large groups of files simultaneously, select them all, right-click the first one, and choose Rename. Type in the new name and press Enter; Windows 7 renames that file. However, it also renames all your *other* selected files to the new name, adding a number as it goes: cat, cat (2), cat (3), cat (4), and so on.

- ✔ Renaming some folders confuses Windows, especially if those folders contain programs. And please don't rename these folders: Documents, Pictures, or Music.

- ✔ Windows won't let you rename a file or folder if one of your programs currently uses it. Sometimes closing the program fixes the problem if you know which one is hanging on to that file or folder. One surefire cure is to restart your PC to release that program's clutches and try again to rename it.

Selecting Bunches of Files or Folders

Although selecting a file, folder, or other object may seem particularly boring, it swings the doors wide open for further action: deleting, renaming, moving, copying, and doing other goodies discussed in the rest of this chapter.

To select a single item, just click it. To select several files and folders, hold down the Ctrl key when you click the names or icons. Each name or icon stays highlighted when you click the next one.

To gather several files or folders sitting next to each other in a list, click the first one. Then hold down the Shift key as you click the last one. Those two items are highlighted, along with every file and folder sitting between them.

Windows 7 lets you *lasso* files and folders as well. Point slightly above the first file or folder you want; then, while holding down the mouse button, point at the last file or folder. The mouse creates a colored lasso to surround your files. Let go of the mouse button, and the lasso disappears, leaving all the surrounded files highlighted.

- ✔ You can drag and drop armfuls of files in the same way that you drag a single file.

- ✔ You can also simultaneously cut or copy and paste these armfuls into new locations using any of the methods described in the "Copying or Moving Files and Folders" section, later in this chapter.

- ✔ You can delete these armfuls of goods, too, with a press of the Delete key.

- ✔ To quickly select all the files in a folder, choose Select All from the folder's Edit menu. (No menu? Then select them by pressing Ctrl+A.) Here's another nifty trick: To grab all but a few files, press Ctrl+A and, while still holding down Ctrl, click the ones you don't want.

Getting Rid of a File or Folder

Sooner or later, you'll want to delete a file that's not important anymore — yesterday's lottery picks, for example, or a particularly embarrassing digital photo. To delete a file or folder, right-click on its name. Then choose Delete from the pop-up menu. This surprisingly simple trick works for files, folders, shortcuts, and just about anything else in Windows.

To delete in a hurry, click the offending object and press the Delete key. Dragging and dropping a file or folder to the Recycle Bin does the same thing.

The Delete option deletes entire folders, including any files or folders stuffed inside those folders. Make sure that you select the correct folder before you choose Delete.

- ✔ After you choose Delete, Windows tosses a box in your face, asking whether you're *sure*. If you're sure, click Yes. If you're tired of Windows' cautious questioning, right-click on the Recycle Bin, choose Properties, and remove the check mark next to Display Delete Confirmation Dialog. Windows now deletes any highlighted items whenever you — or an inadvertent brush of your shirt cuff — press the Delete key.

✔ Be extra sure that you know what you're doing when deleting any file that has pictures of little gears in its icon. These files are usually sensitive hidden files, and the computer wants you to leave them alone. (Other than that, they're not particularly exciting, despite the action-oriented gears.)

FreeCell

✔ Icons with little arrows in their corner (like the one in the margin) are *shortcuts* — push buttons that merely load files. (I cover shortcuts in Chapter 5.) Deleting shortcuts deletes only a *button* that loads a file or program. The file or program itself remains undamaged and still lives inside your computer.

✔ As soon as you find out how to delete files, trot off to Chapter 2, which explains several ways to *un*delete them. (***Hint for the desperate:*** Open the Recycle Bin, right-click your file's name, and choose Restore.)

Copying or Moving Files and Folders

To copy or move files to different folders on your hard drive, it's sometimes easiest to use your mouse to *drag* them there. For example, here's how to move a file to a different folder on your desktop. In this case, I'm moving the Traveler file from the House folder to the Morocco folder.

1. **Aim the mouse pointer at the file or folder you want to move.**

   In this case, point at the Traveler file.

2. **While holding down the right mouse button, move the mouse until it points at the destination folder.**

   As you see in Figure 4-9, the Traveler file is being dragged from the House folder to the Morocco folder. (I describe how to make windows sit neatly next to each other in Chapter 3.)

   Moving the mouse drags the file along with it, and Windows 7 explains that you're moving the file, as shown in Figure 4-9. (Be sure to hold down the right mouse button the entire time.)

Always drag icons while holding down the *right* mouse button. Windows 7 is then gracious enough to give you a menu of options when you position the icon, and you can choose to copy, move, or create a shortcut. If you hold down the *left* mouse button, Windows 7 sometimes doesn't know whether you want to copy or move.

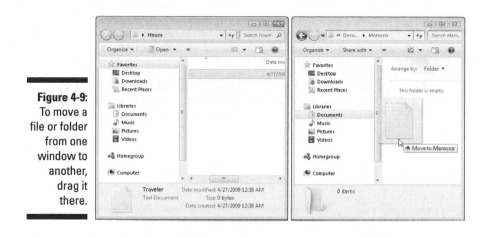

Figure 4-9:
To move a
file or folder
from one
window to
another,
drag it
there.

3. **Release the mouse button and choose Copy Here, Move Here, or Create Shortcuts Here from the pop-up menu.**

Moving a file or folder by dragging it is pretty easy, actually. The hard part is placing both the file and its destination on-screen, especially when one folder is buried deep within your computer.

When dragging and dropping takes too much work, Windows offers a few other ways to copy or move files. Depending on your screen's current layout, some of the following on-screen tools may work more easily:

- **Right-click menus:** Right-click a file or folder and choose Cut or Copy, depending on whether you want to move or copy it. Then right-click on your destination folder and choose Paste. It's simple, it always works, and you needn't place the item and its destination on-screen simultaneously.

- **Menu bar commands:** Click your file and then press Alt to reveal the folder's hidden menus. Click Edit from the menu and choose Copy to Folder or Move to Folder. A new window appears, listing all your computer's drives. Click through the drive and folders to reach the destination folder, and Windows carries out the Copy or Move command. A bit cumbersome, this method works if you know the exact location of the destination folder.

- **Navigation Pane:** Described in Chapter 3, the Computer area displays a list of your drives and folders along the bottom of the Navigation Pane. That lets you drag a file into a folder inside the Navigation Pane, sparing you the hassle of opening a destination folder.

Don't bother reading this hidden technical stuff

You're not the only one creating files on your computer. Programs often store their own information in a *data file*. They may need to store information about the way the computer is set up, for example. To keep people from confusing those files for trash and deleting them, Windows hides them.

You can view the names of these hidden files and folders, however, if you want to play voyeur:

1. **Open any folder, click the Organize button, and choose Folder and Search Options.**

   The Folder Options dialog box appears.

2. **Select the View tab from along the dialog box's top, find the Hidden Files and Folders line in the Advanced Settings section, and click the Show Hidden Files and Folders button.**

3. **Click the OK button.**

The formerly hidden files appear alongside the other filenames. Be sure not to delete them, however: The programs that created them will gag, possibly damaging them or Windows itself. In fact, please click the View tab's Restore Defaults button to hide that stuff again, and click Apply to return the settings to normal.

After you install a program on your computer, don't ever move that program's folder. Programs wedge themselves into Windows. Moving the program may break it, and you'll have to reinstall it. Feel free to move the program's shortcut, though, if it has one.

Seeing More Information about Files and Folders

Whenever you create a file or folder, Windows 7 scrawls a bunch of secret hidden information on it: the date you created it, its size, and even more trivial stuff. Sometimes it even lets you add your own secret information: lyrics and reviews for your music files and folders, or thumbnail pictures for any of your folders.

You can safely ignore most of the information. Other times, tweaking that information is the only way to solve a problem.

To see what Windows 7 is calling your files and folders behind your back, right-click the item and choose Properties from the pop-up menu. Choosing Properties on a Jimi Hendrix song, for example, brings up bunches of details, as shown in Figure 4-10. Here's what each tab means:

✔ **General:** This first tab (shown on the left of Figure 4-10) shows the file's *type* (an MP3 file of the song "Hey Joe"); its *size* (3.27MB); the program that *opens* it (in this case, Windows Media Player); and the file's *location*.

Does the wrong program open your file? Right-click the file, choose Properties, and click the Change button on the General tab. There, you can choose your preferred program from a list.

✔ **Security:** On this tab, you control *permissions:* who can access the file, and what they can do with it — details that become a chore only when Windows 7 won't let your friend (or even you) open the file. If this problem develops, copy the folder to your Public folder, which I cover in Chapter 14. That folder provides a haven where everybody can access the file.

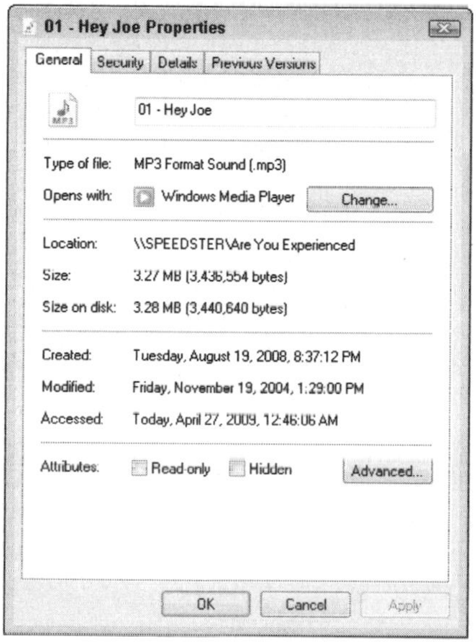

Figure 4-10:
A file's
Properties
page shows
which
program
automati-
cally opens
it, the
file's size,
and other
details.

01 - Hey Joe Properties

General | Security | Details | Previous Versions

01 - Hey Joe

Type of file: MP3 Format Sound (.mp3)

Opens with: Windows Media Player Change...

Location: \\SPEEDSTER\Are You Experienced

Size: 3.27 MB (3,436,554 bytes)

Size on disk: 3.28 MB (3,440,640 bytes)

Created: Tuesday, August 19, 2008, 8:37:12 PM

Modified: Friday, November 19, 2004, 1:29:00 PM

Accessed: Today, April 27, 2009, 12:46:06 AM

Attributes: ☐ Read-only ☐ Hidden Advanced...

OK Cancel Apply

✔ **Details:** True to its name, this tab reveals minute details about a file. On digital photos, for example, this tab lists EXIF (Exchangeable Image File Format) data: the camera model, F-stop, aperture, focal length, and other items photographers love. On songs, this tab displays the song's *ID3 tag* (IDentify MP3): the artist, album title, year, track number, genre, length, and similar information. (I cover ID3 Tags in Chapter 15.)

✔ **Previous Versions:** An obsessive collector, Windows 7 constantly saves previous versions of your files. Made some terrible changes to today's spreadsheet? Take a deep breath, head here, and grab *yesterday's* copy of the spreadsheet. Windows 7's Previous Versions feature works in tandem with trusty System Restore. I cover both of these lifesavers in Chapter 17.

Normally, all these details remain hidden unless you right-click a file and choose Properties. But a folder's Details view can display the details of *all* your files simultaneously, which is handy for quick searches. While in Details view, right-click any word listed at the top of a column, as shown in Figure 4-11. (Click More, at the list's bottom, to see dozens more details, including word count.)

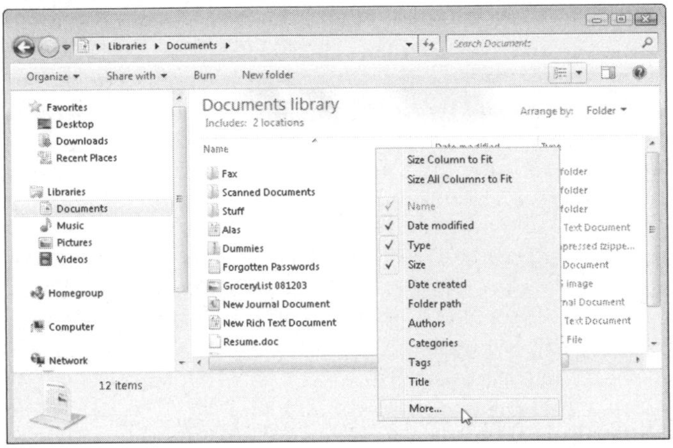

Figure 4-11: Right-click any word along the column's top; a window lets you select which file details to display in the folder.

To switch a folder to Details view, click the arrow by the Views button on the toolbar (shown in the margin.) A menu appears, listing the seven ways a folder can display your files: Extra Large Icons, Large Icons, Medium Icons, Small Icons, List, Details, and Tiles. Try them all to see which view you prefer. (Windows 7 remembers which views you prefer for different folders.)

If you can't remember what a folder's toolbar buttons do, rest your mouse pointer over a button. Windows 7 displays a helpful box summing up the button's mission.

Although some of the additional file information is handy, it can consume a lot of space, limiting the number of files you can see in the window. Displaying only the filename is often a better idea. Then, if you want to see more information about a file or folder, try the following tip.

Folders usually display files sorted alphabetically. To sort them differently, right-click a blank spot inside the folder and choose Sort By. A pop-up menu lets you choose to sort items by size, name, type, and other details.

When the excitement of the Sort By menu wears off, try clicking the words at the top of each sorted column. Click Size, for example, to quickly place the largest files at the list's top. Click Date Modified to quickly sort by the date of their last change, instead.

Writing to CDs and DVDs

Most computers today can write information to a CD or DVD using a flame-less approach known as *burning*. To see whether you're stuck with an older drive that can't burn the discs, remove any discs from inside the drive then open Computer from the Start menu and look at the icon for your CD or DVD drive. You want to see the letters *RW* in the drive icon's name.

 **DVD/CD-RW** If the drive says DVD/CD-RW, like the one in the margin, it can play *and* write to CDs and play but *not* write to DVDs. (I explain how to play DVDs in Chapter 15.)

DVD-RW If your drive says DVD-RW Drive, like the one in the margin, you've hit the jackpot: Your drive can both read and write to CDs *and* DVDs.

TECHNICAL STUFF If your PC has two CD or DVD burners, tell Windows 7 which drive you want to handle the burning chore: Right-click the drive, choose Properties, and click the Recording tab. Then choose your favorite drive in the top box.

Buying the right kind of blank CDs and DVDs for burning

Stores sell two types of CDs: CD-R (short for CD-Recordable) and CD-RW (short for CD-ReWritable). Here's the difference:

- **CD-R:** Most people buy CD-R discs because they're very cheap, and they work fine for storing music or files. You can write to them until they fill up; then you can't write to them anymore. But that's no problem, because most people don't want to erase their CDs and start over. They want to stick their burned disc into the car's stereo or stash it as a backup.

- **CD-RW:** Techies sometimes buy CD-RW discs for making temporary backups of data. You can write information to them, just like CD-Rs. But when a CD-RW disc fills up, you can erase it and start over with a clean slate — something not possible with a CD-R. However, CD-RWs cost more money, so most people stick with the cheaper and faster CD-Rs.

DVDs come in both R and RW formats, just like CDs, so the preceding R and RW rules apply to them, as well. Beyond that, it's chaos: The manufacturers fought over which storage format to use, confusing things for everybody. To buy the right blank DVD, check your DVD burner to see what formats it uses:

DVD-R, DVD-RW, DVD+R, DVD+RW, and/or DVD-RAM. (Most DVD burners from the past few years support *all* of the first four formats, making your choice much easier.)

- ✔ The disc's *x* speed refers to the speed at which it can accept information. For faster disc burning, buy the largest number *x* speed you can find, usually 52x for CDs and 16x for DVDs.

- ✔ Blank CDs are cheap; borrow one from a neighbor's kid to see whether it works in your drive. If it works fine, buy some of the same type. Blank DVDs, by contrast, are more expensive. Ask the store whether you can return them if your DVD drive doesn't like them.

- ✔ For some odd reason, Compact Discs and Digital Video Discs are spelled as "discs," not "disks."

- ✔ Although Windows 7 can handle simple disc-burning tasks, it's extraordinarily awkward at *duplicating* CDs. Most people give up quickly and buy third-party CD-burning software from Roxio or Nero. I explain how Windows 7 creates music CDs in Chapter 15.

- ✔ It's currently illegal to make duplicates of movie DVDs in the United States — even to make a backup copy in case your kids scratch up your new Disney DVD. Windows 7 certainly can't do it, but some programs on Web sites from other countries can.

Copying files from or to a CD or DVD

CDs and DVDs once hailed from the school of simplicity: You simply slid them into your CD player or DVD player. But as soon as those discs graduated to PCs, the problems intensified. When you create a CD or DVD, you need to tell your PC *what* you're copying and *where* you intend to play it: Music for a CD player? Movies for a DVD player? Or simply files for your computer? If you choose the wrong answer, the disc won't work.

Here are the Disc Creation rules:

- ✔ **Music:** To create a CD that plays music in your CD player or car stereo, flip ahead to Chapter 15. You need to fire up the Windows 7 Media Player program and burn an *audio CD*.

- ✔ **Movies and photo slide shows:** To create a DVD with movies or slide shows that play on a DVD player, jump to Chapter 16. You want the *Windows 7 DVD Maker* program.

But if you just want to copy *files* to a CD or DVD, perhaps to save as a backup or to give to a friend, stick around.

Follow these steps to write files to a new, blank CD or DVD. (If you're writing files to a CD or DVD that you've written to before, jump ahead to Step 4.)

Note: If your PC has a third-party disc-burning program, that program may automatically take charge as soon as you insert the disc, bypassing these steps completely. If you want Windows 7 or a different program to burn the disc instead, close the third-party program. Then right-click the drive's icon and choose Open AutoPlay. There, you can tell Windows 7 how to react to an inserted blank disc.

1. **Insert the blank disc into your disc burner and, in the box that appears, choose Burn Files to Disc from the pop-up menu.**

   Windows 7 reacts slightly differently depending on whether you've inserted a CD or DVD, shown in Figure 4-12.

   CD: Windows 7 offers two options:

   - *Burn an Audio CD:* Choosing this option fetches Media Player to create an audio CD that plays music in most CD players. (I describe how to do this task in Chapter 15.)

   - *Burn Files to a Disc:* Choose this option to copy files to the CD.

   DVD: Windows 7 offers two options:

   - *Burn Files to a Disc:* Choose this option to copy files to the DVD.

   - *Burn a DVD Video Disc:* Choosing this option starts Windows 7's DVD Maker program to create a movie or photo slide show, chores I cover in Chapter 16.

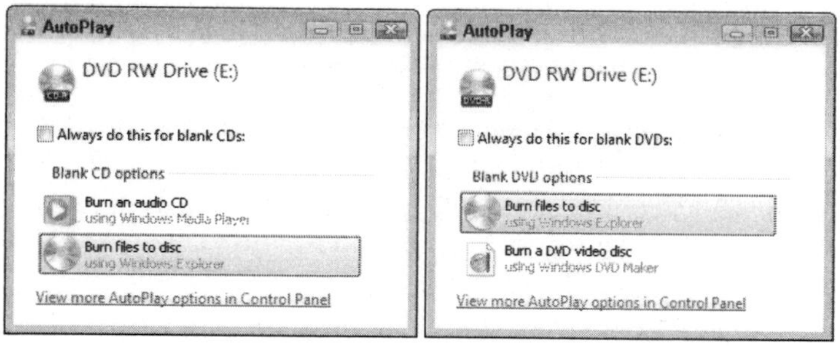

Figure 4-12:
Inserting a blank CD (left) or DVD (right) brings up one of these boxes; choose Burn Files to Disc to copy files to the disc.

2. **Type a name for the disc and describe how you want to use the disc.**

   After you insert the disc and choose Burn Files to a Disc in Step 1, Windows 7 displays a Burn a Disc dialog box and asks you to create a title for the disc.

   Unfortunately, Windows 7 limits your CD or DVD's title to 16 characters. Instead of typing **Family Picnic atop Orizaba in 2009**, stick to the facts: **Orizaba, 2009**. Or, just click Next to use the default name for the disc: the current date.

   Windows can burn the files to the disc two different ways. To decide which method works best for you, it offers you two options:

   - **Like a USB flash drive:** This method lets you read and write files to the disc many times, a handy way to use discs as portable file carriers. Unfortunately, that method isn't compatible with CD or DVD players connected to home stereos or TVs.

   - **With a CD/DVD player:** If you plan to play your disc on your home stereo, choose this method.

   Armed with the disc's name, Windows 7 prepares the disc for incoming files, leaving you with the disc's empty window on-screen, waiting for incoming files.

3. **Tell Windows 7 which files to write to disc.**

   Now that your disc is ready to accept the files, tell Windows 7 what information to send its way. You can do this any of several ways:

   - Right-click the item you want to copy, be it a single file, folder, or selected files and folders. When the pop-up menu appears, choose Send To and select your disc burner from the menu.

   - Drag and drop files and/or folders into the disc burner's open window, or on top of the burner's icon in Computer.

   - Click the Burn button on the toolbar of any folder in your Music folder. This button copies all of that folder's music (or the music files you've selected) to the disc as *files,* readable by some newer car and home stereos that can read WMA or MP3 files.

   - Click the Burn button on the toolbar of any folder in your Picture folder. This copies all that folder's pictures (or the pictures you've highlighted) to the disc for backup or giving to others.

   - Click the Burn button on the toolbar of any folder in your Documents folder. This copies all that folder's files (or any files you've highlighted) to the disc.

   - Tell your current program to save the information to the disc rather than to your hard drive.

   No matter which method you choose, Windows 7 dutifully looks over the information and copies it to the disc you inserted in the first step.

4. Close your disc-burning session by ejecting the disc.

When you're through copying files to the disc, tell Windows 7 you're finished by closing the Computer window: Double-click the little red X in the window's upper-right corner.

Then push your drive's Eject button (or right-click the drive's icon in Computer and choose Eject), and Windows 7 closes the session, adding a finishing touch to the disc that lets it be read in other PCs.

You can keep writing more and more files to the same disc until Windows complains that the disc is full. Then you need to close your current disc, explained in Step 4, insert another blank disc, and start over at Step 1.

If you try to copy a large batch of files to a disc — more than will fit — Windows 7 complains immediately. Copy fewer files at a time, perhaps spacing them out over two discs.

Most programs let you save files directly to disc. Choose Save from the File menu and select your CD burner. Put a disc (preferably one that's not already filled) into your disc drive to start the process.

Working with Flash Drives and Memory Cards

Digital camera owners eventually become acquainted with *memory cards* — those little plastic squares that replaced those awkward rolls of film. Windows 7 can read digital photos directly from the camera, once you find its cable and plug it into your PC. But Windows 7 can also grab photos straight off the memory card, a method praised by those who've lost their camera's special cables.

The secret is a *memory card reader:* a little slot-filled box that stays plugged into your PC. Slide your memory card into the slot, and your PC can read the card's files, just like reading files from any other folder.

Most office supply and electronics stores sell memory card readers that accept most popular memory card formats: Compact Flash, SecureDigital, Mini-Secure Digital, Memory Sticks, and others.

The beauty of card readers is that there's nothing new to figure out: Windows 7 treats your inserted card or floppy just like an ordinary folder. Insert your card, and a folder appears on your screen to show your digital camera photos. The same drag-and-drop and cut-and-paste rules covered earlier in this chapter still apply, letting you move the pictures or other files off the card and into a folder in your Pictures folder.

 Flash drives — also known as thumbdrives — work just like memory card readers. Plug the flash drive into one of your PC's USB ports, and the drive appears as an icon (shown in the margin) in Computer, ready to be opened with a double-click.

 ✔ First, the warning: Formatting a card or disk wipes out all its information. Never format a card or disk unless you don't care about the information it currently holds.

✔ Now, the procedure: If Windows complains that a newly inserted card or floppy isn't formatted, right-click on its drive and choose Format. (This problem happens most often with damaged cards or flash drives.) Sometimes formatting also helps one gadget use a card designed for a different gadget — your digital camera may be able to use your MP3 player's card, for example.

 ✔ Floppy drives, those disk readers from days gone by, still appear on a few older PCs. They work just like memory cards or CDs: Insert the floppy disk into the floppy drive and double-click the floppy drive's icon in Computer to start playing with its files.

 ✔ Press the F5 key whenever you stick in a different floppy disk and want to see what files are stored on it. Windows 7 then updates the screen to show that *new* disk's files, not the files from the first one. (You have to do this step only when working with floppy disks.)

Duplicating a CD or DVD

Windows 7 doesn't have a command to duplicate a CD or DVD. It can't even make a copy of a music CD. (That's why so many people buy CD-burning programs.)

But it can copy all of a CD's or DVD's files to a blank disc using this two-step process:

1. **Copy the files and folders from the CD or DVD to a folder on your PC.**

2. **Copy those same files and folders back to a blank CD or DVD.**

That gives you a duplicate CD or DVD, which is handy when you need a second copy of an essential backup disc.

You can try this process on a music CD or DVD movie, but it doesn't work. (I tried.) It only works when duplicating a disc containing programs or data files.

Part II

Working with Programs and Files

The 5th Wave   By Rich Tennant

"So far he's called up a cobra, 2 pythons, and a bunch of skinks, but still not the file we're looking for."

In this part . . .

The first part of the book explains how to manipulate Windows 7 by poking and prodding its sensitive parts with the mouse.

This part of the book finally lets you get some work done. For example, here's where you find out how to run programs, open existing files, create and save your own files, and print your work when you're through. A primer details the Windows essentials: copying information from one window or program and pasting it into another.

And when some of your files wander (it's unavoidable), Chapter 6 explains how to unleash Windows 7's robotic search hounds to track them down and bring them within reach.

Chapter 5

Playing with Programs and Documents

*I*n Windows, *programs* are your tools: They let you add numbers, arrange words, and shoot spaceships. *Documents,* by contrast, are the things you create with programs: tax forms, heartfelt apologies, and spreadsheets listing high scores.

This chapter starts with the basics of opening programs, creating shortcuts, and cutting and pasting information between documents. Along the way, it throws in a few tricks — how to add things like © to your documents, for example. Finally, it ends with a tour of Windows 7's free programs, showing how to write a letter, calculate your mortgage or gas mileage, or take notes that you spice up with special characters and symbols.

Starting a Program

Clicking the Start button presents the Start menu, the launching pad for your programs. The Start menu is strangely intuitive. For example, if it notices you've been making lots of DVDs, the Start menu automatically moves the Windows DVD Maker icon to its front page for easy access, as shown in Figure 5-1.

Don't see your favorite program on the Start menu's opening list? Click All Programs near the bottom of the Start menu. The Start menu covers up its previously displayed icons with an even *larger* list of programs and category-stuffed folders. Still don't spot your program? Click some of the folders to unveil even *more* programs stuffed inside.

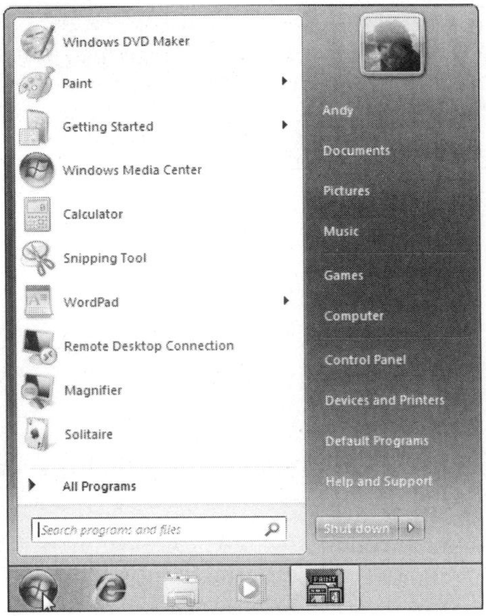

Figure 5-1:
Click the
Start button
and then
click the
program you
want
to open.

When you spot your program, click its name. The program opens onto the desktop, ready for work.

If your program doesn't seem to be living on the Start menu, Windows 7 offers plenty of other ways to open a program, including the following:

- ✔ Open Documents from the Start menu and double-click the file you want to work on. The correct program automatically opens, with that file in tow.

- ✔ Double-click a *shortcut* to the program. Shortcuts, which often sit on your desktop, are handy, disposable push buttons for launching files and folders. (I explain more about shortcuts in this chapter's "Taking the Lazy Way with a Shortcut" section.)

- ✔ If you spot the program's icon on the taskbar — a handy strip of icons lazily lounging along your screen's bottom — click it. The program leaps into action. (I cover the taskbar, including how to customize its row of handy icons, in Chapter 2.)

- ✔ Right-click on your desktop, choose New, and select the type of document you want to create. Windows 7 loads the right program for the job.

- ✔ Type the program's name in the Search box at the bottom of the Start menu and press Enter.

Windows offers other ways to open a program, but these methods usually get the job done. I cover the Start menu more extensively in Chapter 2.

On its front page, the Start menu places *shortcuts* — push buttons — for your most-used programs. Those shortcuts constantly change to reflect the programs you use the most. Don't want the boss to know you play FreeCell? Right-click FreeCell's icon and choose Remove from This List. The shortcut disappears, yet FreeCell's "real" icon remains in its normal spot in the Start menu's Games folder (which hides in the All Programs folder).

Opening a Document

Like Tupperware, Windows 7 is a big fan of standardization. Almost all Windows programs load their documents — often called *files* — exactly the same way:

1. **Click the word File on any program's *menu bar,* that row of staid words along the program's top.**

   If your program hides its menu bar, press Alt to reveal it. Still no menu bar? Then your program might have the rule-breaking Ribbon, a thick bunch of multi-colored symbols along the window's top. If you spot the Ribbon, click the Office button in its corner (shown in the margin) to let the File menu tumble down.

2. **When the File menu drops down, click Open.**

   Windows gives you a sense of déjà vu with the Open window, shown in Figure 5-2: It looks (and works) just like your Documents library, which I cover in Chapter 4.

   There's one big difference, however: This time, your folder displays only files that your program knows how to open — it filters out all the others.

3. **See the list of documents inside the Open dialog box in Figure 5-2? Point at your desired document, click the mouse button, and click the Open button.**

   The program opens the file and displays it on the screen.

Opening a file works this way in most Windows programs, whether written by Microsoft, its corporate partners, or the teenager down the street.

   ✔ To speed things up, double-click a desired file's name; that opens it immediately, automatically closing the Open box.

   ✔ If your file isn't listed by name, start browsing by clicking the buttons shown along the left side of Figure 5-2. Click the Documents library, for example, to see files stored inside.

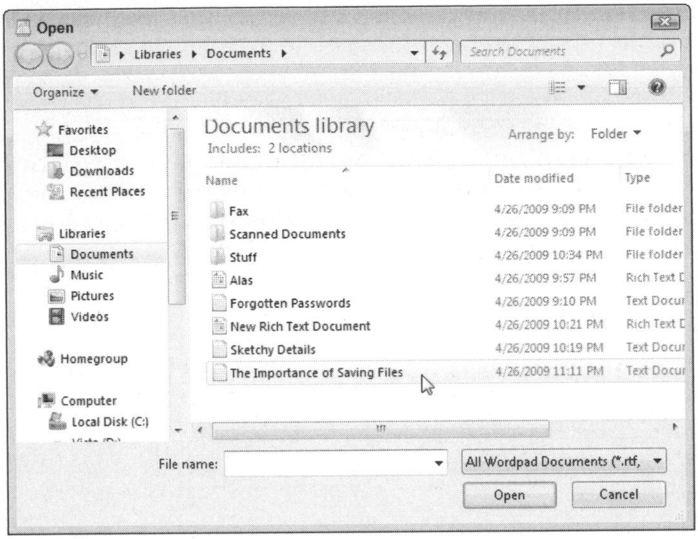

Figure 5-2:
Double-click
the filename
you want
to open.

▶ Puny humans store things in the garage, but computers store their files in neatly labeled compartments called *folders*. (Double-click a folder to see what's stored inside; if you spot your file, open it with a double-click.) If browsing folders gives you trouble, the folders section in Chapter 4 offers a refresher.

▶ Whenever you open a file and change it, even by accident, Windows 7 assumes that you've changed the file for the better. If you try to close the file, Windows 7 cautiously asks whether you want to save your changes. If you changed the file with masterful wit, click Yes. If you made a mess or opened the wrong file, click No or Cancel.

▶ Confused about any icons or commands along the Open box's top or left side? Rest your mouse pointer over the icons, and a little box announces their occupations.

Saving a Document

Saving means to send the work you've just created to a disk or hard drive for safekeeping. Unless you specifically save your work, your computer thinks that you've just been fiddling around for the past four hours. You must specifically tell the computer to save your work before it will safely store it.

Thanks to Microsoft's snapping leather whips, a Save command appears in every Windows 7 program, no matter what programmer wrote it. Here are a few ways to save a file:

- ✔ Click File on the top menu, choose Save, and save your document in your Documents folder or to your desktop for easy retrieval later. (Pressing the Alt key, followed by the letter F and the letter S does the same thing.)

- ✔ Click the Save icon (shown in the margin) on the menu bar.

- ✔ Hold down Ctrl and press S. (S stands for *Save.*)

If you're saving something for the first time, Windows 7 asks you to think up a name for your document. Type something descriptive using only letters, numbers, and spaces between the words. (If you try to use one of the illegal characters I describe in Chapter 4, the Windows Police step in, politely requesting that you use a different name.)

- ✔ Choose descriptive filenames for your work. Windows 7 gives you 255 characters to work with. A file named *June Report on Squeegee Sales* is easier to locate than one named *Stuff.*

When programmers fight over file types

When not fighting over fast food, programmers fight over *formats* — ways to pack information into a file. To accommodate the format wars, some programs have a special feature that lets you open files stored in several different types of formats.

For example, look at the drop-down list box in the bottom-right corner of Figure 5-2. It currently lists All Wordpad Documents (*.rtf), one of several formats used by WordPad. To see files stored in *other* formats, click in that box and choose a different format. The Open box quickly updates its list to show files from that new format, instead.

And how can you see a list of *all* your folder's files in that menu, regardless of their content?

Choose All Documents from the drop-down list box. You'll see all your files, but your program probably won't be able to open all of them and will choke if it tries.

WordPad lists digital photos in its All Documents menu, for example. But if you try to open a photo, WordPad dutifully displays the photo as obscure coding symbols. (If you ever mistakenly open a photo in a program and *don't* see the photo, don't try to save what you've opened. If the program is like WordPad, saving the file will ruin the photo. Simply turn tail and exit immediately with a click on the Cancel button.)

✔ You can save files to any folder, CD, or even a memory card. But files are much easier to find down the road when they stay in the Documents library. (Feel free to save a *second* copy onto your CD as a backup.)

✔ Most programs can save files directly to a CD. Choose Save from the File menu and choose your CD drive from the Navigation Pane's Computer area. Put a CD (preferably one that's not already filled) into your CD-writing drive to start the process.

✔ If you're working on something important (and most things are), choose the program's Save command every few minutes. Or use the Ctrl+S keyboard shortcut (while holding down the Ctrl key, press the S key). Programs make you choose a name and location for a file when you *first* save it; subsequent saves are much speedier.

Choosing Which Program Opens a File

Most of the time, Windows 7 automatically knows which program should open which file. Double-click any file, and Windows tells the correct program to jump in and let you view its contents. But when Windows 7 gets confused, the problem lands in *your* lap.

The next two sections explain what to do when the wrong program opens your file or, even worse, *no* program offers to do the job.

If somebody says something about "file associations," feel free to browse the technical sidebar, "The awkward world of file associations," which explains that awful subject.

The wrong program loads my file!

Double-clicking a document usually brings up the correct program, usually the same program you used to create that document. But sometimes the wrong program keeps jumping in, hijacking one of your documents. (Different brands of media players constantly fight over the right to play your music or videos, for example.)

When the wrong program suddenly begins opening your document, here's how to make the *right* program open it instead:

1. **Right-click your problematic file and select Open With from the pop-up menu.**

   As shown in Figure 5-3, Windows lists a few capable programs, including ones you've used to open that file in the past.

What's the difference between Save and Save As?

Huh? Save as *what?* A chemical compound? Naw, the Save As command just gives you a chance to save your work with a different name and in a different location.

Suppose that you open the *Ode to Tina* file and change a few sentences. You want to save your new changes, but you don't want to lose the original words, either. Preserve *both* versions by selecting *Save As* and typing the new name, *Tentative Additions to Odes to Tina.*

When you're saving something for the *first* time, the Save and Save As commands are identical: Both make you choose a fresh name and location for your work.

2. **Click Choose Default Program and select the program you want to open the file.**

   The Open With window, shown in Figure 5-4, lists more programs. If you spot your favorite program, you *could* double-click it to open your file immediately. But that wouldn't prevent the same problem from recurring. The *next* step tackles that challenge.

   TIP

   If Windows doesn't include your favorite program anywhere on its list, you have to look for it. Choose Default Programs, click the Browse button, and navigate to the folder containing the program you want. (**Hint:** Hover your mouse pointer over the folders to see some of the files and programs inside.)

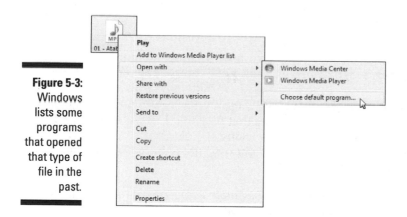

Figure 5-3: Windows lists some programs that opened that type of file in the past.

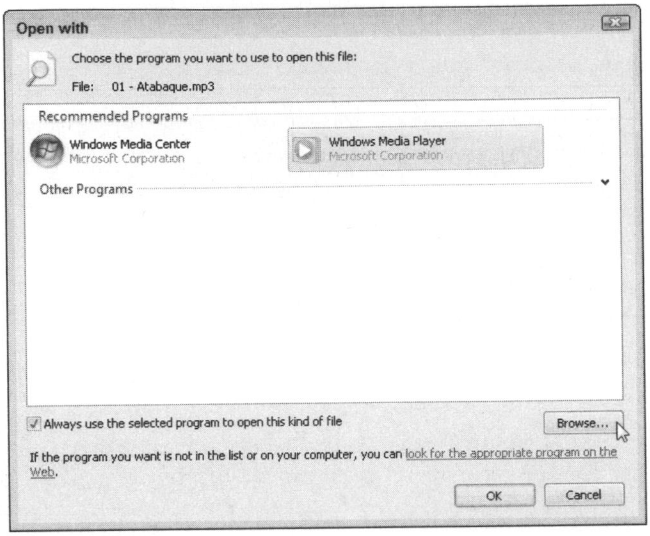

Open with

Choose the program you want to use to open this file:

File: 01 - Atabaque.mp3

Recommended Programs

Windows Media Center
Microsoft Corporation

Windows Media Player
Microsoft Corporation

Other Programs

☑ Always use the selected program to open this kind of file   Browse...

If the program you want is not in the list or on your computer, you can look for the appropriate program on the Web.

OK   Cancel

Figure 5-4:
Choose the
program you
want and
click the
check box
at the
bottom.

3. **Select the Always Use the Selected Program to Open This Kind of File check box and click OK.**

   That checked box makes Windows return top-billing status to your selected program. For example, choosing Paint Shop Pro (and checking the Always box) tells Windows to summon Paint Shop Pro every time you double-click that type of file.

   ✔ Sometimes you'll want to alternate between two programs when working on the same document. To do so, right-click the document, choose Open With, and select the program you need at that time.

   ✔ Occasionally you can't make your favorite program open a particular file because it simply doesn't know how. For example, Windows Media Player can usually play videos, *except* when they're stored in QuickTime, a format used by Microsoft's competition. Your only solution is to install QuickTime (www.apple.com/quicktime) and use it to open that particular video.

   ✔ Can't find *any* program to open your file? Then you're primed for the very next section.

No program will open my file!

It's frustrating when several programs fight to open your file. But it's even worse when *no program* ponies up to the task. Double-clicking your file merely summons the cryptic error message shown in Figure 5-5.

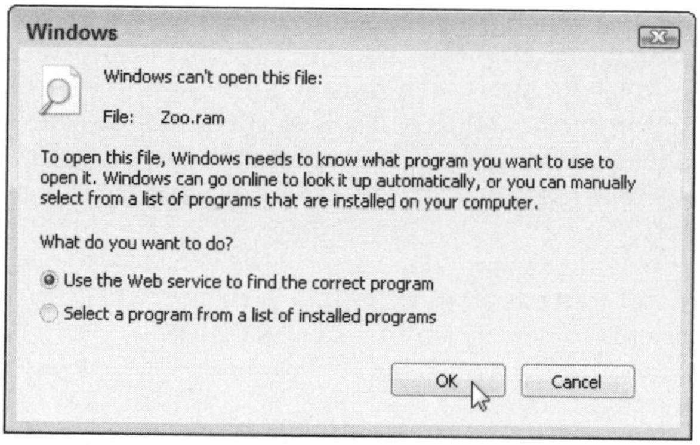

Windows

Windows can't open this file:

File: Zoo.ram

To open this file, Windows needs to know what program you want to use to open it. Windows can go online to look it up automatically, or you can manually select from a list of programs that are installed on your computer.

What do you want to do?

⦿ Use the Web service to find the correct program

◯ Select a program from a list of installed programs

[OK]   [Cancel]

Figure 5-5:
Sometimes Windows refuses to open a file.

If you already know the program needed to open your file, choose the second option: Select a Program from a List of Installed Programs. That summons the familiar window from Figure 5-4, letting you choose your program and click OK to open the file.

TECHNICAL STUFF

The awkward world of file associations

Every Windows program slaps a secret code known as a *file extension* onto the name of every file it creates. The file extension works like a cattle brand: When you double-click the file, Windows 7 eyeballs the extension and automatically summons the proper program to open the file. Notepad, for example, tacks on the three-letter extension .txt to every file it creates. So the .txt extension is associated with Notepad.

Windows 7 normally doesn't display these extensions, isolating users from Windows' inner mechanisms for safety reasons. If somebody accidentally changes or removes an extension, Windows won't know how to open that file.

If you're curious as to what an extension looks like, sneak a peek by following these steps:

1. **Click the Organize button from inside any folder and choose Folder and Search Options from the drop-down menu.**

The Folder Options dialog box appears.

2. **Click the View tab and then click the Hide Extensions for Known File Types box to remove the check mark.**

3. **Click the OK button.**

The files all reveal their extensions — a handy thing to know in technical emergencies.

Now that you've peeked, hide the extensions again by repeating the steps, but put a check mark back in the Hide Extensions for Known File Types box.

The moral? Don't *ever* change a file's extension unless you know exactly what you're doing; Windows 7 will forget what program to use for opening the file, leaving you holding an empty bag.

But if you have no idea which program should open your mystery file, choose the Use the Web Service to Find the Correct Program option and click OK. Windows dashes off to the Internet in search of the right program. If you're lucky, Internet Explorer visits Microsoft's Web site and suggests a place to download a capable program. Download and install the program (after scanning it with a virus-checking program described in Chapter 10), and you've solved the problem.

Sometimes Microsoft routes you directly to a Web site, as shown in Figure 5-6, where you can download a program that opens the file.

Figure 5-6: Windows sometimes helps you find a program for opening an orphaned file.

✔ In Figure 5-6, Microsoft identified a *Real video* file. Microsoft sends you to Real Video's Web site, where you can download and install their free RealPlayer program.

✔ When you visit a Web site to download a suggested program like the RealPlayer and QuickTime movie players, you often find *two* versions: Free and Professional (expensive). The free version often works fine, so try it first.

✔ When trying to open an e-mailed attachment, you might see the error, "This file does not have a program associated with it for performing this action. Create an association in the Folders Options in Control Panel." That complex message simply means that your PC doesn't have the right program installed to open that particular file, which leads to the next bulleted item.

✔ If you can't find *any* program that lets you open your file, you're simply stuck. You must contact the people who gave you that file and ask them what program you need to open it. Then, unfortunately, you'll probably have to buy that program.

Taking the Lazy Way with a Shortcut

Some items are buried *way* too deeply inside of your computer. If you're tired of meandering through the woods to find your favorite program, folder, disk drive, document, or even a Web site, create a *shortcut* — an icon push button that takes you directly to the object of your desires.

Because a shortcut is a mere push button that launches something else, you can move, delete, and copy shortcuts without harming the original. They're safe, convenient, and easy to create. And they're easy to tell apart from the original, because they have a little arrow lodged in their bottom-left corner, such as the FreeCell shortcut shown in the margin.

Follow these instructions to create shortcuts to these popular Windows doodads:

- ✔ **Folders or Documents:** Right-click on the folder or document, choose Send To, and select the Desktop (Create Shortcut) option. When the shortcut appears on your desktop, drag and drop it to a handy corner, the taskbar, the Navigation Pane's Favorites area, or even your Start menu.

- ✔ **Web sites:** See the little icon in front of the Web site's address in Internet Explorer's Address Bar? Drag and drop that little icon to your desktop — or anyplace else. (It helps to drag one of Internet Explorer's window edges inward so that you can see part of your desktop.) You can also add Web sites to Internet Explorer's handy list of Favorites, which I describe in Chapter 8.

- ✔ **Anything on your Start menu:** Hold down the right-mouse button and drag the icon from the Start menu to your desktop. When you release the mouse button, choose Create Link in Desktop.

- ✔ **Nearly anything:** Drag and drop the object to a new place while holding down your right mouse button. When you let go of the mouse button, choose Create Shortcuts Here, and the shortcut appears.

- ✔ **Control Panel:** Found a particularly helpful setting in Control Panel, Windows 7's built-in switch box? Drag the helpful icon onto your desktop, the Navigation Pane's Favorites area, or any other handy spot. The icon turns into a shortcut for easy access.

- ✔ **Disk drives:** Open Computer from the Start menu, right-click the drive you want, and choose Create Shortcut. Windows immediately places a shortcut to that drive on your desktop.

Here are some more tips for shortcuts:

- ✔ For quick CD or DVD burning, put a shortcut to your disc burner on your desktop. Burning files to disc becomes as simple as dragging and dropping them onto the disc burner's new shortcut. (Insert a blank disc into the disc burner's tray, confirm the settings, and begin burning.)

✔ Feel free to move shortcuts from place to place but *don't* move the items they launch. If you do, the shortcut won't be able to find the item, causing Windows to panic, searching (usually vainly) for the moved goods.

✔ Want to see what program a shortcut will launch? Right-click the shortcut and click Open File Location (if available). The shortcut quickly takes you to its leader.

The Absolutely Essential Guide to Cutting, Copying, and Pasting

Windows took a tip from the kindergartners and made *cut and paste* an integral part of life. You can electronically *cut* or *copy* and then *paste* just about anything somewhere else with little fuss and even less mess.

Windows programs are designed to work together and share information, making it fairly easy to put a scanned photo onto your party invitation fliers. You can move files by cutting or copying them from one place and pasting them into another. And you can easily cut and paste paragraphs to different locations within a program.

The beauty of Windows 7 is that, with all those windows on-screen at the same time, you can easily grab bits and pieces from any of them and paste all the parts into a brand-new window.

Don't overlook copying and pasting for the small stuff. Copying a name and address from your address program is much quicker than typing it into your letter by hand. Or, when somebody e-mails you a Web address, copy and paste it directly into Internet Explorer's Address Bar. It's easy to copy most items displayed on Web sites, too (much to the dismay of many professional photographers).

The quick 'n' dirty guide to cut 'n' paste

In compliance with the Don't Bore Me with Details Department, here's a quick guide to the three basic steps used for cutting, copying, and pasting:

1. **Select the item to cut or copy: a few words, a file, a Web address, or any other item.**

2. **Right-click on your selection and choose Cut or Copy from the menu, depending on your needs.**

   Use *Cut* when you want to *move* something. Use *Copy* when you want to duplicate something, leaving the original intact.

Keyboard shortcut: Hold down Ctrl and press X to cut or C to copy.

3. **Right-click on the item's destination and choose Paste.**

You can right-click inside a document, folder, or nearly any other place.

Keyboard shortcut: Hold down Ctrl and press V to paste.

The next three sections explain each of these three steps in more detail.

Selecting things to cut or copy

Before you can shuttle pieces of information to new places, you have to tell Windows 7 exactly what you want to grab. The easiest way to tell it is to *select* the information with a mouse. In most cases, selecting involves one swift trick with the mouse, which then highlights whatever you've selected.

✔ **To select text in a document, Web site, or spreadsheet:** Put the mouse arrow or cursor at the beginning of the information you want and hold down the mouse button. Then move the mouse to the end of the information and release the button. That's it! That selects all the stuff lying between where you clicked and released, as shown in Figure 5-7.

Be careful after you highlight a bunch of text. If you accidentally press the letter *k*, for example, the program replaces your highlighted text with the letter *k*. To reverse that calamity, choose Undo from the program's Edit menu (or press Ctrl+Z, which is the keyboard shortcut for Undo).

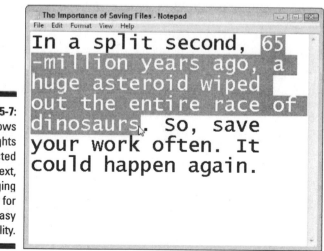

Figure 5-7: Windows highlights the selected text, changing its color for easy visibility.

✔ **To select any files or folders:** Simply click a file or folder to select it. To select *several* items, try these tricks:

- **If all the files are in a row:** Click the first item in the bunch, hold down the Shift key, and then select the last item. Windows highlights the first and last items, as well as everything in between.

- **If the files *aren't* in a row:** Hold down the Ctrl key while clicking each file or folder you want to select.

Now that you've selected the item, the next section explains how to cut or copy it.

✔ After you've selected something, cut it or copy it *immediately*. If you absentmindedly click the mouse someplace else, your highlighted text or file reverts to its boring self, and you're forced to start over.

✔ To delete any selected item, be it a file, paragraph, or picture, press the Delete key.

Cutting or copying your selected goods

After you select some information (which I describe in the preceding section, in case you just arrived), you're ready to start playing with it. You can cut it or copy it. (Or just press Delete to delete it.)

This bears repeating. After selecting something, right-click it. When the menu pops up, choose Cut or Copy, depending on your needs, as shown in Figure 5-8. Then right-click your destination and choose Paste.

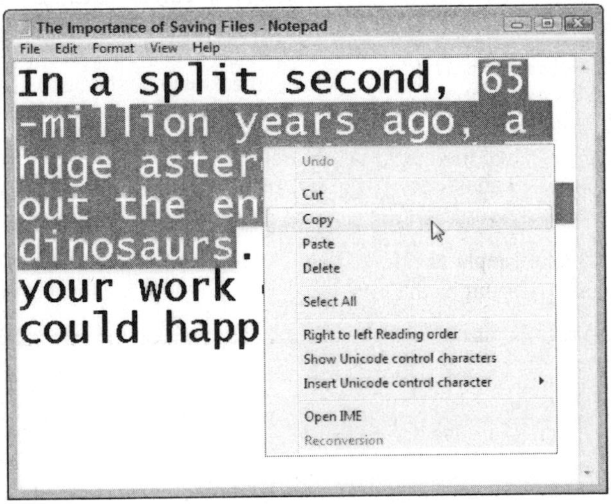

Figure 5-8:
To copy information into another window, right-click your selection and choose Copy.

The Importance of Saving Files - Notepad
File   Edit   Format   View   Help

In a split second, 65
-million years ago, a
huge aster
out the en
dinosaurs.
your work
could happ

Undo
Cut
Copy
Paste
Delete
Select All
Right to left Reading order
Show Unicode control characters
Insert Unicode control character ▸
Open IME
Reconversion

The Cut and Copy options differ drastically. How do you know which one to choose?

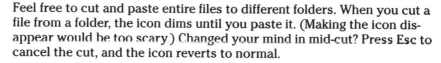

✔ **Choose Cut to move information.** *Cutting* wipes the selected information off the screen, but you haven't lost anything: Windows stores the cut information in a hidden Windows storage tank called the *Clipboard,* waiting for you to paste it.

Feel free to cut and paste entire files to different folders. When you cut a file from a folder, the icon dims until you paste it. (Making the icon disappear would be too scary.) Changed your mind in mid-cut? Press Esc to cancel the cut, and the icon reverts to normal.

✔ **Choose Copy to make a copy of the information.** Compared with cutting, *copying* information is quite anticlimactic. Whereas cutting removes the item from view, copying the selected item leaves it in the window, seemingly untouched. Copied information also goes to the Clipboard until you paste it.

Selecting individual letters, words, paragraphs, and more

When dealing with words in Windows, these shortcuts help you quickly select information:

✔ To select an individual *letter or character,* click in front of the character. Then while holding down the Shift key, press your → key. Keep holding down these two keys to keep selecting text in a line.

✔ To select a single *word,* point at it with the mouse and double-click. The word changes color, meaning it's highlighted. (In most word processors, you can hold down the button on its second click, and then by moving the mouse around, you can quickly highlight additional text word by word.)

✔ To select a single *line* of text, simply click next to it in the left margin. To highlight additional text line by line, keep holding down the mouse button and move the mouse up or down. You can also keep selecting additional lines by holding down the Shift key and pressing the ↓ key or the ↑ key.

✔ To select a *paragraph,* just double-click next to it in the left margin. To highlight additional text paragraph by paragraph, keep holding down the mouse button on the second click and move the mouse.

✔ To select an entire *document,* hold down Ctrl and press A. (Or choose Select All from the Edit menu.)

To copy a picture of your entire Windows desktop (the *whole screen*) to the Clipboard, press the Print Screen key, which is sometimes labeled PrtScrn or something similar. (And, no, the Print Screen key doesn't send anything to your printer.) You can then paste the picture into the Paint program and print it from there.

Pasting information to another place

After you cut or copy information to the Windows Clipboard, it's ready for travel. You can *paste* that information nearly anyplace else.

Pasting is relatively straightforward:

1. **Open the destination window and move the mouse pointer or cursor to the spot where you want the stuff to appear.**

2. **Right-click the mouse and choose Paste from the pop-up menu.**

   Presto! The item you just cut or copied immediately leaps into its new spot.

Or, if you want to paste a file onto the desktop, right-click on the desktop and choose Paste. The cut or copied file appears where you've right-clicked.

- The Paste command inserts a *copy* of the information that's sitting on the Clipboard. The information stays on the Clipboard, so you can keep pasting the same thing into other places if you want.

- Some programs have toolbars along their tops, offering one-click access to Cut, Copy, and Paste, as shown in Figure 5-9.

Figure 5-9:
The Cut, Copy, and Paste buttons.

Windows 7's Free Programs!

Windows 7, the fanciest Windows version yet, comes with a few free programs, such as a music player, DVD burner, and small word processor. These bonus freebies make customers happy and make the government's anti-monopoly departments flap their long black robes.

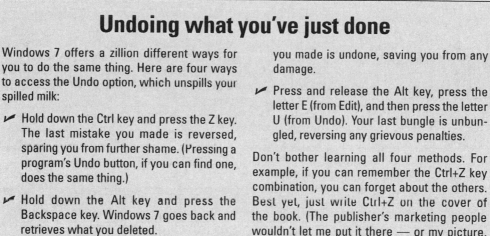

Undoing what you've just done

Windows 7 offers a zillion different ways for you to do the same thing. Here are four ways to access the Undo option, which unspills your spilled milk:

✔ Hold down the Ctrl key and press the Z key. The last mistake you made is reversed, sparing you from further shame. (Pressing a program's Undo button, if you can find one, does the same thing.)

✔ Hold down the Alt key and press the Backspace key. Windows 7 goes back and retrieves what you deleted.

✔ Click Edit and then click Undo from the menu that falls down. The last command you made is undone, saving you from any damage.

✔ Press and release the Alt key, press the letter E (from Edit), and then press the letter U (from Undo). Your last bungle is unbungled, reversing any grievous penalties.

Don't bother learning all four methods. For example, if you can remember the Ctrl+Z key combination, you can forget about the others. Best yet, just write Ctrl+Z on the cover of the book. (The publisher's marketing people wouldn't let me put it there — or my picture, but that's another story.)

Windows 7 comes with far fewer free programs than Windows Vista or Windows XP. Windows 7 dumps Windows Mail (the e-mail program), Windows Photo Gallery (the photo editor), Windows Movie Maker, and Windows Calendar. Microsoft replaced the first three with downloadable programs that I cover in Part V of this book.

This chapter merely focuses on the most useful small freebies: the WordPad word processor, the Calculator, and Character Map.

Writing letters with WordPad

WordPad is nowhere near as fancy as some of the more expensive word processors on the market. It can't create tables or multiple columns, like you see in newspapers or newsletters. Worst of all, there's no spell checker.

WordPad works fine for quick letters, simple reports, and other basic stuff. You can change the fonts, too. And because all Windows users have WordPad on their computers, most computer owners can read anything you create in WordPad.

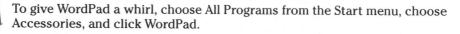

To give WordPad a whirl, choose All Programs from the Start menu, choose Accessories, and click WordPad.

WordPad springs to the screen, but wearing new clothes. In Windows 7, WordPad sports a new icon-filled Ribbon menu across its top, shown in Figure 5-10.

If you've just ditched your typewriter for Windows, remember this: On an electric typewriter, you have to press the Return key at the end of each line, or you start typing off the edge of the paper. Computers avoid that problem by automatically dropping down a line and continuing the sentence. (Tech hipsters call this phenomenon *word wrap*.)

✔ To change fonts in WordPad, select the words you'd like to change (or select the entire document by choosing Select All from the Ribbon's Editing section). Then choose your favorite font from the Font drop-down menu.

✔ WordPad can open files created in Microsoft Word 2007, but it strips away their fancier formatting.

✔ No, there's no way to ditch the WordPad's Ribbon and return to the old menus.

✔ Looking for keyboard shortcut commands to control WordPad? Press Alt, and a letter appears next to each portion of the Ribbon. Press the letter assigned to the Ribbon section you want, and a letter appears next to each command. Press one of those letters to choose that command. (Yes, it's more awkward than the old menu.)

✔ Quickly insert the current day, date, or time into your document by choosing Date and Time from the Ribbon's Insert section. Choose the style of date or time you want from the pop-up menu, and WordPad inserts it into your document.

Figure 5-10:
WordPad's
new Ribbon
emphasizes
buttons
rather than
words, and
it adds
tabs for
switching
between
menus.

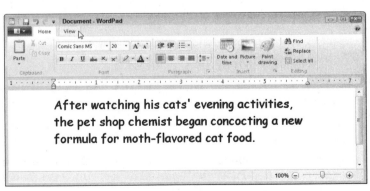

Converting, adding, and balancing with Calculator

For years, Windows' tiny Calculator program looked like it dropped from a Wal-Mart bargain bin. It added, subtracted, multiplied, and divided, but that was about it. The symbols were small and hard to read.

Windows 7 significantly jazzes up Calculator with a new layout; four modes (standard, scientific, programmer, and statistics); data conversion; and templates for calculating gas mileage, leases, and mortgage payments (shown in Figure 5-11).

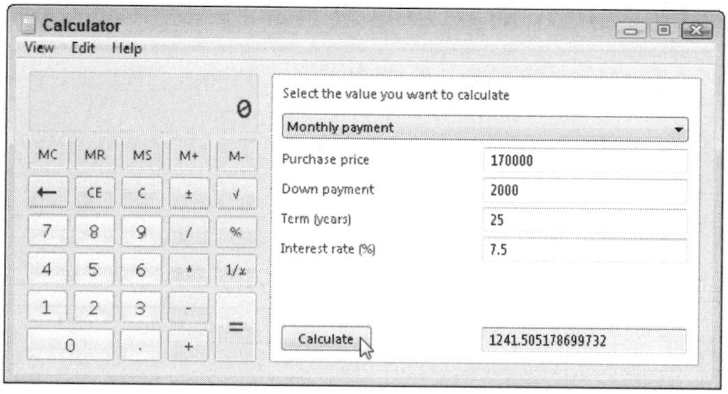

Figure 5-11: Calculator offers templates, which are small forms for oft-used calculations.

Follow these instructions to calculate your mortgage payment based on the purchase price, down payment, and the length of your loan:

1. **Open Calculator by clicking the Start menu, choosing All Programs, choosing Accessories, and clicking Calculator.**

   The Calculator program opens.

2. **Click the View menu, choose Worksheets, and select Mortgage from the pop-up menu.**

   Calculator shows four boxes: Purchase Price, Down Payment, Term, and Interest Rate.

3. **Choose the value you want to calculate from the drop-down list: Down Payment, Monthly Payment, Purchase Price, or Term (years).**

4. **Fill out all four boxes.**

   When you click the Calculate button, Calculator fills out the missing fourth box. (Figure 5-11 shows it calculating the monthly payment.)

Finding symbols like © with Character Map

Character Map lets you insert common symbols and foreign characters into your current document, giving your documents that extra *coup de grâce*. The handy little program displays a box like the one shown in Figure 5-12, listing every available character and symbol.

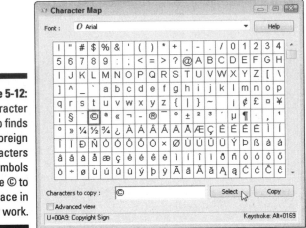

Figure 5-12:
Character
Map finds
foreign
characters
and symbols
like © to
place in
your work.

For example, follow these steps to insert the copyright character (©) somewhere in your carefully crafted letter:

1. **Click the Start menu, choose All Programs, select Accessories, choose System Tools, and select Character Map.**

   Make sure that your current *font* — the name for the style of your letters in your word processor — appears in the Font box.

   If the font you're using in your document isn't showing, click the Font box's down arrow and then scroll down and click your font when it appears in the drop-down list.

2. **Scan the Character Map box until you see the symbol you're after; then pounce on that character with a double-click.**

   The symbol appears in the Characters to Copy box.

3. **Right-click in the document where you want the symbol to appear and choose Paste.**

   The symbol appears, conveniently using the same font as your document.

Chapter 6

Briefly Lost, but Quickly Found

Sooner or later, Windows 7 gives you that head-scratching feeling. "Golly," you say, as your nervous fingers tug on your mouse cord, "that stuff was *right there* a second ago. Where did it go?"

When Windows 7 starts playing hide-and-seek with your information, this chapter tells you where to search and how to make it stop playing foolish games.

Finding Lost Windows on the Desktop

Windows 7 works more like a spike memo holder than an actual desktop. Every time you open a new window, you toss another piece of information onto the spike. The window on top is easy to spot, but how do you reach the windows lying beneath it? If you can see any part of a buried window's edge or corner, a well-placed click will fetch it, bringing it to the top.

When your window is completely buried, look at the desktop's taskbar, that strip along your monitor's bottom edge. (If the taskbar is missing, retrieve it with a press of the Windows key, .) Click your missing window's name on the taskbar to dredge it back to the top. (See Chapter 2 for details about the taskbar.)

Still missing? Try Windows 7's fancy Flip 3D view by holding down the Windows key and pressing Tab. Shown in Figure 6-1, Windows 7 does a magician's shuffle with your windows, letting you see them hanging in the air. While holding down the Windows key, keep pressing Tab (or rolling your mouse's scroll wheel) until your lost window rises to the front of the pack. Let go of the Windows key to place that window at the top of your desktop.

If your older PC can't handle the Flip 3D view (or if your newer PC's graphics card isn't up to snuff), hold down Alt and press Tab for the two-dimensional substitute that works the same or perhaps better. While holding down Alt, keep pressing Tab until Windows 7 highlights your window; let go of Alt to place your newfound window atop your desktop.

If you're convinced a window is open but you still can't find it, spread all your windows across the desktop by right-clicking a blank spot on the taskbar along the desktop's bottom and choosing Show Windows Side By Side from the pop-up menu. It's a last resort, but perhaps you'll spot your missing window in the lineup.

Figure 6-1:
Hold down the Windows key and press Tab repeatedly to cycle through your windows; release the Windows key to drop the front window onto the desktop.

Locating a Missing Program, E-Mail, Song, Document, or Other File

Finding information on the Internet rarely takes more than a few minutes, even though you're searching through millions of Web sites worldwide. But try to find a document on your own PC, and you may spend days — if it even turns up at all.

To solve the search problem, Windows 7 took a tip from Google and created a vast index of both your files and programs. To find one that's missing, open the Start menu and click in the Search box along the Start menu's bottom.

Start typing the first few letters of a word or phrase that appears somewhere inside the file you're looking for. Or type the beginning of a program's name. Either way, as soon as you begin typing, the Start menu begins listing matches. With each letter you type, Windows 7 whittles down the list. After you type enough letters, your lost item floats alone to the top of the list, ready to be opened with a double-click.

For example, typing the first few letters of **Thelonious** into the Start menu's Search box, as shown in Figure 6-2, brought up every mention of Thelonious Monk on my PC.

Figure 6-2: Type the first few letters of a program's name, a word in a document, or a music artist's name, and Windows 7 locates the files.

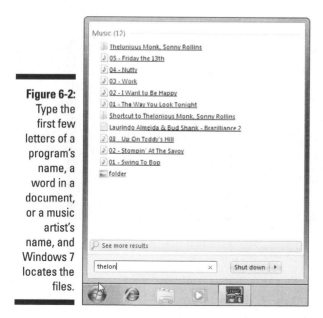

When you spot your file, click its name on the Start menu to open it. To see where your file has been hiding, right-click its name and choose Open File Location from the pop-up menu.

To see *all* of your search results, as well as a snippet of the file your search appeared in, press Enter after typing your word or phrase. Windows 7 brings up a search results window, as shown in Figure 6-3, with more information about your located files.

✔ Windows 7's index includes every file in your Documents, Pictures, Music, and Videos libraries, which makes storing your files in those folders more important than ever. (Windows 7 doesn't let you search through private files stored in accounts of *other* people who may be using your PC.)

✔ The index also includes any files strewn across your desktop, recently deleted files languishing in your Recycle Bin, and any files you're sharing in the *public* folders — the folder that other people on your PC can access. (People on networks connected to your PC can access the public folders, as well.) I explain more about the Public folders in Chapter 13.

✔ If you're searching for a common word and Windows 7 turns up too many files, limit your search by typing a short phrase from your sought-after file: **Just after the cat ate the bamboo**, for example. The more letters of a phrase you type, the better your chances of pinpointing a particular file.

✔ When searching for files, begin typing with the *first* letter of a word or phrase: **b** for bamboo, for example. If you type **amboo**, Windows 7 won't find bamboo, even though bamboo contains that string of letters.

✔ The Search Box ignores capital letters. It considers **Bee** and **bee** to be the same insect.

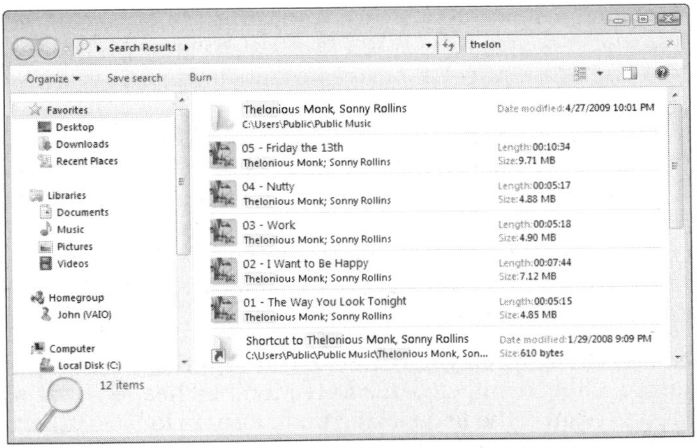

Figure 6-3:
Press Enter after typing a word into the Search box to see more information about the results.

✔ If Windows 7 finds more matches than it can stuff into the small Start menu, shown earlier in Figure 6-2, click See More Results directly above the Search box. That brings up the scrollable window shown in Figure 6-3, making it easier to browse long lists.

✔ Want to route a search to the entire Internet rather than your own PC? After typing your word or phrase, click See More Results to bring up the search results window shown in Figure 6-3. At the bottom of that window is an icon to route your search to the Internet through Internet Explorer. (Chapter 8 explains how to assign your search engine of choice — such as Google — to Internet Explorer.)

Finding a Missing File inside a Folder

The Start menu's Search box probes Windows 7's entire index, making sure that it has looked everywhere. But that's overkill when you're poking around inside a single folder, looking randomly for a missing file. To solve the "sea of filenames in a folder" problem, Windows 7 includes a Search box in every folder's upper-right corner. That Search box limits your search to files within that *particular* folder.

To find a missing file within a specific folder, click inside that folder's Search box and begin typing a word or short phrase from your missing file. As you type letters and words, Windows 7 begins filtering out files that don't contain that word or phrase. It keeps narrowing down the candidates until the folder displays only a few files, including, hopefully, your runaway file.

When a folder's Search box locates too many possible matches, bring in some other helping hands: the headers above each column. (For best results, choose Details from the folder's View icon, which lines up your filenames in one column, as shown in Figure 6-4.) The first column, Name, lists the name of each file; the adjacent columns list specific details about each file.

See the column headers, such as Name, Date Modified, and Type, atop each column? Click any of those headers to sort your files by that term. Here's how to sort by some of the column headers in your Documents folder:

✔ **Name:** Know the first letter of your file's name? Then click here to sort your files alphabetically. You can then pluck your file from the list. Click Name again to reverse the sort order.

✔ **Date Modified:** When you remember the approximate date you last changed a document, click the Date Modified header. That places your newest files atop the list, making them easy to locate. (Clicking Date Modified again reverses the order, a handy way to weed out old files you may no longer need.)

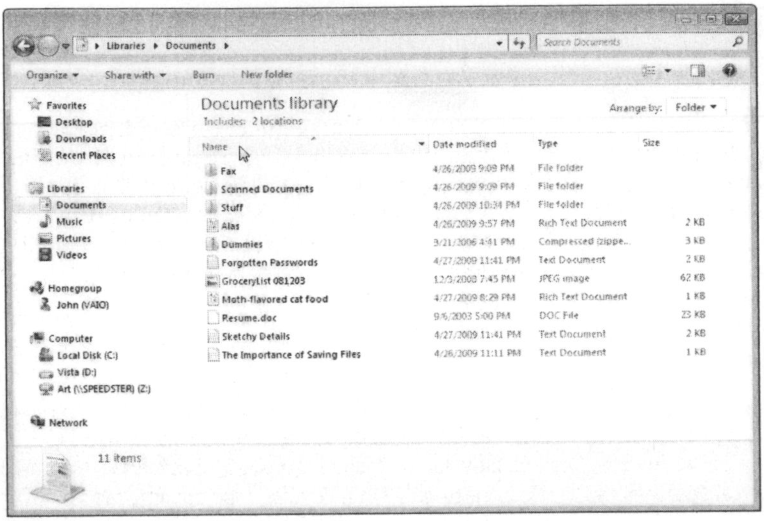

Figure 6-4:
Details view
lets you sort
your files by
name, mak-
ing them
easier to
find.

✔ **Type:** This header sorts files by their contents. All your photos group together, for example, as do all your Word documents. It's a handy way to find a few stray photos swimming in a sea of text files.

✔ **Size:** Sorting here places your 45-page report on one end, with your tiny grocery list on the other.

✔ **Authors:** Microsoft Word and other programs tack your name onto your work. A click on this label alphabetically sorts the files by their creators' names.

✔ **Tags:** Windows 7 often lets you assign tags to your documents and photos, a task I describe later in this chapter. Adding the tags "Moldy Cheese" to that pungent photo session lets you retrieve those pictures by either typing their tags or sorting a folder's files by their tags.

Whether you're viewing your files as thumbnails, icons, or filenames, the column headers always provide a handy way to sort your files quickly.

Folders usually display about five columns of details, but you can add more columns. In fact, you can sort files by their word count, song length, photo size, creation date, and dozens of other details. To see a list of available detail columns, right-click an existing label along a column's top. When the drop-down menu appears, select More to see the Choose Details dialog box. Click to put check marks next to the new detail columns you'd like to see and then click OK.

Folders living outside your libraries *aren't* indexed. (I explain libraries in Chapter 4.) So, searching through them will take a much longer time than searching inside your libraries.

Deep sort

A folder's Details view (shown in Figure 6-4) arranges your files into a single column, with oodles of detail columns flowing off to the right. You can sort a folder's contents by clicking the word atop any column: Name, Date Modified, Author, and so on. But Windows 7's sort features go much deeper, as you'll notice when clicking the little downward-pointing arrow to the right of each column's name.

Click the little arrow by the words *Date Modified*, for example, and a calendar drops down. Click a date, and the folder quickly displays files modified on that particular date, filtering out all the rest. Beneath the calendar, check boxes also let you view files created Today, Yesterday, Last Week, Earlier This Month, Earlier This Year, or simply A Long Time Ago.

Similarly, click the arrow next to the Authors column header, and a drop-down menu lists the authors of every document in the folder. Click the check boxes next to the author names you'd like to see, and Windows 7 immediately filters out files created by other people, leaving only the matches. (This feature works best with Microsoft Office documents.)

These hidden filters can be dangerous, however, because you can easily forget that you've turned them on. If you spot a check mark next to any column header, you've left a filter turned on, and the folder is hiding some of its files. To turn off the filter and see *all* that folder's files, click the check mark next to the column header and examine the drop-down menu. Click any checked boxes on that drop-down menu; that removes their check marks and removes the filter.

Arranging and Grouping Files

Sorting your folders by their name, date, or type, described in the previous section, provides enough organization for most people. To please the meticulous, Windows 7 also lets you organize your files two other ways: *arranging* and *grouping*. What's the difference?

✔ **Arranging:** Arranging (known as "stacking" in Windows Vista), works much like organizing stray papers into piles on your office desk. You might pile them up by the date you created them, for example, tossing today's work in one big pile, and last week's work in another. Or you might want to put all your unpaid bills in one pile, and the bank statements in another.

Windows 7 normally displays items alphabetically in folders, but you can arrange them in other ways that make them easier to find. To arrange your photos by the month you snapped them, for example, click the button next to Arrange By in your photo library's upper-right corner and then choose Month from the drop-down menu, as shown in Figure 6-5.

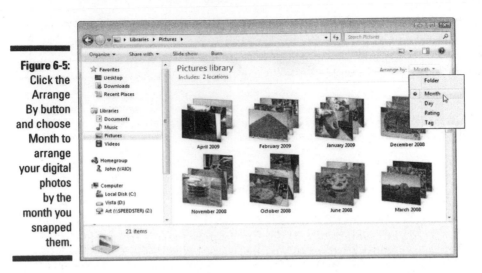

Figure 6-5: Click the Arrange By button and choose Month to arrange your digital photos by the month you snapped them.

✔ **Grouping:** Windows 7's Grouping function also clumps similar items together. But instead of stacking the files into tall piles, Windows 7 spreads them out flat, keeping related items next to each other. Grouping items by Date Modified, shown in Figure 6-6, groups your files by date but places a label above each group: Last Week, Earlier This Month, Earlier This Year, and others.

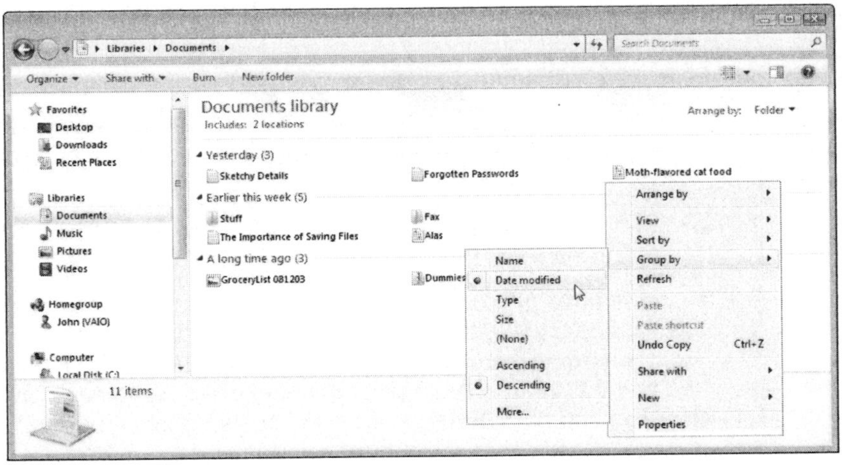

Figure 6-6: Right-click a blank part of a folder and choose Group By to organize your work into groups of similar files.

There's no right or wrong time to choose Sort, Group, or Arrange. It's up to your own preference and the files you're dealing with at the time. Think of Windows 7 as a card shuffler, able to quickly stack all your Costa Rica vacation photos into one stack. To see your photos, click the stack.

Want your folder to return to its *un*-arranged and *un*-grouped look? To return to a normal view, press Alt, and click the View menu. When the drop-down menu appears, choose Clear Changes from the Arrange By menu, and choose (None) from the Group By menu.

Finding Lost Photos

Windows 7 indexes your e-mail down to the last word, but it can't tell the difference between your Yosemite photos and your photo shoot at Dog Beach. When it comes to photos, the ID work lies in your hands, and these four tips make the chore as easy as possible:

- **Tag your photos.** When you connect your camera to your PC, as described in Chapter 16, Windows 7 graciously offers to copy your photos to your PC. Before copying, Windows 7 asks you to tag these pictures. That's your big chance to type a *tag* — a computer term for a word or short phrase describing your file. Tags give Windows 7 something to index, making the photos easier to retrieve later.

- **Store shooting sessions in separate folders.** Windows 7's photo importing program, covered in Chapter 16, automatically creates a new folder to store each session, named after the current date and the tag you choose. But if you're using some other program to dump photos, be sure to create a new folder for each session. Then name the folder with a short description of your session: Sushi Dinner, Parboiling Potatoes, or Truffle Hunt.

- **Sort by date.** Have you stumbled onto a massive folder that's a huge mishmash of digital photos? Here's a quick sorting trick: Repeatedly click the View icon (shown in the corner) from the folder's top menu until the photos morph into identifiable thumbnails. Then right-click a blank part of the folder, choose Sort By, and select either Date Modified or Date Taken. Sorting the photos by date usually lines them up in the order you snapped them, turning chaos into organization.

- **Rename your photos.** Instead of leaving your Belize vacation photos named IMG_2421, IMG_2422, and so on, give them meaningful names: Select all the files in your Belize folder by clicking the Organize button and choosing Select All. Then right-click the first picture, choose Rename, and type **Belize**. Windows names them as Belize, Belize (2), Belize (3), and so on.

Following those four simple rules helps keep your photo collection from becoming a jumble of files.

Be *sure* to back up your digital photos to a portable hard drive, CDs, DVDs, or another backup method I describe in Chapter 12. If they're not backed up, you'll lose your family history when your PC's hard drive eventually crashes.

Finding Other Computers on a Network

A *network* is simply a group of connected PCs that can share things, such as your Internet connection, files, or a printer. Most people use a network every day without knowing it: Every time you check your e-mail, your PC connects to another PC on the Internet to grab your waiting messages.

Much of the time, you don't need to care about the other PCs on your network. But when you want to find a connected PC, perhaps to grab the files from the PC in your family room, Windows 7 is happy to help.

The new Homegroup network in Windows 7 makes it easier than ever to share files with other Windows 7 PCs. Creating a Homegroup is as simple as entering the same password on every PC.

To find a PC on your Homegroup or traditional network, open any folder and look at the bottom of the Navigation Pane along the folder's left edge, as shown in Figure 6-7.

Click Homegroup in the Navigation Pane to see a list of other Windows 7 PCs in your Homegroup; click Network to see every PC that's connected to your own PC in a traditional (but more difficult to set up) network. To browse files on any of those PCs in either category, just double-click their names.

Figure 6-7:
To find computers connected to your PC through a network, click the Navigation Pane's Network category.

I walk through the steps of creating both your own Homegroup and a traditional network in Chapter 14.

Finding Information on the Internet

The handy Search box on the Start menu lets you quickly search for bits of information on your PC. But when you want to search the Internet, fire up your Web browser. (The icon for Internet Explorer lives on your taskbar, usually near the Start button.)

Type your query into the Search box in Internet Explorer's upper-right corner, press Enter, and your favorite search engine displays the results. (I explain more about Internet Explorer, including how to make the Search box use your favorite search engine, in Chapter 8.)

Saving Your Searches

When you find yourself repeatedly searching for the same pieces of information, save yourself time by *saving* your search. Once you save your search, Windows 7 keeps it current, automatically adding any newly created items that fit your search criteria.

Rebuilding the index

When the Windows 7 Search feature slows down considerably or doesn't seem to find files you *know* are in the pile, tell Windows 7 to rebuild the index from scratch.

Although Windows 7 re-creates its index in the background while you keep working, avoid slowing down your PC by sending a rebuild command in the evening. That way, Windows 7 can toil while you sleep, ensuring that you'll have a complete index the next morning.

Follow these steps to rebuild your index:

1. **Open the Start menu and click the Control Panel.**

   The Control Panel appears in a window.

2. **Open the Indexing Options icon.**

   Don't spot it? Type **Indexing Options** in the Search box until its icon appears; then click the icon.

3. **Click the Advanced button and then click the Rebuild button.**

   Windows 7 warns you, just as I do, that rebuilding the index takes a *long* time.

4. **Click OK.**

   Windows 7 begins indexing anew, waiting until it's finished with the new index before it deletes the old one.

Save search

To save a search, type the search words or phrase in the Start menu's Search box and press Enter. When the search results window appears (shown previously in Figure 6-3), click the Save Search button (shown in the margin). Type a name for your saved search in the Save As box and then click Save. Your search now appears in your Navigation Pane's Favorites area.

Click your saved search's name, and it opens like any other folder, but with the contents of your search already inside. Tired of seeing an old search on the Favorites list? Right-click its name and choose Remove. (That deletes only the search, not the files listed inside.)

Chapter 7

Printing Your Work

*O*ccasionally you'll want to slip something away from your PC's whirling electrons and onto something more permanent: a piece of paper.

This chapter tackles that job by explaining all you need to know about printing. Here, you find out how to make that troublesome document fit on a piece of paper without hanging off the edge.

I also cover the mysterious *print queue,* a little-known area that lets you cancel documents mistakenly sent to the printer — before they waste all your paper.

Printing Your Masterpiece

Windows 7 shuttles your work off to the printer in any of a half-dozen different ways. Chances are good that you'll be using these methods most often:

- ✔ Choose Print from your program's File menu.
- ✔ Click the program's Print icon, usually a tiny printer.
- ✔ Right-click your document icon and choose Print.
- ✔ Click the Print button on a program's toolbar.
- ✔ Drag and drop a document's icon onto your printer's icon.

If a dialog box appears, click the OK button, and Windows 7 immediately begins sending your pages to the printer. Take a minute or so to refresh your coffee. If the printer is turned on (and still has paper and ink), Windows handles everything automatically. If your coffee cup is still full, keep on working or playing FreeCell. Windows prints your work in the background.

If the printed pages don't look quite right — perhaps the information doesn't fit on the paper correctly or it looks faded — then you need to fiddle around with the print settings or perhaps change the paper quality, as described in the next sections.

TIP

- ✔ If you stumble upon a particularly helpful page in the Windows Help system, right-click inside the topic or page and choose Print. (Or, click the page's Print icon, if you spot one.) Windows prints a copy for you to tape to your wall or stick in this book.

- ✔ For quick-'n'-easy access to your printer, add a printer shortcut to your desktop: Open the Start menu, choose Devices and Printers, right-click your printer's icon, and choose Create Shortcut. To print things, just drag and drop their icons onto your printer's new desktop shortcut. (Right-click the shortcut icon and choose Printing Properties to adjust your printer's settings, as well.)

- ✔ To print a bunch of documents quickly, select *all* their icons. Then right-click the selected icons and choose Print. Windows 7 quickly shuttles all of them to the printer where they emerge on paper, one after the other.

- ✔ Still haven't installed a printer? Flip to Chapter 11, where I explain how to plug one in and make Windows 7 embrace it.

Adjusting how your work fits on the page

In theory, Windows *always* displays your work as if it were printed on paper. Microsoft's marketing department calls it *What You See Is What You Get,* forever disgraced with the awful acronym WYSIWYG and its awkward pronunciation: "wizzy-wig." If what you see on-screen *isn't* what you want to see on paper, a trip to the program's Page Setup dialog box, shown in Figure 7-1, usually sets things straight.

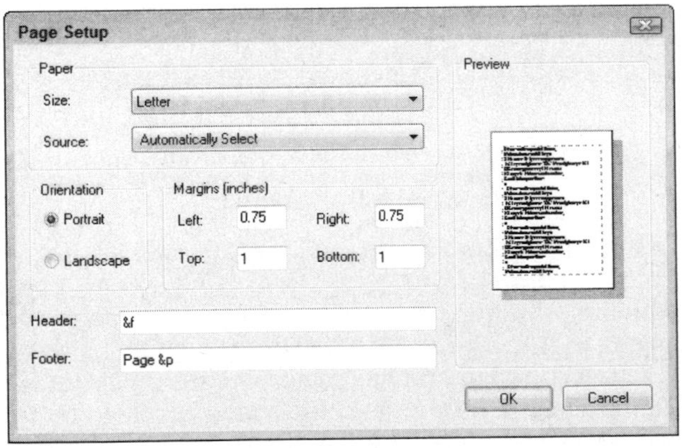

Figure 7-1:
The Page Setup dialog box allows you to adjust the way your work fits onto a piece of paper.

Page Setup	
Paper	**Preview**
Size: Letter	
Source: Automatically Select	
Orientation / **Margins (inches)**	
◉ Portrait Left: 0.75 Right: 0.75	
◯ Landscape Top: 1 Bottom: 1	
Header: &f	
Footer: Page &p	
	OK Cancel

Peeking at your printed page *before* it hits paper

Printing often requires a leap of faith: You choose Print from the menu and close your eyes while the thing prints. If you're blessed, the page looks fine. But if you're cursed, you've wasted another sheet of paper.

The Print Preview option, found on nearly every program's File menu, foretells your printing fate *before* the words hit paper. Print Preview compares your current work with your program's page settings and then displays a detailed picture of the printed page. That preview makes it easy to spot off-kilter margins, dangling sentences, and other printing fouls.

Different programs use slightly different Print Preview screens, with some offering more insight than others. But almost any program's Print Preview screen lets you know whether everything will fit onto the page correctly.

If the preview looks fine, choose Print at the window's top to send the work to the printer. If something looks wrong, however, click Close to return to your work and make any necessary adjustments.

Page Setup, found on nearly any program's File menu, offers several ways to flow your work across a printed page (and subsequently your screen). Page Setup dialog boxes differ among programs and print models, but the following list describes the options that you'll find most often and the settings that usually work best:

- ✔ **Size:** This option lets your program know what size of paper lives inside your printer. Leave this option set to Letter for printing on standard, 8.5-x-11-inch sheets of paper. Change this setting if you're using legal-size paper (8.5 x 14), envelopes, or other paper sizes. (The nearby sidebar, "Printing envelopes without fuss," contains more information about printing envelopes.)

- ✔ **Source:** Choose Automatically Select or Sheet Feeder unless you're using a fancy printer that accepts paper from more than one printer tray. People who have printers with two or more printer trays can select the tray containing the correct paper size. Some printers offer Manual Paper Feed, making the printer wait until you slide in that single sheet of paper.

- ✔ **Header/Footer:** Type secret codes in these boxes to customize what the printer places along the top and bottom of your pages: page numbers, titles, and dates, for example, as well as their spacing. For example, notice the *&f* in the Header text box and *Page &p* in the Footer text box of Figure 7-1? That means to print the file's name along the page's top (the header), and the word *Page* followed by the page number along the bottom (the footer).

Unfortunately, different programs use different codes for their header and footer. If you spot a little question mark in the Page Setup dialog box's top-right corner, click it; then click inside the Header or Footer box for clues. No little question mark? Then press F1 and search for **page setup** in the program's Help menu.

✔ **Orientation:** Leave this option set to Portrait to print normal pages that read vertically like a letter. Choose Landscape only when you want to print sideways, which is a great way to print wide spreadsheets. (If you choose Landscape, the printer automatically prints the page sideways; you don't need to slide the paper sideways into your printer.)

✔ **Margins:** Feel free to reduce the margins to fit everything on a single sheet of paper. You may need to change them for homework requirements, as well.

✔ **Printer:** If you have more than one printer installed on your computer or network, click this button to choose which one to print your work. Click here to change that printer's settings as well, a job discussed in the next section.

When you're finished adjusting settings, click the OK button to save your changes. (Click the Print Preview button, if it's offered, to make sure that everything looks right.)

To find the Page Setup box in some programs (including Internet Explorer), click the little arrow next to the program's Printer icon and choose Page Setup from the menu that drops down.

Printing envelopes without fuss

Although clicking *Envelopes* in a program's Page Setup area is fairly easy, printing addresses in the correct spot on the envelope is extraordinarily difficult. Some printer models want you to insert envelopes upside down, while others prefer right side up. Your best bet is to run several tests, placing the envelope into your printer's tray in different ways until you finally stumble on the magic method. (Or you can pull out your printer's manual, if you still have it, and pore over the "proper envelope insertion" pictures.)

After you've figured out the correct method for your particular printer, tape a successfully printed envelope above your printer and add an arrow pointing to the correct way to insert it.

Should you eventually give up on printing envelopes, try using Avery's mailing labels. Buy your preferred size of Avery labels and then download the free Avery Wizard from Avery's Web site (www.avery.com/us/software/index.jsp). Compatible with Microsoft Word, the wizard places little boxes on your screen that precisely match the size of your particular Avery labels. Type the addresses into the little boxes, insert the label sheet into your printer, and Word prints everything onto the little stickers. You don't even need to lick them.

Or do as I did: Buy a little rubber stamp with your return address. It's much faster than stickers or printers.

Adjusting your printer's settings

When you choose Print from many programs, Windows offers one last chance to spruce up your printed page. The Print dialog box, shown in Figure 7-2, lets you route your work to any printer installed on your computer or network. While there, you can adjust the printer's settings, choose your paper quality, and select the pages (and quantities) you'd like to print.

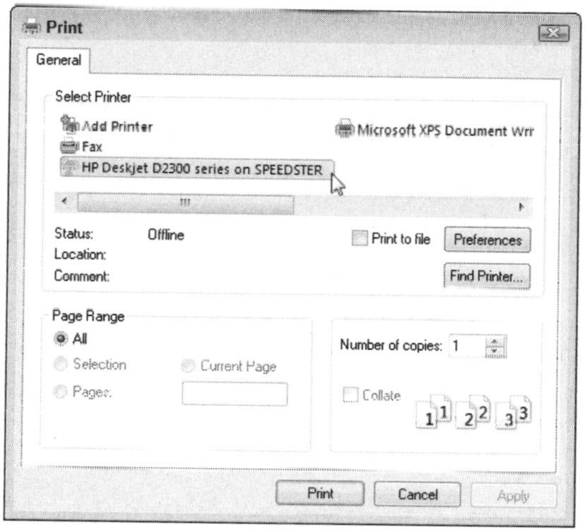

Figure 7-2:
The Print
dialog box
lets you
choose your
printer and
adjust its
settings.

You're likely to find these settings waiting in the dialog box:

- ✔ **Select Printer:** Ignore this option if you have only one printer because Windows chooses it automatically. If your computer has access to more than one printer, click the one that should receive the job. Choose Fax to send your work as a fax through Windows Fax and Scan program.

  The printer called Microsoft XPS Document Writer sends your work to a specially formatted file, usually to be printed or distributed professionally. Chances are good that you'll never use it.

- ✔ **Page Range:** Select All to print your entire document. To print just a few of its pages, select the Pages option and enter the page numbers you want to print. For example, enter **1-4, 6** to leave out page 5 of a 6-page document. If you've highlighted a paragraph, choose Selection to print that particular paragraph — a great way to print the important part of a Web page and leave out the rest.

- ✔ **Number of Copies:** Most people leave this set to 1 copy, unless everybody in the boardroom wants their own copy. You can choose Collate only if your printer offers that option. (Most don't, leaving you to sort the pages yourself.)

✓ **Preferences:** Click this button to see a dialog box like the one in Figure 7-3, where you can choose options specific to your own printer model. The Printing Preferences dialog box typically lets you select different grades of paper, choose between color and black and white, set the printing quality, and make last-minute corrections to the page layout.

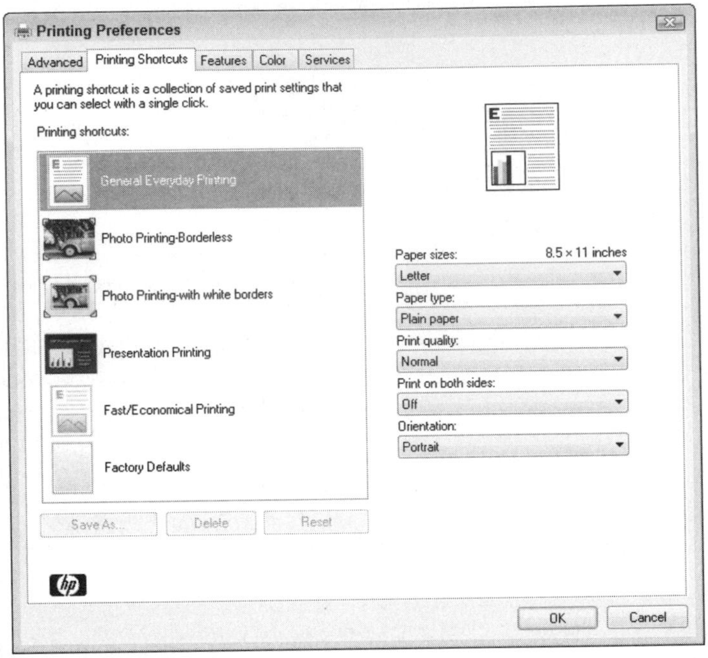

Figure 7-3:
The Printing
Preferences
dialog box
lets you
change
settings
specific to
your printer,
including
the paper
type and
printing
quality.

Canceling a print job

Just realized you sent the wrong 26-page document to the printer? So you panic and flip the printer's off switch. Unfortunately, many printers automatically pick up where they left off when you turn them back on, leaving you or your co-workers to deal with the mess.

To purge the mistake from your printer's memory, follow these steps:

1. **Click Start and choose Devices and Printers.**

2. **Right-click your printer's name or icon and choose See What's Printing.**

   The handy *print queue* appears, as shown in Figure 7-4.

3. **Right-click your mistaken document and choose Cancel to end the job. Repeat with any other listed unwanted documents.**

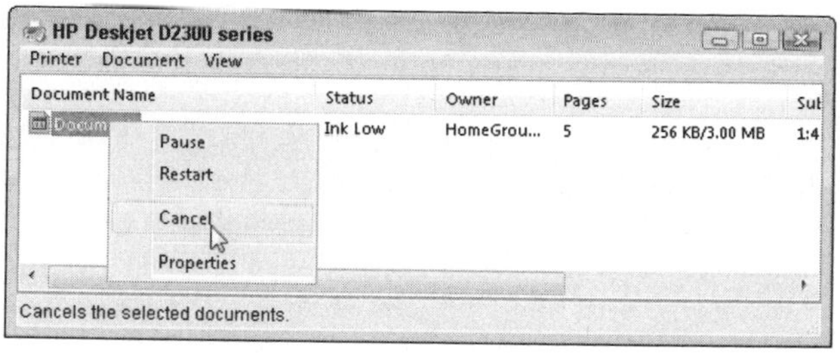

HP Deskjet D230U series

Printer   Document   View

Document Name		Status	Owner	Pages	Size	Sub
Docum		Ink Low	HomeGrou...	5	256 KB/3.00 MB	1:4
	Pause					
	Restart					
	Cancel					
	Properties					

Cancels the selected documents.

Figure 7-4:
Use the
print queue
to cancel a
print job.

Your printer queue can take a minute or two to clear itself. (To speed things up, click View and choose Refresh.) When the print queue is clear, turn your printer back on; it won't keep printing that same darn document.

✔ The print queue, also known as the print *spooler,* lists every document waiting patiently to reach your printer. Feel free to change their printing order by dragging and dropping them up or down the list. (You can't move anything in front of the currently printing document, though.)

✔ Sharing your printer on the network? Print jobs sent from other PCs end up in *your* print queue, so *you'll* need to cancel the botched ones. (And networked folks who share *their* printer will need to delete your botched print jobs, as well.)

✔ If your printer runs out of paper during a job and stubbornly halts, add more paper. Then to start things flowing again, open the print queue, right-click your document, and choose Restart. (Some printers let you push an Online button to begin printing again.)

✔ You can send items to the printer even when you're working in the coffee shop with your laptop. Later, when you connect the laptop to your printer, the print queue notices and begins sending your files. (Beware: When they're in the print queue, documents are formatted for your specific printer model. If you subsequently connect your laptop to a *different* printer model, the print queue's waiting documents won't print correctly.)

Printing a Web page

Although information-chocked Web pages look awfully tempting, *printing* those Web pages is rarely satisfying because they look so awful on paper. When sent to the printer, Web pages often run off the page's right side, consume zillions of additional pages, or are much too small to read.

To make matters worse, all those colorful advertisements can suck your printer's color cartridges dry fairly quickly. Only four things make for successfully printed Web pages, and I rank them in order of success:

- **Use the Web page's built-in Print option.** Some Web sites, but not all, offer a tiny menu option called Print This Page, Text Version, Printer-Friendly Version, or something similar. That option tells the Web site to strip out its garbage and reformat the page so that it fits neatly onto a sheet of paper. This option is the most reliable way to print a Web page.

- **Choose Print Preview from your browser's File or Print menu.** After 15 years, some Web page designers noticed that people want to print their pages, so they tweaked the settings, making their pages *automatically* reformat themselves when printed. If you're lucky, a clean look in the Print Preview window means you've stumbled onto one of those printer-friendly sites.

- **Copy the portion you want and paste it into WordPad.** Try selecting the desired text from the Web page, copying it, and pasting it into WordPad or another word processor. Delete any unwanted remnants, adjust the margins, and print the portion you want. Chapter 5 explains how to select, copy, and paste.

- **Copy the entire page and paste it into a word processor.** Although it's lots of work, it's an option. Choose Select All from Internet Explorer's Edit menu. Then choose Copy (which is also on the Edit menu) or press Ctrl+C. Next, open Microsoft Word or another full-featured word processor and paste the Web page inside a new document. By hacking away at the unwanted portions, you can sometimes end up with something printable.

These tips may also come in handy for moving a Web page from screen to paper:

- If you spot an E-Mail option but no Print option, e-mail the page to yourself. You may have better success printing it as an e-mail message.

- To print just a few paragraphs of a Web page, use the mouse to select the portion you're after. (I cover selecting in Chapter 5.) Choose Print from Internet Explorer's File menu to open the Print dialog box, shown earlier in Figure 7-2, and then select the Selection option in the Page Range box.

- If a Web page's table or photo insists on vanishing off the paper's right edge, try printing the page in Landscape mode rather than Portrait. See the "Adjusting how your work fits on the page" section, earlier in this chapter, for details on Landscape mode.

Troubleshooting your printer

When you can't print something, start with the basics: Are you *sure* that the printer is turned on, plugged into the wall, full of paper, and connected securely to your computer with a cable?

If so, then try plugging the printer into different outlets, turning it on, and seeing whether its power light comes on. If the light stays off, your printer's power supply is probably blown.

Printers are almost always cheaper to replace than repair. But if you've grown fond of your printer, grab an estimate from a repair shop — if you can find one — before discarding it.

If the printer's power light beams brightly, check these things before giving up:

- ✔ Make sure that a sheet of paper hasn't jammed itself inside the printer. (A steady pull usually extricates jammed paper; sometimes opening and closing the printer's lid starts things moving again.)

- ✔ Does your inkjet printer still have ink in its cartridges? Does your laser printer have toner? Try printing a test page: Click the Start menu and open Devices and Printers. Right-click your printer's icon, choose Printer Properties, and click the Print Test Page button to see whether the computer and printer can talk to each other.

- ✔ Try updating the printer's *driver,* the little program that helps it talk with Windows 7. Visit the printer manufacturer's Web site, download the newest driver for your particular printer model, and run its installation program. (I cover drivers in Chapter 12.)

Finally, here are a couple of tips to help you protect your printer and cartridges:

- ✔ Turn off your printer when you're not using it. Inkjet printers, especially, should be turned off when they're not in use. The heat tends to dry the cartridges, shortening their life.

- ✔ Don't unplug your inkjet printer to turn it off. Always use the on/off switch. The switch ensures that the cartridges slide back to their home positions, keeping them from drying out or clogging.

Choosing the right paper for your printer

If you've strolled the aisles at an office-supply store lately, you've noticed a bewildering array of paper choices. Sometimes the paper's packaging lists its application: Premium Inkjet Paper, for example, for high-quality memos. Here's a list of different print jobs and the types of paper they require. Before printing, be sure to click the Printer's Preferences section to select the grade of paper you're using for that job.

✔ **Junk:** Keep some cheap or scrap paper around for testing the printer, printing quick drafts, leaving desktop notes, and printing other on-the-fly jobs. Botched print jobs work great here; just use the paper's other side.

✔ **Letter quality:** Bearing the words Premium or Bright White, this paper works fine for letters, reports, memos, and other things designed for showing to others.

✔ **Photos:** You can print photos on any type of paper, but they look like photos only on actual photo-quality paper — the expensive stuff. Slide the paper carefully into your printer tray so that the picture prints on the glossy, shiny side. Some photo paper requires placing a little cardboard sheet beneath it, which helps glide the paper smoothly through the printer.

✔ **Labels:** They've never sent me a T-shirt, but I still say that Avery's Wizard program (www.avery.com) makes it easy to print Avery labels and cards. The wizard teams up with Microsoft Word to mesh perfectly with Avery's preformatted mailing labels, greeting cards, business cards, CD labels, and many others.

✔ **Transparencies:** For powerful PowerPoint presentations, buy special transparent plastic sheets designed to be used with your type of printer. Make sure the transparency is compatible with your printer, be it laser or inkjet.

Before plunking down your money, make sure that your paper is designed specifically for your printer type, be it laser or inkjet. Laser printers heat the pages, and some paper and transparencies can't take the heat.

Part III
Getting Things Done on the Internet

The 5th Wave   By Rich Tennant

"Face it Vinnie—you're gonna have a hard time getting people to subscribe online with a credit card to a newsletter called, 'Felons Interactive.'"

In this part . . .

The Internet used to be clean, quiet, and helpful, just like a new library. You could find detailed information about nearly anything, read newspapers and magazines from around the world, listen to music in the media section, or quietly browse the card catalogs.

Today, this wonderful global library has been bombarded with noisy people who toss ads in front of what you're trying to read. Some won't even let you close that book you inadvertently opened — the book keeps opening back up to the wrong page. Pickpockets and thieves stalk the halls.

This part of the book helps you turn the Internet back into that quiet, helpful library it once was. It shows how to stop pop-up ads, browser hijackers, and spyware. It explains how to send and receive e-mail so that you can keep in touch with friends.

Finally, it shows you how to stay safe using Windows 7's User Account Protection, firewall, security center, and other tricks to help bring back the Internet you love.

Chapter 8

Cruising the Web

· ·

· ·

*E*ven when being installed, Windows 7 starts reaching for the Internet, hungry for any hint of a connection. After connecting with the Internet, Windows 7 kindly nudges your computer's clock to the correct time. Some motives are less pure: Windows 7 also checks in with Microsoft to make sure that you're not installing a pirated copy.

This chapter explains how to connect with the Internet, visit Web sites, and find all the good stuff online. For ways to keep out the bad stuff, be sure to visit Chapter 10 to get a quick primer on safe computing. The Internet is full of bad neighborhoods, and that chapter explains how to avoid viruses, spyware, hijackers, and other Internet parasites.

Once your computer is wearing its appropriate helmet and kneepads, however, hop onto the Internet and enjoy the ride.

What Is the Internet?

Today, most people take the Internet for granted, much like they do a telephone line. Instead of marveling at the Internet's internal gearing, they've grown accustomed to this new land called *cyberspace* and its healthy stock of attractions:

- ✔ **Library:** The Internet is stuffed with educational material: classic books, hourly news updates, foreign language dictionaries, specialized encyclopedias, and more. Visit RefDesk (`www.refdesk.com`) for a detailed list of some of the Internet's best free reference materials.

- ✔ **Store:** Although the Internet seemed like a novelty ten years ago, today the Internet revolves around making money. You can purchase nearly anything available in stores (and some things *not* sold in stores) on the Internet and ship it to your thatch hut. Sites like Amazon (`www.amazon.com`) even let you listen to song snippets and read reviews before putting that John Coltrane CD on your credit card.

- ✔ **Communicator:** Many people treat the Internet as a private postal service for sending messages to friends, co-workers, and even strangers around the world. Unfortunately, unwelcome marketers do the same, sending people increasingly desperate, unsolicited sales pitches known as *spam*. (I cover downloadable e-mail programs that are compatible with Windows 7 in Chapter 9.)

- ✔ **Time waster:** When sitting in a waiting room, everybody naturally reaches for the magazine table. The Internet, too, offers zillions of ways to waste time. Jumping from one Web site to another is much like flipping pages in a magazine, but each flip often reveals a completely different, yet oddly related, subject that brims with fascinating information. Or at least it seems so at the time.

- ✔ **Entertainment:** The Internet brings not only a movie's show times into your home, but also its trailers, cast lists, reviews, and celebrity gossip. If you're tired of movies, browse for online games, research exotic travel destinations, or look up sporting statistics.

Simply put, the Internet is a 24-hour international library that's stocked with something for everyone.

- ✔ Just as a television channel surfer flips from channel to channel, a Web surfer jumps from page to page, sampling the vast and esoteric piles of information.

- ✔ Almost every government but China loves the Internet. In the United States, the FBI shares pictures of its ten most wanted criminals (`www.fbi.gov`), and the Internal Revenue Service (`www.irs.ustreas.gov`) lets Internet users make free copies of tax forms 24 hours a day. Protesting a parking ticket? Your city's Web site probably hands you the right number to call faster than the phone book.

- ✔ Universities and scientists love the network, too, because they can file grant forms more quickly than ever. Worried about the goo coagulating in the crevices of your bromeliads? The Internet's famed botanical site (www. botany.net) enables researchers to study everything from Australian acacias to zoosporic fungi.

✔ Most computer companies support their products on the Internet. Visitors can swap messages with technicians and other users about their latest computing woes. You may be able to download a fix or uncover the magic sequence of keystrokes that solves a problem.

What's an ISP, and Why Do I Need One?

Everybody needs three things to connect to the Web: a computer, Web browser software, and an Internet service provider (ISP).

You already have the computer, and Windows 7 comes with a Web browser called Internet Explorer. (Europeans finding themselves with a brower-less version of Windows 7 should contact their PC's manufacturer for assistance.)

That means most people need to find only an ISP. Although television signals come wafting through the air to your TV set for free, you must pay an ISP for the privilege of surfing the Web. Specifically, you pay the ISP for a *password* and an *account name*. When your computer connects to your ISP's computers, Internet Explorer automatically enters your password and account name, and you're ready to surf the Web.

Don't know which ISP to choose? First, different ISP's serve different geographical areas. Ask your friends, neighbors, or local librarians how they connect and whether they recommend their ISP. Call several ISPs for a rate quote and then compare rates. Most bill on a monthly basis; if you're not happy, you can always switch.

✔ Although a few ISPs charge for each minute you're connected, most charge a flat monthly fee between $15 and $50 for unlimited service. Make sure that you know your rate before hopping aboard, or you may be surprised at the month's end.

✔ ISPs let you connect to the Internet in a variety of ways. The slowest ISPs require a dialup modem and an ordinary phone line. Faster still are *broadband* connections: special DSL or ISDN lines provided by some phone companies, and the even faster cable modems, supplied by your cable company. When shopping for broadband ISPs, your geographic location usually determines your options, unfortunately.

Setting Up Internet Explorer the First Time

This part's easy. Windows 7 constantly looks for a working Internet connection in your PC. If it finds one, through a wired or wireless network, broadband (cable or DSL), or wireless hotspot, you're set: Windows 7 passes the news along to Internet Explorer, and your PC can connect to the Internet immediately. That means you needn't wade through this section.

If Windows 7 can't find the Internet, though — a frequent occurrence for people connecting through phone lines — the job's up to you, with the aid of this section.

To guide you smoothly through the turmoil of setting up an Internet connection, Windows 7 passes you a questionnaire, quizzing you about the details. After a bit of interrogation, Windows 7 helps connect your computer to your ISP so that you can Web surf like the best of them.

If you're having trouble connecting to the Internet through a home network, see Chapter 14 for troubleshooting details.

To transfer your existing Internet account settings to or from another computer, use the Easy Transfer program, covered in Chapter 19. The program copies one PC's Internet settings into the other PC, sparing you the bother of following these steps.

Here's what you need to set up a dialup Internet connection:

- ✔ **Your username, password, and access phone number.** If you don't have an ISP yet, Windows 7 finds you one, so grab a pencil and paper. (The suggested ISPs might be a tad pricey, however.)

- ✔ **A plugged-in modem.** If you're planning on connecting to the Internet through phone lines, you need a dialup modem. To see whether your PC already has a dialup modem, look for a telephone jack on the back of your computer, near where all the other cables protrude. Then connect a standard phone cable between that jack (the computer's jack says *Line,* not *Phone*) and the phone jack in your wall. No dialup modem? Buy one that plugs into your USB port, giving you a jack to plug in your phone line.

Whenever your Internet connection gives you log-on problems, head here and run through the following steps. The wizard walks you through your current settings, letting you make changes. Summon the wizard by following these steps:

1. **Click the Start button, choose Control Panel, and in the Network and Internet section, choose Connect to the Internet.**

   The Connect to the Internet window appears, asking which way you want to connect:

   - **Broadband (PPPoE):** Choose this if you subscribe to one of the few broadband ISPs requiring a username and password. (Some call this Point-To-Point Protocol over Ethernet.) If you click this, enter your username and password in the boxes and click Connect to hitch up to the Internet.

   - **Dial-up:** Click this if you connect to the Internet through the plain old telephone lines, then move to the next step.

   - **Wireless:** If your PC has a wireless Internet adapter, Windows 7 begins sniffing out wireless signals as soon as you install the operating system on your PC. If it's having trouble, though, turn to Chapter 14 and check out the section on connecting wirelessly. (I offer laptop-specific help in Chapter 22.)

   If Windows 7 does find a *wireless* network, by chance, you're in luck. You can hop aboard the signal by double-clicking the network's name. (I cover wireless networks in Chapter 14.)

2. **Choose Dial-Up.**

   If you're not choosing wireless or broadband (PPPoE), dialup is your only Internet connection option. To speed things along, Windows 7 passes you a questionnaire, shown in Figure 8-1, ready for you to enter your dialup ISP's information.

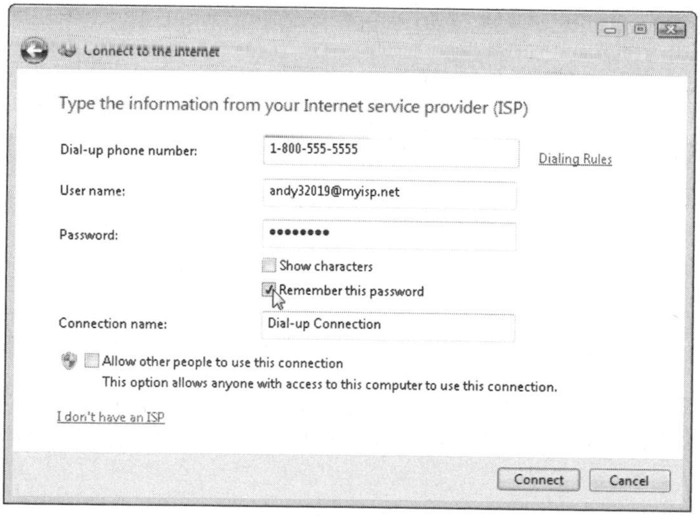

Figure 8-1:
Enter your ISP's dialup phone number, your username, and your password.

> Connect to the Internet
>
> Type the information from your Internet service provider (ISP)
>
> Dial-up phone number: 1-800-555-5555   Dialing Rules
>
> User name: andy32019@myisp.net
>
> Password: ••••••••
>
> ☐ Show characters
> ☑ Remember this password
>
> Connection name: Dial-up Connection
>
> ☐ Allow other people to use this connection
>   This option allows anyone with access to this computer to use this connection.
>
> I don't have an ISP
>
> Connect   Cancel

3. **Enter your dialup ISP's information.**

   Here's where you enter three all-important pieces of information and pick a couple more settings:

   - **Dial-Up Phone Number:** Enter the phone number your ISP gave you, complete with the area code.

   - **User Name:** This isn't necessarily your own name, but the user-name your ISP assigned to you when giving you the account. (It's often the first part of your e-mail address, as well.)

   - **Password:** Type your password here. To make sure that you're entering your password correctly, select the Show Characters check box. Then deselect the check box when you've entered the password without typos.

   Be sure to select the Remember This Password check box. That keeps you from reentering your name and password each time you want to dial the Internet. (*Don't* select that check box if you don't want your roommate or others to be able to dial your connection.)

   - **Connection Name:** Windows 7 names your connection *Dial-Up Connection*. Change it to something more descriptive if you're juggling dialup accounts from several ISPs.

   - **Allow Other People to Use This Connection:** Check this option to let people with other user accounts on your PC log on with this connection.

   Clicking the I Don't Have an ISP link brings up a window where you can insert a setup CD given to you by your ISP.

   Click the Dialing Rules link, next to the phone number. There, you can enter key details like your country, area code, and whether you need to dial a number to reach an outside line. Windows remembers this information, making sure that it dials a 1 if you're dialing outside your area code, for example. Laptoppers should visit Dialing Rules for every city they visit.

4. **Click the Connect button.**

   Your PC connects to the Internet. To test your connection, load Internet Explorer from the Start menu, if it's not already loaded, and see if it lets you visit Web sites.

In the future, connect to the Internet by simply loading Internet Explorer. Your PC automatically dials the Internet using the connection you've created here.

Don't be afraid to bug your ISP for help. Most ISPs come with technical support lines. A member of the support staff can talk you through the installation process. Don't stick with an ISP that's unfriendly or that won't help you connect.

Sometimes Internet Explorer doesn't automatically hang up the phone when you're done browsing. To make your PC hang up when you close Internet Explorer, choose Internet Options from the program's Tools menu and click the Connections tab. Click the Settings button and then the Advanced button. Finally, select the Disconnect When Connection May No Longer Be Needed check box and click OK.

Navigating the Web with Internet Explorer 8

Your Web browser is your Internet surfboard — your transportation to the Internet's millions of Web sites. Internet Explorer comes free with Windows 7, so many people use it out of convenience. Other people prefer browsers published by other software companies, such as Mozilla's Firefox (www.get firefox.com).

Simply put, you're not forced to stick with Internet Explorer 8, the version of Internet Explorer introduced in Windows 7. Feel free to try competing Web browsers, as they all do pretty much the same thing: take you from one Web site to another.

But I want to see some pop-ups!

Early versions of Internet Explorer had no way to stop pop-up advertisements from exploding across your screen. Internet Explorer now offers a pop-up ad blocker that stops 90 percent of them. To make sure that it's turned on, choose Pop Up Blocker from Internet Explorer's Tools menu and make sure that no check mark appears in the Turn Off Pop-Up Blocker check box.

If you *want* to see pop-ups on certain sites, that same menu lets you choose Pop-Up Blocker Settings. Type the Web site address, and Internet Explorer allows that site's pop-ups to pop unblocked.

If a site tries to send a pop-up ad or message, Internet Explorer places a strip along its top edge saying, A pop-up was blocked. To see this pop-up or additional options, click here. Click the strip to do any one of these three things: temporarily allow that pop-up to appear, always allow pop-ups from that particular site, or change the pop-up blocker's settings.

Finally, to stop the informational strip from making that obnoxious pop noise when it stops a pop-up, choose Pop-Up Blocker from Internet Explorer's Tools menu, choose Pop-Up Blocker Settings, and remove the check mark from the Play a Sound When a Pop-Up Is Blocked check box.

Moving from Web page to Web page

All browsers work basically the same way. Every Web page comes with a specific address, just like houses do. Internet Explorer lets you move between pages in three different ways:

✔ By pointing and clicking a button or link that automatically whisks you away to another page

✔ By typing a complicated string of code words (the Web address) into the Address box of the Web browser and pressing Enter

✔ By clicking the navigation buttons on the browser's toolbar, which is usually at the top of the screen

Clicking links

The first way is the easiest. Look for *links* — highlighted words or pictures on a page — and click them. See how the mouse pointer turned into a hand (shown in the margin) as it pointed at the word *Books* in Figure 8-2? Click that word to see a Web page with more information about my books. Many words on this page are links, as well; the mouse pointer becomes a hand when it's near them, and the words become underlined. Click any linked word to see pages dealing with that link's particular subject.

Web page designers get mighty creative these days, and without the little hand pointer, it's often hard to tell where to point and click. Some buttons look like standard elevator buttons; others look like fuzzy dice or tiny vegetables. But when you click a button, the browser takes you to the page relating to that button. Clicking the fuzzy dice may bring up a betting-odds sheet for local casinos, for example, and vegetables may bring information about the local farmers market.

Figure 8-2:
When the mouse pointer becomes a hand, click the word or picture to go to a Web page with more information about that item.

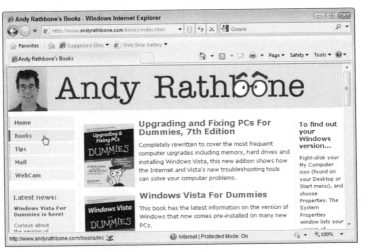

Typing Web addresses in the Address box

The second method is more difficult. If a friend gives you a napkin with a cool Web page's address written on it, you need to type the Web site's address into your browser's Address box. You'll do fine, as long as you don't misspell anything. See the address for my Web site along the top of Figure 8-4 (later in the chapter)? I typed www.andyrathbone.com into the Address box. When I pressed Enter, Internet Explorer scooted me to my Web page. (You don't need to type the http:// part, thank goodness.)

Using Internet Explorer's toolbar

Finally, you can maneuver through the Internet by clicking various buttons on Internet Explorer's toolbar, which sits at the top of the screen. Table 8-1 offers a handy reference of the important navigation buttons.

Hover your mouse pointer over a confusing Internet Explorer button to see its purpose in life.

Table 8-1	Navigating with Internet Explorer's Buttons	
This Button . . .	*Is Called This . . .*	*And It Does This . . .*
(Back button)	Back	Pointed and clicked yourself into a dead end? Click the Back button to head for the last Web page you visited. If you click the Back button enough times, you wind up back at your home page, where you began.
(Forward button)	Forward	After you click the Back button, you can click Forward to revisit a page, too.
☆ Favorites	Favorites	Clicking the Favorites button along the top reveals the Favorites list, a list of links that *could* lead to your favorite Web sites. (Microsoft stuffs the center with its own Web sites; feel free to delete them and add your own by clicking the Add to Favorites button.)
☆ (Add to Favorites button)	Add to Favorites Bar	See a site you want to visit later? Click this star with a green arrow on it to add your currently viewed Web page to your Favorites Bar — that strip near the top of Internet Explorer. (The Favorites Bar isn't related to the Favorites area found in every folder's Navigation Pane.)

(continued)

Table 8-1 *(continued)*

This Button . . .	Is Called This . . .	And It Does This . . .
Suggested Sites ▼	Suggested Sites	Internet Explorer will bug you to turn on this feature. When turned on, Suggested Sites robotically eavesdrops on your browsing habits and suggests other sites you may enjoy.
Get More Add-ons ▼	Get More Add-Ons	These mini-programs enhance your Web browsing experience by performing single tasks: adding an Amazon link to a book mentioned on a Web page, for example, so you can purchase it. (*Tip:* Look for add-ons that block advertisements.)
[Home icon] ▼	Home	If you get lost while exploring the Internet, return to familiar territory by clicking the Home button along the program's top. (Click the arrow next to the button to change your *home page* — the first page you see when loading Internet Explorer — to the currently displayed site.)
[RSS icon] ▼	RSS Feed	When this orange button lights up, you know the site offers Real Simple Syndication (RSS), a quick way to read the site's headlines without actually visiting. To see the headlines, click Favorites and click the Feeds tab. (Again, Microsoft stuffs feeds from its own sites in your folder; feel free to delete them and add your own.)
[Web Slices icon] ▼	Web Slices	Microsoft's clone of the RSS feed system also offers a quick way to read sites' headlines without visiting. (Web Slices also appear in the Favorites area's Feeds tab.)
[Read Mail icon]	Read Mail	This does absolutely nothing . . . until you install an e-mail program, a chore I tackle in Chapter 9. (Unlike previous Windows versions, Windows 7 lacks an e-mail program.)
[Print icon] ▼	Print	Click here to print the Web site as you see it. (Click the tiny arrow to its right for printing options, including seeing a preview.)

This Button . . .	Is Called This . . .	And It Does This . . .
Page ▼	Page	These options relate to the current page: Enlarging its text size, for example, or saving it as a file.
Safety ▼	Safety	Click here to delete your browsing history, browse in private (handy for bank sites), or check suspicious Web sites for danger.
Tools ▼	Tools	This button opens a menu full of Internet Explorer tweaks, letting you make adjustments to the pop-up blocker and phishing filter, among others.
⊙	Help	Flummoxed? A click here brings up Internet Explorer's Help menu.

Making Internet Explorer open to your favorite site

Your Web browser automatically displays a Web site when you first log on. That Web site is called your *home page,* and you can tell Internet Explorer to use any site you want for your home page by following these steps:

1. **Visit your favorite Web site.**

   Choose any Web page you like. I like Google News (http://news. google.com) so Internet Explorer always opens with the latest headlines.

2. **Choose the tiny arrow to the right of the Home icon and choose Add or Change Home Page.**

   The new, security-conscious Internet Explorer asks whether you'd like to use that Web page as your only home page or add it to your home page tabs. (You can have several home pages, each with its own tab along the page's top.)

3. **Click Use This Webpage As Your Only Home Page and click Yes.**

   When you click Yes, shown in Figure 8-3, Internet Explorer always opens to the page you're currently viewing.

   Clicking No sticks with your current home page, which starts out as The Microsoft Network (www.msn.com).

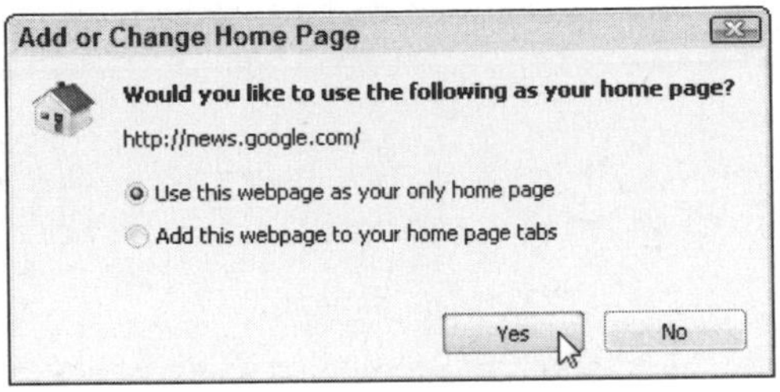

Figure 8-3:
Click
Use This
Webpage
As Your Only
Home Page,
and Internet
Explorer
always
opens to
that page.

Add or Change Home Page

Would you like to use the following as your home page?

http://news.google.com/

◉ Use this webpage as your only home page

○ Add this webpage to your home page tabs

[Yes]   [No]

After Internet Explorer remembers your chosen home page, you can move around the Internet, searching for topics in Google (www.google.com) or other search engines, simply pointing and clicking different links.

✔ A home page of a Web site is its "cover," like the cover of a magazine. Whenever you jump to a Web site, you usually jump to the site's home page, and you can start browsing from there.

✔ If your home page is suddenly hijacked to a different site and these instructions don't fix it, then it's probably been hijacked by evil forces. Head to Chapter 10 and read the section on staying safe on the Internet, especially the portions on removing hijackers and spyware.

✔ Internet Explorer lets you choose several pages as home pages, simultaneously loading each one and placing a tab atop each page for switching between them. To add home pages to your collection, choose Add This Webpage to Your Home Page Tabs in Step 3 of the preceding list (Figure 8-3).

Revisit favorite places

Sooner or later, you'll stumble across a Web page that's indescribably delicious. To make sure that you can find it again later, add it to Internet Explorer's built-in list of favorite pages by following these steps:

⭐ Favorites

1. Click the Favorites button on Internet Explorer's toolbar.

A little menu drops down.

2. Click Add to Favorites.

A box appears, offering to name the Web page by its title — the words that appear on the tab at the page's top. Feel free to right-click the title and shorten the wording so that the title fits better on the narrow Favorites menu.

When you're happy with the name, click the Add button to add the page to your Favorites list.

Whenever you want to return to that page, click the Favorites button. When the Favorites menu drops down, click your favorite site's name.

 Librarian-types like to organize their menu of favorite links: Click the Favorites button, click the arrow by the Add to Favorites button, and choose Organize Favorites. That lets you create folders for storing similar and group-related links in single folders.

Don't see your favorites on the drop-down menu when you click the Favorites button? Click the Favorites tab at the menu's top to switch to them. (You may be looking at the History tab, covered in the sidebar, or the RSS feeds tab, which lists a site's headlines.)

Finding things on the Internet

When searching for a book in a library, you usually head straight for the computerized index. To find a particular Web site on the Internet, you should head for an index, as well. To help you out, Internet Explorer lets you access an Internet index — known as a search engine — through the Search box in its top-right corner.

Internet Explorer's secret history of your Web visits

Internet Explorer keeps a record of every Web site you visit. Although Internet Explorer's History list provides a handy record of your computing activities, it's a spy's dream.

To keep tabs on what Internet Explorer is recording, click your Favorites button and click the History icon on the drop-down menu. Internet Explorer lists every Web site you've visited in the past 20 days. Feel free to sort the entries by clicking the little arrow to the right of the word History. You can sort them by date, alphabetically, most visited, or by the order you've visited on that particular day — a handy way to jump back to that site you found interesting this morning.

To delete a single entry from the history, right-click it and choose Delete from the menu. To delete the entire list, exit the Favorites area. Then choose Internet Options from the Tools menu and click the Delete button in the Browsing History section. A menu appears, letting you delete your History and other items.

To turn off the History, click the Settings button instead of the Delete button. Then in the History section, change the Days to Keep Pages in History option to 0.

Type a few words into the Search box about what you're seeking — **exotic orchids,** for example — and press Enter. Internet Explorer fires your search off to Bing, Microsoft's own search engine. Don't like Bing? You can change that search engine to Google (www.google.com) or any other search engine you like.

In fact, you can add a variety of search engines, for example, routing most of your searches to Google but sending searches for books and CDs to Amazon. Follow these steps to customize Internet Explorer's Search box to your liking:

1. **Click the downward-pointing arrow on the Search box's right edge.**

   A drop-down menu appears.

2. **Choose Find More Providers.**

   Internet Explorer visits Microsoft's Web site and lists a few dozen popular search engines.

3. **Click the Add to Internet Explorer button next to your favorite search engine.**

   A dialog box opens, asking whether you want to add that search provider.

   If you want your searches to all go to one search engine — Google, for example — also select the check box labeled Make This My Default Search Provider before you go to Step 4. That option tells Internet Explorer to automatically send all your searches to that provider.

4. **Click the Add button.**

5. **Feel free to add any other search engines you like, as well.**

   To add any other search engines, repeat Steps 3 and 4. They'll all appear on the Search box's drop-down menu, as shown in Figure 8-4.

Figure 8-4: Stock your Search box with different search engines for searching different places.

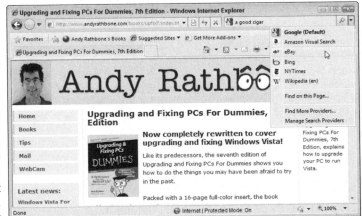

- ✔ You can change your default search engine at any time by choosing Manage Search Providers from the bottom of the drop-down menu in Figure 8-4. A window appears, listing all your search engines; click your favorite, and Internet Explorer sends it all your searches.

- ✔ If Google finds Web sites in foreign languages, it often translates them into your own language for you.

- ✔ Sometimes Google brings up a Web site that's been updated and no longer lists what you're searching for. If that happens, click the Cached link instead of the site's name. That brings up a snapshot of the Web site as it looked when it contained what you're searching for.

- ✔ On the Google home page, you can enter your search term and then click the I'm Feeling Lucky button, and Google displays the site most likely to contain what you're after. This option works best when you're searching for common information.

- ✔ The new Accelerators in Internet Explorer 8 offer another way to search for information. When you highlight words on a Web page, a little arrow appears; click it to see a pop-up menu with suggestions on what to do with those words: You can look them up on a map, search for more information about them, write them up on a blog, and more. Accelerators come stocked with links to Microsoft's own Web sites, but you can add others by choosing Add Accelerators from the pop-up menu.

The Web Page Says It Needs a Weird Plug-In Thing!

Computer programmers abandoned their boring old TV sets and turned to their exciting new computers for entertainment. Now, they're trying to turn their computers back into TV sets. They're using fancy programming techniques called Java, Flash, RealPlayer, QuickTime, Silverlight, and other goodies to add animation, movies, and flashing advertisements to the Internet.

Programmers create little software tidbits called *plug-ins* that allow your computer's Web browser to display these flashy items. You'll know when you're installing a plug-in when Internet Explorer sticks a threatening notice in your face, as shown in Figure 8-5.

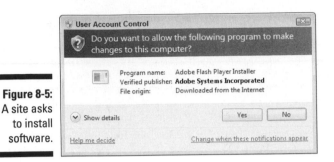

Figure 8-5:
A site asks
to install
software.

WARNING!

What's the problem? If Internet Explorer says it needs a plug-in or the latest version of the software, click the Install or Yes button — *only if you can trust the program.* Although it's often difficult to tell the good programs from the evil ones, I explain in Chapter 10 how to judge a plug-in's trustworthiness. The following plug-ins are both free and safe:

✔ **QuickTime (www.apple.com/quicktime):** The free version of QuickTime plays some video formats that Microsoft's Media Player can't handle.

✔ **RealPlayer (www.real.com):** Although I hate many things about this software, sometimes it's the only way to see or view some things on the Internet. Be sure to download the *free* version, no matter now much the Real folks try to hide it behind the pay version on the Web site.

✔ **Adobe Flash (www.adobe.com/products/flashplayer):** This double-edged free download plays the most distracting advertisements on Web sites as well as most online videos and animations.

✔ **Microsoft Silverlight (www.silverlight.net):** Microsoft's challenge to the hugely popular Flash, this software also plays movies and ads.

✔ **Adobe Acrobat Reader (www.adobe.com/products/reader):** Another popular freebie, Acrobat Reader lets you view documents as if they're printed on paper. (Sometimes it doesn't let you copy parts of them, though, or read them with your word processor.)

WARNING!

Beware of sites that try to slip in other programs when you download the plug-in. For example, some programs try to sneak in their partner's toolbar along with their plug-in. Examine the check boxes carefully and deselect any that you don't want, need, or trust before you click the Install or Download button. If it's too late, I describe how to remove unwanted add-ons in the "Removing Unneeded Plug-Ins" section, later in this chapter.

Saving Information from the Internet

The Internet places a full-service library inside your house, with no long checkout lines. And just as every library comes with a copy machine, Internet Explorer provides several ways for you to save interesting tidbits of information for your personal use. (Check your country's copyright laws for specifics.)

The following sections explain how to copy something from the Internet onto your computer, whether it's an entire Web page, a single picture, a sound or movie, or a program.

I explain how to print a Web page (or information it contains) in Chapter 7.

Saving a Web page

Hankering for a handy Fahrenheit/Centigrade conversion chart? Need that Sushi Identification Chart for dinner? Want to save the itinerary for next month's trip to Norway? When you find a Web page with indispensable infor- mation, sometimes you can't resist saving a copy onto your computer for further viewing, perusal, or even printing at a later date.

When you save a Web page, you're saving the page as it *currently exists* on your screen. To see any subsequent changes, you must revisit the actual site.

Saving your currently viewed Web page is easy:

| Page ▾ |

1. **Click Internet Explorer's Page button, and choose Save As from the overly crowded drop-down menu.**

   When the Save Webpage box appears, Internet Explorer enters the Web page's name in the File Name text box, as shown in Figure 8-6.

   To save the entire page as a single file in your Documents folder, click Save. But if you want to save the file in a different place or in a different format, move to Step 2.

2. **Select a location in the Navigation Pane to save the file.**

   Internet Explorer normally saves the Web page in your Documents folder, which is accessible from the Navigation Pane that hitches itself to every folder's left edge. To save the Web page in a different place, perhaps Downloads, click the Downloads item in the Navigation Pane's Favorites section.

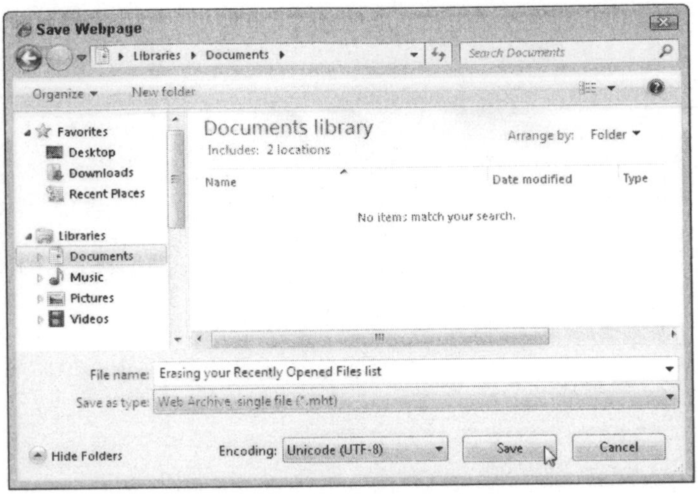

Figure 8-6:
Internet
Explorer's
Web
Archive
format
saves the
page to a
single file.

3. **Choose how you want to save the page in the Save As Type drop-down list.**

   Internet Explorer offers *four* different ways to save the Web page:

   - **Web Archive, Single File (*.mht):** This default choice saves an exact copy of the Web page packed neatly into a single file named after the Web page's title. Unfortunately, only Internet Explorer can open this type of file, ruling out its use by people who use other Web browsing programs.

   - **Webpage, Complete (*.htm;*.html):** More awkward but more compatible, this option saves the Web page in two separate pieces: a folder containing the page's images and a link that tells the computer to display that folder's contents. It's unwieldy, but it can be opened in any Web browser.

   - **Webpage, HTML Only (*.htm;*.html):** This option saves the page's text and layout but strips away the images. It's handy for stripping pictures and advertisements from tables, charts, and other formatted chunks of text.

   - **Text File (*.txt):** This option scrapes all the text off the page and dumps it into a Notepad file without taking many pains to preserve the formatting. It's handy for saving very simple lists but not much else.

4. **Click the Save button when you're done.**

To revisit your saved Web page, open your Downloads folder and click the saved file. Internet Explorer leaps back to life and displays the page.

Saving text

To save just a little of the text, select the text you want to grab, right-click it, and choose Copy. (I explain how to select text in Chapter 5.) Open your word processor and paste the text into a new document and save it in your Documents folder with a descriptive name.

To save *all* the text from a Web site, it's easiest to save the entire Web page, as described in the previous section.

To save a Web site's text but strip all the formatting and fonts, paste the copied text into Notepad. Then copy it from Notepad and paste it into the word processor of your choice.

Saving a picture

As you browse through Web pages and spot a picture that's too good to pass up, save it to your PC: Right-click the picture and choose Save Picture As, as shown in Figure 8-7.

The Save Picture window appears, letting you choose a new filename for the picture or stick with the filename used by the Web page. Click Save to place your pilfered picture in your Pictures folder.

The crowded right-click menu shown in Figure 8-7 offers other handy options, as well, letting you choose to print or e-mail the picture or even set it as your desktop's background.

Remember the little picture by your name on Windows 7's Welcome screen? Feel free to use any picture from the Internet. Right-click the new picture and save it to your Pictures folder. Then use the Control Panel (see Chapter 11) to transform that picture into your new user account picture.

Downloading a program, song, or other type of file

Sometimes downloading is as easy as clicking a Web site's Click to Download Now button. The Web site asks where to save your file, and you choose your Downloads folder for easy retrieval. The file arrives in a few seconds (if you have a cable modem) or a few minutes to hours (if you have a dialup modem).

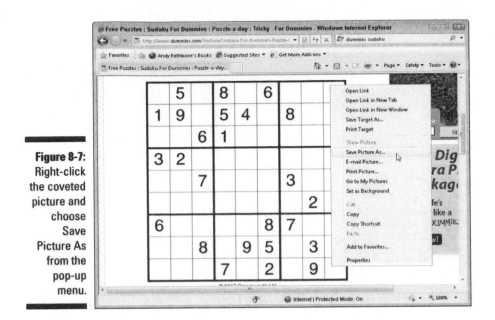

Figure 8-7:
Right-click
the coveted
picture and
choose
Save
Picture As
from the
pop-up
menu.

But sometimes downloading takes a few extra steps:

1. **Right-click the link pointing to your desired file and choose Save Target As.**

   For example, to download a song from a Web site, right-click its link (the song title, in this case). Then choose Save Target As from the pop-up menu, similar to the menu shown earlier in Figure 8-7.

   When you try to download a program, Windows asks whether you want to Save the File or Run It from Its Current Location. Choose Save the File.

2. **Navigate to your Downloads folder, if necessary, and click the Save button.**

   Windows 7 normally offers to save the incoming file into the same folder your last download landed in, saving you the trouble of navigating to it. (You can see Downloads listed in the folder's Navigation Pane in Figure 8-8.) But if you prefer to download it to a different place — your Music library, for example, when downloading a song — navigate to that location and click the Save button.

No matter what type of file you're downloading, Windows 7 begins copying the file from the Web site to your hard drive. A window appears to tell you when it finishes downloading, and you can click the Open Folder button to open the folder harboring your downloaded file.

✔ Before running any downloaded programs, screen savers, themes, or other items, be sure to scan them with your antivirus program. Windows 7 doesn't come with one built-in, leaving it up to you to purchase one.

✔ Many downloaded programs come packaged in a tidy folder with a zipper on it, known as a *Zip file*. Windows 7 treats them like normal folders; just double-click them to see inside them. (The files are actually compressed inside that folder to save download time, if you care about the engineering involved.) To extract copies of the zipped files, right-click the zipped file and choose Extract All.

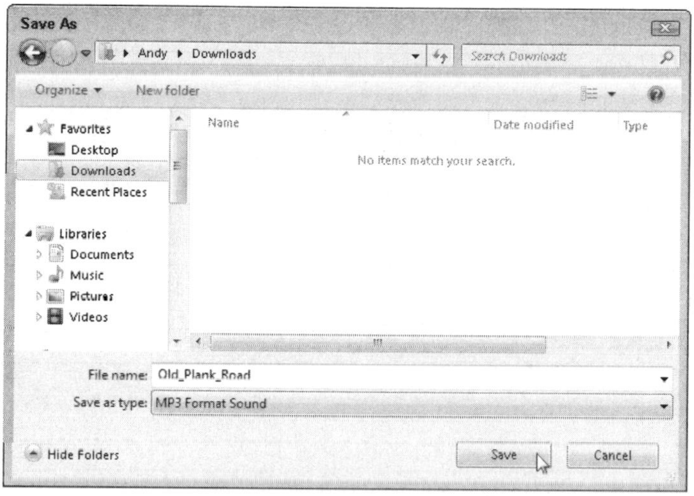

Figure 8-8: Navigate to a folder or library and click the Save button.

It Doesn't Work!

If something doesn't work, don't feel bad. The Internet has been around for a while, but this whole Web thing is relatively new, complicated, and changing quickly. It's not supposed to work as smoothly as a television yet, and it isn't something you can figure out overnight. This section explores common problems and possible solutions.

The person holding the Administrator account — usually the computer's owner — is the only one who is authorized to make some of the changes I describe in this section. If a mean message pops up, waving its finger and mumbling about administrator restrictions, you're locked out. Better find the computer's owner to proceed.

Here are some general tips that you may want to try before you explore the following sections:

- ✔ When a Web site gives you problems, try emptying Internet Explorer's wastebasket. Click Internet Explorer's Tools button, choose Internet Options, and click the Delete button. Put a check mark in the check box called Temporary Internet Files, remove check marks from items you *don't* want to delete, and click the Close button. Revisit the problematic site and try again.

- ✔ If your connection settings seem askew, try setting up your Internet connection again. Described in the "Setting Up Internet Explorer the First Time" section, earlier in this chapter, the steps guide you through your current settings, letting you change things that look suspicious.

- ✔ Think you've messed up Internet Explorer beyond repair? When all seems lost, return the program to its original settings by doing this: Click Tools, choose Internet Options, click the Advanced tab, and click Reset. This wipes out *all* of your settings, including your list of favorite sites.

- ✔ If you can't connect to the Internet at all, your best bet is to call your ISP's tech support number and ask for help. (Be sure to call your Internet service provider, not Microsoft.)

- ✔ If a page doesn't seem to display correctly, look for Internet Explorer's warning strip along the page's top. Click the strip and tell Internet Explorer *not* to block what it's trying to block.

Removing Unneeded Plug-Ins

Lots of Web sites install little programs inside Internet Explorer to help you navigate the Web or play with some Web sites. Not all of those little programs are well behaved. To help you pry off the leeches, Internet Explorer lets you see a list of all the currently installed little programs, called *add-ons.*

To see what's hanging onto your copy of Internet Explorer, click the program's Tools button and choose Manage Add-ons. Internet Explorer's Manage Add-ons window appears, as shown in Figure 8-9, letting you see all add-ons, toolbars, search engines, and more.

Most add-ons listed in the Manage Add-ons window are fine. (The ones from Microsoft are generally harmless.) But if you spot an add-on that you don't recognize, or that you think is causing problems, look up its name in Google (www.google.com) to see what most people say about it. If you find one that seems bad, click its name and click the Disable button.

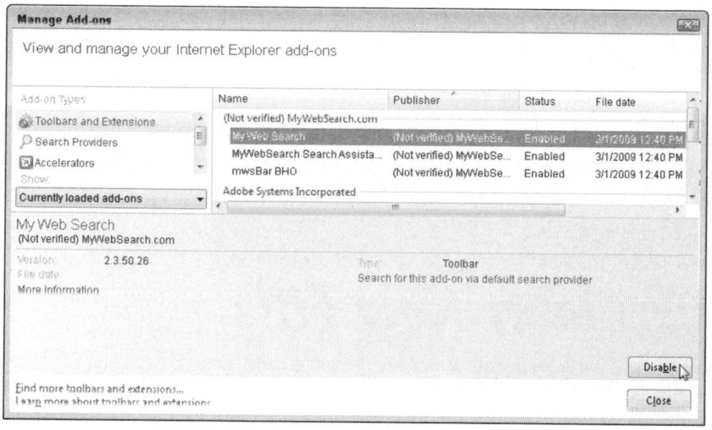

Figure 8-9:
Select a
suspicious
add-on and
click the
Disable
button.

If disabling the add-on keeps something from working correctly, return to the
Manage Add-ons window, click the add-on's name, and click the Enable button.

Managing add-ons turns into a game of trial and error, but it's a handy way to
disable a rogue add-on installed by a nasty Web site.

The Pages Won't All Fit on My Screen

Some people can afford huge monitors that pack lots of information onto
the screen. Other folks have smaller monitors that simply don't have the
real estate to display everything. So, how does a Web site reshape itself to fit
every viewer's screen? It can't.

Some fit squarely onto smaller monitors but leave white space along the
edges of larger monitors. Others try to guess a monitor's size and automatically resize themselves to fit. Others simply fall off your screen's right edge.

The best way to fight back is to experiment with your *screen resolution* — the
amount of information your screen can display. Although I describe the process in Chapter 11, here are the quick-and-dirty steps:

1. **Right-click a blank part of your desktop and choose Screen
   Resolution.**

2. **Click in the Resolution box to see the sliding control.**

3. **Slide the Resolution bar to adjust your Screen Resolution.**

   Sliding the bar upward packs more information onto the screen but
   makes everything smaller. Sliding it downward makes everything larger
   but sometimes leaves parts of the screen hanging off the edge.

Although the resolution setting of 800 x 600 pixels works well for average to small monitors, many sites now pack their information into a resolution of 1024 x 768 pixels.

If a Web page still seems too small to read, enlarge its text and images by holding down the Ctrl key and pressing +. (Hold down Ctrl and press – to shrink them; hold down Ctrl and press 0 [zero] to return the letters to normal.)

Internet Explorer Now Fills My Entire Screen!

Internet Explorer normally lives safely within its own menu-filled window. But occasionally it swells up to fill the entire screen, neatly trimming away both your menus and the desktop's taskbar. Full-screen mode looks great for movies, but the scarcity of menus leaves you with no way to switch to a different program.

To switch out of full-screen mode, press F11. That toggles full-screen mode, putting your menus back within reach. Press F11 again to watch the movie.

Even when Internet Explorer runs in full-screen mode, a press of the Windows key ( ) always fetches the Start menu and taskbar, which is handy for running a quick program and then returning to your full-screen Internet Explorer.

Chapter 9

Sending and Receiving E-Mail

A Web browser turns the Internet into a multimedia magazine, but an e-mail program turns it into your personalized post office, where you never need to fumble for a stamp. Windows 7, unfortunately, leaves you fumbling for something else: an e-mail program to send and receive your e-mail.

To replace your missing e-mail program, Microsoft hopes that you'll download and install Microsoft's free Windows Live Mail. You'll find mentions of Windows Live scattered throughout the Windows 7 menus, just begging for a click.

This chapter describes Windows Live Mail, as well as some alternative e-mail programs you may prefer. If you take the plunge on Windows Live Mail, this chapter describes how to download and install the program, set it up to work with a new or existing e-mail address, and keep your e-mail flowing in both directions.

Understanding E-Mail Options in Windows 7

E-mail programs come in two types: programs you fiddle with on a Web site and standalone programs that run on your PC. Both varieties attract fans, for the reasons I outline in the following sections.

Web-based e-mail

Web-based e-mail programs, such as those offered by Google (www.gmail.com), Yahoo! (http://mail.yahoo.com), and AOL (www.aol.com), let you send and receive e-mail directly from a Web site. To check or send e-mail, you visit the Web site, enter your name and password, and begin trawling through your waiting e-mail messages.

- ✔ **Pros:** Web-based programs let you access your e-mail from any PC that's connected to the Internet, be it in your home, in a hotel, or at a friend's house. Web-based e-mail programs also come in handy if you own several PCs: All your mail stays in one place, rather than being scattered between your desktop and laptop PC.

- ✔ **Cons:** Because your e-mail lives on the Web, not on your own PC, you can't browse your e-mail unless you're connected to the Internet. If the Internet is down, or your laptop is out of range of a wireless connection, you can't look up that phone number your friend e-mailed you last week. Your e-mail is more difficult to back up. Finally, most Web-based e-mail services pay their way by stuffing ads alongside your e-mail.

 If you're curious about Web-based e-mail, Google's Gmail easily wins as my favorite. It's fairly easy to set up, automatically filters out most of the spam, works with several mobile phones, and gives you 7GB of storage space.

Plus, Gmail is expandable. You can set it up to fetch and store e-mail from your other e-mail addresses, if you want. Gmail's search feature works as quickly and efficiently as Google's Web search. It lets you receive file attachments up to 25MB — more than enough for a handful of full-size digital photos.

One more thing: Gmail is free.

PC-based e-mail programs

If you've worked with Windows before, you're probably familiar with one of its built-in e-mail programs: either Outlook Express or Vista's Windows Mail. These programs store your e-mail on your own PC rather than on a Web site.

- ✔ **Pros:** Many e-mail programs that run on a PC, including Windows Live Mail, can send and receive e-mail from addresses other than their own. (For example, if you already have an AOL e-mail address, you can set up Windows Live Mail to send and receive e-mail from that address, all without ever creating a Windows Live Mail address.)

  Also, unlike Web sites, which sometimes change their menus, e-mail programs stay the same, letting you grow familiar with the controls.

✔ **Cons:** PC-based e-mail programs are more difficult to set up. They don't work with all e-mail addresses, because some unfriendly companies like Yahoo! make you pay for the privilege of sending or receiving e-mail through a program rather than through their Web site.

Although Windows Live Mail works much like both Windows XP's Outlook Express and Windows Vista's Windows Mail, it's certainly not the only free e-mail program. Its biggest competition comes from Thunderbird (www.mozilla.com/thunderbird), released by the same people behind the Firefox Web browser.

If you're not happy with Windows Live Mail but still want an e-mail program living on your PC, try Thunderbird (www.getthunderbird.com).

Installing Windows Live Mail

Windows 7 introduces a first hurdle to putting your e-mail in order. You must set up your Internet account, a task I describe in Chapter 8, before you can download the Windows Live Mail program.

When your Internet connection is flowing smoothly, follow these steps to download and install Windows Live Mail:

1. **Visit the Windows Live Web site (http://explore.live.com) and download the Windows Live Essentials 2011 installation program.**

   Save the incoming installation program in your Downloads folder, accessible from every folder's Navigation Pane, which is that strip along the left edge.

2. **Double-click the installation program in your Downloads folder.**

   The program wears the icon shown in the margin and goes by the name wlsetup-web. Windows 7 may become alarmed at a program trying to install itself on your PC and toss up a warning screen. If so, click Yes, and the installation program begins.

3. **Choose the Windows Live programs you want to install, and click Install.**

   The sneaky Microsoft tries to make you install *all* of its Live programs, as I describe in the nearby sidebar. Remove the check marks next to the programs you don't want, but be sure to leave the check mark next to the Mail program.

4. **Remove the check marks from the form's boxes to keep your existing search provider and home page, if desired, and then click Continue.**

   Search engines and home pages are big moneymakers, making them lucrative targets for hijacking: Every company wants to change them to its *own* services.

So, when you install any Windows Live program, Microsoft tries to set your Internet search provider to its *own* search engine (called Bing), and it wants to set your browser's home page to the Microsoft Network (MSN). If you're happy with your browser's current search engine and home page, remove the check marks from those two check boxes at this stage in the installation process.

5. **If you're unhappy with your e-mail address or need another one, create a Windows Live account. (Windows Live can use your existing e-mail address, if you prefer.) Otherwise, click Close.**

Windows Live Mail can send and receive e-mail from many e-mail addresses other than Microsoft's own, and the program probably works fine with your current e-mail address. But if you don't have an e-mail address or you want an additional one, click Sign Up to create a Windows Live e-mail address. (An e-mail account from Microsoft's Hotmail service can double as a Windows Live e-mail account.)

What are those other Windows Live programs?

Google, the search engine giant, began offering a suite of free online programs several years ago. When the programs proved popular (and profitable), Microsoft created its competing Windows Live programs. When you ask to download Windows Live Mail (or any other Microsoft Live program), the installation program offers to tack on all these free downloadable programs:

- **Messenger:** This little window on your desktop lets you type in short messages to your buddies, much like sending text messages through a cell phone.

- **Mail:** Covered in this chapter, Mail lets you send, receive, store, and organize your e-mail.

- **Photo Gallery and Movie Maker:** These two programs offer simple editing tools to spruce up your photos and videos, as well as share them online. (I cover both programs in Chapter 16.)

- **Writer:** Contrary to its name, Writer isn't a word processor but a blog editor: A tool for posting text and photos to online diaries known as blogs. It's compatible with big-league blogging services like WordPress, Blogger, LiveJournal, TypePad, SharePoint, Windows Live, and others.

- **Family Safety:** This program lets you monitor your kids' computer activity, limiting their access at certain times.

- **Messenger Companion:** This places a little window inside Internet Explorer, where you can share links with friends.

- **Windows Live Mesh:** Here, Microsoft gives you storage space accessible through any computer connected to the Internet.

- **Bing Bar:** Here, Microsoft wants you to change your search engine to Microsoft's own search engine, called Bing.

When running the Windows Live installation program, remove check marks from the programs you don't want.

When you're through, the Windows Live Mail icon appears on your Start menu, and you're ready to set it up.

Setting Up Windows Live Mail

Unless you created a Windows Live Mail account, the Windows Live Mail program doesn't know your e-mail address, nor where to send and receive your e-mail. To give the program that information, you must fill out its entrance forms, detailed in this section.

If you choose to install a competing e-mail program, you'll also follow steps similar to these that force you to enter the same information.

Follow these steps to tell Windows Live Mail to begin handling your e-mail:

1. **Open Windows Live Mail.**

   To call up Windows Live Mail for the first time, open the Start menu and click the Windows Live Mail icon (shown in the margin). If you don't see this icon, choose All Programs and click the Windows Live Mail icon that lurks inside.

   Windows Live Mail hops onto the screen, ready to be set up to send and receive your e-mail, as shown in Figure 9-1.

   If the screen in Figure 9-1 doesn't appear automatically, open Windows Live Mail, click Accounts from the top menu, and click the Email icon. The window appears, ready to add an e-mail account.

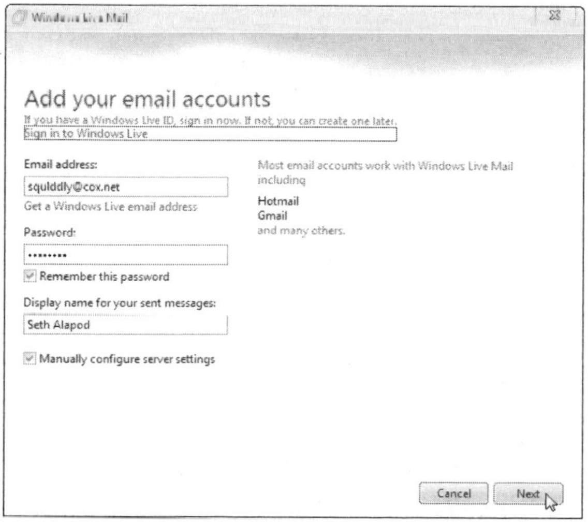

Figure 9-1: When loaded for the first time, Windows Live Mail offers to set up your e-mail account.

Add your email accounts

If you have a Windows Live ID, sign in now. If not, you can create one later.
Sign in to Windows Live

Email address:
squiddly@cox.net
Get a Windows Live email address

Password:
••••••••
☑ Remember this password

Display name for your sent messages:
Seth Alapod

☑ Manually configure server settings

Most email accounts work with Windows Live Mail including

Hotmail
Gmail
and many others.

Cancel   Next

2. **Type your e-mail address, password, and display name in the first three boxes.**

   If you signed up for a Windows Live Account or if you're planning on using your Hotmail account, simply click Next, and you're through: Windows Live Mail fills out all this window's settings for you.

   If you're using any other e-mail address, though, Windows Live Mail needs to know these three things:

   - **E-Mail Address:** Your e-mail address is your username, the @ sign, and your internet service provider (ISP), all information that your ISP or e-mail service must provide you with. For example, if your username is *jeff4265* and your ISP's name is *charternet.com,* type **jeff4265@charternet.com** into the E-Mail Address text box.

   - **Password:** You probably created this online when signing up for an account. Or, you may have received this password from your ISP along with your username. Either way, it's probably *case sensitive* (meaning the password **Onions** is different than **onions**). Select the Remember Password check box to fetch your mail automatically in the background, without having to enter your password every time.

   - **Display Name:** This name appears in the From text box of all your e-mail, so most people simply type their own name. Names like *DragonSlayer* may come back to haunt you.

   If you're using a different e-mail address, however, move to Step 3.

3. **Select the check box labeled Manually Configure Server Settings for E-Mail Account and then click Next.**

   The window shown in Figure 9-2 appears.

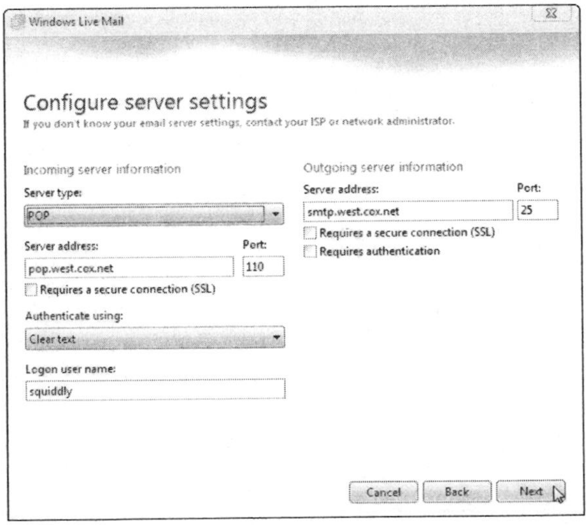

Figure 9-2:
Fill in your
incoming
and out-
going mail
server
information.

4. **Choose your server type and the names for your incoming and outgoing mail servers and click Next.**

   Easily the most agonizing portion of the e-mail experience, the window in Figure 9-2 asks for your e-mail server information. That consists of these things:

   - **Incoming server information:** You must type in your incoming mail server's name and whether it supports POP3, IMAP, or HTTP.

   - **Outgoing server information:** Type your outgoing mail server's name here. It's usually a string of words with periods between them, and one word is **SMTP.**

   - **Login ID (if different from e-mail address):** The program automatically places the first portion of your e-mail address in this box. Don't change it unless your ISP specifically tells you to enter something different.

   This window reeks of other confusing settings having to do with secure connections, port numbers, and other odd terms. Don't change them unless your ISP specifically says to change them.

   Some ISPs mail you these settings and instructions through the post office. If yours didn't, head for your ISP's Web site and look in the support section. If you *still* can't find this information, call your ISP's tech support folks and ask them for their mail server's *name* and *type*. (They've answered this question many times.)

   To give you a fighting chance, I've stocked Table 9-1 with the server information required by some common e-mail services.

Table 9-1	E-Mail Settings for Popular ISPs		
Service	*E-Mail Type*	*Incoming Mail Server*	*Outgoing Mail Server*
Google Gmail (See the Gmail sidebar for additional settings.)	POP3	pop.gmail.com	smtp.gmail.com
America Online (AOL) (See the AOL sidebar for additional settings.)	IMAP	imap.aol.com	smtp.aol.com
Yahoo! Mail Plus (See the Yahoo! sidebar for other settings.)	POP3	plus.pop.mail.yahoo.com	plus.smtp.mail.yahoo.com

5. Click Finish.

The last window simply congratulates you on setting up your e-mail. Unfortunately, it doesn't let you know if you typed anything wrong in Steps 2 or 3. That happens the first time you try to send or receive mail, described in the "Composing and sending an e-mail" section, later in this chapter.

Something not working correctly? These tips can help you fight your way through some stubborn situations:

✔ Are your settings not working? Then change them from within Windows Live Mail. Right-click your account name from the program's left side and choose Properties. The information you've entered in these four steps appears on the tabs marked General, Servers, and Advanced.

✔ Own more than one e-mail account? Add the second account by clicking Accounts from the top menu and choosing Email. That puts you right back at Step 1, letting you enter the information for your second e-mail address.

✔ The first e-mail account you set up in Windows Live Mail is your *default* account — the one listed as the return address on every e-mail you send. To grant default status to a different e-mail account, right-click that other account's name from Windows Live Mail's left side and choose Set as Default Account from the pop-up menu.

✔ Back up these settings to avoid the hassle of ever filling them out again: Click the Menu icon in the program's top, left corner, choose Options, and choose Email. Click your account's name, then click the Export button to save your account information as an IAF (Internet Account File). To import those settings back into Windows Live Mail — or into your laptop's mail program — follow the same steps, but choose Import instead of Export.

Sending and Receiving E-Mail in Windows Live Mail

The Windows Live Mail screen, shown in Figure 9-3, splits your e-mail into three sections: The Folder pane, along the left edge, automatically stores and sorts your e-mail into folders and accounts; the Message list section, in the middle, lets you see and tinker with your list of e-mail messages; finally, the Reading pane section, along the right, shows the contents of the currently selected message. (The program also displays a small appointment calendar along the right edge.)

Folder pane   Message list   Reading pane

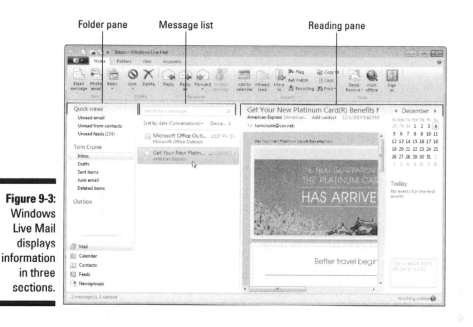

Figure 9-3:
Windows
Live Mail
displays
information
in three
sections.

Finishing up your Gmail account in Windows Live Mail

After you set up your Gmail account, you need to jump through a few extra hoops before it works with Windows Live Mail:

1. **Sign in to your Gmail account (www. gmail.com), click the Settings link at the top of the page, and click the Forwarding and POP/IMAP link.**

2. **Select the Enable POP for All Mail option and click the Save Changes button.**

3. **Open Windows Live Mail, right-click your Gmail account name in the left pane, and choose Properties.**

4. **When the Properties window appears, click the Servers tab.**

5. **In the Outgoing Mail Server section, select the My Server Requires Authentication check box and click Apply.**

6. **Click the Advanced tab.**

7. **In the Server Port Numbers section, select both check boxes called This Server Requires a Secure Connection (SSL).**

   The Incoming Mail port changes to 995.

8. **In the Outgoing mail (SMTP) box, change the number 25 to 465.**

9. **Click Apply, click OK, and click Close.**

Finishing up your AOL account in Windows Live Mail

Even after completing every step in the "Setting Up Windows Live Mail" section, your AOL e-mail account won't work correctly until you jump through the following additional hoops:

1. **Right-click your AOL account from Windows Live Mail's leftmost pane, choose Properties, and click the Servers tab.**

2. **In the Outgoing Mail Server section, click the My Server Requires Authentication box and click Apply.**

3. **Click the Advanced tab.**

4. **In the Outgoing Mail (SMTP) box, change the number to 587 and click Apply.**

5. **Click the IMAP tab and deselect the Store Special Folders on IMAP Server check box.**

6. **Click Apply, click OK, and click Close.**

If a message asks you to download folders from the mail server, click Yes.

The folders in Windows Live Mail's Folder pane work much like traditional inboxes and outboxes for sorting memos. Double-click any e-mail account's name to peek inside, and you're in for a pleasant surprise. Unlike your own office, Windows Live Mail automatically sorts your information into the following folders:

Send/
Receive ▾

✔ **Inbox:** When you connect to the Internet, Windows Live Mail grabs any waiting e-mail and places it in your Inbox folder. On PCs with a broadband Internet connection, Windows Live Mail checks for new mail every 10 minutes — or whenever you click the Send/Receive button (shown in the margin) on the toolbar.

You can change your 10-minute wait by clicking the Menus button along the program's top left (shown in the margin), choosing Options, choosing Mail, and changing the number of minutes in the Check for New Messages Every X Minutes box.

✔ **Drafts:** When you're midway through writing an e-mail and want to finish it later, click the Save button (shown in the margin) atop your e-mail window. Windows Live Mail saves a copy of the letter in your Drafts folder for retrieval later.

✔ **Sent Items:** *Every* piece of e-mail you've sent lingers in here, leaving a permanent record. (To kill any embarrassing e-mail from any folder, right-click the offending e-mail and choose Delete.)

✔ **Junk Email:** Windows Live Mail sniffs out potential junk mail and drops suspects into this folder. Peek in here every once in a while to make sure nothing lands in here by mistake.

✔ **Deleted Items:** The Deleted Items folder serves as Windows Live Mail's Recycle Bin, letting you retrieve accidental deletions. To delete something permanently from the Deleted Items folder, right-click it and choose Delete from the pop-up menu.

To keep deleted mail from cluttering your Deleted Items folder, click the Menus icon, choose Options, choose Mail, click the Advanced tab, and click the Maintenance button. From there, select the check box called Empty Messages from the 'Deleted Items' Folder on Exit.

✔ **Outbox:** When you send or reply to a message, Windows Live Mail immediately tries to connect to the Internet and send it. If you're already connected, Windows Live Mail fires it off to its recipient. Not connected? Your message lingers here. Try clicking the Send/Receive button to connect to the Internet and send it on its way.

To see the contents of any folder, click it. That folder's contents spill out to the right. Click any e-mail, and its contents appear in the Reading pane to the far right.

Want to transfer all your filed e-mail from one computer to another? I explain that chore in Chapter 19.

Finishing up your Yahoo! Mail Plus account in Windows Live Mail

Only *paid* Yahoo! accounts known as Yahoo! Mail *Plus* work with Windows Live Mail. After paying Yahoo! a fee and following the steps in the "Setting Up Windows Live Mail" section, you must jump through these extra hoops before your account works with Windows Live Mail:

1. **Right-click your Yahoo! account from Windows Live Mail's leftmost pane, choose Properties, and click the Servers tab.**

2. **In the Outgoing Mail Server section, click the My Server Requires Authentication box and click Apply.**

3. **Click the Advanced tab.**

4. **Enter 465 in the Outgoing mail (SMTP) field.**

5. **Under Incoming Mail (SMTP), select the check box labeled This Server Requires a Secure Connection (SSL).**

   The Incoming Mail port changes to 995.

6. **Click Apply, click OK, and click Close.**

Composing and sending an e-mail

Ready to send your first e-mail? After you've set up Windows Live Mail with your e-mail account, follow these steps to compose your letter and drop it in the electronic mailbox, sending it through virtual space to the recipient's computer:

1. **Open Windows Live Mail and click the Email Message icon on the program's menu bar.**

   Don't like mice? Hold down Ctrl and press N to open a new e-mail. Either way, a New Message window appears, as shown in Figure 9-4.

   If you've set up more than one account, as described in the previous section, Windows Live Mail automatically addresses the mail with your *default* account — usually the first e-mail account you created in Windows Live Mail.

   To send your mail from one of your other e-mail accounts, should you have one, click the downward-pointing arrow in the From box — the box currently listing your e-mail address — and select the preferred account.

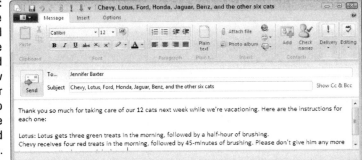

Figure 9-4: Click the Email Message icon, and a window appears for you to compose and send e-mail.

2. **Type your friend's e-mail address into the To box and press Tab to move to the Subject box.**

   If you know that the person's e-mail address is already in your list of Contacts, speed things up by doing this: Click the To button (shown in the margin), and a window appears, listing your contacts' names and e-mail addresses. Click your contact's name, click the window's To button, and click OK. That program addresses your e-mail to that person, just as if you'd type it in manually.

   Repeat the process for each person you'd like to receive the mail.

Bcc...

Sending or forwarding a message to several people? Preserve their privacy by clicking the Bcc button (shown in the margin) instead of the To button. That still sends them the same message but hides their e-mail addresses from each other, preserving their privacy. (If your Bcc button is missing, reveal it by clicking Show Cc & Bcc to the right of the Subject box.)

Cc...

To let *everybody* see each other's e-mail addresses, select their names and click the To or Cc button, shown in the margin. (Unless the recipients all know each other, this is considered bad etiquette.)

3. **Fill in the Subject box.**

   Although optional, the Subject line lets your friends know why you're bugging them. That makes it easier for your friends to sort their mail.

4. **Type your message into the large box at the window's bottom.**

   Type as many words as you want. There's no limit.

5. **(Optional) Attach any files or photos to your e-mail, if desired, as described in this chapter's upcoming sections, "Attaching a file or files to an e-mail" and "Embedding photos in an e-mail."**

   Most ISPs balk at sending files larger than about 5MB, which rules out most MP3 files and some digital photos. I describe sending and receiving attachments in more detail later in this chapter.

6. **Click the Send button along the box's left side.**

   Whoosh! Windows Live Mail dials your modem, if necessary, and whisks your message through the Internet to your friend's mailbox. Depending on the speed of the Internet connection, mail can arrive anywhere from 5 seconds later to a few days later, with a few minutes being the average.

For some reason, Windows Live Mail doesn't automatically check your spelling before you send your message. To turn on the spell checker, click the Menus icon at the top of the window, choose Options, click Mail, click the Spelling tab, and select the Always Check Spelling Before Sending check box.

Reading a received e-mail

If you keep Windows Live Mail running while you're connected to the Internet, you'll know when a new letter arrives. Your computer makes a little hiccup to herald its arrival.

To check for any new mail when Windows Live Mail isn't running, load the program from the Start menu. When it loads, click the Send/Receive button. Windows Live Mail logs on to the Internet, sends any outgoing mail you have sitting around, and grabs any incoming mail to place in your Inbox.

Exactly what do I need to send e-mail?

To send e-mail to a friend or foe with Windows Live Mail, you need three things:

✔ **An e-mail account:** This chapter describes how to set up Windows Live Mail to work with your e-mail account. Most ISPs (Internet service providers, covered in Chapter 8) give you a free e-mail address along with your Internet access.

✔ **Your friend's or foe's e-mail address:** Find out your friends' e-mail addresses by simply asking them. (Or import the addresses from another e-mail program, as I describe in this chapter's Managing Your Contacts section.) An address consists of a *username* (which occasionally resembles the person's real name), followed by the @ sign, followed by the name of your friend's ISP. The e-mail address of an America Online user with the username of Jeff9435 would be `jeff9435@aol.com`. (Unlike your local post office, e-mail doesn't tolerate any spelling errors. Precision is a must.)

✔ **Your message:** Here's where the fun finally starts: typing your letter. After you type the person's e-mail address and your message, click the Send button. Windows Live Mail routes your message in the right direction.

You'll find people's e-mail addresses on business cards, Web sites, and even return addresses. When an e-mail arrives in Windows Live Mail, click the words Add Contact next to the sender's e-mail address. Then Windows Live Mail adds that person's name and e-mail address to your list of contacts.

If you misspell part of an e-mail address, your sent message bounces back to your own Inbox, with a confusing *undeliverable* message attached. Check the spelling of the address and try again. If it bounces again, humble yourself: Pick up the phone and ask the person to confirm his or her e-mail address.

Follow these steps to read the letters in your Inbox and either respond or file them away:

1. **Open Windows Live Mail and click your Inbox.**

   Windows Live Mail shows you the messages in your Inbox, and they look something like Figure 9-5. Each subject is listed, one by one, with the newest one at the top.

   To find a particular e-mail quickly, type the sender's name or a keyword in the Search box, shown atop the list of received e-mails in Figure 9-5. (You can also search for e-mails directly from the Start menu's Search box.)

2. **Click any message's subject to read it.**

   Click any message, and Windows Live Mail spills that message's contents into the Reading pane along the window's right side, as shown in Figure 9-5, ready for you to examine. Or, to see the entire message in its own window, double-click it.

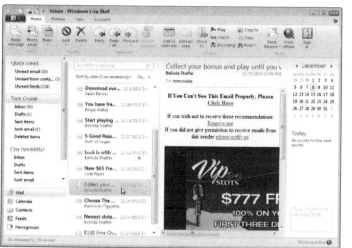

Figure 9-5:
Your incoming mail appears in the Inbox; the highlighted mail's contents appear to the right.

3. **From here, Windows Live Mail leaves you with several options, and you can access each of them from one of these buttons along the e-mail's top edge:**

- **Nothing:** Undecided? Don't do anything, and the message simply sets up camp in your Inbox folder until you delete it.

- **Reply:** Click the Reply button along the top of Windows Live Mail, and a new window appears, ready for you to type in your response. The window is just like the one that appears when you first compose a message but with a handy difference: This window is pre-addressed with the recipient's name and the subject. Also, the original message usually appears at the bottom of your reply for reference.

- **Reply All:** Some people address e-mails to several people simultaneously. If you see several other people listed on an e-mail's To line, you can reply to all of them by clicking Reply All instead of Reply.

- **Forward:** Received something that a friend would like? Click Forward to send the e-mail to that friend.

- **Add to Calendar:** Windows Live Mail includes a basic calendar for keeping appointments. Click this button to fetch a new window, where you can embed the e-mail's message into the date of your choice.

- **Delete:** Click the Delete button to toss the message into your Deleted Items folder. Your deleted messages sit inside the folder until you right-click the Deleted Items folder and choose Empty 'Deleted Items' Folder. For automatic deletion, click the Menus icon, select Options, click the Advanced tab, click Maintenance, and choose Empty Messages from the Deleted Items folder on Exit.

- **Junk:** Windows Live Mail filters out spam, but if you stumble upon a piece it missed, click the Junk button on the Windows Live Mail toolbar. That quickly moves the odiferous e-mail out of your Inbox and into your Junk folder.

- **Print:** Click the Menu icon, click Print, and Windows Live Mail shoots your opened message to the printer to make a paper copy.

- **Previous/Next:** Click one of these arrow icons to see either your next waiting message or the one you just read. (If you don't see these, drag open your e-mail window a little wider.)

These tips help you wring the most work out of Windows Live Mail:

- ✔ When viewing a received e-mail, click the words Add Contact (located to the right of the name of the sender) to place that sender's name and e-mail address in your contacts list. Then that person's name and e-mail address will be one click away when you click the To button in a new e-mail.

- ✔ To organize your incoming messages, right-click your Inbox and choose New Folder to create another folder inside it. Create as many folders as you need to categorize your spam offers.

- ✔ To move an e-mail into another folder, drag it there from the Inbox.

- ✔ Some people's e-mails contain not only words, but a file, which computer folk refer to as an *attachment*. Attachments cause enough problems to warrant their own section, which appears next.

- ✔ If you ever receive an unexpected e-mail from a bank, eBay, or any other money-oriented Web site, think twice before clicking any of the e-mail's Web links. A criminal industry called *phishing* sends e-mails that try to trick you into entering your name and password on a phony Web site. That gives your coveted information to the evil folk, who promptly steal your money. Windows Live Mail sends you a warning when it spots suspicious phishing e-mails; I write more about phishing in Chapter 10.

- ✔ When you see a little red *X* in place of a picture or photo on your e-mail, that means Windows Live Mail is blocking it. To view the image, click the blue message Show Images that appears in the yellow banner atop the message. To keep Windows Live Mail from blocking images, click the Menus button (shown in the margin), choose Options, choose Safety Options, click the Security tab, and deselect the check box called Block Images and Other External Content in HTML Email.

Sending and Receiving Files through E-Mail

Like a little pair of movie tickets slipped into the envelope of a thank-you note, an *attachment* is any type of file that piggybacks onto an e-mail message. You can send or receive any type of file as an attachment. When sent, the attachments look like icons neatly tacked to the top of your e-mail.

Attachments work fine for transporting files, but they're a pretty boring tool for sending digital photos. To spice things up, Windows Live Mail offers an option to *embed* photos directly into your e-mail: Rather than display photos as boring icons, Windows Live Mail puts thumbnails of each photo directly into your e-mail for quick and easy viewing.

Whether you're attaching or embedding files, beware of one thing: Many ISPs limit the size of an attachment to 5MB or less — a small handful of digital photos. (Google's Gmail lets you send attachments up to 25MB to other Gmail accounts.)

The next sections explain how to send and receive attachments, as well as how to send and receive digital photos embedded inside an e-mail.

Attaching a file or files to an e-mail

Email message

To e-mail any file to somebody, begin by creating your new e-mail: Click the Email button, as described in the "Composing and sending an e-mail" section, earlier in this chapter. When the New Message window appears, type your message as usual.

When you're ready to add a file as an attachment, follow these steps:

Attach file

1. **Click the Attach File button and locate the file or files you want to send.**

   A window appears, conveniently opening to show the Navigation Pane and its libraries, stuffed with your documents, music, photos, and video files. Browse the files and folders in your libraries until you find the ones you want to e-mail.

2. **To attach a single file, double-click its name. To attach several files, select them all and then click the Open button.**

   Oddly enough, clicking the Open button doesn't *open* any files. Instead, it attaches the files to your e-mail message.

No matter which method you choose, Windows Live Mail tacks on the file or files to your e-mail. You can spot an attached file's name — adjacent to a paperclip icon — below the mail's subject line, shown in Figure 9-6. (The mouse pointer is pointing to it.)

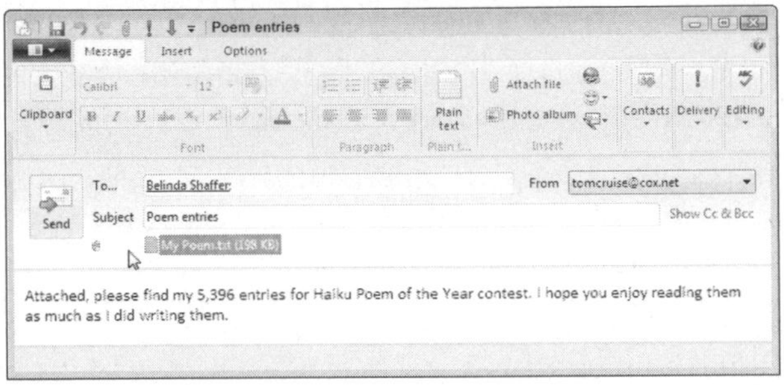

Figure 9-6:
Attached files appear listed in the Attach line of an e-mail.

Accidentally added the wrong file? Remove it by right-clicking its name and choosing Remove.

3. Click the Send button.

Windows Live Mail whisks off your mail and its attachment to the recipient.

The preceding steps let you add an attachment while you're composing an e-mail, but you can send a file through either of these methods, too:

✔ Right-click a file's name from within its folder, choose Send To from the pop-up menu, and select Mail Recipient. Windows Live Mail (or whatever e-mail program you've installed) opens a new e-mail window with that file already attached.

✔ While your new e-mail message is open on the screen, drag and drop a file anywhere into its window. That file appears as an attachment, ready to be sent.

Saving an attached file

Saving attached files that you've received is easier than sending them. To save an attachment, follow these steps:

1. Open the e-mail with the attachment.

The attached file appears as a name with a paperclip next to it, shown earlier in Figure 9-6.

2. **Right-click the attached file's name and choose Save As from the pop-up menu.**

   Have several attached files? Then hold down Ctrl and click them all. Then right-click the selected files and choose Save As from the menu.

   Either way, the Save Attachment As window appears, letting you choose a place to save your incoming goods. Save incoming pictures in the Pictures library; most other items go in the Documents library.

3. **Choose a place to save the file, and click Save.**

   Windows Live Mail saves a copy of the file in your chosen spot, leaving a copy of the file still attached to the e-mail as a backup.

E-mail makes it easy to exchange files with friends around the world. Files are so easy to send, in fact, that virus writers quickly picked up on the trend, creating viruses that spread themselves by mailing a copy of themselves to everybody in the recipient's address book.

That brings me to the following warnings:

- If a friend sends you an attached file unexpectedly, *don't open it.* E-mail your friend and ask whether he or she *really* sent it. That attachment may be sent by a virus without your friend knowing about it. To be safe, drag received attachments onto your desktop and scan them with your antivirus program before opening. Don't open them directly from the e-mail itself.

- To prevent you from opening a virus, Windows Live Mail refuses to let you open almost *any* attached file. If Windows Live Mail won't let you open a file you're expecting from a friend, turn off that protection: On the Home tab, click the Junk icon, then choose Safety Options. Click the Security tab, and deselect the check box labeled Do Not Allow Attachments to Be Saved or Opened That Could Potentially Be a Virus.

Embedding photos in an e-mail

To make things easy, send your digital photos as attachments as described in the previous section. But if you have a Windows Live e-mail address, you can embed the photos in your e-mail, instead.

If you still want to proceed, follow these steps to place thumbnails of photos directly inside your e-mail, as shown in Figure 9-7, all neatly aligned in a grid.

Figure 9-7:
Embedded
photos
appear in
the e-mail
itself; click
beneath a
photo to add
a caption.

The recipient can then view the thumbnails, click any thumbnail to see a larger version of a picture, or even watch an online slide show within 90 days. After 90 days, though, they can't see the pictures any longer.

To embed photos into an e-mail, follow these steps:

1. **In Windows Live Mail, click the Photo Email button.**

   The Add Photos window appears, conveniently opening to show your Pictures library.

2. **Choose the photo or photos you want to attach, and click Open.**

   To attach a *single* photo, click its name and click Open.

   To attach *several* photos, hold down the Ctrl key while clicking your photos. Then click the Open button.

   No matter which method you choose, clicking Open tells Windows Live Mail to embed the photo(s) in your e-mail, as shown previously in Figure 9-7.

3. **Add title, if desired, by clicking Enter Album Name Here and typing your words.**

You don't need to type more than one line of text.

4. **Add your recipient's e-mail addresses and enter a subject.**

   Click the To button and choose recipient's names from your contacts, then type a subject into the Subject line.

5. **Choose your message's recipient in the To: box, fill out the subject, and click Send to deliver your e-mail.**

   Windows Live Mail whisks off your mail and its photos to the recipient.

Saving embedded photos

To save photos visibly embedded in your e-mail or on a Website, right-click them and choose Save Picture As from the pop-up menu. When the Save Picture window appears, type a name for the incoming photo, click the Pictures library, and click Save.

If you've received embedded photos sent through a Windows Live Mail account, save the photos by following these steps:

1. **Open the e-mail with the embedded photos.**

   The e-mail almost looks like a Web page, as shown in Figure 9-7. Actually, it is, in a way: The e-mail contains a link to Microsoft's Web site, where the photos are actually stored.

2. **Click the Download All link then click Save.**

   After entering your Windows Live Mail name and password, and clicking Save, the Save As window appears, letting you choose a folder to receive the incoming photos. Navigate to your Pictures library, the handy storage spot for all your digital photos. Don't have a Windows Live e-mail account? Then you can only download the pictures individually by right-clicking and choosing Save Picture As.

3. **Click Save.**

   Windows Live Mail downloads a copy of the photos to your chosen spot, leaving a copy of the photos still attached to the e-mail for safekeeping. The photos come packaged in a "zipped" file; to unzip them from their container, right-click the newly received zip file and choose Extract All.

Although Windows Live Mail can be handy for e-mailing a batch of digital photos, keep this in mind: Microsoft puts a one-month deadline on downloading the photos. After that, the high-resolution ones are deleted, leaving you with only the embedded thumbnail versions.

Finding lost mail

Eventually, an important e-mail will disappear into a pile of folders and filenames. Windows 7 offers you several ways to retrieve it:

✔ **Windows Live Mail's Search box:** Atop the program's middle pane lives the Search box. Type in a name or word from an e-mail, and the Search box fetches every match. See the little blue box that appears below the Search box? That box's menu lets you choose whether to search a specific folder or all your mail.

✔ **Folder's Search box:** If you've saved your e-mail in a particular folder, click that folder and then type your search in the Search box. The box limits its search to that particular folder.

✔ **The Start menu's Search box:** Don't know which folder houses your lost e-mail? The Start menu's Search box, which I cover in Chapter 6, constantly indexes your e-mail — and the Start menu's Search box works like a mini-Google to find it.

Managing Your Contacts

Windows Vista stored your contacts as separate files in a Contacts folder. Windows Live Mail does the same thing unless you sign in with a Windows Live e-mail account. The Windows Live e-mail account lets you store your contacts in *two* places: within the program itself and online. When you sign in to Windows Live Mail, the online version mimics your desktop version, complete with the same contacts and even the same sent and received e-mails.

To see your list of contacts in Windows Live Mail on your PC, click the Contact icon (shown in the margin) at the bottom of the left pane. The Windows Live Contacts window appears, listing everybody you've added to your Contacts list.

You can beef up your list of contacts several ways:

✔ **Let Windows Live Mail do it automatically.** When you respond to somebody for the third time, Windows Live Mail automatically tosses that person's name and e-mail address into your Contacts list. If Windows Live Mail ever stops doing that, fix it: Click the Menus icon, choose Options, click Mail, click the Send tab, and select the check box called Automatically Put People I Reply to in My Address Book After the Third Reply.

✔ **Import an old address book.** To import an Address Book file from another computer, open your list of contacts, and click the Import icon. From here, you can import contacts from a variety of different file formats. (Of course, that means you first need to *export* those contacts from your other program in either a WAB, VCF, or CSV.)

✔ **Add contacts manually.** When somebody hands you a business card, you must enter the information by hand. From inside Windows Live Mail's Contacts window, click the Contact icon. Type in the person's name and e-mail address, or create a detailed dossier by filling out every box in every section. Click Add Contact when you're through.

These other tasks come in handy when you find yourself staring into your Contacts window:

✔ To send a quick message to a contact in your Contacts window, click that person's name, and choose Send Email. Windows Live Mail calls up a handy, preaddressed New Message window, ready for you to type your message and click Send.

✔ To back up your Contacts list, click the Export icon a top the menu bar, and export them as either CSV (Comma Separated Values) or VCF (Business Card or vCards) files. (In case of disaster, you can import either of those files back into the program.)

Reducing Your Spam

Unfortunately, you can never completely banish spam from your Inbox. Believe it or not, some people still buy things from spammers, making the junk e-mails profitable enough for spammers to continue. Scowl at any neighbors who confide that they've bought a spammer's merchandise.

Luckily, Windows Live Mail has wised up a bit when it comes to recognizing spam. In fact, when the program spots an e-mail that smells suspiciously like spam, it sends you a message, shown in Figure 9-8, and deposits the suspect into your Junk E-mail folder.

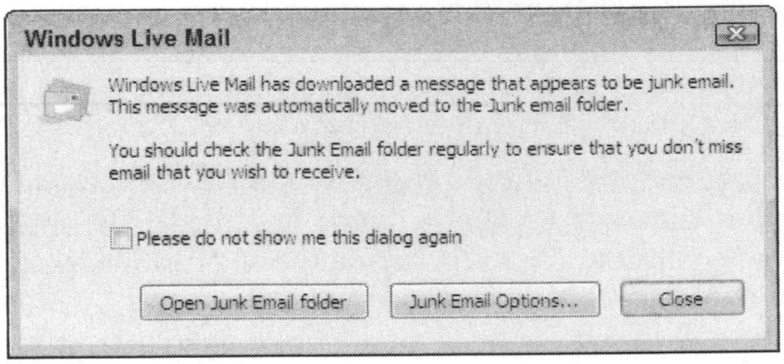

Figure 9-8:
Windows
Live Mail's
spam filter
automati-
cally moves
spam to
your Junk
Email folder.

Windows Live Mail

Windows Live Mail has downloaded a message that appears to be junk email.
This message was automatically moved to the Junk email folder.

You should check the Junk Email folder regularly to ensure that you don't miss
email that you wish to receive.

☐ Please do not show me this dialog again

[Open Junk Email folder] [Junk Email Options...] [Close]

If you spot mail in the Junk E-mail folder that's *not* junk, click the good piece of mail and click the Not Junk button on the toolbar. Windows Live Mail quickly whisks that piece of mail back into your Inbox.

Although you can't completely stop spam, you can weed out much of it by following these rules:

✔ Give your e-mail address only to close friends, relatives, and trusted business contacts. Don't give it to strangers or post it on Web sites.

✔ Create a second, *disposable* e-mail account to use when signing up for online offers, filling out online forms, or carrying out any short-term correspondence. Delete that address once it's plagued with spam, and create a new one.

✔ Never post your real e-mail address in an Internet chat forum, news-group, or other public conversation area. And never respond to a spam-mer, even if it's to click the Unsubscribe link. Clicking that link merely adds you to the spammer's list of confirmed e-mail addresses.

✔ See whether your ISP offers built-in spam filtering. The filters work so well that many spammers now try to evade the filters by using nonsensi-cal words. If they do make it through, the nonsense in the subject gives it away as being spam.

Chapter 10

Safe Computing

· ·

· ·

*L*ike driving a car, working with Windows is reasonably safe, as long as you stay clear of the wrong neighborhoods, obey traffic signals, and don't steer with your feet while you stick your head out the sunroof.

But in the world of Windows and the Internet, there's no easy way to recognize a bad neighborhood, spot the traffic signals, or even distinguish between your feet, the steering wheel, and the sunroof. Things that look totally innocent — a friend's e-mail or a program on the Internet — may be a virus or prank that sneakily rearranges everything on your dashboard or causes a crash.

This chapter helps you recognize the bad streets in Windows' virtual neighborhoods and explains the steps you can take to protect yourself from harm and minimize any damage.

Understanding Those Annoying Permission Messages

After 20 years of Windows development, Windows 7 is still pretty naive. Oh, it's much better than Vista, of course. But sometimes when you run a program or try to change settings on your PC, Windows 7 can't tell whether *you're* doing the work or a *virus* is attempting to mess with your PC.

Windows 7's solution? When Windows 7 notices anybody (or anything) trying to change something that can potentially harm Windows or your PC, it darkens the screen and flashes a message asking for permission, like the one shown in Figure 10-1.

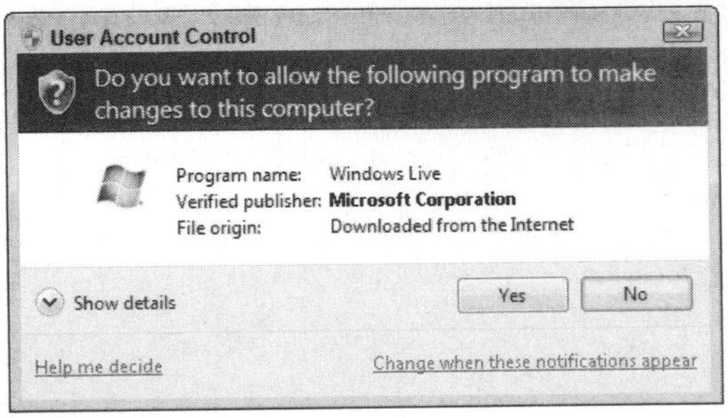

Figure 10-1: Click No if this message appears unexpectedly.

If one of these permission messages appears out of the blue, Windows 7 may be warning you about a bit of nastiness trying to sneak in. So click No to deny it permission. But if *you're* trying to do something specific with your PC and Windows 7 puts up its boxing gloves, click Yes, instead. Windows 7 drops its guard and lets you in.

If you don't hold an Administrator account, however, you can't simply click Yes. You must track down an Administrator account holder and ask her to type her password.

Yes, a dimwitted security-guard robot polices Windows 7's front door, but it's also an extra challenge for the people who write the viruses.

Windows 7's permission screens are called *User Account Control* or *User Account Protection,* depending on the person you're asking.

Assessing Your Safety in the Action Center

Take a minute to check your PC's safety with Windows 7's Action Center. Part of the Control Panel, the Action Center displays any problems it notices with Windows 7's main defenses, and provides handy, one-button fixes for the situations. Its taskbar icon, the white flag shown in the margin, always shows the Action Center's current status.

Turning off permissions

Toning down the nagging permission screens leaves your PC more vulnerable to the dark forces of computing. But if you find yourself grinding your teeth more than working, Administrator account holders may adjust Windows 7's paranoia level by following these steps:

1. **Click the Start button, choose Control Panel, and then click System and Security.**

   The Control Panel, which I explain in Chapter 11, lets you tweak how Windows runs on your PC.

2. **In the Action Center section, click Change User Account Control Settings.**

   A scroll bar appears on the screen, set three-quarters of the way up to Default.

3. **To relax User Account Control, slide the scroll bar down; to increase its strictness, slide it up.**

   The scroll bar offers four settings:

   Always Notify Me When: This setting makes for a very secure PC but a very difficult work environment stuffed with false alarms.

Default: This setting is a nice balance between safe and nag-free. Windows 7 comes set to this option.

Notify Me Only When Programs Try to Make Changes to My Computer (Do Not Dim My Desktop): Less secure, this setting warns you only when a program tries to make changes. (Plus, it doesn't blacken the desktop during a warning.)

Never Notify Me When: The least secure, this setting stops warning you when you or programs make changes. You must restart your PC before it takes effect.

Choose the setting that makes you the most comfortable. I leave mine set at the default level because it strikes a good balance between security and comfort.

4. **Click OK after choosing your comfort level.**

If you change your mind, turn the Permissions screens back on by following Steps 1 through 4, making sure to return to the Default setting in Step 3.

The Action Center window, shown in Figure 10-2, color codes problems by their severity; a blood red band shows critical problems requiring immediate action, and a yellow band means the problem needs attention soon.

For example, Figure 10-2 shows a red band by the first item, Virus Protection. The second item, Set Up Backup, wears a yellow band.

All these defenses should be up and running for maximum safety, because each protects you against different things.

If any of your computer's big cannons aren't loaded and pointing in the right direction, the Action Center's tiny taskbar icon, shown in the margin, appears with a red X across the flag.

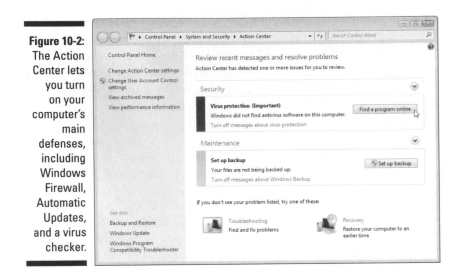

When you spot that red flagged icon on your taskbar, follow these steps to visit the Action Center and fix the problem:

1. **Click the taskbar's red-flagged Action Center icon and choose Open Action Center from the pop-up menu.**

   The Action Center, shown earlier in Figure 10-2, hops on-screen to display your computer's status in both security and maintenance.

   Security messages: The Activity Center can show problems in any of these categories, but rarely shows more than one or two at a time:

   • *Windows Update:* Windows Update program automatically visits Microsoft through the Internet, downloads any new safety patches, and installs them, all for free and all without any effort on your part.

   • *Internet Security Settings:* This category covers protection settings for Internet Explorer, which help keep nasties from attaching themselves to your Web browser.

   • *Network Firewall:* Windows 7's new, more powerful firewall monitors every connection arriving in and leaving your PC. When the firewall notices an unrequested connection trying to enter, it blocks it, stopping potential intruders.

   • *Spyware and Related Protection:* Windows 7 includes a spyware remover called Windows Defender, and the Activity Center shouts out if it's not running correctly.

   • *User Account Control:* Activity Center lets you know if something's wrong with User Account Control, described in the previous section, and its nagging permission screens.

- *Virus Protection:* Windows 7 lacks a virus checker, but it checks to see whether you've installed one. If the Action Center notices you haven't bought an antivirus program or kept its subscription fees paid, the Action Center hoists the red flag.

Maintenance: In addition to monitoring security issues, the Activity Center monitors these three maintenance tasks:

- *Windows Backup:* Windows Backup (covered later in this chapter) automatically creates copies of your important files to fall back on in case of emergency.

- *Windows Troubleshooting:* When Windows notices problems with your PC or its programs, it sends up a message offering to troubleshoot them. If you clicked that message away in frustration, you can come here to take Windows up on its offer.

   Don't see your previous offer of troubleshooting help? In the left pane of the Action Center window, click View Archived Messages. A window appears, listing all the offers of help Windows has given you for past problems.

- *Check for Updates:* This means Windows Update and Windows Defender have stopped checking for newly updated software.

2. **Click the button next to flagged items to fix any potential security problems.**

   Whenever you notice that one of Windows 7's defenses is turned off in the Action Center, click the button next to the item. For example, in Figure 10-2, clicking the buttons named Find a Program Online and Set Up Backup will either fix the problem automatically or let you flip the right switch to set things straight.

By following the two preceding steps, your computer will be much safer than under any other version of Microsoft Windows.

Changing the firewall settings

Just about everybody has dropped a fork to pick up the phone, only to hear a recorded sales pitch. That's because telemarketers run programs that sequentially dial phone numbers until somebody answers. Internet troublemakers run similar programs that automatically try to break into every computer that's currently connected to the Internet.

Broadband Internet users are especially vulnerable because their computers are constantly connected to the Internet. That increases the chances that hackers will locate them and try to exploit any available vulnerability.

That's where Windows Firewall comes in. The firewall sits between your computer and the Internet, acting as an intelligent doorman. If something tries to connect, but you or one of your programs didn't request it, the firewall stops the connection.

Occasionally, however, you'll *want* another computer to interact with your computer over the Internet. You may be playing a multiplayer game, for example, or using a file-sharing program. To stop the firewall from blocking those programs, add their names to the firewall's Exceptions list by following these steps:

1. **Choose Control Panel from the Start menu, click System and Security, and click the Windows Firewall icon (shown in the margin).**

   The Windows Firewall window appears, showing the Windows 7 settings for two different types of networks you might connect with:

   - **Home or Work (Private):** Since home and work networks are more secure, Windows Firewall relaxes its grip enough to let you share files with the PCs of co-workers and family members.

   - **Public:** Public networks, like those found in coffee shops and airports, aren't secure. So, the firewall tightens its grip, forbidding the PCs around you from seeing or grabbing any of your PC's information.

2. **On the Windows Firewall window's left side, click the words Allow a Program or Feature Through Windows Firewall.**

   Shown in Figure 10-3, Windows Firewall lists every program currently allowed to communicate through its firewall. (Windows 7 adds many of its programs automatically, so don't be surprised to see a zillion programs already listed.)

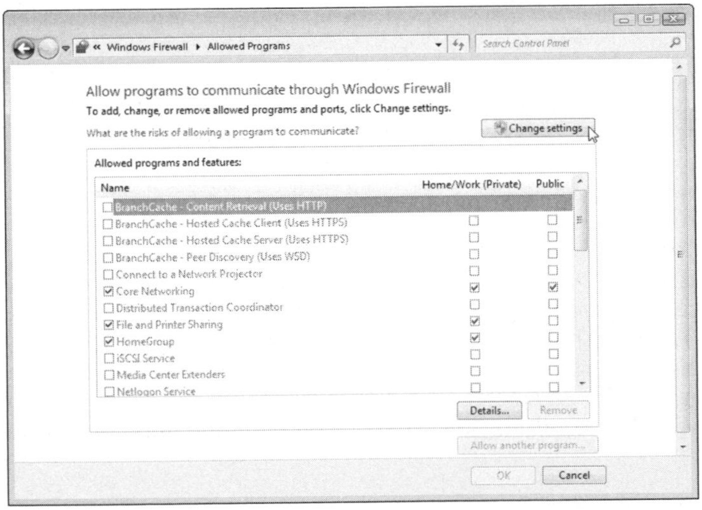

Figure 10-3:
Click the
Change
Settings
button to
add a pro-
gram to the
firewall's
Exceptions
list.

Change settings

3. **Click the Change Settings button.**

   Click Continue or enter an Administrator account's password if the Windows 7 permissions screen nags you.

4. **Click the Allow Another Program button, select the program (or click Browse to locate the program), and click OK.**

   If you click Browse, you'll find almost all of your programs living in your C drive's Program Files folder. Your program's name bears the same icon you see on its Start menu entry.

   The firewall adds your selected program to its Exceptions list and begins allowing other computers to connect to it.

   ✔ Don't add programs to the Exceptions list unless you're *sure* the firewall is the problem. Each time you add a program to the list, you're leaving your computer slightly more vulnerable.

   ✔ If you think you've messed up the firewall's settings, it's easy to revert to its original settings. In Step 1 earlier in this section, click the Restore Defaults button from the list in the window's left pane. When the Restore Defaults window appears, click the new Restore Defaults button, and click the next window's Yes button to complete the changes. The firewall removes *all* the changes you or your programs have made, letting you start from scratch.

Changing Windows Update settings

Whenever somebody figures out a way to break into Windows, Microsoft releases yet another patch to keep Windows users safe. Unfortunately, the bad folks find holes in Windows as quickly as Microsoft can patch them. The result? Microsoft ends up releasing a constant stream of patches.

In fact, the flow of patches became so strong that many users couldn't keep up. Microsoft's solution is to make Windows Update work *automatically:* Whenever you go online, whether to check e-mail or browse the Web, your computer automatically visits Microsoft's Windows Update site and downloads any new patches in the background.

When your computer's through downloading the new patches, it installs them at 3 a.m. to avoid disturbing your work. Occasionally, you're prompted to restart your computer the next morning to make the patches start working; other times, you don't even notice the action taking place.

Windows 7's Action Center, covered earlier in this chapter, explains how to make sure that Windows Update is up and running. But if you want to adjust its settings, perhaps not installing new patches until you've had a chance to review them, follow these steps:

1. **Click the Start button, choose All Programs, and choose Windows Update.**

   The Windows Update window appears.

   Not sure whether Windows Update is *really* checking for updates? Click the Check for Updates link in the window's left pane. Windows Update will drop by Microsoft to see if any updates await.

2. **Choose Change Settings from the leftmost pane.**

   The Change Settings page appears, as shown in Figure 10-4.

3. **If needed, choose Install Updates Automatically (Recommended).**

   Normally turned on by default, the Install Updates Automatically (Recommended) option keeps your PC updated automatically.

   At this step, some experienced computer users select the option Download Updates but Let Me Choose Whether to Install Them. That option gives them a chance to ogle the incoming patches before giving the okay to install them.

4. **Click OK to save your changes.**

   Chances are good that you won't need to make any changes. But night owls might want to change the 3 a.m. automatic installation time by clicking the drop-down lists in the Install New Updates area.

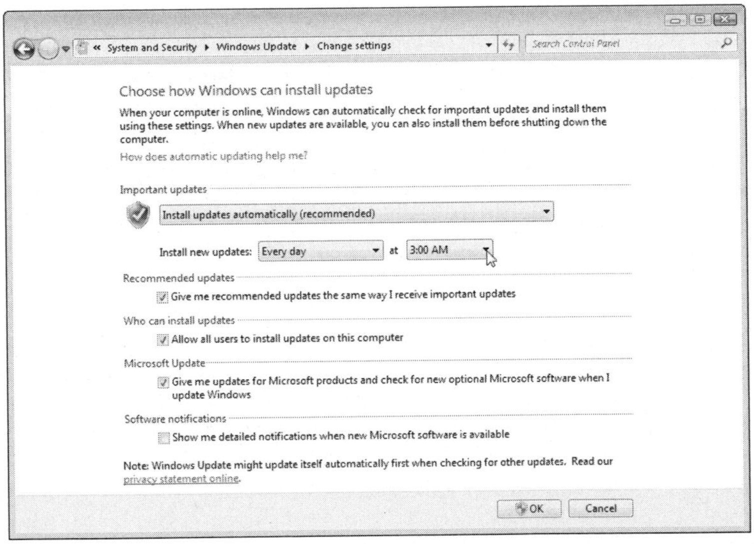

Figure 10-4:
Choose
Install
Updates
Auto-
matically
(Recom-
mended).

(Screenshot of the Windows Update "Change settings" page)

Choose how Windows can install updates

When your computer is online, Windows can automatically check for important updates and install them using these settings. When new updates are available, you can also install them before shutting down the computer.

How does automatic updating help me?

Important updates

Install updates automatically (recommended)

Install new updates: Every day at 3:00 AM

Recommended updates

☑ Give me recommended updates the same way I receive important updates

Who can install updates

☑ Allow all users to install updates on this computer

Microsoft Update

☑ Give me updates for Microsoft products and check for new optional Microsoft software when I update Windows

Software notifications

☐ Show me detailed notifications when new Microsoft software is available

Note: Windows Update might update itself automatically first when checking for other updates. Read our privacy statement online.

OK   Cancel

Avoiding viruses

When it comes to viruses, *everything* is suspect. Viruses travel not only in e-mail messages, programs, files and thumbdrives, but also in screen savers, themes, toolbars, and other Windows add-ons.

If you think you have a virus and you don't have an antivirus program, unplug your PC's network or telephone cable before heading to the store and buying an antivirus program. Install and run your new antivirus program *before* reconnecting your computer to the Internet. (You may need to plug in the cable while the newly installed antivirus program fetches its updates.)

McAfee offers a free virus-removal tool that removes more than 50 common viruses. Downloadable from `http://vil.nai.com/vil/stinger`, it's a handy tool for times of need.

Can't afford an antivirus program, or don't want to pay subscription fees? Check out free antivirus programs like Microsoft's Windows Security Essentials, (`www.microsoft.com/security`), ClamWin (`www.clamwin.com`), avast! Home Edition (`www.avast.com`), AVG Anti-Virus Free Edition (`http://free.avg.com`), or Avira AntiVir Personal (`www.free-av.com`). Be prepared to see some nag screens from some of these, asking you to upgrade to the paid version.

No matter what antivirus program you own, follow these rules to reduce your risk of infection:

- ✔ Make sure your antivirus program scans everything you download, as well as anything that arrives through e-mail or a messaging program.

- ✔ Only open attachments that you're *expecting*. If you receive something unexpected from a friend, don't open it. Instead, e-mail or phone that person to see whether he or she *really* sent you something.

- ✔ Don't install *two* virus checkers, because they often quarrel. If you want to test a different program, first uninstall your existing one from the Control Panel's Programs area. (You may need to restart your PC afterward.) It's then safe to install another virus checker that you want to try.

- ✔ Simply buying an antivirus program isn't enough. Most paid programs also require an annual fee to keep your virus checker smart enough to recognize the latest viruses. Without the most up-to-date virus definitions, virus checkers detect only old viruses, not the new ones sprouting daily on the Internet. (The newest viruses always spread most quickly, causing the most damage.)

Staying Safe on the Internet

The Internet is not a safe place. Some people design Web sites specifically to exploit the latest vulnerabilities in Windows — the ones Microsoft hasn't yet had time to patch. This section explains some of Internet Explorer's safety features, as well as other safe travel tips when navigating the Internet.

Avoiding evil add-ons and hijackers

Microsoft designed Internet Explorer to let programmers add extra features through *add-ons*. By installing an add-on program — toolbars, stock tickers, and program launchers, for example — users can wring a little more work out of Internet Explorer. Similarly, many sites use *ActiveX* — a fancy word for little programs that add animation, sound, video, and other flashy tricks to a Web site.

Unfortunately, dastardly programmers began creating add-ons and ActiveX programs that *harm* users. Some add-ons spy on your activities, bombard your screen with additional ads, redirect your home page to another site, or make your modem dial long-distance numbers to porn sites. Worst yet, some renegade add-ons install themselves as soon as you visit a Web site — without asking your permission.

Windows 7 packs several guns to combat these troublemakers. First, if a site tries to sneak a program onto your computer, Internet Explorer quickly blocks it and sends a warning (shown in Figure 10-5) across the top of Internet Explorer's screen. Clicking the warning reveals your options, as shown in Figure 10-6.

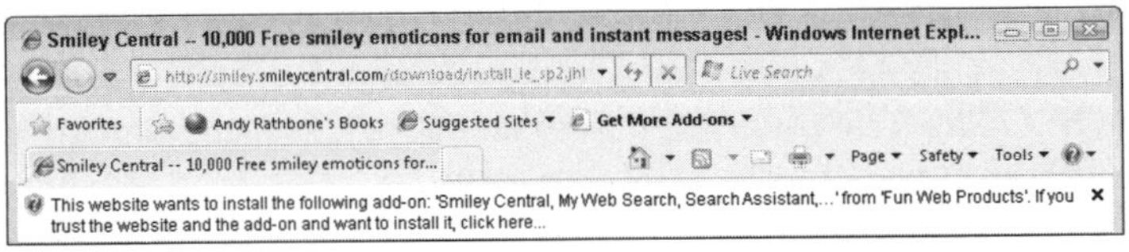

Figure 10-5:
Internet Explorer blocks a program.

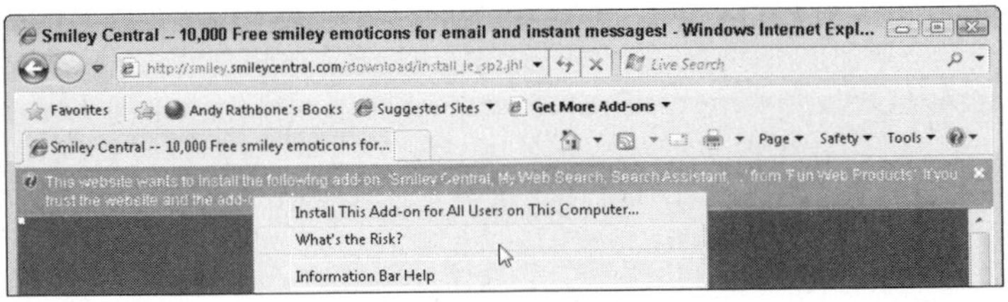

Figure 10-6:
The warning strip shows your options.

WARNING!

Unfortunately, Internet Explorer can't tell the good downloads from the bad, leaving the burden of proof to you. So, if you see a message like the one shown in Figure 10-5 and you *haven't* requested a download, chances are good that the site is trying to harm you: Don't download the program or install the ActiveX control. Instead, click one of your Favorite links or your Home icon to quickly move to a new Web site.

If a bad add-on creeps in somehow, you're not completely out of luck. Internet Explorer's Add-On Manager lets you disable it. To see all the add-on programs installed in Internet Explorer (and remove any that you know are bad, unnecessary, or just plain bothersome), follow these steps:

Tools ▾

1. **Click Internet Explorer's Tools menu and choose Manage Add-Ons.**

   The Manage Add-Ons window appears, as shown in Figure 10-7, letting you see all currently loaded add-ons.

2. **Click the add-on that gives you trouble and click the Disable button.**

   Can't find the unwanted add-on? Click the Show drop-down menu to toggle between seeing All Add-Ons, Currently Loaded Add-Ons, Run Without Permission, and Downloaded Controls.

   When you spot the name of an unwanted toolbar or other bad program, purge it by clicking its name and clicking the Disable button.

3. **Repeat the process for each unwanted add-on and then click the Close button.**

   You may need to restart Internet Explorer for the change to take effect.

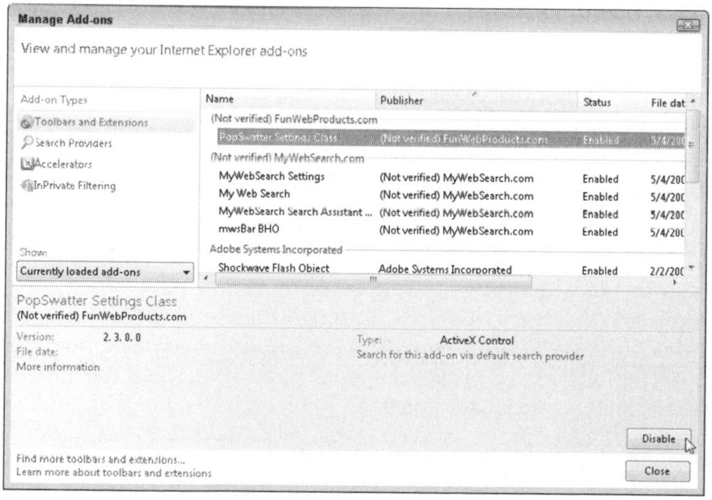

Figure 10-7: Internet Explorer's Manage Add-Ons window lets you see all installed add-ons and disable the ones you don't like.

Setting Internet Explorer's security zones

Chances are good that you won't need to fiddle with Internet Explorer's security zones. They come preset to offer the most protection with the least amount of effort. But if you're curious about Internet Explorer's zones, choose Internet Options from the program's Tools menu, and click the Security tab.

Internet Explorer offers four security zones, each offering a different level of protection. When you add different Web sites to different zones, Internet Explorer treats those sites differently, placing restrictions on some and lifting restrictions for others. Here's the rundown:

✔ **Internet:** Unless you change Internet Explorer's zones, Internet Explorer treats every Web site as if it were in this zone. This zone offers medium-high security, which works very well for most needs.

✔ **Local Intranet:** This zone is intended for Web sites running on an *internal* network. (Home users rarely have to deal with intranets because they're mostly found in corporations and large businesses.) Because internal Web sites are created in-house and are self-contained, this zone removes some restrictions, letting you do more things.

✔ **Trusted Sites:** Putting sites in here means you trust them *completely*. (I don't trust any Web site completely.)

✔ **Restricted Sites:** If you don't trust a site at all, place it in here. Internet Explorer lets you visit it, but not download from it or use any of its *plug-ins* — small downloadable programs adding extra graphics, animation, and similar enhancements. I used to place a few sites in here to strip their pop-up ads, but Internet Explorer's built-in pop-up blocker now eliminates the need.

If you fiddled with the security settings and think you've changed them for the worse, you're not stuck. Just click the Security tab's button called Reset All Zones to Default Level.

Not all add-ons are bad. Many good ones let you play movies, hear sounds, or view special content on a Web site. Don't delete an add-on simply because it's listed in the Add-On Manager.

✔ In the rare instance that disabling an add-on prevents an important Web site from loading, click that add-on's name in Step 2 of the preceding steps and click the Enable button to return it to working order.

✔ How the heck do you tell the good add-ons from the bad? Unfortunately, there's no sure way of telling, although the name listed under Publisher provides one clue. Do you recognize the publisher or remember installing its program? Instead of scratching your head later, think hard before installing things Internet Explorer has tried to block.

✔ Don't like Internet Explorer's accelerators that show up every time you right-click inside a Web page? Dump them by clicking the Accelerators add-on category, which you can see in the left pane in Figure 10-7. Right-click each accelerator you don't use and choose Remove from the pop-up menu.

✔ Make sure that Internet Explorer's pop-up blocker runs by choosing Pop-Up Blocker from the Tools menu. If you see Turn Off Pop-Up Blocker in the pop-up menu, you're all set. If you see Turn On Pop-Up Blocker, click the command to turn it back on.

Avoiding phishing scams

Eventually, you'll receive an e-mail from your bank, eBay, PayPal, or a similar Web site announcing a problem with your account. Invariably, the e-mail offers a handy link to click, saying that you must enter your username and password to set things in order.

Don't do it, no matter how realistic the e-mail and Web site may appear. You're seeing an ugly industry called *phishing:* Fraudsters send millions of these messages worldwide, hoping to convince a few frightened souls into typing their precious account name and password.

How do you tell the real e-mails from the fake ones? It's easy, actually, because *all* these e-mails are fake. Finance-related sites may send you legitimate history statements, receipts, or confirmation notices, but they will never, ever e-mail you a link for you to click and enter your password. If you're suspicious, visit the company's *real* Web site — by typing the Web address by hand. Then look for the security area and forward the e-mail to the company and ask whether it's legitimate. Chances are, it's not.

Windows 7 employs several safeguards to thwart phishing scams:

✔ When you first run Internet Explorer, make sure its SmartScreen filter is turned on by clicking Safety from the top menu and highlighting SmartScreen Filter. If you see a pop-up option to Turn Off SmartScreen Filter, the filter's already turned on.

✔ Internet Explorer examines every Web page for suspicious signals. If a site seems suspicious, Internet Explorer's Address Bar — the normally white area that lists the Web site's address — turns yellow. Internet Explorer sends a pop-up warning that you're viewing a suspected phishing site.

✔ Internet Explorer compares a Web site's address with a list of verified phishing sites. If it finds a match, the Phishing Filter keeps you from entering, as shown in Figure 10-8. Should you ever spot that screen, close the Web page.

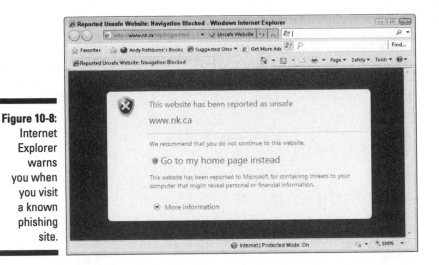

Figure 10-8:
Internet
Explorer
warns
you when
you visit
a known
phishing
site.

So, why can't the authorities simply arrest those people responsible? Because Internet thieves are notoriously difficult to track down and prosecute. The reach of the Internet lets them work from any place in the world.

- ✔ If you've already entered your name and password into a phishing site, take action immediately: Visit the *real* Web site and change your password. Change your username, too, if possible. Then contact the company involved and ask it for help. It may be able to stop the thieves before they wrap their electronic fingers around your account.

- ✔ You can warn Microsoft if you spot a site that smells suspiciously like phish. Choose SmartScreen Filter from Internet Explorer's Safety menu and choose Report Unsafe Website. Internet Explorer takes you to Microsoft's SmartScreen Filter Web site. Telling Microsoft of suspected phishing sites helps them warn other visitors.

- ✔ To find out more about phishing, drop by the Anti-Phishing Working Group (www.antiphishing.org).

Avoiding and removing spyware and parasites with Windows Defender

Spyware and *parasites* are programs that latch onto Internet Explorer without your knowledge. The sneakiest programs may try to change your home page, dial toll numbers with your modem, or spy on your Web activity, sneaking your surfing habits back to the spyware program's publisher.

Most spyware programs freely admit to being spies — usually on the 43rd page of the 44-page agreement you're supposed to read before installing the program.

Nobody wants these ugly programs, of course, so the creators do tricky things to keep you from removing them. That's where the Windows Defender program comes in. It stops some spyware from installing itself automatically and pries off spyware that has already latched onto your PC. Best yet, Windows Update keeps Windows Defender up-to-date to recognize and destroy the latest strains of spyware.

To make Windows Defender scan your PC immediately, a potential solution when your PC's acting strange, follow these steps:

1. **Click the Start menu, type** Windows Defender **into the Search box, and click its name in the list.**

    Windows Defender no longer lives on the Start menu, like it did in Windows Vista. Nor is it listed under any category in the Control Panel. Unfortunately, typing its name into the Search box is the quickest way to locate the program.

2. **Click the Windows Defender's Scan button on the top menu.**

    Windows Defender immediately performs a quick scan of your PC. When it's through, move to Step 3.

3. **Click Tools, choose Options, and select the Automatically Scan My Computer (Recommended) check box, and then click Save.**

    That schedules automatic scans to run at 2 a.m. every day, an easy way to help keep your PC safe.

Several other antispyware programs can also scan your computer for spyware, carefully snipping out any pieces that they find. Some programs are free in the hopes that you'll buy the more full-featured version later. Ad-Aware (www.lavasoft.com) and Spybot – Search & Destroy (www.safer-net working.org) are two of the most popular programs.

Don't be afraid to run more than one spyware scanner on your PC. Unlike antivirus programs, antispyware programs are compatible with each other. Each does its own scan, killing off any spyware it finds.

Setting Up Parental Controls

A feature much-welcomed by parents and much-booed by their children, Windows 7's Parental Controls offer several ways to police how people can access the computer, as well as the Internet. In fact, people who share their PCs with roommates may enjoy the Parental Controls, as well.

The Parental Controls in Windows 7 are nowhere near as comprehensive as the version found in Windows Vista. They no longer let you filter Web site viewing by categories, for example, or list the Web sites and programs accessed by your children. Instead, Parental Controls offer only these three categories:

- ✔ **Time Limits:** You can define certain hours when children (or other account holders) may log on to the PC.

- ✔ **Games:** Some over-the-counter computer games come with rating levels. This area lets you choose which rating level your children may play, helping to keep them away from mature or violent content.

- ✔ **Allow or block programs:** Don't want anybody digging into your checkbook program? This category lets you set certain programs as off-limits, while allowing access to others.

To set Parental Controls, you must own an Administrator account. (I explain the types of accounts in Chapter 13.) If everybody shares one PC, make sure that the other account holders — the children or your roommates, usually — have Standard accounts. If your children have their own PCs, create an Administrator account on their PCs for yourself and change their accounts to Standard.

To set up Parental Controls, follow these steps:

1. **Open the Start menu, choose Control Panel, locate the User Accounts and Family Safety section, and choose Set Up Parental Controls For Any User.**

   If Windows 7's built-in policeman says, "A program needs your permission to continue," feel free to click the Continue button.

2. **Click the user account you want to restrict.**

   Windows 7 lets you add Parental Controls to only one user account at a time, a process that would have caused considerable grief for Mr. and Mrs. Brady.

   When you choose a User account, the Parental Controls screen appears, as shown in Figure 10-9. The next steps take you through each section of the controls.

3. **Turn the Parental Controls on or off.**

   The Parental Controls area first presents two switches, letting you toggle the controls between On and Off. Turn them on to enforce the rules you'll be setting up; click Off to temporarily suspend them.

4. **Choose the categories you'd like to enforce and set the limits.**

   Click any of these three categories and make your changes:

   • **Time limits:** This option fetches a grid, letting you click the hours when your child should be restricted from using the PC. (The clicked squares darken, representing forbidden hours. The remaining squares are fair game.) This offers an easy way to make the PC off-limits after bedtime, for example.

   • **Games:** You may allow or ban *all* games here, restrict access to games with certain ratings (ratings appear on most software boxes), and block or allow individual games.

   • **Allow and Block Specific Programs:** Here's where you can keep the kids out of your checkbook program, for example. You can block *all* programs, or you can allow access to only a handful of programs by selecting the boxes next to their names in a long list.

5. **Click OK to exit Parental Controls.**

Third-party programs can add extra controls to Parental Controls, adding Web filtering, for example, to keep your children away from certain Web sites.

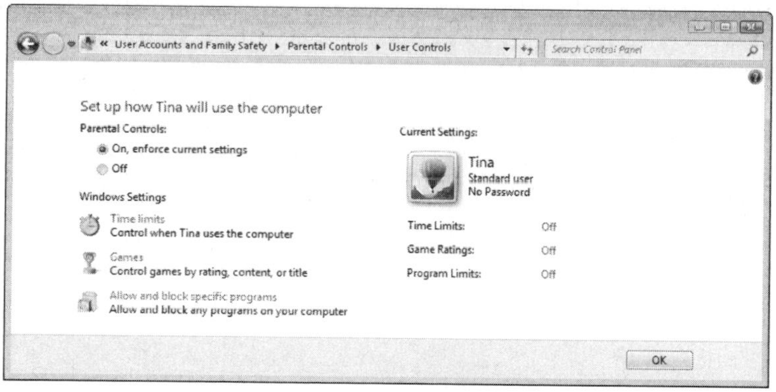

Figure 10-9: Windows 7 lets you set controls on how your children (or any other Standard user account) may use the PC.

Encrypting your PC with BitLocker

Windows 7's BitLocker feature scrambles the contents of your PC's hard drive. Then it quickly unscrambles it whenever you enter your user account's password. Why bother? To keep your information safe from thieves. If they steal your PC or even its hard drive, they won't be able to access your data, and its stash of passwords, credit-card numbers, and other personal information.

Unfortunately, BitLocker provides more protection than most people need, which is why BitLocker comes only in Windows 7's Ultimate and Enterprise versions. It's difficult for non-techies to set up, and if you ever lose your password, you've lost all your data, as well. BitLocker also requires your PC to be set up in a special way, with an extra *partition* — a separate storage area — on your hard drive. For full protection, it requires a PC with a special chip, something not found on many PCs today.

If you're interested in BitLocker, take your PC to your office's information technology person and ask for help and advice on setting it up. Or, as a start, try out BitLocker on a portable flash drive. Because many flash drives live in pockets and keychains, they're much more likely to fall into a stranger's hands. If you're comfortable using your flash drive only on PCs running Windows 7 or Windows Vista, follow these steps to encrypt your flash drive with BitLocker:

1. **Insert your flash drive into your PC's USB port, click Start, click Computer, and find your drive's icon.**

2. **Right-click the drive's icon and choose Turn On BitLocker from the pop-up menu.**

3. **When the BitLocker Drive Encryption window appears, choose Use a Password to Unlock the Drive, enter a password, and click Next.**

    The program offers tips for choosing a strong password.

4. **Choose Print the Recovery Key, and click Next.**

    This important step prints a sequence of characters to type in should you lose your password.

5. **Click the Start Encrypting button and wait for the encryption to finish.**

The next time you insert your flash drive into a PC running Windows 7 or Windows Vista, you — or the thief — must enter the password entered in Step 3, or the drive's contents will stay encrypted and inaccessible. (**Warning:** Drives encrypted with BitLocker can't be opened on any Apple computers or PCs running Windows XP or earlier Windows versions.)

Part IV
Customizing and Upgrading Windows 7

The 5th Wave   By Rich Tennant

"Jeez— I thought the Registry just defined the wallpaper on the screen."

In this part . . .

When your life changes, you want Windows 7 to change with it, and that's where this part of the book comes in. Here's where you discover Windows 7's reorganized Control Panel, which lets you change nearly everything but your computer's disposition.

Chapter 12 describes easy click-through tune-ups you can perform to keep your computer in top shape, backed up, and running smoothly. If you're sharing your computer with others, you discover how to dish out user accounts to each of them, with *you* deciding who can do what.

Finally, when you're ready to buy that second (or third, fourth, or fifth) computer, a chapter walks you through linking them all to create a home network, where they can all share the same Internet connection, printer, and files.

Chapter 11

Customizing Windows 7 with the Control Panel

Anybody who's seen a science-fiction movie knows that robots come with secret control panels, the best of which include an emergency Off switch. Windows 7's Control Panel lives in plain sight, thankfully, living one click away on the Start menu.

Inside the Control Panel, you can find hundreds of switches and options that let you customize the look, feel, and vibe of Windows 7. This chapter explains the switches and sliders you'll want to tweak, and it steers you away from the ones to avoid.

I also list shortcuts that whisk you directly to the right Control Panel setting, bypassing the long, twisting corridors of menus. Still can't find a setting? Type its name in the Control Panel's Search box that lives in the window's upper-right corner.

One word of caution, however: Some of the Control Panel's settings can be changed only by the person holding the almighty Administrator account — usually the computer's owner. If Windows 7 refuses to open the Control Panel's hatch, call the PC's owner for help.

Finding the Right Switch in the Control Panel

Flip open the Start menu and choose the Control Panel, and you can while away an entire work week opening icons and flipping switches to fine-tune Windows 7. Part of the attraction comes from the Control Panel's magnitude: It houses more than *50* icons, and some icons summon menus with more than two dozen settings and tasks.

To save you from searching aimlessly for the right switch, the Control Panel lumps similar items together in its Category view, shown in Figure 11-1.

Figure 11-1: Windows 7 makes settings easier to find by grouping them into categories.

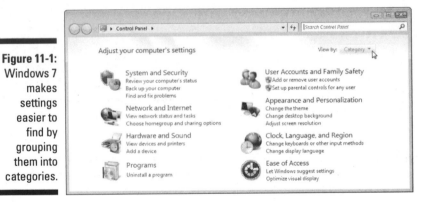

 Below each category's name live shortcuts for that category's most popular offerings. The System and Security category icon in Figure 11-1, for example, offers shortcuts to check for the latest security updates, as well as to evaluate your PC's current security status.

Some controls don't fall neatly into categories, and others merely serve as shortcuts to settings found elsewhere. To see these and every other icon the Control Panel offers, choose either Large Icons or Small Icons from the View By dropdown list, shown in the top-right corner of Figure 11-2. The window quickly displays *all* umpteen-zillion Control Panel icons, as shown in Figure 11-2. (To pack them all into one window, choose Small Icons.)

Don't think something's astray if your Control Panel differs from the one in Figure 11-2. Different programs, accessories, and computer models often add their own icons to the Control Panel. Different versions of Windows 7, which I describe in Chapter 1, also leave out some of the icons seen here.

 Rest your mouse pointer over any confusing icon or category in the Control Panel, and Windows 7 thoughtfully explains its meaning in life.

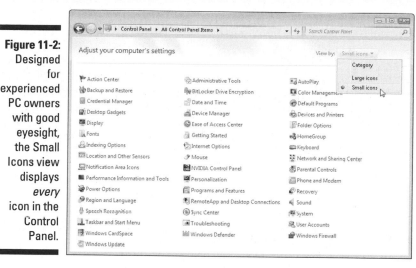

Figure 11-2: Designed for experienced PC owners with good eyesight, the Small Icons view displays *every* icon in the Control Panel.

The Control Panel gathers all of Windows 7's main switches into one well-stocked panel, but it's certainly not the only way to change Windows 7's settings. You can almost always jump to these same settings by right-clicking the item you want to change — be it your desktop, Start menu, or a folder — and choosing Properties from the pop-up menu.

The rest of this chapter lists the Control Panel's categories shown in Figure 11-1, the reasons you'd ever want to visit them, and any shortcuts that jump straight to the setting you need.

System and Security

Like a '67 Mustang, Windows 7 needs occasional maintenance. In fact, a little bit of maintenance can make Windows 7 run so much more smoothly that I devote the best of Chapter 12 to that subject. There, you discover how to speed up Windows, free up hard drive space, back up your data, and create a safety net called a Restore Point.

This category's security section contains a full brigade of soldiers. I've written field manuals for them in Chapter 10: Windows Firewall, Windows Update, Windows Defender, and Parental Controls.

User Accounts and Family Safety

I explain in Chapter 13 how to create separate accounts for other people to use your computer. That lets them use your PC but limits the amount of damage they can do to Windows and your files.

Here's a refresher if you don't want to flip ahead to that chapter: Choose Control Panel from the Start menu. Then, under the User Accounts and Family Safety category, click Add or Remove User Accounts.

That opens the Manage Accounts area, where you can not only create new accounts but also change existing ones, including their name, password, or Start menu picture.

The Control Panel's User Accounts and Family Safety category also includes a link to the Security section's Parental Controls area, where you can place limits on how and when your kids access your PC. I explain Parental Controls in Chapter 10.

Network and Internet

Windows 7 normally reaches out and touches other PCs and the Internet automatically. Plug an Internet connection into your PC, and Windows 7 quickly starts slurping information from the Web. Plug in another PC, and Windows 7 wants to connect the two with a Homegroup or another type of network. (I explain Homegroups in Chapter 13.)

But should Windows 7 botch the job, turn to the Control Panel's Network and Internet category: Choose Control Panel from the Start menu and choose the Network and Internet category.

I devote Chapter 14 completely to networking; the Internet gets its due in Chapter 8.

Changing Windows 7's Appearance (Appearance and Personalization)

One of the most popular categories, Appearance and Personalization lets you change the look, feel, and behavior of Windows 7 in a wide variety of ways. Inside the category await these seven icons:

✔ **Personalization:** Pay dirt for budding interior designers, this area lets you stamp your own look and feel across Windows. Hang a new picture or digital photo across your desktop, choose a fresh screen saver, and change the colors of Windows 7's window frames. (To head quickly to this batch of settings, right-click a blank part of your desktop and choose Personalize.)

✔ **Display:** While personalization lets you fiddle with colors, the Display area lets you fiddle with your monitor itself. For example, it lets you enlarge the text to soothe tired eyes, adjust the screen resolution, and adjust the connection of an additional monitor.

✔ **Desktop Gadgets:** Covered in Chapter 2, this area manages the miniprograms called *gadgets* that live on your desktop. (To jump quickly to this area, right-click the desktop and choose Gadgets.)

✔ **Taskbar and Start menu:** Ready to add your *own* photo to that boring picture atop your Start menu? Want to customize the taskbar living along your desktop's bottom edge? I cover both these things in Chapter 2, in the sections on the Start menu and taskbar. (To jump quickly to this area, right-click the Start button and choose Properties.)

✔ **Ease of Access Center:** Designed to help people with special needs, this shortcut leads to the Ease of Access Center category. There, you find settings to make Windows more navigable by the blind, the deaf, and people with other physical challenges. Because Ease of Access exists as its own category, I describe it in its own section later in this chapter.

✔ **Folder Options:** Visited mainly by experienced users, this area lets you tweak how folders look and behave. (To jump quickly to Folder Options, open any folder, click Organize, and choose Folder and Search options.)

✔ **Fonts:** Here's where you preview, delete, or examine fonts that spruce up your printed work.

In the next few sections, I explain the Appearance and Personalization tasks that you'll reach for most often.

Changing the desktop background

A *background,* also known as wallpaper, is simply the picture covering your desktop. To change it, follow these steps:

Jump to Step 3 by right-clicking your desktop, choosing Personalize, and selecting Desktop Background.

1. **Click the Start menu, choose Control Panel, and select the Appearance and Personalization category.**

   The Control Panel opens to display its Appearance and Personalization category.

2. **Choose Change Desktop Background from the Personalization category.**

   The window shown in Figure 11-3 appears.

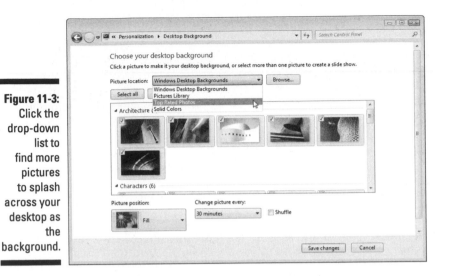

Figure 11-3: Click the drop-down list to find more pictures to splash across your desktop as the background.

3. Click a new picture for the background.

Be sure to click the drop-down list, shown in Figure 11-3, to see all the available photos, colors, paintings, and light auras that Windows 7 offers. To rummage through folders not listed, click Browse. Feel free to search your own Pictures library for potential backgrounds.

Background files can be stored as BMP, GIF, JPG, JPEG, DIB, or PNG files. That means you can choose a background from nearly any photo or art found on the Internet or shot from a digital camera.

When you click a new picture, Windows 7 immediately places it across your desktop. If you're pleased, jump to Step 5.

4. Decide whether to fill, fit, stretch, tile, or center the picture.

Not every picture fits perfectly across the desktop. Small pictures, for example, need to be either stretched to fit the space or spread across the screen in rows like tiles on a floor. When tiling and stretching still look odd or distorted, try the Fill or Fit option to keep the perspective. Or, try centering the image and leaving blank space around its edges.

You can automatically switch between images by choosing more than one photo (hold down Ctrl while clicking each one). The picture then changes every 30 minutes unless you change the time in the Change Picture Every drop-down list.

5. Click Save Changes to save your new background.

Did you happen to spot an eye-catching picture while Web surfing with Internet Explorer? Right-click that Web site's picture and choose Set As Background. Sneaky Windows copies the picture and splashes it across your desktop as a new background.

Choosing a screen saver

In the dinosaur days of computing, computer monitors suffered from *burn-in:* permanent damage when an oft-used program burned its image onto the screen. To prevent burn-in, people installed a screen saver to jump in with a blank screen or moving lines. Today's monitors no longer suffer from burn-in problems, but people still use screen savers because they look cool.

Windows comes with several built-in screen savers. To try one out, follow these steps:

Jump to Step 3 by right-clicking your desktop, choosing Personalize, and choosing Screen Saver.

1. **Open the Control Panel from the Start menu and select the Appearance and Personalization category.**

   The Appearance and Personalization category opens to show its offerings.

2. **Choose Change Screen Saver from the Personalization area.**

   The Screen Saver Settings dialog box appears.

3. **Click the downward-pointing arrow in the Screen Saver box and select a screen saver.**

   After choosing a screen saver, click the Preview button for an audition. View as many candidates as you like before making a decision.

   Be sure to click the Settings button because some screen savers offer options, letting you specify the speed of a photo slide show, for example.

4. **If desired, add security by selecting the On Resume, Display Logon Screen check box.**

   This safeguard keeps people from sneaking into your computer while you're fetching coffee. It makes Windows ask for a password after waking up from screen saver mode. (I cover passwords in Chapter 13.)

5. **When you're done setting up your screen saver, click OK.**

If you *really* want to extend your monitor's life (and save electricity), don't bother with screen savers. Instead, click Change Power Settings in Step 3. The resulting Select a Power Plan window lets you choose the Power Saver plan, which tells Windows 7 to turn off your monitor when you haven't touched a key for 5 minutes, and to put your PC to sleep after 15 minutes of inaction. (Lengthen or decrease the times by clicking Change Plan Settings in the Power Saver area.)

Changing the computer's theme

Themes are simply collections of settings: You can save your favorite screen saver and desktop background, for example, as one theme, letting you switch easily between different themes.

To try one of Windows 7's built-in themes, right-click your desktop and choose Personalize. Windows 7 lists its token bundled themes shown in Figure 11-4, as well as an option to create your own. Click any theme, and Windows 7 tries it on immediately.

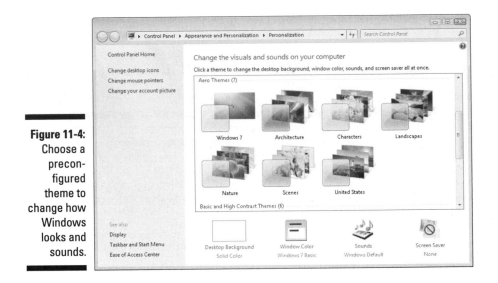

Figure 11-4: Choose a preconfigured theme to change how Windows looks and sounds.

The window offers these themes, with options listed along the window's bottom.

- ✔ **My Themes:** Themes you've personally created appear here.

- ✔ **Aero Themes:** This category includes Windows 7's bundled themes, including its original one, meant for PCs with powerful graphics.

- ✔ **Basic and High Contrast Themes:** Although this features high-contrast themes for the visually impaired, productivity hounds jump on the Windows Classic theme that brings a retro-yet-super-speedy look and feel to Windows 7.

Instead of choosing from the pre-assembled themes, feel free to make your own by clicking the buttons (shown along the bottom of Figure 11-4) for changing the Desktop Background, Window Color, Sounds, and Screen Saver.

After creating your perfect theme, save your work by clicking Save Theme and typing a name.

- ✔ Tired of Windows 7's built-in themes? Find dozens more by clicking Get More Themes Online in the My Themes section.

- ✔ If you enjoy Windows 7's tools for creating themes, take a step up with a third-party program like WindowBlinds (www.windowblinds.net). You can download Themes created by WindowBlinds aficionados at WinCustomize (www.wincustomize.com).

- ✔ Before you begin downloading themes from the Web or e-mail attachments, be sure that you're using an updated antivirus program. Viruses sometimes masquerade as themes.

Changing the screen resolution

One of Windows 7's many change-it-once-and-forget-about-it options, *screen resolution* determines how much information Windows 7 can cram onto your monitor at one time. Changing the resolution either shrinks windows to pack more of 'em on-screen, or it enlarges everything at the expense of desktop real estate.

To find your most comfortable resolution — or if a program or game mutters something about you having to change your *screen resolution* or *video mode* — follow these steps:

Right-click a blank part of your desktop and choose Screen Resolution to jump to Step 3.

1. **Choose Control Panel from the Start menu and select the Appearance and Personalization category.**

   You see the Appearance and Personalization area, which lists the main ways you can change Windows 7's appearance.

2. **In the Display area, choose Adjust Screen Resolution.**

   The Screen Resolution window appears, as shown in Figure 11-5.

3. **To change the screen resolution, click the Resolution drop-down list and use your mouse to drag the little bar between High and Low.**

   Watch the little preview screen near the window's top change as you move the mouse. The more you slide the bar upward, the larger your monitor grows. Unfortunately, the more information Windows 7 can pack onto your monitor, the smaller that information appears.

There's no right or wrong choice here, but here's a word of advice: Most Web sites won't fit onto your screen well at 640 x 480 pixels. A setting of 800 x 600 is better, and 1024 x 768, Windows 7's favorite, will accommodate just about any Web size you visit.

4. **View your display changes by clicking the Apply button, then click the Keep Changes button to authorize the change.**

When Windows 7 makes drastic changes to your display, it gives you 15 seconds to click a Keep Changes button approving the change. If your change leaves your monitor unreadable, you won't see the on-screen button. After a few seconds, Windows notices that you didn't click the approval button and reverts to your original setup.

5. **Click OK when you're done tweaking the display.**

After you change your video resolution once, you'll probably never return here. Unless you plug a second monitor into your PC, of course, which I describe in the sidebar.

Figure 11-5:
The higher the screen resolution, the more information Windows can squeeze onto your monitor.

Hardware and Sound

Windows 7's Hardware and Sound category, shown in Figure 11-6, shows some familiar faces. The Display icon, for example, also appears in another category.

This category controls the parts of your PC you can touch or plug in. You can control your display here, as well as your mouse, speakers, keyboard, printer, telephone, scanner, digital camera, game controllers, and, for you graphic artists out there, digital pen.

You won't spend much time in here, though, especially coming in through the Control Panel's doors. Most settings appear elsewhere, where a mouse-click will bring you directly to the setting you need.

Whether you arrive at these pages through the Control Panel or a shortcut, the following sections explain the most popular reasons for visiting here.

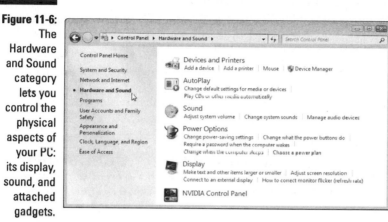

Figure 11-6:
The Hardware and Sound category lets you control the physical aspects of your PC: its display, sound, and attached gadgets.

Adjusting volume and sounds

The Sound area lets you adjust your PC's volume, as well as connect seven speakers and a subwoofer to your PC, a feature much loved by World of Warcraft enthusiasts.

To turn down your PC's volume knob, shown in Figure 11-7, click the little speaker by your clock and slide down the volume. No speaker on your taskbar? Restore it by right-clicking the taskbar's clock, choosing Properties, and turning on the Volume setting.

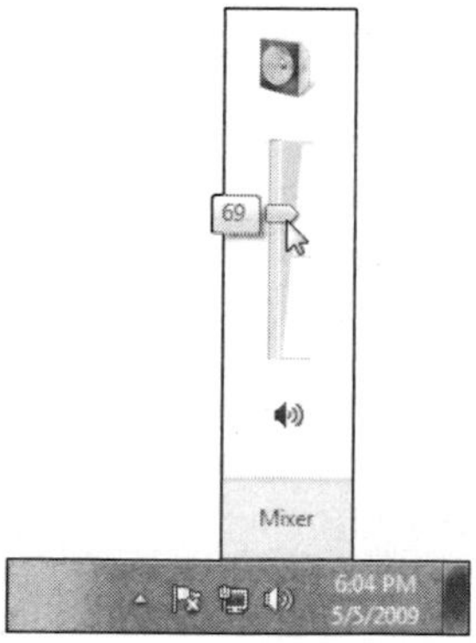

Figure 11-7:
Click the speaker icon and move the sliding control to adjust your PC's volume.

To mute your PC, click the little speaker icon at the bottom of the sliding control, shown in Figure 11-7. Clicking that icon again removes the gag.

Windows 7 one-ups Windows XP by letting you set different volumes for different programs. You can quietly detonate explosives in Minesweeper while still allowing Windows Mail to loudly announce any new messages. To juggle volume levels between programs, follow these steps:

Right-clicking the little speaker icon next to your clock and choosing Open Volume Mixer jumps you ahead to Step 3.

1. **Choose Control Panel from the Start menu and select the Hardware and Sound category.**

   The Control Panel's Hardware and Sound area (shown earlier in Figure 11-6) displays its tools.

2. **Double-click the Sound icon and then click Adjust System Volume.**

   The Volume Mixer appears, as shown in Figure 11-8, listing each noise-maker on your PC.

3. **Slide any program's control up or down to muzzle it or raise it above the din.**

   Close the Volume Mixer by clicking the little red X in its corner.

Doubling your workspace with a second monitor

Blessed with an extra monitor, perhaps a left-over from a deceased PC? Connect it to your PC, place it aside your first monitor, and you've doubled your Windows desktop: Windows 7 stretches your workspace across both monitors. That lets you view the online encyclopedia in one monitor while writing your term paper in the other.

To perform these video gymnastics, your PC needs a video card with two *ports,* and those ports must match your monitor's *connectors* — technical topics all covered in my book *Upgrading & Fixing PCs For Dummies,* 7th Edition (Wiley Publishing, Inc).

After you plug in the second monitor, right-click a blank part of your desktop and choose Screen Resolution. The Screen Resolution window shows a second on-screen monitor next to your first. (Click the Detect button if the second monitor doesn't appear on-screen.) Drag and drop the on-screen monitors to the right or left until they match the physical placement of the real monitors on your desk. Then click OK. (That bit of clickery lets Windows expand your newly widened desktop in the correct direction.)

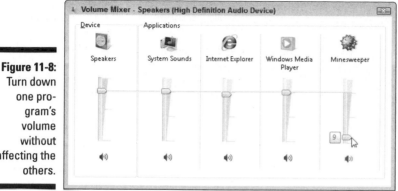

Figure 11-8:
Turn down
one pro-
gram's
volume
without
affecting the
others.

Installing or setting up speakers

Most PCs come with only two speakers. Some PCs today come with four, and PCs that double as home theaters or gaming rigs sometimes have up to eight. To accommodate the variety of setups, Windows 7 includes a speaker setup area, complete with a speaker test.

If you're installing new speakers, or you're not sure your old ones are working, follow these steps to introduce them properly to Windows 7.

Right-click your taskbar's Speaker icon and choose Playback Devices to jump to Step 3.

1. **Click the Start button, choose Control Panel, and select the Hardware and Sound category.**

   The familiar Hardware and Sound category from Figure 11-6 appears.

2. **In the Sound area, choose Manage Audio Devices.**

   The Sound dialog box appears, open to the Playback tab, which lists your speakers.

3. **Click your speaker or speaker's icon, and click the Configure button.**

   The Speaker Setup dialog box appears, as shown in Figure 11-9.

4. **Click the Test button, adjust your speaker's settings, and click Next.**

   Windows 7 walks you through selecting your number of speakers and their placement and then plays each one in turn so that you can hear whether they're in the correct locations. Then the program leaves you back at Figure 11-9.

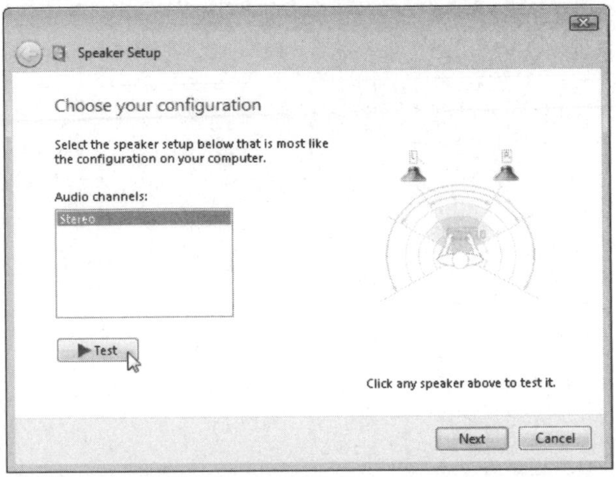

Figure 11-9:
Click the
Test button
to hear your
speakers.

5. **Click the tabs for any other sound devices you want to adjust. When you're through adjusting, click the OK button.**

Feel free to check your microphone volume by clicking the Recording tab, for example, as well as tabs for any other gadgetry you can afford.

If your speakers and microphone don't show up as devices, Windows 7 doesn't know they're there. That usually means you need to install a new driver, an annoying journey I walk you through in Chapter 12.

Adding a printer

Quarrelling printer manufacturers couldn't agree on how printers should be installed. As a result, you install your printer in one of two ways:

- Some printer manufacturers say simply to plug in your printer, usually by pushing its connector into a little rectangular USB port. Turn on your PC, and Windows 7 automatically recognizes and embraces your new printer. Add any needed ink cartridges, toner, or paper, and you're done.

- Other manufacturers take an uglier approach, saying you must install their bundled software *before* plugging in your printer. And if you don't install the software first, the printer may not work correctly.

The only way to know how your printer should be installed is to check the printer's manual. (Sometimes this information appears on a colorful, one-page Installation Cheat Sheet packed in the printer's box.)

If your printer didn't come with installation software, install the cartridges, add paper to the tray, and follow these instructions to put it to work:

1. **With Windows 7 up and running, plug your printer into your PC and turn on the printer.**

   If your printer's rectangular connector slides into a rectangular hole or *port* on your PC, you have a *USB printer,* the type used by almost all printers today. Windows 7 may send a message saying that your printer is installed successfully, but follow the next step to test it.

   If your elderly printer's evil-looking, pronged connector pushes into a long oval connector full of holes, it plugs into your PC's *printer port.* (That connector is called *LPT1:* or *parallel* in computer language.)

2. **Click the Start menu and choose Devices and Printers.**

   The Control Panel displays its categories of devices, including your printer, if you're lucky. If you spot your USB printer listed by its model or brand name, right-click its icon, choose Printer Properties, and click the Print Test Page button. If it prints correctly, you're finished. Congratulations.

   When you create a Homegroup, described in Chapter 13, your USB printer is automatically available to every Windows 7 computer on a network.

   If your printer's name doesn't appear, though, move to Step 3.

   Test page *didn't* work? Check that all the packaging is removed from inside your printer and that it has ink cartridges. If it still doesn't print, your printer is probably defective. Contact the store where you bought it and ask who to contact for assistance.

   Windows 7 lists a printer named Microsoft XPS Document Writer that's not really a printer. Choosing to print to that printer creates a special file much like Adobe's PDF files, which require a special program to view and print. Windows 7 can view or print XPS files; Windows XP, by contrast, first requires you to download and install Microsoft's XPS Viewer (www.microsoft.com/downloads).

3. **Click the Add a Printer button from the Printers window's top menu, and choose Add a Local Printer.**

   If you're installing a printer on a *network,* see Chapter 14 for the lowdown.

4. **Choose how you've connected the printer to your PC and click Next.**

   Choose LPT1 (the oblong connector). If you're using a USB printer, click Cancel, install the printer's software, and start over. No software? You need to download it from the printer manufacturer's Web site.

5. **Choose your printer's port and click Next.**

   When Windows 7 asks which printer port to use, choose LPT1: (Printer Port).

6. **Click your printer's manufacturer and model names when you see them listed and click Next.**

   The Add Printer dialog box lists the names of printer manufacturers on the left; choose yours from the list. The right side of the box lists that manufacturer's printer models. (Windows 7 knows how to talk to hundreds of different printer models.)

   Windows 7 may ask you to stick the appropriate setup CD into a drive. Stuck? Click the Windows Update button; Windows 7 connects to the Internet to find software for that printer.

   After a moment, you see the new printer listed. If Windows 7 offers to print a test page, take it up on the offer.

That's it. If you're like most people, your printer will work like a charm. If it doesn't, I've stuffed some tips and fix-it tricks in the printing section in Chapter 7.

If you have two or more printers attached to your computer, right-click the icon of your most oft-used printer and choose Set As Default Printer from the menu. Windows 7 then prints to that printer automatically, unless you tell it otherwise.

✔ To remove a printer you no longer use, right-click its name in Step 2, and then choose Delete from the menu. That printer's name no longer appears as an option when you try to print from a program. If Windows 7 asks to uninstall the printer's drivers and software, click Yes — unless you think you may install that printer again sometime.

✔ You can change printer options from within many programs. Choose File in a program's menu bar (you may need to press Alt to see the menu bar) and then choose Print Setup or choose Print. That area lets you change things such as paper sizes, fonts, and types of graphics.

✔ To share a printer quickly over a network, create a Homegroup, which I describe in Chapter 13. Your printer immediately shows up as an installation option for all the computers on your network.

✔ If your printer's software confuses you, try clicking the Help buttons in its dialog boxes. Many buttons are customized for your particular printer model, and they offer advice not found in Windows 7.

Installing or adjusting other computer parts

The Control Panel's Hardware and Sound category lists the Devices and Printer area, home to many items tethered to most PCs. The following sections explain how to tweak other computer gadgets you may find listed in the Devices and Printers window.

If the window doesn't list one of your gadgets — your keyboard, for example — view the Control Panel with its small icon view, shown earlier in Figure 11-2. That lets you see a clickable icon for each one of your plugged-in gadgets.

Mouse

To change your mouse settings, open the Control Panel's Hardware and Sound category, open the Devices and Printers area, right-click the mouse icon, and choose Mouse Settings.

There, in the Mouse Properties window, you'll find lots of settings for standard-issue, two-button mice, but most are frivolous (dressing up your mouse pointer's arrow, for example).

Southpaws should visit here to swap their mouse buttons. Select the Switch Primary and Secondary Buttons check box. (The change takes place immediately, even before you click Apply, so be sure to click with the newly swapped button.)

People with slow fingers should fine-tune their double-click speed. Test your current speed by double-clicking the little folder in the Double-Click Speed area. If the folder opens, your settings are fine. If it doesn't open, though, slow down the speed with the sliding control until it opens and closes at your double-clicking pace.

Owners of mice with extra buttons or wireless connections often find extra settings in here, as well.

Scanners and Cameras

To install scanners or cameras, just plug them in and turn them on. Windows 7 almost always recognizes and greets them by name. On the rare occasion that Windows doesn't recognize your model, though, take these extra steps to fetch the Scanner and Camera Installation Wizard:

1. **Open the Start menu and choose Control Panel.**

2. **Type** View Scanners and Cameras **in the Search box; then click the View Scanners and Cameras icon.**

   The Scanners and Cameras window appears, listing all the attached scanners and cameras Windows 7 currently recognizes.

3. **Click the Add Device button and click Next.**

   Windows brings up its Scanner and Camera Installation Wizard, the magical communicator between Windows 7 and elderly scanners and cameras that Windows 7 can't recognize.

4. **Choose the manufacturer and model, and click Next.**

   Click the manufacturer's name on the window's left side and choose the model on the right.

5. **Type a name for your scanner or camera (or keep the suggested name), click Next, and click Finish.**

   If you've turned on your camera or scanner and plugged in its cable correctly, Windows should recognize it and place an icon for it in both your Computer area and your Control Panel's Scanners and Cameras area.

Unfortunately, the installation of older cameras and scanners doesn't always work this easily. If Windows doesn't automatically accept your gear, fall back on the scanner or camera's bundled software. The scanner or camera may still work — you just won't be able to use Windows 7's built-in software tools to grab its images.

Chapter 16 explains how to grab photos from a digital camera, and that chapter's camera tips apply to scanners: Windows 7 treats digital cameras and scanners the same way.

Keyboard

If your keyboard is not working or is not plugged in, your computer usually tells you as soon as you turn on your PC's power. The freshly awaked PC spits out a startled Keyboard Error message and asks you to press the Esc key. If Windows can't find the keyboard, either, then it's time to buy a new one. Windows 7 should recognize the new keyboard as soon as you plug it in.

If your new keyboard comes with extra buttons along the top for things like Internet, Email, or Volume, you need to install the keyboard's bundled software to make those buttons work. (Wireless keyboards almost always require their own software, as well.)

Windows 7 offers some minor keyboard tweaks like changing how fast the keys rrrrrrrepeat when you hold them down. To find the settings, click the Start menu, choose Control Panel, type **Keyboard** in the Control Panel's Search box, and double-click the Keyboard icon when it appears.

Windows Mobility Center

The Mobile PC area, shown only on laptops, lets you adjust the settings cherished by laptop owners: adjusting the screen's brightness, quickly changing the sound volume in crowded coffee shops, saving battery power, connecting to wireless networks, and setting up external displays or projectors. I cover most of these settings in Chapter 22.

Clock, Language, and Region

Microsoft designed this area mostly for laptoppers who frequently travel to different time zones and locations. Otherwise, you touch this information only once — when first setting up your computer. Windows 7 subsequently remembers the time and date, even when your PC is turned off.

 To drop by here, choose Control Panel from the Start menu and click the Clock, Language, and Region category. Two sections appear:

- ✔ **Date and Time:** This area is fairly self-explanatory. (Clicking your taskbar's clock and choosing Change Date and Time Settings lets you visit here, as well.)

- ✔ **Region and Language Options:** Traveling in Italy? Click this category's icon and choose Italian from the Region and Language window's Format section. Windows switches to that country's currency symbols and date format. While you're at the Region and Language window, click the Location tab and choose Italy — or whatever country you're currently visiting.

If you're bilingual or multilingual, you should also visit this area when you're working on documents that require characters from different languages.

Adding or Removing Programs

Whether you've picked up a new program or you want to purge an old one, the Control Panel's Programs category handles the job fairly well. One of its categories, Programs and Features, lists your currently installed programs, shown in Figure 11-10. You click the one you want to discard or tweak.

The next two sections describe how to remove or change existing programs and how to install new ones.

Removing or changing programs

To remove a troublesome program or change its settings, follow these steps:

1. **Choose the Control Panel from the Start menu and, in the Programs section, choose Uninstall a Program.**

   The Uninstall or Change a Program window appears, as shown in Figure 11-10, listing your currently installed programs, their publisher, size, installation date, and version number.

 To free up disk space, click the Installed On or Size column header to find old or large programs. Then uninstall those forgotten programs you never or rarely use.

2. **Click the unloved program and then click its Uninstall, Change, or Repair button.**

   The menu bar above the programs' names always displays an Uninstall button, but when you click certain programs, you may also see buttons for Change and Repair. Here's the rundown:

   - **Uninstall:** This completely removes the program from your PC. (Some programs list this button as Uninstall/Change.)

   - **Change:** This lets you change some of the program's features or remove parts of it.

   - **Repair:** A handy choice for damaged programs, this tells the program to inspect itself and replace damaged files with new ones. You might need to have the program's original CD handy, though.

3. **When Windows asks whether you're *sure*, click Yes.**

   Depending on which button you've clicked, Windows 7 either boots the program off your PC or summons the program's own installation program to make the changes or repair itself.

   After you delete a program, it's gone for good unless you kept its installation CD. Unlike other deleted items, deleted programs don't linger inside your Recycle Bin.

Always use the Control Panel's Uninstall or Change a Program window to uninstall unwanted programs. Simply deleting their files or folders won't do the trick. In fact, doing so often confuses your computer into sending bothersome error messages.

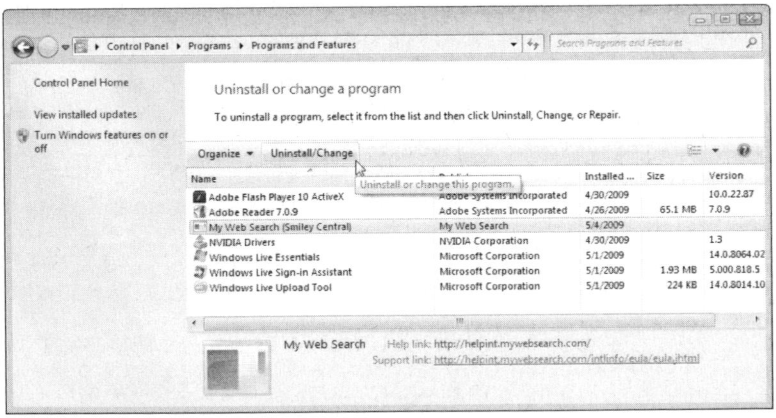

Figure 11-10:
The Uninstall or Change a Program window lets you remove any of your currently installed programs.

Adding new programs

Chances are good that you'll never have to use this option. Today, most programs install themselves automatically as soon as you slide their discs into your PC's drive. If you're not sure whether a program has installed, click the Start button and poke around in your All Programs menu. If it's listed there, the program has installed.

But if a program doesn't automatically leap into your computer, here are some tips that can help:

✔ You need an Administrator account to install programs. (Most computer owners automatically have an Administrator account.) That keeps the kids, with their Limited or Guest accounts, from installing programs and messing up the computer. I explain User accounts in Chapter 13.

✔ Downloaded a program? Windows 7 usually saves them in your Downloads folder, accessible by clicking your username on the Start menu. Double-click the downloaded program's name to install it.

✔ Many eager, newly installed programs want to add a desktop shortcut, Start menu shortcut, *and* a Quick Launch toolbar shortcut. Say "no" to all but the Start menu. All those extra shortcuts clutter your computer, making programs difficult to find. (If any program adds these shortcuts, you can safely delete them by right-clicking the shortcut and choosing Delete.)

✔ It's always a good idea to create a restore point before installing a new program. (I describe creating restore points in Chapter 12.) If your newly installed program goes haywire, use System Restore to return your computer to the peaceful state of mind it enjoyed before you installed the troublemaker.

Add/remove parts of Windows 7

Just as you can install and uninstall programs, you can remove parts of Windows 7 need. You can remove the games, for example, to keep employees from playing them at the office. Don't use Media Player? Give it the axe, as well.

Before removing Internet Explorer, make sure to download a replacement Web browser like Firefox (www.getfirefox.com).

To see what parts of itself Windows 7 has left off your computer or to remove unwanted components that Windows 7 *has* installed, follow these steps:

1. **Click the Start menu, choose Control Panel, and click the Programs icon.**

2. **In the Programs and Features area, choose Turn Windows Features On or Off and click Continue (if prompted).**

    Windows brings up a window listing all its features. The features with check marks by their names are already installed. No check mark? Then that feature's not installed. If you see a box that's filled — neither empty nor checked — then double-click the component to see what's installed and what's left out.

When a program doesn't have an installation program . . .

Sometimes programs — especially small ones downloaded from the Internet — don't come with an installation program. If you've downloaded one of these low-budget creations to your computer, create a new folder for it and move the downloaded file inside. (Be sure to scan any downloaded file with your antivirus program.) Then try double-clicking the program's file. (It's usually the file with the fanciest icon.) One of two things may happen:

✔ **The program may simply start running.** That means you're done — the program doesn't need to be installed. (Drag and drop its program icon to your Start button to add it to the Start button menu.) If you need to uninstall the program, just right-click it and choose Delete. These types of programs rarely appear on your Change or Remove a Program list.

✔ **The program may start installing itself.** That also means you're done. The program's installation program takes over, sparing you any more trouble. To uninstall the program, use the Control Panel's Uninstall a Program option.

But if the program comes in a *zipped* folder — the folder icon bears a little zipper — you have an extra step. Right-click the zipped folder, choose Extract All, and then click Extract. Windows automatically *unzips* the folder's contents and places them into a new folder, usually named after the program. From there, you can either run the program directly or, if it has an installation program, run the installation program.

3. **To add a component, click in its empty check box. To remove an installed component like Windows Games, deselect its check box.**

4. **Click the OK button.**

   Windows 7 adds or removes the program. (You may need to insert your Windows 7 DVD during the process.)

Modifying Windows 7 for the Physically Challenged

Nearly everybody finds Windows 7 to be challenging, but some people face special physical challenges, as well. To assist them, the Control Panel's Ease of Access area offers a variety of changes.

If your eyesight isn't what it used to be, you may appreciate the ways to increase the text size on your PCs.

Choosing the default program

Microsoft lets computer vendors replace Internet Explorer, Media Player, Outlook Express, and Windows Messenger with different programs from other companies. Your new computer may come with the Firefox Web browser, for example, instead of Microsoft's Internet Explorer. Some PCs may come with both browsers installed.

When more than one program can handle a task — opening a Web link, for example — Windows 7 needs to know which program it should summon. That's where the Windows 7 program defaults area comes in. To choose your default programs, click the Start button, select Default Programs, and choose Set Your Default Programs.

The Set Your Default Programs window lists programs along the right edge. Click the program you use the most and then choose Set This Program As Default. Repeat for any other listed programs that you prefer over Windows 7's bundled programs and then click OK.

Follow these steps to modify the settings in Windows 7:

1. **Choose Control Panel from the Start menu, select the Ease of Access category, and choose Ease of Access Center.**

   The Ease of Access Center appears, as shown in Figure 11-11. Windows 7's ethereal voice kicks in, explaining how to change its programs.

2. **Choose the Get Recommendations to Make Your Computer Easier to Use link.**

   Look for the link called Get Recommendations to Make Your Computer Easier to Use (shown with the mouse pointing to it in Figure 11-11). That makes Windows 7 give you a quick interview so that it can gauge what adjustments you may need. When it's through, Windows 7 automatically makes its changes, and you're done.

   If you're not happy with the changes, move to Step 3.

3. **Make your changes manually.**

   The Ease of Access Center offers these toggle switches to make the keyboard, sound, display, and mouse easier to control:

   • **Start Magnifier:** Designed for the visually impaired, this option magnifies the mouse pointer's exact location.

   • **Start Narrator:** Windows 7's awful built-in narrator reads on-screen text for people who can't view it clearly.

- **Start On-Screen Keyboard:** This setting places a clickable keyboard along the screen's bottom, letting you type by pointing and clicking.

- **Set up High Contrast:** This setting eliminates most screen colors, but helps vision-impaired people view the screen and cursor more clearly.

Choose any of these options to turn on the feature immediately. Close the feature's window if the feature makes matters worse.

If you're still not happy, proceed to Step 4.

4. **Choose a specific setting in the Explore All Settings area.**

Here's where Windows 7 gets down to the nitty gritty, letting you optimize Windows 7 specifically for the following things:

- Blindness or impaired vision

- Using an alternative input device rather than a mouse or keyboard

- Adjusting the keyboard and mouse sensitivity to compensate for limited movements

- Turning on visual alerts instead of sound notifications

- Making it easier to focus on reading and typing tasks

Some centers that assist physically challenged people may offer software or assistance for helping you make these changes.

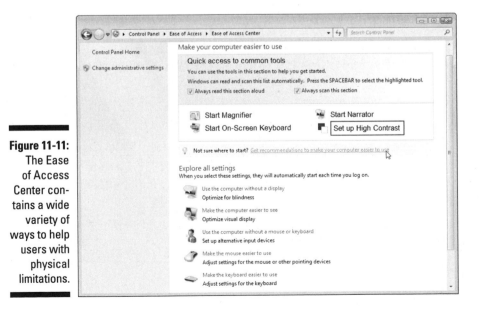

Figure 11-11:
The Ease of Access Center contains a wide variety of ways to help users with physical limitations.

Chapter 12

Keeping Windows from Breaking

*I*f something in Windows is already broken, hop ahead to Chapter 17 for the fix. But if your computer seems to be running reasonably well, stay right here. This chapter explains how to keep it running that way for the longest time possible.

This chapter is a checklist of sorts, with each section explaining a fairly simple and necessary task to keep Windows running at its best. There's no need to call in a techie because much of this upkeep takes place using either Windows 7's built-in maintenance tools or standard household cleaners. For example, when your hard drive is running low on space, you run Windows 7's built-in Disk Cleanup program to remove the detritus.

This chapter also helps you fix the annoying and ubiquitous "bad driver" problem by explaining how to put a fresh driver behind the wheel.

Finally, you discover a quick way to clean your mouse — a necessary but oft-overlooked task that keeps the pointer on target. (Feel free to grab the vacuum cleaner and suck all the cookie crumbs out of your keyboard during the same cleaning spree.)

In addition to the checklist this chapter offers, make sure that the Windows Update and Windows Defender programs are running on autopilot, as I describe in Chapter 10. Those programs go a long way to keeping your computer running safely and securely.

Creating a Restore Point

When your computer is ailing, System Restore (which I cover more thoroughly in Chapter 17) provides a magical way to go back in time to when your computer was feeling better. Although Windows 7 creates restore points automatically, feel free to create your own. A restore point lets you return your PC to a point in its history when *you* know it was working. Follow these steps:

1. **Open the Start menu, right-click Computer, and choose Properties.**

   The System window appears, displaying your PC's vital stats.

2. **From the System window's left panel, choose System Protection.**

   The System Properties window appears. Look for the Create button near the bottom.

3. **Click the Create button to fetch the System Protection window, type a name for your new restore point, and then click the System Protection window's Create button to save the restore point.**

   Windows 7 creates a restore point with your chosen name, leaving you with a bunch of open windows to close.

By creating your own restore points on good days, you'll know immediately which ones to use on bad days. I describe how to resuscitate your computer with System Restore in Chapter 17.

Tuning Up Windows 7 with Built-In Maintenance Tools

Windows 7 contains a slew of tools for keeping Windows 7 running smoothly. Several run automatically, limiting your work to checking their On switches. Others help you prepare for global warming by backing up your PC's files. To check them out, click the Start menu, choose Control Panel, and select the System and Security category.

You'll need these tools most often:

- ✔ **Backup and Restore:** The Windows 7 backup program works much better than the one included with Windows Vista. It's still free, leaving you no excuse not to back up your files. All hard drives eventually die, and you've stored lots of memories on yours.

- ✔ **System:** Technical support people thrive in this crawlspace. The System area lists your version of Windows 7, your PC's horsepower and networking status, and a scorecard rating of what Windows thinks of your PC's performance.

✔ **Windows Update:** This tool lets Microsoft automatically siphon security fixes into your PC through the Internet, usually a good thing. Here's where you can turn Windows Update back on, if it's not running.

✔ **Power Options:** Not sure whether your PC or laptop is sleeping, hibernating, or just plain turned off? Chapter 2 explains the difference, and this section lets you determine your PC's degree of lethargy when you press its Off button. (Or, if you're a laptop owner, when you close its lid.)

✔ **Administrative Tools:** One gem lives in this complicated grab bag of tech tools: The Disk Cleanup program deletes your PC's garbage to give you more storage space on your PC's hard drive.

I describe these tasks more fully in the next five sections.

Backing up your computer

Your hard drive will eventually die, unfortunately, and it will take everything down with it: years of digital photos, songs, letters, financial records, scanned memorabilia, and anything else you've created or stored on your PC.

That's why you must back up your files on a regular basis. When your hard drive finally walks off the stage, your backup copy lets you keep the show on the road.

Windows 7's solution is its bundled backup program, which runs roughshod over its awkward predecessor from Windows Vista. The new backup program is simple to figure out, automatically runs on schedule, and backs up everything you need.

Before you can use Windows Backup, you need three things:

✔ **A CD burner, a DVD burner, or an external hard drive:** Windows 7's free backup program can write to CDs and DVDs — if you're willing to sit by your PC, hand-feeding those discs to your PC. But for dependable, automatic backups, nothing beats a portable hard drive: a hard drive in a little box. Buy one that plugs into your computer's FireWire or USB 2.0 port, and Windows 7 recognizes it on the spot.

If you're backing up your PC to a portable hard drive, plug the hard drive into your PC before running the backup program.

✔ **An Administrator account:** You must be logged on to the computer with an Administrator account. I explain passwords and user accounts in Chapter 13.

✔ **The Windows 7 backup and restore program:** The free backup and restore program in every version of Windows 7 can automatically back up any or all of your work. But it won't do anything until you set it up the first time.

Follow these steps to make your computer back up your work automatically each month (good), week (better), or evening (best):

1. **Open the Backup and Restore program.**

   Click the Start button, choose Control Panel, select the System and Security category, and click Backup and Restore.

   If you've previously set up the backup program, you can change the program's settings by clicking the words Change Settings. Then proceed to Step 3 to choose a new backup location or schedule.

   If you haven't already, click the words Create a System Repair Disc in the window's left panel. That lets you burn a CD or DVD with a program to reinstall Windows 7 with the System Image you'll be creating as part of your backup. Write *Repair Disc Windows 7* on the disc and save it in a safe place.

2. **Click Set Up Backup from the Backup and Restore window's upper-right corner.**

   The thoughtful program asks where you want to save the files by presenting you with a dialog box, as shown in Figure 12-1.

3. **Select the location where you want to save your backup and click Next.**

   Windows 7 lets you save your backup nearly anywhere: CDs, DVDs, flash drives, portable hard drives, or even a drive stored on a second PC that's linked through a *network* (see Chapter 14).

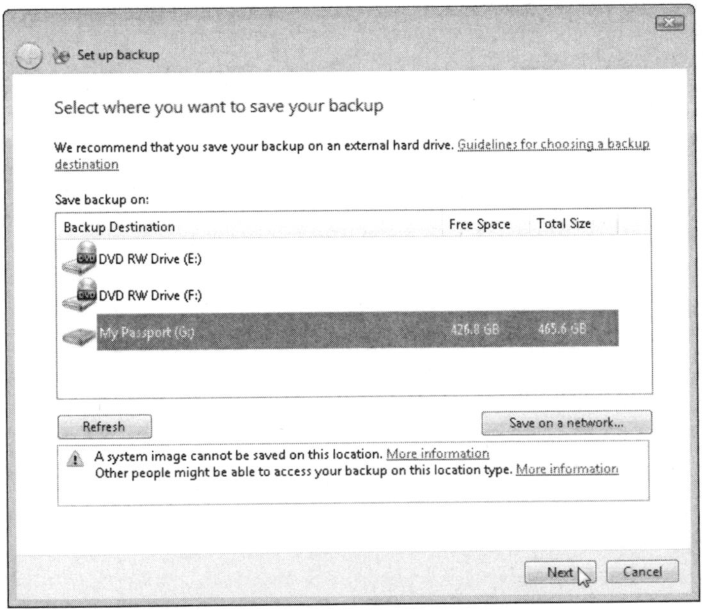

Figure 12-1:
Choose where you want to save your files.

Set up backup

Select where you want to save your backup

We recommend that you save your backup on an external hard drive. Guidelines for choosing a backup destination

Save backup on:

Backup Destination	Free Space	Total Size
DVD RW Drive (E:)		
DVD RW Drive (F:)		
My Passport (G:)	426.8 GB	465.6 GB

Refresh   Save on a network...

⚠ A system image cannot be saved on this location. More information
Other people might be able to access your backup on this location type. More information

Next   Cancel

Although your choice depends on the amount of information you're backing up, the best solution is a *portable hard drive:* a hard drive in a box that you plug into one of your PC's USB or FireWire ports. Windows 7 quickly assigns the new drive a letter, and the drive appears as a backup location.

If you can't afford a portable hard drive, and you don't have another PC connected through a network, then CDs or DVDs are the next best thing.

If you try to save to a networked drive on another PC, Windows 7 asks for an Administrator account's username and password on the other PC.

4. **Choose what you want to back up and click Next.**

   Windows offers you two options:

   - **Let Windows Choose:** The easiest choice, this backs up everything: your Documents; your Music, Pictures, and Video libraries; and everything on your desktop. If you have a large second hard drive in your PC devoted to backups, the program also creates a *system image* — an exact copy of the drive Windows 7 lives on.

   - **Let Me Choose:** A treat tossed in for techies, this option lets you pick and choose what to back up and what to leave behind.

5. **Review your settings, adjust the schedule for how often to back up (if needed), and click the Save Settings and Run Backup button.**

   Windows 7 normally backs up automatically every Sunday at 7 p.m., as shown in Figure 12-2. To change that, click the Change Schedule link and then choose the day and time for the Backup program to kick in. For example, to schedule a backup every evening at midnight, choose Daily from the How Often menu and choose 12 AM (midnight) from the What Time menu.

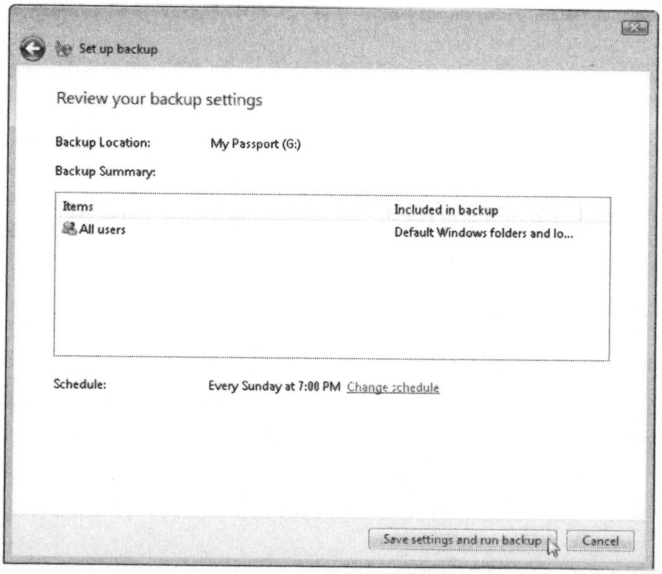

Figure 12-2:
Click
Change
Schedule to
change the
frequency,
day, and
time of your
automatic
backups.

Set up backup

Review your backup settings

Backup Location: My Passport (G:)

Backup Summary:

Items	Included in backup
All users	Default Windows folders and lo...

Schedule: Every Sunday at 7:00 PM Change schedule

Save settings and run backup   Cancel

You can schedule a backup time to take place while you're still working on your PC, but your PC will be sluggish.

When you click the Save Settings and Run Backup button, Windows 7 immediately starts its backup — even if one isn't scheduled yet. That's because the ever-vigilant Windows 7 wants to make sure that it grabs everything right now — before something goes wrong.

6. **Restore a few files to test your backup.**

   Now it's time to make sure that everything worked. Repeat the first step, but choose Restore Files. Follow Windows 7's menus until you can browse the list of backed-up files. Restore a test file to make sure that it's copied back to its original place.

   ✔ Theoretically, Windows wakes up from Sleep or Hibernate mode to back up your PC in the evenings. Realistically, though, some older PCs keep napping. If yours doesn't wake up during a test run, leave the PC *turned on* during the scheduled backup time. Most PCs consume less power than a light bulb. (Please turn off your computer's monitor, though.)

   ✔ Windows 7 saves your backup in a file named Windows 7 in the location you choose in Step 3. Don't move that file, or Windows 7 may not be able to find it again when you choose to restore it.

Finding technical information about your computer

If you ever need to look under Windows 7's hood, heaven forbid, select the Control Panel's System and Security category and choose System. Shown in Figure 12-3, the System window offers an easily digestible technical briefing about your PC's viscera:

   ✔ **Windows Edition:** Windows 7 comes in several versions. To jog your memory, Windows 7 lists the version that's running on your PC.

   ✔ **System:** Here, Windows 7 rates your PC's strength — its *Windows Experience Index* — on a scale of 1 (frail) to 7.9 (robust). Your PC's type of *CPU* (central processing unit) also appears here, as well as its amount of memory.

   ✔ **Computer Name, Domain, and Workgroup Settings:** This section identifies your computer's name and *workgroup,* a term used when connecting to other computers in a network. (I cover networks in Chapter 14.)

   ✔ **Windows Activation:** To keep people from buying one copy of Windows 7 and installing it on several PCs, Microsoft requires Windows 7 to be *activated,* a process that chains it to a single PC.

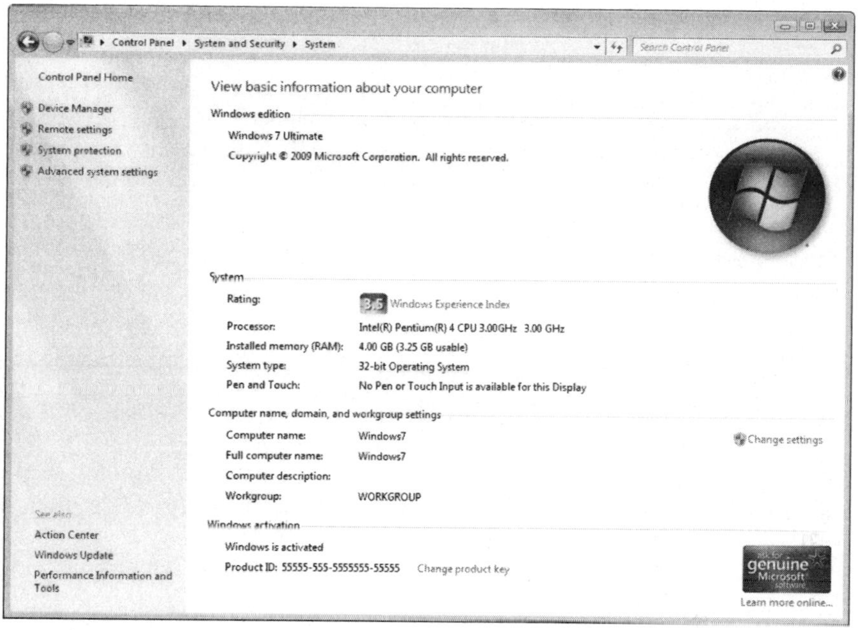

Figure 12-3:
Clicking the
System icon
brings up
technical
information
about your
PC.

The pane along the left also lists some more advanced tasks you may find handy during those panic-stricken times when something's going wrong with your PC. Here's the rundown:

- ✔ **Device Manager:** This option lists all the parts inside your computer, but not in a friendly manner. Parts with exclamation points next to them aren't happy. Double-click them to see Windows 7's explanation of why they're not working correctly. (Sometimes a Troubleshoot button appears by the explanation; click the button to diagnose the problem.)

- ✔ **Remote Settings:** Rarely used, this complicated setup lets other people control your PC through the Internet, hopefully to fix things. If you can find one of these helpful people, let them walk you through this procedure over the phone or through an instant messaging program.

- ✔ **System Protection:** This option lets you create restore points (described in this chapter's first section). You can also come here and use a restore point to take your PC back to another point in time — hopefully when it was in a better mood.

- ✔ **Advanced System Settings:** Professional techies spend lots of time in here. Everybody else ignores it.

Most of the stuff listed in Windows 7's System area is fairly complicated, so don't mess with it unless you're sure of what you're doing or a technical support person tells you to change a specific setting. If you want a taste of it, check out the sidebar on adjusting visual effects.

Speeding up your PC by toning down the visual effects

As it frantically crunches numbers in the background, Windows 7 tries to project a navel-gazing image of inner peace. Its menus and windows open and close with a fade; aesthetically pleasing shadows surround each menu and the mouse pointer. If your video card possesses enough oomph, Windows 7 makes the window borders translucent, allowing part of the desktop to glow from behind.

All these extra visual decisions require extra calculations on Windows 7's part, however, slowing it down a bit. To change Windows 7's attitude from peaceful to performance, head for the Control Panel's System and Security category, choose System, and click Advanced System Settings in the left pane. When the System Properties box opens to the Advanced tab, click the Settings button in the Performance area.

For fastest action, which is handy for slow laptops, choose the Adjust for Best Performance option. Windows quickly strips away all the visuals and reverts to Classic mode — a faster way of working that mimics earlier, no-frills Windows versions. To return to a prettier, but slower, Windows, choose the Let Windows Choose What's Best for My Computer option.

Freeing up space on your hard drive

Windows 7 grabs quite a bit of space on your hard drive, although it's nowhere near as hoggy as Windows Vista. If programs begin whining about running out of room on your hard drive, this solution grants you a short reprieve:

1. **Click the Start button and choose the Control Panel's System and Security category. Then, in the Administrative Tools category, choose Free Up Disk Space.**

   If your PC has more than one disk drive, Windows 7 asks which drive to clean up. Leave the choice set to (C:), and click OK.

   The Disk Cleanup program calculates how much disk space you can save.

2. **Select the check boxes for all the items and then click OK.**

   Windows 7 presents the Disk Cleanup dialog box, shown in Figure 12-4. Select all the check boxes and then click OK. As you select a check box, the Description section explains what's being deleted.

   If you spot a Clean Up System Files button, click it, too. It deletes detritus created by your PC, not you.

3. **Click the Delete Files button when Windows 7 asks whether you're sure.**

   Windows 7 proceeds to empty your Recycle Bin, destroy leftovers from old Web sites, and remove other hard drive clutter.

For a shortcut to Disk Cleanup, click the Start menu and type **disk cleanup** in the Search box.

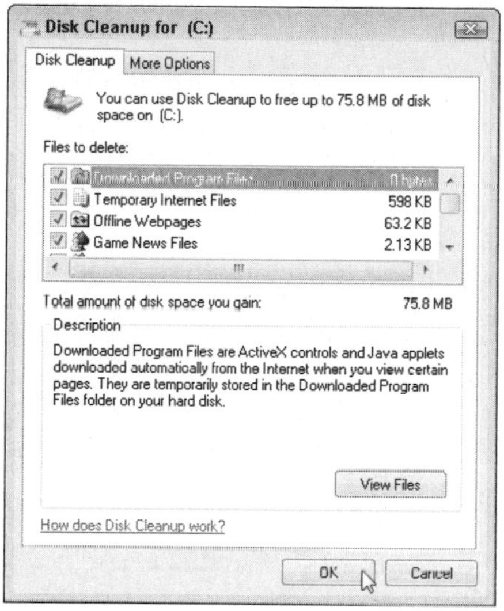

Figure 12-4: Make sure that all the check boxes are selected.

Empowering your power button

Normally, a press of a PC's power button turns off your PC, whether or not Windows 7 is ready. That's why you should always turn off Windows 7 with its *own* Off button, found by clicking the Start menu and clicking Shut Down. That gives Windows 7 time to prepare for the event.

To avoid jolting Windows 7 with an unexpected shutdown, consider reprogramming your laptop or PC's power button so that it doesn't turn off your PC at all. Instead, it makes your PC sleep or hibernate to save power.

If you're a laptop owner, this area also lets you control what happens when you shut the lid: Should your PC turn off or hibernate?

To change your power button's mission, follow these steps:

1. **Click the Start button, choose Control Panel, and select the System and Security category.**

2. **Choose Power Options.**

   The Power Options window appears.

3. **From the left side panel, click Choose What the Power Button Does, and apply your changes.**

   A window appears, offering a menu where you can tell your PC's or laptop's Power button to either Sleep, Hibernate, Shut Down your PC, or Do Nothing, which prevents people from turning off your PC. (I describe the difference between Sleep and Hibernate in Chapter 2.)

   Laptops offer an extra menu option on this page: You can make the laptop behave differently according to whether it's plugged in or running on batteries.

   Laptop owners also find a menu letting them choose their laptop's behavior when they close its lid. (The menu offers different behaviors depending on whether your laptop's plugged in or not.)

   For extra security, click Require a Password so that anybody waking up your PC needs your password to see your information.

4. **Click the Save Changes button.**

For quick access to this area, type **Power Options** into the Start menu's Search box.

Setting up devices that don't work (fiddling with drivers)

Windows comes with an arsenal of *drivers* — software that lets Windows communicate with the gadgets you plug into your PC. Normally, Windows 7 automatically recognizes your new part, and it works. Other times, Windows 7 heads to the Internet and fetches some instructions before finishing the job.

But occasionally, you'll plug in something that's either too new for Windows 7 to know about or too old for it to remember. Or perhaps something attached to your PC no longer works right, and odd messages grumble about "needing a new driver."

In these cases, it's up to you to track down and install a Windows 7 driver for that part. The best drivers come with an installation program that automatically places the software in the right place. The worst drivers leave all the grunt work up to you.

If Windows 7 doesn't automatically recognize and install your newly attached piece of hardware — even after you restart your PC — follow these steps to locate and install a new driver:

1. **Visit the part manufacturer's Web site and download the latest Windows 7 driver.**

You often find the manufacturer's Web site stamped somewhere on the part's box. If you can't find it, search for the part manufacturer's name on Google (www.google.com) and locate its Web site.

Look in the Web site's Support, Downloads, or Customer Service area. There, you usually need to enter your part's name, its model number, and your computer's operating system (Windows 7) before the Web site coughs up the driver.

No Windows 7 driver listed? Try downloading a Windows Vista driver instead because they usually work just as well. (Be sure to scan *any* downloaded file with a virus checker.)

2. **Run the driver's installation program.**

Sometimes clicking your downloaded file makes its installation program jump into action, installing the driver for you. If so, you're through. If not, head to Step 3.

If the downloaded file has a little zipper on the icon, right-click it and choose Extract All to *unzip* its contents into a new folder. (Windows 7 names that new folder after the file you've unzipped, making it easy to relocate.)

3. **Click the Start menu, open the Control Panel, choose the Hardware and Sound category, and select Device Manager from the Devices and Printers section.**

The Device Manager appears, listing an inventory of every part inside or attached to your computer.

4. **Click anywhere inside the Device Manager window. Then click Action from the Device Manager's menu bar, and choose Add Legacy Hardware from the drop-down menu.**

The Add Hardware Wizard guides you through the steps of installing your new hardware and, if necessary, installing your new driver.

✔ Avoid problems by keeping your drivers up-to-date. Even the ones packaged with newly bought parts are usually old. Visit the manufacturer's Web site and download the latest driver. Chances are good that it fixes problems earlier users had with the first set of drivers.

✔ Problems with the new driver? Click the Start menu, choose Control Panel, and select the System and Security category. In the System area, choose Device Manager and double-click the part name — *Keyboards,* for example — on the window's left side. Windows 7 reveals the make and model of your part. Double-click the part's name and click the Driver tab on the Properties box. Keep your breathing steady. Finally, click the Roll Back Driver button. Windows 7 ditches the newly installed driver and returns to the previous driver.

Cleaning Your Mouse

If your mouse pointer jumps around on-screen or doesn't move at all, your mouse is probably clogged with desktop gunk. Follow these steps to degunkify it:

1. **Turn the mouse upside down and clean off any dirt stuck to the bottom.**

   Your mouse must lie flat on its pad to work correctly.

2. **Inspect the bottom of your mouse.**

   If your mouse has a little ball on the bottom, proceed to Step 3.

   If your mouse has a little light on the bottom, proceed to Step 4.

3. **Cleaning a mouse that has a ball:**

   Twist off the mouse's little round cover and remove the ball. Wipe off any crud from the ball and blow dust out of the hole. A little air blower, sold at office and computer stores, works well here. (It also blows off the dust layers clogging your computer's air vents.)

   Pull out any stray hairs, dust, and roller goo. A cotton swab moistened with alcohol cleans the most persistent goo from the little rollers. (The rollers should be smooth and shiny.) Dirty rollers cause the most mouse problems.

   Replace the cleaned ball into the cleaned hole and reinsert the clean little round cover.

4. **Cleaning an optical mouse:**

   An *optical mouse* replaces the old-fashioned rubber ball with a tiny laser. With no moving parts, optical mice rarely need cleaning. But if yours is acting up, remove any stray hairs clinging to the bottom around the light.

   Also, make sure that the mouse rests on a textured surface that's not shiny. If your desktop is glass or shiny (polished wood grain, for example), put your mouse on a mouse pad for better results.

If your newly cleaned mouse still has problems, it may be time for a new one. But before shelling out the cash, check these things:

- ✔ Wireless mice go through batteries fairly quickly. If your mouse doesn't have a connecting cord, it's wireless. Check its battery and make sure that it's within range of its receiving unit. (The receiving unit plugs into your PC, perhaps in the back.)

- ✔ Check your mouse's settings: Click Start and then choose Devices and Printers. Right-click your mouse's icon, choose Settings, and look through the check boxes to see whether any of the offered settings match the symptoms of your particular problem. Sometimes deselecting a check box can solve a problem — removing pointer "ghosts" that follow your arrow across the screen, for example.

Chapter 13

Sharing One Computer with Several People

In This Chapter

▶ Understanding user accounts

▶ Setting up, deleting, or changing user accounts

▶ Logging on at the Welcome screen

▶ Switching quickly between users

▶ Sharing files between account holders

▶ Understanding passwords

*W*indows 7 allows several people to share one computer, without letting anybody peek into anybody else's files.

The secret? Windows 7 grants each user his or her own *user account,* which neatly separates that person from other users. When people log on using their own user account, the computer looks tailor-made for them: It displays their personalized desktop background, menu choices, programs, and files — and it forbids them from seeing items belonging to other users.

This chapter explains how to set up a separate user account for everybody in the house, including the computer's owner, family members or roommates, and even occasional visitors who ask to check their e-mail.

You'll also discover how to break down some of those walls to share information between accounts, letting everybody see your vacation photos, but keeping your love letters off-limits.

Understanding User Accounts

Windows 7 wants you to set up a *user account* for everybody who uses your PC. A user account works like a cocktail-party name tag that helps Windows recognize who's sitting at the keyboard. Windows 7 offers three types of user accounts: Administrator, Standard, and Guest. To begin playing with the PC, people click their account's name when Windows 7 first loads, as shown in Figure 13-1.

Who cares? Well, Windows 7 gives each type of account permission to do different things on the computer. If the computer were a huge apartment building, the Administrator account would belong to the manager, each tenant would have a Standard account, and Guest accounts would belong to visitors trying to use the bathroom in the lobby. Here's how the different accounts translate into computer lingo:

- ✔ **Administrator:** The administrator controls the entire computer, deciding who gets to play with it and what each user may do on it. On a computer running Windows 7, the owner usually holds the almighty Administrator account. He or she then sets up accounts for each household member and decides what they can and can't do with the PC.

- ✔ **Standard:** Standard accounts can access most of the computer, but they can't make any big changes to it. They can't install programs, for example, but they can still run them. (Windows XP referred to Standard accounts as Limited accounts.)

- ✔ **Guest:** Guests can play with the computer, but the computer doesn't recognize them by name. Guest accounts function much like Standard accounts, but with no privacy: Anybody can log on with the Guest account, and the desktop will look the way the last guest left it. It's great for Web browsing, but not much else.

Figure 13-1:
Windows 7
lets users
log on under
their own
accounts.

Here are some ways accounts are typically assigned when you're sharing the same computer under one roof:

- ✔ In a family, the parents usually hold Administrator accounts, the kids usually have Standard accounts, and the babysitter logs on using the Guest account.

- ✔ In a dorm or shared apartment, the computer's owner holds the Administrator account, and the roommates have either Standard or Guest accounts, depending on their trustworthiness level (and perhaps how clean they've left the kitchen that week).

To keep others from logging on under your user account, you must protect it with a password. (I describe how to choose a password for your account in this chapter's "Setting Up Passwords and Security" section.)

Guest accounts can't dial up the Internet. They can only access the Web if your PC has a broadband connection — a connection that's always turned on.

When you created new accounts in Windows XP, they were always made Administrator accounts — unless you clicked the Limited button. Windows 7 reverses that to add a layer of security. When you create a new account, it's automatically granted *Standard* account status — Windows 7's relative equivalent of XP's Limited account. To create an Administrator account in Windows 7, you must specifically choose the Administrator account option.

Giving yourself a Standard account

Whenever an evil piece of software slips into your computer — and you're logged in as an administrator — that evil software holds as much power as you do. That's dangerous because Administrator accounts can delete just about anything. And that's why Microsoft suggests creating *two* accounts for yourself: an Administrator account and a Standard account. Then log on with your Standard account for everyday computing.

That way, Windows 7 treats you just like any other Standard user: When the computer is about to do something potentially harmful, Windows 7 asks you to type the password of an Administrator account. Type your Administrator account's password, and Windows 7 lets you proceed. But if Windows 7 unexpectedly asks for permission to do something odd, you know something may be suspect.

This second account is inconvenient, no doubt about it. But so is reaching for a key whenever you enter your front door. Taking an extra step is the price of extra security.

Setting Up or Changing User Accounts

Being second-class citizens, Standard account holders lack much power. They can run programs and change their account's picture, for example, or even change their password. But the administrators hold the *real* power: They can create or delete any user account, effectively wiping a person's name, files, and programs off the computer. (That's why you should never upset a computer's administrator.)

If you're an administrator, create a Standard user account for everybody who's sharing your computer. That account gives them enough control over the computer to keep them from bugging you all the time, yet it keeps them from accidentally deleting your important files or messing up your computer.

Follow these steps to add another user account to your PC or change an existing account:

1. **Click the Start menu, choose Control Panel, and choose Add or Remove User Accounts, which appears under the User Accounts and Family Safety category.**

   The Manage Accounts window pops up, as shown in Figure 13-2.

2. **Create a new account, if desired.**

   If you click Create a New Account, shown in Figure 13-2, Windows lets you choose between creating a Standard and creating an Administrator account. Choose Standard User unless you have an important reason to create another Administrator account. Type a name for the new account and click the Create Account button — you're finished.

   To tweak the settings of an existing account, move to Step 3.

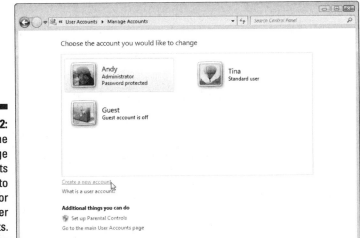

Figure 13-2: Use the Manage Accounts window to create or change user accounts.

3. **Click the account you want to change.**

Click either the account's name or photo. Windows 7 displays a page with that user account's photo and lets you tweak the account's settings in any of these ways:

- **Change the Account Name:** Here's your chance to correct a misspelled name on an account. Or, feel free to jazz up your account name, changing Jane to Crystal Powers.

- **Create/Change a Password:** Every account should have a password to keep out other users. Here's your chance to add one or change the existing one.

- **Remove the Password:** You shouldn't use this option, but password-protected accounts offer this option, just in case.

- **Change the Picture:** Any account holder can change his own picture, so you needn't bother with this one — unless, of course, you somehow know more about computers than your kid.

- **Set Up Parental Controls:** An Easter egg for parents, Parental Controls lets you choose the hours that an account holder may access the PC, as well as limit the programs and games the account holder may run. I cover Parental Controls in Chapter 10.

- **Change the Account Type:** Head here to promote a Standard user of high moral character to an Administrator account or bump a naughty administrator down to Standard.

- **Delete the Account:** Don't choose this setting hastily, as deleting somebody's account also deletes all their files. Even System Restore can't retrieve the files of a deleted account holder.

- **Manage Another Account:** Save your current crop of changes and begin tweaking somebody else's account.

4. **When you're through, close the window by clicking the red X in its top-right corner.**

Any changes made to a user's account take place immediately.

Switching Quickly between Users

Windows 7 enables an entire family, roommates, or employees in a small office to share a single computer. Best yet, the computer keeps track of everybody's programs while different people use the computer. Mom can be playing chess and then let Jerry log on to check his e-mail. When Mom logs back on a few minutes later, her chess match is right where she left it, pondering the sacrifice of her rook.

Known as *Fast User Switching*, switching between users works fairly easily. While holding down the Windows key (it's usually between your keyboard's Ctrl and Alt keys), press the letter L. Wham! The Switch User button appears, letting you hand over the reins to any other account holder.

When that person finishes, he can log off normally: Click the little arrow next to the Start button's Shut Down button (shown in the margin) and choose Log Off from the pop-up menu. Then you can log back on and see your desktop, just as you left it.

Keep these tips in mind when managing other account holders on your PC:

✔ With all this user switching, you may forget whose account you're actually using. To check, open the Start menu. The current account holder's name and picture appear at the menu's top right corner. Also, Windows 7's opening screen lists the words "logged on" beneath the picture of every user who's currently logged on.

✔ Don't restart the PC while another person's still logged on in the background, or that person will lose any work he hasn't saved. (Windows 7 warns you before restarting the PC, giving you a chance to ask the other person to save his work.)

✔ You can also switch users by clicking the Start button and clicking the little arrow by the Start menu's Lock sign (shown in the margin). When the menu appears, click Switch User instead of Log Off.

✔ If you need to change a security setting while your child's logged on, you don't need to switch to your Administrator account. Just sit down at the PC and begin changing the setting: Like your child, you see a message asking for an administrator's password. Type your administrator password, and Windows 7 lets you change the setting, just as if you'd logged on under your own account.

✔ Fast User Switching slows down older computers that lack gobs of memory. If your computer runs slowly with more than one person logged on, avoid Fast User Switching. Log on one person at a time and then log off when you're done to give somebody else some keyboard time.

Sharing Files among Account Holders

Normally the Windows user account system keeps everybody's files separate, effectively thwarting Jack's attempts to read Jill's diary. But what if you're co-writing a report with somebody, and you both want access to the same file? Sure, you can e-mail the file back and forth to each other, or you can store the file on a flash drive and carry the flash drive from PC to PC.

The big problem with Standard accounts

Standard account holders have no problem accessing their own files. But they can't do anything that affects other users — for example, delete a program or change one of the computer's security settings. If they try, Windows 7 freezes the screen, demanding an administrator's password. That's when the administrator must walk over to type it in.

While some people appreciate the extra security, others feel like a slave to their PC. You have several ways to make Windows 7 less demanding:

✔ **Upgrade everybody to Administrator accounts.** The upgrades allow *any* user to type a password and override the security screens. Beware, though: This option also lets any user do *anything* on your PC, including delete your entire user account and your personal files.

✔ **Adjust User Account Protection.** Slide this toggle switch, described in Chapter 10, to adjust 7's attitude. Slide it to the bottom,

and Windows 7 stops caring: It no longer displays permission screens, disabling Windows 7's attempts to keep your PC secure. Slide it to the top, and Windows 7 questions *anything* that could put your PC at risk.

✔ **Live with it.** You could just put up with Windows 7's nag screens as the price to pay for a secure computer in today's world. Juggle your own security and convenience levels and then make your own decision.

If you've turned off User Account Protection and want to turn it back on, head for the Control Panel, select the User Accounts and Family Safety category, choose User Accounts, and then choose Change User Account Control Settings. Slide the toggle switch up two bars to the Default setting (the setting with a dark bar) and then click OK.

But for an easier way, place a copy of that file in a *Public* folder in your library. That file then shows up in *everybody's* library, where anybody can view, change, or delete it. Here's how to find the Public folders living in your libraries and copy files into them for sharing with others:

1. **Open any folder and navigate to the folder containing the files you'd like to share.**

   No folder already open on your desktop? Then open one by clicking the library icon (shown in the margin) on your taskbar.

2. **Double-click the word Libraries in the folder's Navigation Pane to see your four libraries.**

   Double-clicking the word Libraries toggles the view of your libraries, either showing or hiding the names of your four libraries: Documents, Music, Pictures, and Videos.

3. **Double-click the library where you want to share your files.**

   Double-click the Music library, for example, and the Music library reveals the two folders it displays: My Music and Public Music.

Every one of your four libraries constantly displays the contents of a Public folder, as well as the contents of your own personal folder.

The beauty of Public folders is that their contents appear in *everybody's* library. If John puts a music file into his Public Music folder, it will automatically appear in Becky's Public Music library, too, because Becky's library also displays the Public Music folder's contents.

4. **Copy the file or folder you want to share to the appropriate library's Public folder.**

   You can drag and drop the item directly into the folder's icon on the Navigation Pane. Once the item is in the Public folder, it automatically appears in everybody's library, where they can open, change, or even delete it. (Because it can be deleted, it's sometimes wiser to *copy* items into the Public folder rather than *move* them.)

Here are some other Public folder tips:

✔ To see exactly what items you're sharing, examine your own libraries, displayed in every folder's Navigation Pane. For example, to see what music you're sharing publicly, double-click the word Music in your library and then click Public Music. The contents of that folder can be accessed, changed, or deleted by anybody.

✔ If you find some things in your Public folder you don't want to share anymore, move them back into your own folder. For example, move that Beatles album from your Music library's Public Music folder to your Music library's My Music folder.

✔ If you connect your PCs through a network, which I describe in Chapter 14, you can create a *Homegroup* — a simple way of sharing files between PCs in the home. After you create a Homegroup, everybody on any PC in your home can share *everything* in the libraries you choose. It's a simple and convenient way to share all your photos, music, and videos.

Changing a User Account's Picture

Okay, now the important stuff: changing the dorky picture that Windows automatically assigns to your user account. For every newly created user account, Windows 7 dips into its image bag and adds a random picture of flowers, animals, soccer balls, or some similarly boring image. Feel free to change the picture to something more reflective of the Real You: You can use digital camera photos, as well as any pictures or graphics found on the Internet.

To change your user account's picture, click the Start button and click your picture at the menu's top. When the User Accounts window appears, click the Change Your Picture option. Windows 7 lets you choose from its current stock, shown in Figure 13-3.

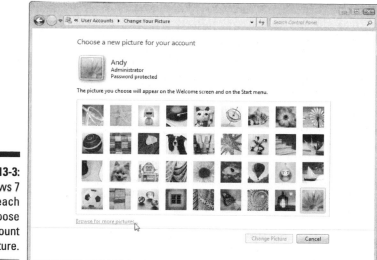

Figure 13-3:
Windows 7 lets each user choose an account picture.

To assign a picture that's *not* currently shown, select Browse for More Pictures, shown in Figure 13-3. A new window appears, this time showing the contents of your Pictures library. (Your digital camera usually stores its pictures there.) Click a desired picture from the folder and choose Open. Windows 7 quickly slaps that picture atop your Start menu.

Here are a few more options:

- You can also grab any picture off the Internet and save it to your Pictures folder for use as your user account picture. (Right-click the Internet picture and choose Save Picture As.)
- Don't worry about choosing a picture that's too big or too small. Windows 7 automatically shrinks or expands the image to fit the post-age-stamp-sized space.
- All users may change their pictures — Administrator, Standard, and Guest accounts. (Pictures are about the only thing that guests *are* allowed to change.)

Setting Up Passwords and Security

There's not much point to having a user account if you don't have a password. Without one, Charles from the next cubicle can click your account on the logon screen, giving him free reign to snoop through your files.

Administrators, especially, should have passwords. If they don't, they're automatically letting anybody wreak havoc with the PC: When a permission's screen appears, anybody can just press Enter at the password screen to gain entrance.

To create or change a password, follow these steps:

1. **Open the Start menu, choose Control Panel, select the User Accounts and Family Safety category, and choose User Accounts.**

   The User Accounts screen opens.

2. **Choose Change Your Password.**

   People who haven't created a password should instead choose Create a Password for Your Account.

3. **Make up an easy-to-remember password and type it into the New Password text box, and then retype the same characters into the Confirm New Password text box below it.**

   Retyping the password eliminates the chance of typos.

   Changing an existing password works slightly differently: The screen shows a Current Password box where you must first type your existing password. (That keeps pranksters from sneaking over and changing your password during lunch hours.)

4. **In the Type a Password Hint text box, type a clue that helps you remember your forgotten password.**

   Make sure that the clue works only for you. Don't enter "My hair color," for example. If you're at work, enter **My cat's favorite food** or **The director of my favorite movie**. If you're at home, choose something only you — not the kids — know. And don't be afraid to change your password every once in a while, too. You can find out more about passwords in Chapter 2.

5. **When the User Accounts screen returns, choose Create a Password Reset Disk from along the screen's left side.**

   Windows 7 walks you through the process of creating a Password Reset Disk from a floppy, a memory card, or a USB flash drive.

When you forget your password, you can insert your Password Reset Disk as a key. Windows 7 will let you in to choose a new password, and all will be joyous. Hide your Password Reset Disk in a safe place, because it lets *anybody* into your account.

Chapter 14

Connecting Computers with a Network

- -

In This Chapter

▶ Understanding a network's parts

▶ Choosing between wired and wireless networks

▶ Understanding a network's parts

▶ Setting up a small network

▶ Connecting wirelessly

▶ Creating a Homegroup to share files

▶ Sharing an Internet connection, files, and printers on a network

▶ Troubleshooting a network

- -

*B*uying that second PC brings you yet another computing problem: How can two PCs share the same Internet connection and printer? And how do you share your files between your two PCs?

The solution involves a *network*. When you connect two or more computers with a cable, Windows 7 introduces them to each other and lets them swap information, share an Internet connection, and print with the same printer.

If your computers live too far apart to extend a cable, go *wireless*. Also known as *Wi-Fi*, this option lets your computers chatter through the airwaves like radio stations that broadcast and take requests.

This chapter explains several ways to link a handful of computers so that they can share things. Be forewarned, however: This chapter contains some pretty advanced stuff. Don't tread here unless you're running an Administrator account and you don't mind doing a little head-scratching as you wade from conceptualization to actualization to, "Hey, it works!"

Understanding a Network's Parts

A *network* is two or more computers that have been connected so that they can share things. Although computer networks range from pleasingly simple to agonizingly complex, they all have three things in common:

- ✔ **A network adapter:** Every computer on your network needs its own network adapter. Adapters come in two main forms. A *wired* network adapter is a special jack where you plug in a cable to connect one computer with the other computers. A *wireless* network adapter translates your computer's information into radio signals and broadcasts them to the other computers. (Feel free to mix wired and wireless adapters; they get along fine.)

- ✔ **A router:** When you connect two computers with a single cable or with wireless connections, each computer is smart enough to swap messages with the other one. But the easiest way by far to share Internet signals and files comes from an electronic traffic cop in the form of a little box called a *router*. Each computer connects to the router, which sends the right messages to the right computer.

- ✔ **Cables:** Wireless networks don't require cables. But wired networks need cables to connect the computers' network adapters to each other or to the router.

Most networks resemble a spider, as shown in Figure 14-1, with each computer's cable connecting to the router in the center.

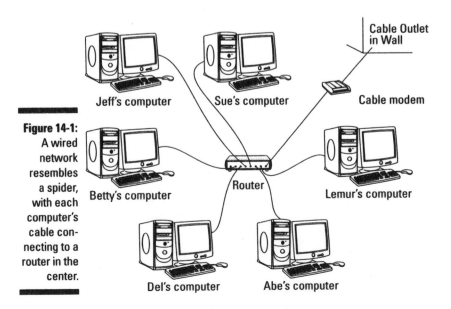

Figure 14-1: A wired network resembles a spider, with each computer's cable connecting to a router in the center.

A wireless network looks identical but without the cables. Or, you can mix wired and wireless adapters to create a network resembling Figure 14-2. Many routers today come with built-in wireless access, letting your PCs connect to them with both wired and wireless adapters.

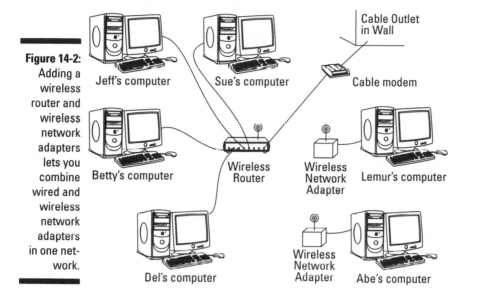

Figure 14-2: Adding a wireless router and wireless network adapters lets you combine wired and wireless network adapters in one network.

Windows 7 divides its attention among networked computers quite well. It lets every networked computer share a single Internet connection, for example, so that everyone can surf the Internet or check their e-mail simultaneously. Everyone can share a single printer, as well. If two people try to print something simultaneously, Windows stashes one person's files until the printer is free and then prints them when the printer's ready.

Setting Up a Small Network

If you're trying to set up a lot of computers — more than ten — you probably need a more advanced book. Networks are fairly easy to set up, but sharing their resources can be scary stuff, especially if the computers contain sensitive material. But if you're just trying to set up a few computers in your home or home office, this information may be all you need.

Choosing between wired and wireless networks

Today, *wireless* (also known as *Wi-Fi*) is the buzzword, and it's easy to see why. You can easily string cables between computers that sit on the same desk or live in one room, but cables quickly become messy when computers live in separate rooms. The solution comes with wireless network adapters, which convert the information to radio waves and broadcast the waves to other computers on the network. The wireless adapters on the other computers catch the waves and convert them back into information.

But just as radio broadcasts fade as you drive out of the city, wireless signals fade, as well. The more they fade, the slower the connection becomes. If your wireless signals pass through more than two or three walls, your computers may not be able to communicate. Also, wireless networks take longer to set up because they have *a lot* more settings to tweak.

Wired connections work more quickly, efficiently, securely, and inexpensively than wireless. But if your spouse wants the cables removed from the hallways, wireless may be your best option. Remember, you can set up adjacent computers with cables and use wireless for the rest.

To use wireless with broadband Internet access, buy a router with a built-in wireless access point. If you live in a big home, ask the salesperson about a "wireless signal booster" that can increase your range.

So without further blabbing, here's a low-carb, step-by-step list of how to set up a small and inexpensive network. The following sections show how to buy the three parts of a network — network adapters, cables (or wireless connections), and a router for moving information between each computer. I explain how to install the parts and, finally, how to make Windows 7 create a network out of your handiwork.

 You can find more detailed instructions about home networking in my book *Upgrading & Fixing PCs For Dummies* (Wiley Publishing, Inc.).

Buying parts for a network

Walk into the computer store, walk out with this stuff, and you're well on your way to setting up your network:

Fast Ethernet or 100BaseT cable: Buy a cable for each PC that won't be using wireless. You want an *Ethernet* cable, which resembles phone cable but with slightly thicker jacks. Ethernet cable is sometimes called Ethernet RJ-45, Cat 5, Cat 5e, Cat 6, Fast Ethernet, LAN cable, 100BaseT cable, or 1000BaseT cable. The names usually include a number relating to the cable's speed rating: 10, 100, or 1,000. (Big numbers are faster, so opt for the fastest you find.)

Some of today's newer homes come conveniently prewired with network jacks in the wall, sparing their owners the bother of buying and stringing long cables from room to room. If your computers live too far apart for cables, buy a wireless network adapter, described next.

Network adapters: Each computer on the network needs its own network adapter, and those gadgets come in two main varieties: wired and wireless. Most computers come with a built-in wired network adapter, sparing you the cost. Most newer laptops come with both wired *and* wireless adapters preinstalled, letting you connect either way.

If you need to buy a network adapter, keep these factors in mind:

- ✔ A wired adapter needs a 10/100 Ethernet connector. These adapters can plug into a USB port, plug inside one of your desktop computer's unused slots, or even piggyback on your home's power or telephone lines.

- ✔ The adapter's box should say that it's *Plug and Play* and supports Windows 7. (Adapters that support Windows Vista should also work, but save your receipt, just in case.)

Router: Most of today's routers come with built-in wireless, and some even come with a built-in broadband modem. The most expensive part of your network, your choice of router depends on your Internet connection and network adapters:

- ✔ Broadband Internet users should purchase a router that has enough ports for each networked computer. If you need a wireless connection, buy a router with built-in wireless access. Figure 14-3 shows where to plug in the router's cables.

- ✔ Routers usually include ports for either four or eight wired connections. Wireless routers can shuffle connections between dozens of wirelessly connected computers.

Figure 14-3:
Your router needs a numbered port for every PC's cable, and it needs a WAN port for your broadband modem.

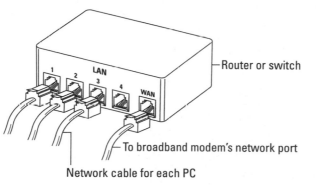

Router or switch

To broadband modem's network port

Network cable for each PC

Buying the same brand of wireless router and wireless network adapter makes them easier to set up.

That's the shopping list. Drop this list onto the copy machine at the office and take it to the computer store.

Installing a wired network

After you've bought your network's parts, you need to plug everything into the right place. Windows 7 — as well as XP and Vista — should automatically recognize the newly installed network adapters and embrace them gleefully.

1. **Turn off and unplug all the computers on your soon-to-be network.**

   Turn 'em all off; unplug them as well.

2. **Turn off all the computers' peripherals — printers, monitors, modems, and anything else that's attached.**

3. **Install the network adapters, if necessary.**

   Plug the USB adapters into your computers' USB ports. If you're using adapter cards in a desktop PC, remove each computer's case and push the card into the proper size of slot. (If you live in a static-prone environment, ground yourself first by touching the side of the computer's case.)

   If a card doesn't seem to fit into a slot, don't force it. Different types of cards fit into different types of slots, and you may be trying to push the wrong type of card into the wrong type of slot. See whether it fits into another slot more easily. Shameless plug: My book *Upgrading & Fixing PCs For Dummies* explains slots and cards in much more detail.

4. **Replace the computers' cases, if necessary, and connect a network cable between each computer's adapter and the router.**

   Unless you're using wireless adapters, you may need to route cables under carpets or around doorways. (Routers have power cords that need to be plugged into a wall outlet as well.)

5. **Broadband Internet users should plug their modems into the router's WAN port.**

   Most routers label their cable modem's port with the letters WAN (wide area network). The router's other ports, labeled LAN (local area network), are numbered. You can plug any PC into any of the numbered ports. (You can leave any unused numbered ports empty.)

   Dialup modem owners can keep the modem plugged into the computer. When that computer is turned on and connected to the Internet, Windows 7 allows each networked computer to share its dialup Internet connection.

The easiest way to connect two computers

Sometimes you simply need to link two computers, quickly and easily, to move information from one computer to another (from an old computer to a new one, for example). You don't need expensive equipment, just a special breed of cable called a *crossover Ethernet* cable. Be sure to emphasize *crossover* or *crossed* cable when shopping at the computer store; a regular Ethernet cable won't work.

Connect the crossed cable between the two computers' network adapters, and Windows 7 creates a quick network between the two computers. If one computer connects to the Internet, the other computer should be able to find and share its Internet connection.

For linking two PCs on the cheap, that cable may be all you need.

6. **Turn on the router, the computers, and the computers' peripherals.**

   Turn on the router first, then the computers and their monitors, printers, modems, and whatever else happens to be connected to them.

7. **Select a location for your network.**

   When Windows 7 wakes up and notices the newly attached network equipment, it asks you for your network's *location:* Home, Work, or Public Location. Choose whether you're working at home or work (safe) or in public (much less safe), and Windows 7 automatically adds the proper security level to protect you.

If all goes well, Windows 7 wakes up, notices its newly installed network adapter, and automatically sets up the applicable connections. If your computer's network adapter came with an installation CD, insert it now. (If the setup program doesn't run automatically, double-click the disc's Setup file to install the software.)

If all *doesn't* go well, you probably need a new driver for your network adapter, a task I cover in Chapter 12.

Windows 7 does a reasonably good job of casting its networking spells on your computers. If the computers are all connected correctly and restarted, chances are good that they wake up in bondage with each other. If they don't, try restarting them all again.

Keep these things in mind when setting up your network:

✔ If you choose Home as your network location in Step 7, Windows asks if you'd like to create a *Homegroup* to share files with the computer's user accounts, as well as with your networked PCs. Take it up on its offer and move ahead to the section "Setting Up a Homegroup," later in this chapter.

✔ After you create a Homegroup, Windows 7 automatically shares three of your libraries with every networked PC: your Music, Pictures, and Video libraries. Any files you place inside those folder are available to everybody on your PC as well as anybody connected to the network. (I explain more about sharing files, folders, printers, and other items later in the section "Connecting to and Sharing Files with Windows XP and Windows Vista PCs.")

✔ Windows XP names its shared folder *Shared Documents*. Windows Vista and Windows 7 name their shared folders as *Public,* instead. But both do the same thing: They provide a place to share files with other people on the same PC, as well as on the same network.

✔ To see other PCs connected to your PC through the network, open any folder and click the Network link in the Navigation Pane on the left.

✔ If your PCs can't see each other, make sure that each PC uses the same workgroup name, covered in the "Workgroup names and Windows XP" sidebar.

Workgroup names and Windows XP

Like children and pets, networks need names. A network's name is called a *workgroup,* and for some reason, Microsoft used different workgroup names in different versions of Windows. That causes problems if you have any Windows XP Home PCs on your network.

Windows XP Home PCs automatically use MSHOME as their workgroup name; Windows XP Professional, Windows Vista, and Windows 7 PCs use WORKGROUP as their workgroup name. The result? Put a Windows 7 PC and a Windows XP Home PC on the same network, and they can't find or talk with each other: One PC searches in vain for other MSHOME PCs, and the other looks for WORKGROUP PCs.

The solution is to give them both the *same* workgroup name, a fairly easy task with these steps:

1. **On your Windows XP Home PC, click the Start menu, right-click My Computer, and choose Properties.**

   The System Properties window appears, revealing basic techie information about your PC.

2. **Click the Computer Name tab and click the Change button.**

   The Computer Name Changes dialog box appears.

3. **In the bottom box, change the Workgroup name to** WORKGROUP.

   That puts Windows XP Home in the same workgroup as the rest of your PCs.

   Tip: Be careful in this step to change the PC's *workgroup* name, not its *computer* name — they're different things.

4. **Click OK to close the open windows and, when asked, click the Restart Now button to restart your PC.**

   Repeat these steps for any other Windows XP Home PCs on your network, making sure that the name WORKGROUP appears in each Workgroup box.

Connecting Wirelessly

Setting up your own wireless home network takes two steps:

1. Set up the wireless router or wireless access point to start broadcasting and receiving information to and from your PCs.

2. Set up Windows 7 on each PC to receive the signal and send information back, as well.

This section covers both of those daunting tasks.

Setting up a wireless router or access point

Wireless connections bring a convenience felt by every cell phone owner. But with computers, a wireless connection is more complicated to set up than a wired connection. You're basically setting up a radio transmitter that broadcasts to little radios attached to your PCs. You need to worry about signal strength, finding the right signal, and even entering passwords to keep outsiders from listening in.

Wireless transmitters, known as *wireless access points* (WAPs), come built into most routers today. Unfortunately, different brands of wireless equipment come with different setup software, so there's no way I can provide step-by-step instructions for setting up your particular router.

However, the setup software on every model of router requires you to set up these three things:

✔ **Network name (SSID):** Enter a short, easy-to-remember name here to identify your particular wireless network. Later, when connecting to the wireless network with your computer, you'll select this same name to avoid accidentally connecting with your neighbor's wireless network.

✔ **Infrastructure:** Choose Infrastructure instead of the alternative, Ad Hoc.

✔ **Security:** This option encrypts your data as it flies through the air. Most routers offer at least three types of security: WEP is barely better than no password, WPA is much better, and WPA2 is better still. Look to see which of those three acronyms your PC's wireless network adapter supports, and choose the best of the three. (Your router's security can only be as good as your wireless network adapter's security, or they can't communicate.)

Many routers include an installation program to help you change these settings; other routers contain built-in software that you access with Windows' own Web browser.

As you enter settings for each of the three settings, write them on a piece of paper: You must enter these same three settings when setting up your PC's wireless connection, a job tackled in the next section. You'll also need to pass out that information to any houseguests who want to check their e-mail on their laptops.

Setting up Windows 7 to connect to a wireless network

After you've set up your router or wireless access point to broadcast your network, you must tell Windows 7 how to receive it.

To connect to a wireless network, either your own or one in a public place, follow these steps:

1. **Turn on your wireless adapter, if necessary.**

   Many laptops turn off their wireless adapters to save power. To turn it on, open the Windows Mobility Center by holding down the   key and pressing X, and click the Turn Wireless On button. Not listed? Then you need to pull out your laptop's manual, unfortunately.

   If your taskbar contains a wireless network icon (shown in the margin), click it to jump to the description in Step 3. That icon is a handy way to connect wirelessly at coffee shops, airports, and hotels.

2. **Open the Start menu, choose Control Panel, choose Network and Internet, and click Network and Sharing Center.**

   The Network and Sharing Center window appears, as shown in Figure 14-4.

3. **Choose Connect to a Network.**

   A window appears in your desktop's bottom-right corner, listing all the wireless networks your PC finds within range, as shown in Figure 14-5. Don't be surprised to see several networks listed, as your neighbors are probably seeing your network listed, as well.

   When you hover your mouse pointer over a network's name, Windows 7 sums up the connection four ways, all shown in Figure 14-5:

   - **Name:** This is the network's name, also known as its *SSID* (Service Set Identifier). Because wireless networks overlap, network names let you connect to the specific network you want. Choose the SSID name you gave your wireless router when you set it up, for example, or select the name of the wireless network at the coffee shop or hotel.

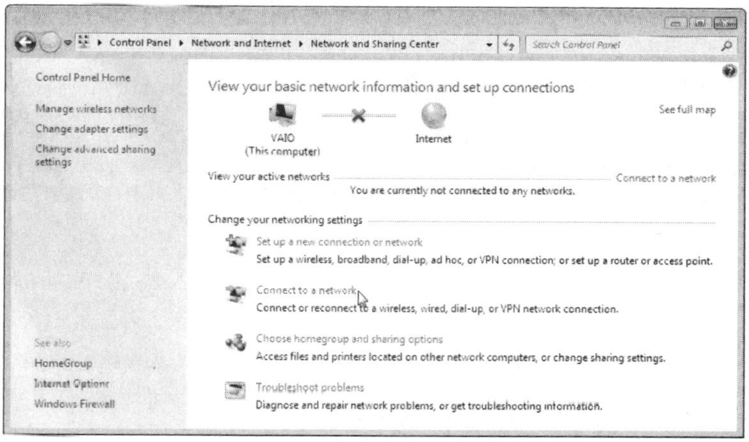

Figure 14-4:
A starting point for diagnosing network problems, the Network and Sharing Center lets you tweak your network's settings.

- **Signal Strength:** These green vertical bars work much like a cell phone's signal strength meter: More bars means a stronger connection that's labeled as Excellent. Connecting to networks with two bars or less will be frustratingly sporadic, and labeled Poor.

- **Security Type:** Networks listed as Unsecured Network don't require a password. That means you can hop aboard and start surfing the Internet for free — even if you don't know who owns the network. However, the lack of a password means that other people can eavesdrop. Unsecured networks work fine for quick Internet access, but they aren't safe for online shopping. A security protected network, by contrast, is safer, as the network's password filters out all but the most dedicated snoops.

- **Radio Type:** This lists the speed of the signal. 802.11g is fast, 802.11n is faster still, and 802.11b is slow.

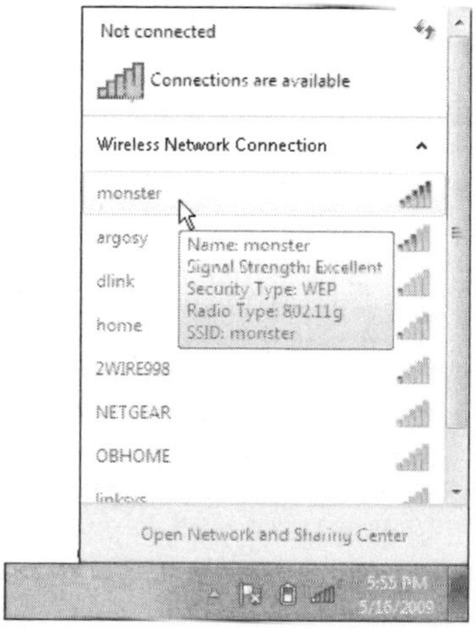

Figure 14-5:
Windows lists every wireless network within range.

4. **Connect to the desired network by clicking its name and clicking Connect.**

   If you spot your network's name, click it, and then click the Connect button that appears.

   If you're connecting to an *unsecured network* — a network that doesn't require a password — you're done. Windows 7 warns you about connecting to an unsecured network, but a click of the Connect button lets you connect anyway. (Don't do any shopping or banking on an unsecured connection.)

   If you select the adjacent Connect Automatically check box before clicking the Connect button, Windows automatically connects to that network whenever it's in range, sparing you the process of manually connecting each time.

   Clicking the two blue arrows in the upper-right corner, shown in Figure 14-5, tells Windows to search again for available networks — a handy trick when you've moved to a spot that may offer better reception.

   If you *don't* spot your desired network's name, jump ahead to Step 6.

5. **Enter a password, if needed.**

   When you try to connect to a security-enabled wireless connection, Windows 7 asks you to enter a "network security key" or "passphrase" — technospeak for "password." Here's where you type the password you entered into your router when setting up your wireless network.

   If you're connecting to somebody *else's* password-protected wireless network, pull out your credit card. You need to buy some connection time from the people behind the counter.

   Don't see your wireless network's name? Then move to the next step.

6. **Connect to an unlisted network.**

   If Windows 7 doesn't list your wireless network's name, two culprits may be involved:

   • **Low signal strength.** Like radio stations and cell phones, wireless networks are cursed with a limited range. Wireless signals travel several hundred feet through open air, but walls, floors, and ceilings severely limit their oomph. Try moving your computer closer to the wireless router or access point. (Or just move to a different spot in the coffee shop.) Keep moving closer and clicking the Refresh button (shown in margin) until your network appears.

   • **It's hiding.** For security reasons, some wireless networks don't broadcast their names, so Windows lists an invisible networks' name as Other Network. To connect to an unnamed network, you must know the network's *real* name and type in that name before connecting. If you think that's your problem, move to the next step.

7. **Click a wireless network listed as Other Network.**

When asked, enter the network's name (SSID) and, if required, its password, described in Step 5. Once Windows 7 knows the network's real name and password, Windows 7 will connect. Without that name or password, however, you're locked out.

8. **Change to a home or work network, if needed.**

When you connect wirelessly, Windows 7 sometimes assumes you're connecting to a public network, so it adds an extra layer of security. That security makes it more difficult to share files, which is usually why you're setting up a home network in the first place.

Fix that by switching to a home or work network: Call up the Network and Sharing Center (as described in Step 2) and then click the words Public Network — if you spot it in the View Your Active Networks section — to change the setting. When the Set Network Location window appears, choose Home Network or Work Network, depending on your location.

Choose Home or Work *only* when connecting to a wireless connection within your home or office. Choose Public for all others to add extra security.

After you've connected all your PCs, every networked PC should be able to connect to the Internet. However, you still need to tell your Windows 7 PCs to share their files with your other PCs. To do that, create a Homegroup, covered in the next section.

If you're still having problems connecting, try the following tips:

✔ When Windows 7 says that it can't connect to your wireless network, it offers to bring up the Network troubleshooter. The Network troubleshooter mulls over the problem and then says something about the signal being weak. It's really telling you this: Move your PC closer to the wireless transmitter.

✔ If you can't connect to the network you want, try connecting to one of the unsecured networks, instead. Unsecured networks work fine for casual browsing on the Internet.

✔ Windows can remember the name and password of networks you've successfully connected with before, sparing you the chore of reentering all the information. Your PC can then connect automatically whenever you're within range.

✔ Cordless phones and microwave ovens, oddly enough, interfere with wireless networks. Try to keep your cordless phone out of the same room as your wireless PC, and don't heat up that sandwich when browsing the Internet.

✔ If networks leave you wringing your hands, you need a book dealing more specifically with networks. Check out my other book, *Upgrading & Fixing PCs For Dummies.*

Setting Up a Homegroup

Networks can be notoriously difficult to set up. To solve the problem of cranky networks and their even crankier owners, Microsoft added *Homegroups* to Windows 7. A new way of networking, Homegroups offer a simple way to let every PC in the house share files, including music, photos, and movies, and even the household or office printer.

The catch? Homegroups only work with other Windows 7 PCs, unfortunately. But even if you have only one Windows 7 PC in your home network, set up its Homegroup anyway to gain these two big benefits:

- ✔ Homegroups let every user account on that Windows 7 PC share their files more quickly and easily with each other — much more easily than in Windows Vista or Windows XP.

- ✔ Creating a Homegroup lets your PC share files with older PCs still running Windows Vista or Windows XP and their clunkier file sharing methods.

Here's how to set up a new Homegroup on a Windows 7 PC, as well as how to join an existing Homegroup:

1. **Click the Library icon on your taskbar to launch your Libraries window.**

   Actually, you can open any folder on your PC. Or just click the Start button and choose Computer. Either way, you'll spot the word HomeGroup in the Navigation Pane along the open folder's left side.

2. **Right-click the Homegroup link in the Navigation Pane and click the Create a Homegroup button.**

   If you see a Join Now button, click it, instead: Somebody has already created a Homegroup on your network. After clicking the Join Now button, move to the next step.

   If you don't spot the words Create a HomeGroup on the right-click menu, your Homegroup is already set up; choose Change HomeGroup Settings, instead, and move to the next step.

3. **Decide what items to share on your Homegroup, and click Next or Save Changes.**

   Shown in Figure 14-6, the window lets you select the items you want to share with your Homegroup brethren. (If you clicked Change HomeGroup Settings in the previous step, your window will look slightly different than this one.)

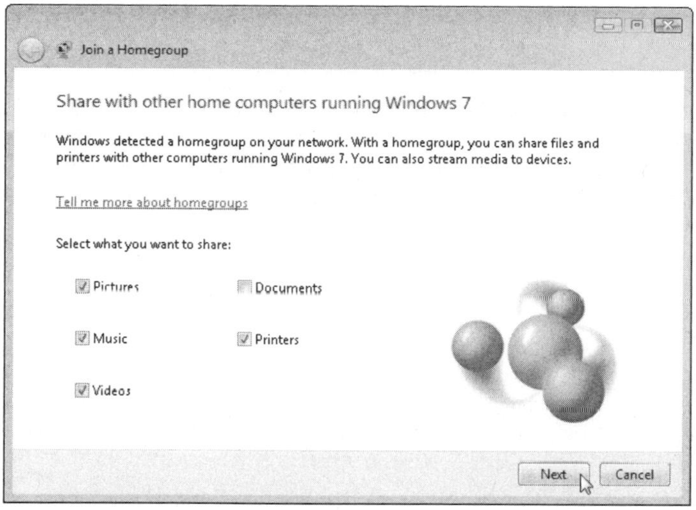

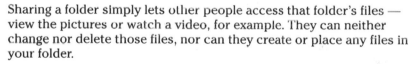

Figure 14-6:
Select or
deselect
check boxes
next to any
items you
don't want
shared.

Windows 7 normally shares your Pictures, Music, and Videos libraries, as well as any printer that's attached to any PC on your Homegroup. Most people leave their Documents library unshared because it usually contains more private items.

Select an item's check box to share it; remove the check mark to stop sharing.

Sharing a folder simply lets other people access that folder's files — view the pictures or watch a video, for example. They can neither change nor delete those files, nor can they create or place any files in your folder.

4. **Process the password and click Finish.**

For this step, how you process the password depends on whether you're creating or joining a Homegroup:

- **Creating a Homegroup:** Windows 7 spits out a customized password, shown in Figure 14-7. The password contains a mixture of numbers and letters, both upper- and lowercase, so write it down carefully. You need to type it into each Windows 7 PC within your Homegroup.

- **Joining a Homegroup:** Type in the password given out by the PC that created the Homegroup. (To see the password, head to the PC that created the Homegroup, right-click the word Homegroup in the Navigation Pane, and choose View HomeGroup Password.)

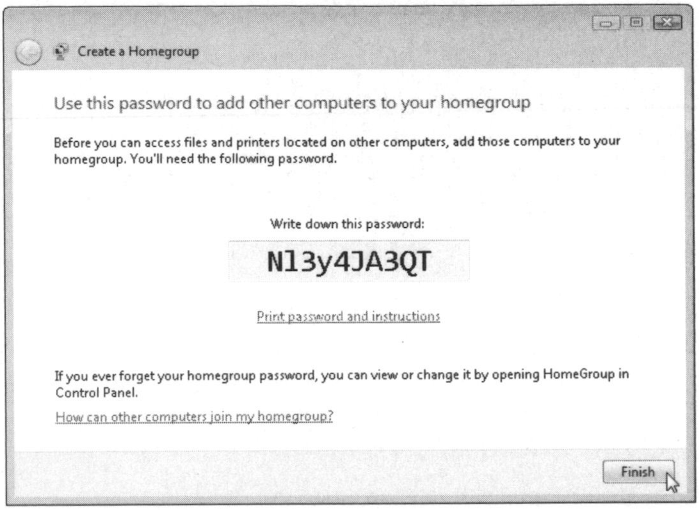

Figure 14-7:
Carefully
write
down the
password
and then
type it into
the other
Windows 7
PCs in your
Homegroup.

Create a Homegroup

Use this password to add other computers to your homegroup

Before you can access files and printers located on other computers, add those computers to your homegroup. You'll need the following password.

Write down this password:

N13y4JA3QT

Print password and instructions

If you ever forget your homegroup password, you can view or change it by opening HomeGroup in Control Panel.

How can other computers join my homegroup?

Finish

When you're through with these steps, you've created or joined a Homegroup that's accessible from the Navigation Pane of every Windows 7 PC on your network. You've also set up your PC to allow its Music, Photos, and Videos libraries to be shared, something I describe in the next section.

- ✔ When you create or join a Homegroup, you're choosing what libraries to share only from your *own* account. If other account holders on that PC also want to share their libraries, they should do this: Open any folder, right-click Homegroup in the Navigation Pane, and choose Change HomeGroup Settings. There, they can add check marks to the items they want to share and then click Save Changes.

- ✔ Changed your mind about what to share on your PC? Follow the steps in the preceding paragraph to change the check boxes next to your own folders.

- ✔ Forgot the all-important Homegroup password? It's available on any PC on the Homegroup: Open any folder, right-click the word Homegroup in the Navigation Pane, and then choose View the HomeGroup Password.

- ✔ PCs running Windows 7 Starter Edition can't create a Homegroup, but they can join one. (That version of Windows might be sold on some *net-books,* which are tiny, inexpensive laptops.)

Sharing Files within a Homegroup

Windows 7 does an admirable job of isolating user accounts, so no one can mess with anybody else's files or settings. But what if you *want* to step outside of your sandbox and share files with somebody else's account? After all, vacation photos aren't much good unless you can share them.

The answer comes with Windows 7's new *Homegroup* feature. After one account holder on your PC has created a Homegroup, described in the previous section, everybody can share their music, videos, photos, and documents with everybody else on the PC, as well as everyone on the network.

This section explains how to share certain items, *not* share other items, and how to access files shared by other users on your PC and network.

Choosing what items to share in a Homegroup

Like the best types of mailing lists, Homegroups are *opt-in,* meaning Windows 7 won't share your items until you decide you *want* to share them, and you must specify exactly *which* items you want to share. Here's how to choose the items you want to add to your Homegroup, making them available to others:

1. **Open any folder, right-click the word Homegroup in the Navigation Pane, and choose Change HomeGroup Settings from the pop-up menu.**

   A window appears, similar to the one shown earlier in Figure 14-6, listing your four main libraries: Pictures, Documents, Music, and Videos.

2. **Select the check boxes beside the libraries you want to share and then click Save Changes.**

   Most people choose to share everything but their Documents library, which usually contains more sensitive information than the others. The Printers check box should stay selected, if it's listed, in case any networked Windows 7 PCs want to print to it later.

A short while after you click Save Changes, everybody else on your PC may access the libraries you've chosen to share, as well as everything inside those libraries. (That's why most people share only their Music, Pictures, and Videos libraries, and leave their Documents folder private.)

Can other people mess up my shared files?

When you share libraries on Homegroups, you want the benefits of sharing: You want your family to marvel over your photos of Costa Rican tree frogs, for example. But you don't want anybody to delete or mess up your original files. Will sharing your files allow people to delete them or draw moustaches on your photos?

No. That's because Homegroups show the contents of a *library* (which I cover in Chapter 4). And libraries actually show the contents of at least *two* folders: Your own folder, and one that's called *Public*. The library displays the contents of both folders in one window, but it treats the two folders very differently. Here's the scoop:

✔ **Your own folder:** When you place a file or folder into one of your libraries, Windows automatically places the item in your *own* folder. If you've chosen to share that folder through the Homegroup, other people can *see* that folder's files, *view* the photos, *hear* the music, or *watch* the videos. They can

even make copies of them to do with as they please. But they can't change or delete any of your *original* files, thankfully.

✔ **Public:** In addition to displaying the contents of your folder, libraries display the contents of a second folder, known as the Public folder. The Public folder remains fair game for anybody and everybody. Anything you place inside the Public folder can be changed or deleted by anybody else. But since you made the decision to put it in the Public folder rather than in your own folder, you want that to happen: You *want* somebody to offer advice to your term paper, for example, or to touch up your photos and burn them to a DVD.

So, when you want to collaborate with others on a file, place that item in your library's Public folder, a task I explain in the section on letting others change your shared files in Chapter 13.

Things you choose to share can't be deleted or changed by others unless you specifically want those things to be changed. And for the full story on letting people change your files, drop by the sidebar "Can other people mess up my shared files?"

Accessing what others have shared

To see the shared libraries of other people on your PC and network, click the word Homegroup, found in the Navigation Pane of every folder. The right side of the window, shown in Figure 14-8, promptly lists the names and androgynous icons of every account holder who's chosen to share their files.

You may also spot names of account holders on *networked* Windows 7 PCs — PCs connected to your PC either wirelessly or with cables — who've chosen to share their libraries.

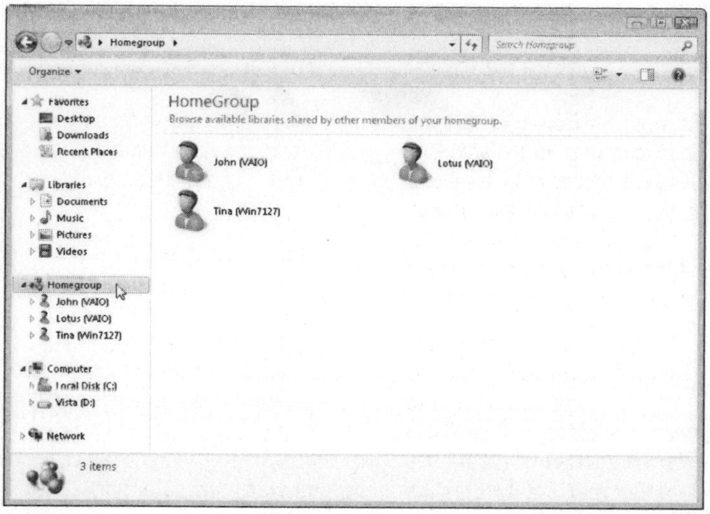

Figure 14-8: Click the word Homegroup to see any account holders who've shared their libraries.

To browse the libraries shared by another person within the Homegroup, double-click that person's name from the Homegroup window. The window promptly displays that person's shared libraries, as shown in Figure 14-9, ready to be browsed as if they were your own.

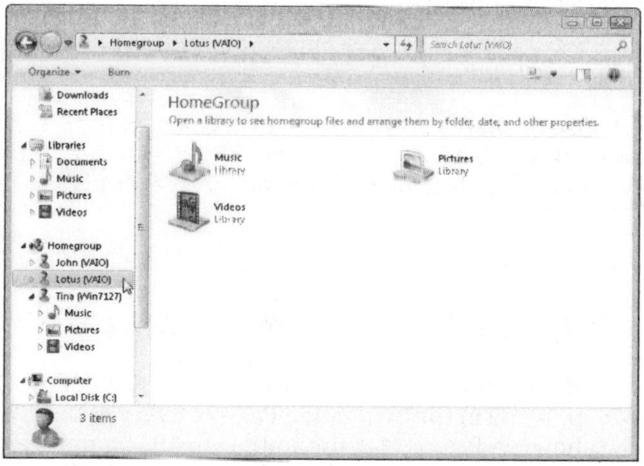

Figure 14-9: Click a person's name to see her shared libraries.

You can do more than browse those libraries, as described here:

- **Opening:** To open a file on a shared library, double-click its icon, just as you would any other file. The appropriate program opens it. If you see an error message, the sharing person created the file using a program you don't own. Your solution? Buy or download the program from the Internet or ask the person to save the file in a format that one of your programs can open.

- **Copying:** To copy a file from one person's Homegroup, drag it into your own library: Point at the file you want and, while holding down the mouse button, point at your own library. Let go of the mouse button, and Windows 7 copies the file into your library. Alternatively, select the file and press Ctrl+C to copy it; then go into the folder where you want to put the copied file and press Ctrl+V to paste it.

- **Deleting or changing:** You can delete or change some, but not all, of the items in another person's Homegroup. I explain why in the sidebar "Can other people mess up my shared files?"

Homegroups work only with Windows 7 PCs, unfortunately. Holdouts still clinging to Windows Vista or Windows XP can still share files and folders through a network by copying them into their Public or Shared Documents folders.

Connecting to and Sharing Files with Windows XP and Windows Vista PCs

Setting up a Homegroup makes it easy for people running Windows 7 to share files, folders, and even printers. Different account holders on the same PC can share files by clicking Homegroup in the Navigation Pane and choosing another account holder's name to see his or her shared files.

But you still have a little work to do before you can share files with any Windows XP or Windows Vista PCs on your network:

1. First, you need to tell your Windows 7 PCs to show themselves to those older PCs and to begin sharing their files.

2. Second, you need to know where to find those files from your Windows XP and Vista PCs.

3. Finally, you need to know how to find the shared folders living on your Windows XP and Vista PCs.

The next three sections tackle each of those chores in order.

Letting older PCs notice your Windows 7 PCs

Windows 7 PCs rely on their own Homegroup community. Because it's protected by a password, the rules are relaxed, and it's easy for Windows 7 PCs to share information.

In fact, PCs running Windows XP or Vista won't even be able to notice Windows 7 PCs on the network until you follow these steps:

Be sure to create a Homegroup on your Windows 7 PC, described in the previous section, before following these steps.

1. **Create a working network on your Windows XP and Windows Vista PCs.**

   I describe how to create networks on Windows XP and Windows Vista in my books *Windows XP For Dummies* and *Windows Vista For Dummies* (both from Wiley Publishing, Inc.).

2. **Join that network with your Windows 7 PCs, as I describe earlier in this chapter.**

   Windows 7 PCs can join a wired or wireless network. Once they've joined, you must tell your Windows 7 PCs to start sharing their files with the PCs running older versions of Windows.

3. **On your Windows 7 PC, click the Start button, choose Control Panel, choose Network and Internet, and choose Network and Sharing Center.**

   The Network and Sharing Center appears, shown earlier in Figure 14-4.

   A quick way to open the Network and Sharing Center is to click one of your taskbar's network adapter icons, shown in the margin, and choose Open Network and Sharing Center from the pop-up menu.

4. **Click the Change Advanced Sharing Settings link in the Network and Sharing Center's left pane.**

   The Advanced Sharing Settings window appears, shown in Figure 14-10, offering a plethora of options.

5. **Change these items in the Advanced Sharing Settings window:**

   The first three options will probably already be turned on, but check them anyway.

   • **Network Discovery:** Turn on this setting. The computer equivalent of letting people tap other folks on the shoulder, this option lets your Windows 7 PC and your networked PCs find each other on the network.

- **File and Printer Sharing:** Turn on file and printer sharing. Now that the PCs have found each other by name, this setting lets them see each other's files and printer, as well.

- **Public Folder Sharing:** Turn on sharing to let anyone with network access read and write files in the Public folders.

- **Password Protected Sharing:** The clincher, this should be turned *off,* or people on Windows XP and Vista PCs will face a name/password prompt when they want access to your Public folders.

If you own an Xbox 360 game machine, feel free to turn on Media Streaming, as well. That lets your Xbox access music, pictures, and videos stored on your Windows 7 PC.

6. **Click Save Changes.**

Windows 7 saves your new settings, allowing other PCs on your network to share the files in the Public folders of your Windows 7 PCs.

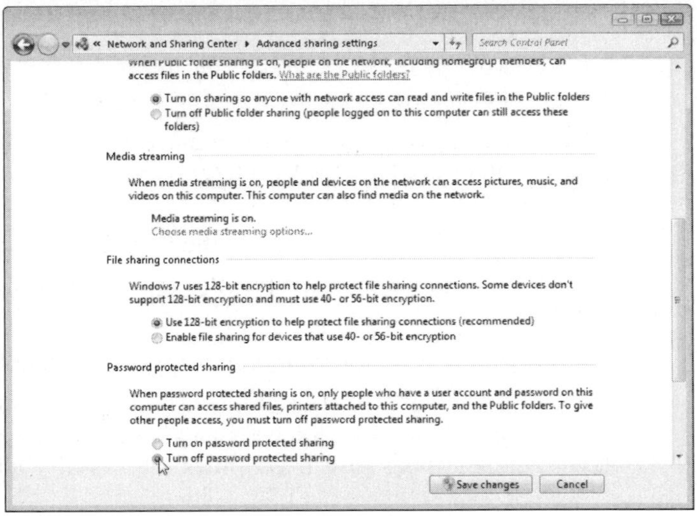

Figure 14-10:
Tell your
Windows 7
PC to begin
sharing its
files with
older PCs.

Be sure to change only the settings on the Home or Work (Current Profile) section of the Advanced Sharing Settings window. The lower portion of that window, called Public, dictates how your PC should behave when connected to *Public* networks. You don't want to share your laptop's files with everybody in the coffee shop.

Accessing a Windows 7 PC's shared files from an older PC

After you've followed the steps in the previous section, PCs running Windows XP and Vista can see and access files placed in the any of the Public folders on Windows 7 PCs. However, those PCs need to know exactly where to look, and you need to make sure you've placed your file in a place they can spot.

Here's how to accomplish both of those tasks:

1. **On your Windows 7 PC, place the file you want to share inside one of your Public folders.**

   Your libraries each show the contents of at least two folders: your own folder and a public folder. Any items you want to share with Windows XP or Vista PCs must go in the Public folder.

   I explain how to put items in your Public folder in Chapter 13, in the section on letting others change your shared files, but here's a synopsis:

   Double-click the word Libraries in your Navigation Pane to see your four folders: Documents, Music, Pictures, and Videos.

   Double-click the library where you want to place a shared file. Two folders will appear. If you double-click Music, for example, you'll see My Music and Public Music.

   Place the music files you want to share in the Public Music folder.

2. **On your Windows XP or Windows Vista PC, find the Windows 7 PC's Public folder.**

   The process differs depending on your Windows version. Here's the scoop:

   • **Windows Vista:** Click the Start button, and choose Network. The Network window appears, listing all of your networked PCs. Double-click the name of your Windows 7 PC, double-click the Users folder, and you see its Public folder inside.

   • **Windows XP:** Click Start and choose My Networked Places. If you spot your Windows 7 PC listed, double-click its name, double-click the Users folder, and you see its Public folder.

   If your Windows XP PC still can't find the Windows 7 PC, click Start, right-click My Networked Places, and choose Search For Computers. Click the Search button without entering anything in the Search box. Windows XP lists all your networked PCs. Double-click the name of your Windows 7 PC, and you see the coveted Public folder waiting inside.

3. **From your Windows XP or Windows Vista PC, open the Public folder and open the folder containing the shared file or files.**

   If you double-click the Public folder, you see a list of *all* the Public folders on that Windows 7 PC. Double-click the one you want, be it Music, Video, Pictures, or Documents. Inside, you find the shared files. You can open them from there with a double-click, or you can copy them to your own PC.

Accessing a Windows XP or Vista PC's shared files from your Windows 7 PC

This section walks you through placing items you want to share in the proper folders on the Windows XP and Windows Vista PCs and then fetching them from the Windows 7 PC. Here's what to do:

1. **On your Windows XP or Vista PC, place the files you want to share in your PC's shared folder.**

   The shared folder lives in different places on Windows XP and Vista, and goes by two different names.

   - **Windows XP:** Click Start and open My Computer. The shared folder is called *Shared Documents*.

   - **Windows Vista:** Click Start and open Computer. The shared folder lives in the folder's Favorite Links area along the folder's left edge. The shared folder is called *Public*.

2. **On your Windows 7 PC, double-click the networked PC holding those files.**

   Open any folder — a click on the taskbar's Library folder will do — and look at the Network listing on the Navigation Pane along the folder's left edge. The Network area lists all your networked PCs, including any Windows XP or Windows Vista PCs.

3. **Click the name of the Windows XP or Vista PC with your files.**

   The folder's right side shows that PC's shared folders. The shared folder on Windows XP is called SharedDocs; Vista's shared folder is called Public, as shown in Figure 14-11.

4. **Double-click the shared folder to see the shared files inside.**

   Double-click the file you're after, and you can edit it from its spot on the other PC. Or, feel free to copy the file to your own PC.

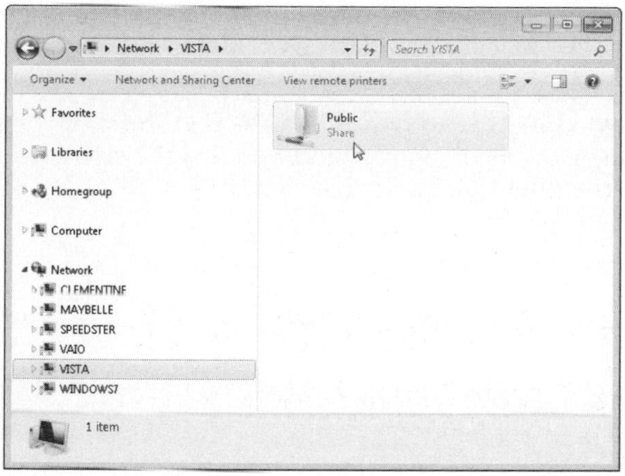

Figure 14-11:
Click the
networked
Windows
XP or
Windows
Vista PC's
name to see
its shared
folder.

Sharing a Printer on the Network

Windows 7 brings a welcome new ease to sharing a printer with other PCs. Many households or offices have several computers but only one printer. (I explain how to install a printer in Chapter 11.) Naturally, most people want to share that one printer with the other PCs.

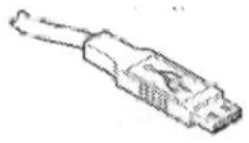

If you've turned on the Homegroups, covered earlier in this chapter, Windows 7 makes sharing a printer extraordinarily easy. Once you plug a USB printer — the kind with the connector shown in the margin — into one of your Windows 7 PCs, you're set: Windows 7 automatically recognizes the newly plugged-in printer as soon as it's turned on.

Plus, your Windows 7 PC quickly spreads the news to all your networked Windows PCs. Within minutes, that printer's name and icon appear on all of those PCs, and in all their programs' print menus.

To make sure, here's how to see that printer on your other networked Windows PCs:

 ✔ **Windows 7:** Click the Start button and choose Devices and Printers. The networked printer appears in the Printers and Faxes section.

 ✔ **Windows Vista:** Click the Start button, choose Control Panel, and open the Hardware and Sound category. Choose Printers to see the printer's icon.

 ✔ **Windows XP:** Click the Start button, choose Control Panel, and open the Printers and Hardware category. Choose Printers and Faxes to see the new printer's icon.

Deleting files from a networked PC

Normally, anything you delete on your own PC ends up in your Recycle Bin, giving you a last chance at retrieval. That's not true when you're working on a file within a *networked* PC's folder.

When you delete a folder on a networked PC's folder, the file is gone for good — it doesn't hop into the Recycle Bin of your own PC *or* the networked PC. Beware.

What's not simple, though, is when you want to share a printer that's plugged into a Windows XP or Windows Vista PC on your network. Should you be in that situation, here's how to access it:

1. **Share the printer with your network.**

   I explain how to share printers attached to Windows XP in my book *Windows XP For Dummies*.

   To share a printer attached to a Windows Vista PC, click the Start menu, choose Control Panel, select the Hardware and Sound category, and choose Printers. Right-click the printer's icon and choose Sharing. Select the Share This Printer option and click OK.

2. **On your Windows 7 PC, click the Start button and choose Devices and Printers.**

   The Devices and Printers window appears, showing the gadgets plugged into your PC. (Ignore the Microsoft XPS Document Writer because it's not a real printer.)

   Add a printer

3. **Click the Add a Printer button and choose Add a Network, Wireless or Bluetooth Printer. Select your networked printer, then click Next.**

   Your PC glances around the network for the other PCs' shared printer. If your PC finds the printer, it lists the printer's name. Click its name and click Next to install it, letting the printer install its driver if necessary. You're finished with these steps, but print a test page, if asked, to make sure all is well.

   If your PC *doesn't* find the printer, however, move to the next step.

4. **Choose The Printer That I Want Isn't Listed, and then click Browse to go to the shared printer.**

   Clicking the Browse button fetches a list of your networked PCs. Double-click the name of the PC with the attached printer, and Windows 7 lists the printer's name.

5. **Double-click the shared printer's icon and click Next.**

   Windows 7 finally connects to your networked printer. You may also need to install that printer's software on your PC before it can print to the networked printer.

Troubleshooting a Network

Setting up a network is the hardest part of networking. After the computers recognize each other (and connect to the Internet, either on their own or through the network), the network usually runs fine. But when it doesn't, here are some things to try:

✔ Make sure that each PC on the network has the same workgroup name. Open the Start menu, right-click Computer, and choose Properties. Choose Change Settings, click the Change button, and make sure that the name WORKGROUP appears in each PC's Workgroup box.

✔ Turn off every computer (using the Start menu's Shut Down option, of course), the router, and the broadband modem (if you have one). Check their cables to make sure that everything's connected. Turn on the modem, wait a minute, turn on the router, wait another minute, and then begin turning on the computers.

✔ Right-click the network icon in your taskbar, and choose Troubleshoot Problems. The Windows troubleshooters become a little better with each new release, and the Windows 7 troubleshooters are the best yet.

Can I get in trouble for looking into the wrong networked computer?

People usually *tell* you where to find files and things on your computers attached to the network. But if nobody's dropped you a hint, feel free to grab a torch and go spelunking on your own by browsing the Network area in a folder's Navigation Pane. If you're worried about getting into trouble, the rule is simple: Windows 7 rarely lets you peek into networked areas where you're not supposed to be.

In fact, Windows 7 is so security conscious that it often keeps you from seeing things that you *should* be able to see. (That's when you call on the office administrator or the computer's owner and ask for help.) If you try to peek inside a forbidden computer, you simply see an access denied message. No embarrassing sirens or harm done.

If you find yourself in a folder where you obviously don't belong — for example, the folder of employee evaluations on your supervisor's computer — quietly bring it to the administrator's attention.

Part V
Music, Movies, Memories (And Photos, Too)

The 5th Wave   By Rich Tennant

"A brief announcement class — An open faced peanut butter sandwich is not an appropriate replacement for a missing mousepad."

In this part . . .

*U*p until now, the book has covered the boring-but-necessary stuff: adjusting your computer so that you can get your work done. This part of the book lets you turn your computer into an entertainment center:

- ✔ Watch DVDs on your PC or laptop.

- ✔ Create greatest hits CDs for your car stereo.

- ✔ Organize a digital photo album from your digital camera.

- ✔ Edit camcorder videos into something people *want* to watch.

- ✔ Create DVDs to display your edited movies or photo slide shows.

When you're ready to play for a while, flip to this part of the book for a helping hand.

Chapter 15

Playing and Copying Music in Media Player

*W*indows 7's Media Player 12 is a big bundle of buttons that reveals how much money you've spent on your computer. On expensive computers, Media Player rumbles like a home theater. On cheap ones, it sounds like a cell phone's ring tone.

Media Player plays CDs, DVDs, MP3s, and videos; organizes them all into a tidy library; and can copy and burn your CDs. But because Media Player still won't work with either Apple's iTunes or Microsoft's own Zune, most folks stick with their music player's own software, leaving Media Player unclicked.

If you're curious about what Media Player can do, this chapter explains how to do those things the player can do well.

This chapter's last section introduces Windows Media *Center,* a completely different program than Windows Media Player. Windows Media Center lets you watch and record live TV shows on your PC — provided your PC has the right equipment.

Running Media Player for the first time

The first time you open Windows 7's Media Player, an opening screen asks how to deal with Media Player's privacy, storage, music store, and other settings:

✔ **Recommended Settings:** Designed for the impatient, this option loads Media Player with Microsoft's chosen settings in place. Media Player sets itself up as the default player for all your music and video (robbing iTunes of that job, if you currently rely on iTunes or another media player). It sweeps the Internet to update your songs' title information, and it tells Microsoft what you're listening to and watching. Choose Express if you're in a hurry; you can always customize the settings some other time.

✔ **Custom Settings:** Aimed at the fiddlers and privacy conscious, this choice lets you fine-tune Media Player's behavior. A series of screens lets you choose the types of music and video Media Player can play and how much of your listening habits should be sent to Microsoft. Choose this option only if you have time to wade through several minutes of boring option screens.

If you later want to customize any Media Player settings — either those chosen for you in Express setup or the ones you've chosen in Custom setup — click the Organize button and choose Options.

Stocking Media Player's Library

When you begin using Media Player, the program automatically sorts through your libraries' stash of digital music, pictures, videos, and recorded TV shows, automatically cataloging everything into Media Player's *own* library. But if you've noticed that some of your PC's media is missing from Media Player's library, you can tell Media Player where to find those missing items by following these steps:

 You can load Media Player by clicking its icon in the taskbar.

> Organize ▾

1. **Click the Organize button and choose Manage Libraries from the drop-down menu to reveal a pop-out menu.**

   The pop-out menu lists the four types of media that Media Player can handle: Music, Videos, Pictures, and Recorded TV.

2. **From the pop-out menu, click the name of the library that's missing files.**

   A window appears, shown in Figure 15-1, listing the folders monitored by your chosen library. For example, the Music library normally monitors the contents of your My Music folder and the Public Music folder.

   But if you're storing items elsewhere — perhaps on a portable hard drive — here's your chance to give the player directions to that other media stash.

Music Library Locations

Change how this library gathers its contents

When you include a folder in a library, the files appear in the library, but continue to be stored in their original locations.

Library locations

My Music C:\Users\Andy\Music	Default save location	Add...
Public Music C:\Users\Public\Music		Remove

Learn more about libraries

OK   Cancel

3. **Click the Add button, select the folder with your files, click the Include Folder button, and click OK.**

   Clicking the Add button brings the Include Folder window to the screen. Navigate to the folder you'd like to add — the folder on your portable hard drive, for example — and click the Include Folder button. Media Player immediately begins monitoring that folder, adding its music to its library.

   To add music from even more folders or drives — perhaps a folder on another networked Windows 7 PC or a flash drive — repeat these steps until you've added all the places Media Player should search for media.

   To stop Media Player from monitoring a folder, follow these steps, but in Step 3, click the folder you no longer want monitored, and click the Remove button shown in Figure 15-1.

When you run Media Player, the program shows the media it has collected (shown in Figure 15-2), and it continues to stock its library in the following ways:

✔ **Monitoring your libraries:** Media Player constantly monitors your Music, Pictures, and Videos libraries, as well as any other locations you've added. Media Player automatically updates *its* library whenever you add or remove files from *your* libraries. (You can change what libraries and folders Windows 7 monitors by following the three preceding steps.)

✔ **Monitoring the Public folder:** Media Player automatically catalogs anything placed into your PC's Public folder by another account holder on your PC, or even by somebody on a networked PC.

Windows Media Player

Figure 15-2:
Click an
item from
the left to
see its con-
tents on the
right.

✔ **Adding played items:** Anytime you play a music file on your PC or the
Internet, Windows 7 adds the song or its Internet location to its library
so that you can find it to play again later. Unless specifically told to,
Windows 7 *doesn't* add played items that live on networked PCs, USB
flash drives, or memory cards.

✔ **Ripped music from CD:** When you insert a music CD into your CD drive,
Windows 7 offers to *rip* it. That's computereze for copying the CD's
music to your PC, a task described in the "Ripping (Copying) CDs to
Your PC" section, later in this chapter. Any ripped music automatically
appears in your Media Player Library. (Media Player won't copy DVD
movies to your library, unfortunately.)

✔ **Downloaded music and video from online stores:** Media Player lets you
shop from a variety of online stores (but not iTunes). When you buy a
song, Media Player automatically stocks its library with your latest
purchase.

Feel free to repeat the steps in this section to search for files whenever you
want; Media Player ignores the ones it has already cataloged and adds any
new ones.

You'll notice a few new surprises in Media Player 12 in the form of *codecs* —
the way different file formats store their music and movies. Media Player 12
recognizes more types of sound and video than before.

Unlike Media Player 11, Media Player 12 no longer offers an advanced editor
for changing a song's *tags,* which are described in the sidebar. Instead, the
player edits them for you automatically from an online database.

What are a song's tags?

Inside every music file lives a small form called a *tag* that contains the song's title, artist, album, and other related information. When deciding how to sort, display, and categorize your music, Windows Media Player reads those tags — *not* the songs' filenames. Most portable music players, including the iPod, also rely on tags.

Tags are so important, in fact, that Media Player visits the Internet, grabs song information, and automatically fills in the tags when it adds files to its library.

Many people don't bother filling out their songs' tags; other people update them meticulously. If your tags are already filled out the way you prefer, stop Media Player from messing with them: Click the Organize button, choose Options,

click the Library tab, and deselect the check box next to Retrieve Additional Information From the Internet. If your tags are a mess, leave that check box selected so that Media Player will clean up the tags for you.

If Media Player makes a mistake, fix the tags yourself: Right-click the song (or, in the case of an album, the selected songs) and choose Find Album Info. When a window appears listing Media Player's guess as to the song or album, choose Edit. A new window appears, where you can fill in the album, artist, genre, tracks, title, contributing artist, and composer. Click Done when you're through tidying up the information.

Browsing Media Player's Libraries

 Unlike Media Player 11, which tried to integrate all its controls in one window, Media Player 12 wears two distinct faces: The Library face and the Now Playing face. You switch between the two parts of the program by clicking the tiny icon shown in the margin.

The Media Player Library window is where the behind-the-scenes action takes place. There, you organize files, create playlists, burn or copy CDs, and choose what to play. The Now Playing window, by contrast, shows what's currently playing by displaying a video or an album cover from your currently playing song. On-screen controls let you adjust the volume, skip between listed songs or videos, pause the action, or even launch multicolored kaleidoscopic visualizations while listening to music.

When first loaded, Media Player displays your Music library, appropriately enough. But Media Player actually holds several libraries, designed to showcase not only your music but photographs, video, and recorded TV shows as well.

All your playable items appear in the Navigation Pane along the window's left, shown in Figure 15-3. The pane's top half shows your own media collection, called simply Library. The bottom half, called Other Libraries, lets you browse the collections of other people using your PC, as well as people sharing their media from networked Windows 7 PCs.

Figure 15-3:
Click the
type of
media
you're
interested
in browsing
from the
Navigation
Pane along
the left.

Media Player organizes your media into these categories:

- ✔ **Playlists:** Like playing albums or songs in a certain order? Click the Save List button atop your list of songs to save it as a playlist that shows up in this category.

- ✔ **Music:** All your digital music appears here. Media Player recognizes most major music formats, including MP3, WMA, WAV, and even 3GP files used by some cell phones. (It finally recognizes non-copy-protected AAC files, sold by iTunes, but it can't recognize popular lossless or uncompressed formats like FLAC, APE, or OGG.)

- ✔ **Videos:** Look here for videos you've saved from a camcorder or digital camera, or for videos you've downloaded from the Internet. Media Library recognizes AVI, MPG, WMV, ASF, DivX, some MOV files, and a few other formats.

- ✔ **Pictures:** Media Player can display photos individually or in a simple slide show, but your Pictures library, described in Chapter 16, handles photos better. (Media Player can't turn photos right-side up, for example, a feat done easily in your Pictures folder.)

- ✔ **Recorded TV:** Recorded television shows appear here — if your PC has the equipment needed to record them. (I describe Windows 7's built-in TV recorder, Media Center, in this chapter's last section.)

- ✔ **Other Media:** Items that Media Player doesn't recognize hide in this area. Chances are, you won't be able to do much with them.

- ✔ **Other Libraries:** Here, you'll find media appearing on other Windows 7 PCs in your Homegroup — a type of network I describe in Chapter 14.

- ✔ **Media Guide:** This opens the doors to Microsoft's online music stores.

Yes, Media Player spies on you

Just like your bank, credit card company, and grocery store club card, Media Player spies on you. Media Player's 6,000-word online Privacy Statement boils down to this: Media Player tells Microsoft every song, file, or movie that you play. Some people find that creepy, but if Microsoft doesn't know what you're playing, Media Player can't connect to the Internet and retrieve applicable artist information and artwork.

If you don't care that Microsoft hums along to your CDs, don't bother reading any further. If you *do* care, choose your surveillance level: Click the Organize button, choose Options, and click the Privacy tab. Here's the rundown on the Privacy tab options that cause the biggest ruckus:

✔ **Display media Information from the Internet:** If this option is selected, Media Player tells Microsoft what CD or DVD you're playing and retrieves doodads to display on your screen: CD covers, song titles, artist names, and similar information.

✔ **Update Music Files by Retrieving Media Info from the Internet:** Microsoft examines your files, and if it recognizes any, it fills in the songs' tags with the correct information. (For more information on tags, see the "What are a song's tags?" sidebar.)

✔ **Send Unique Player ID to Content Providers:** Known in the biz as *data mining,* this option lets other corporations track how you use Media Player. To leave yourself out of their databases, leave this option blank.

✔ **Cookies:** Like several other Windows 7 programs, Media Player tracks your activity with little files called *cookies.* Cookies aren't necessarily bad, as they help Media Player keep track of your preferences.

✔ **History:** Media Player lists the names of your recently played files for your convenience — and the possible guffaws of your co-workers or family. To keep people from seeing the titles of music and videos you've recently played, remove *all* the checkmarks from this section, and click the two buttons called Clear History and Clear Caches.

After you click a category, Media Player's Navigation Pane lets you view the files in several different ways. Click Artist in the Navigation Pane's Music category, for example, and the pane shows the music arranged alphabetically by artists' first names.

Similarly, clicking Genre in the Music category separates songs and albums by different types of music. Instead of just showing a name to click — blues, for example — Media Player arranges your music into piles of covers, just as if you'd sorted your albums or CDs on your living room floor.

To play anything in Media Player, right-click it and choose Play. Or, to play all your music from one artist or genre, right-click the pile and choose Play All.

Controlling Your Now Playing Items

Media Player offers the same basic controls when playing any type of file, be it a song, video, CD, DVD, or photo slide show. Figure 15-4 shows Media Player open to its Now Playing window as it plays an album. The labels in the figure explain each button's function. Or, rest your mouse pointer over an especially mysterious button, and Media Player displays a pop-up explanation.

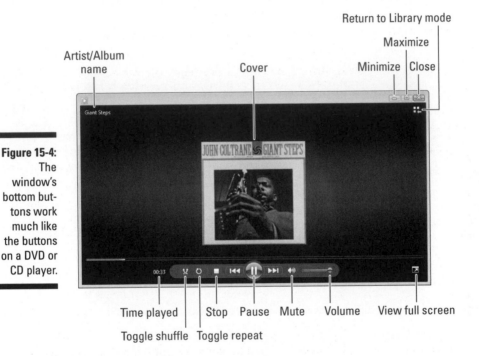

Figure 15-4:
The window's bottom buttons work much like the buttons on a DVD or CD player.

The buttons along the bottom work like those found on any DVD or CD player, letting you play, stop, rewind, fast-forward, and mute the current song or movie. For even more controls, right-click anywhere in the Now Playing window. A menu appears, offering to perform these common tasks:

- ✔ **Show List:** Shows the playlist along the right side, handy for jumping directly to different songs.

- ✔ **Full Screen:** Enlarges the window to fill the screen.

- ✔ **Shuffle:** Plays songs randomly.

- ✔ **Repeat:** Loops the same song.

- ✔ **Visualizations:** Choose between showing the album cover, wavy lines, groovy spirals, dancing waves, or other freaky eye games.

- ✔ **Enhancements:** Opens an equalizer, balance adjuster, playback speed, volume balancer, and other sound options.

- ✔ **Lyrics, Captions or Subtitles:** Display these items, if they're available, which come in handy when watching foreign films or practicing for Karaoke night.

- ✔ **Shop for More Music:** Head to Microsoft's WindowsMedia.com Web site to buy songs or albums from online stores.

- ✔ **Always Show Now Playing on Top:** Keeps the window above your other windows on the desktop.

- ✔ **More Options:** Brings up the Options page, where you can tweak Media Player's habits when ripping CDs, stocking your Media Player Library, and other tasks.

- ✔ **Help with Playback:** Fetches the Help program to deal with head-scratchers.

The Now Playing controls disappear from the screen when you haven't moved the mouse for awhile. To bring them back, move your mouse pointer over the Now Playing window.

To return to the Media Player Library, click the Library toggle icon in the window's top-right corner.

Playing CDs

As long as you insert the CD in the CD drive correctly (usually label-side up), playing a music CD is one of Media Player's easiest tasks. You drop it into your CD drive, and Media Player jumps to the screen to play it, usually identifying the CD and its musicians immediately. In many cases, it even tosses a picture of the cover art on the screen.

The controls along the bottom, shown earlier in 15-4, let you jump from track to track, adjust the volume, and fine-tune your listening experience.

If for some odd reason Media Player doesn't start playing your CD, look at the Library item in Media Player's Navigation Pane, along the left side of the window. You should spot either the CD's name or the words *Unknown Album*. When you spot the listing, click it and then click Media Player's Play button to start listening.

To make Media Player automatically play your music CD when inserted, click the Start menu, choose Default Programs, and choose Change AutoPlay settings. Then, in the Audio CD category, select Play Audio CD Using Windows Media Player from the drop-down list. Click the Save button to save your handiwork.

Press F7 to mute Media Player's sound and pick up that phone call.

Want to copy that CD to your PC? That's called *ripping,* and I cover ripping in the "Ripping (Copying) CDs to Your PC" section, later in this chapter.

Playing DVDs

Media Player plays DVDs as well as CDs, letting your laptop do double-duty as a portable DVD player. Grab your favorite DVD, some headphones, and watch what *you* like during that next long flight.

Although Media Player plays, burns, and copies CDs, it can't copy a DVD's movie to your hard drive, nor can it duplicate a movie DVD. (Remember the somber FBI warning at the beginning of each DVD?)

Those dastardly DVD region codes

If you watch many foreign films, Media Player will eventually send you a nasty error message, saying "Your system is set to DVD region 1. To play this DVD, set your system to region 4." Your own region numbers will vary, depending on your geographic location and your particular DVD.

When you click the error message's OK button, a new window pops up automatically and allows you to type your newly required region into the New Region text box. When you click OK, Media Player finally lets you watch the DVD.

The catch? Your DVD player only lets you switch regions *four* times before refusing to switch anymore — even if you reinstall Windows or install the drive into another PC.

The solution? If you're playing lots of movies from two different regions, consider buying and installing a second DVD drive in your PC so you'll have one for each region. Also, some companies sell software that legally bypasses region coding, letting you play all regions. As a last resort, you can do something called "flashing your drive's firmware," a technically challenging process discussed by folks who hang out at www.rpc1.org.

When you insert the DVD, Media Player jumps to the screen and begins playing the movie. Media Player's controls work very much like your TV's DVD player, with the mouse acting as your remote. Click the on-screen words or buttons to make the DVD do your bidding.

To play the DVD in full-screen mode, hold down the Alt key and press Enter. Media Player fills the screen with the movie. (Hold down Alt and press Enter to revert to normal playback inside a window.) To make Media Player's on-screen controls disappear, don't touch your mouse for a few seconds; jiggle the mouse to bring the controls back in view.

Playing Videos and TV Shows

Many digital cameras can capture short videos as well as photos, so don't be surprised if Media Player places several videos in its library's Video section. Media Player also lists videos you've created in Microsoft's Movie Maker Live, a downloadable program that I cover in Chapter 16.

Playing videos works much like playing a digital song. Click Videos in the Navigation Pane along Media Player's left side. Double-click the video you want to see, and start enjoying the action, as shown in Figure 15-5.

Figure 15-5:
Move the mouse over the video to make the controls appear.

Media Player lets you watch videos in several sizes. Hold down Alt and press Enter to make it fill the screen, just as when watching a DVD. (Repeat those keystrokes to return to the original size.)

✔ To make the video adjust itself automatically to the size of your Media Player window, right-click the video as it plays, choose Video from the pop-up menu, and select Fit Video to Player on Resize.

✔ When downloading video from the Internet, make sure that it's stored in Windows Media format. Media Player can't play videos stored in some QuickTime or RealVideo formats. Those two competing formats require free players available from Apple (`www.apple.com/quicktime`) or Real (`www.real.com`). Make sure that you download the *free* versions — those sites often try to sucker you into buying their pay versions.

✔ When choosing video to watch on the Internet, your connection speed determines its quality. If you have a dialup connection, watch the video's 56K version. Broadband users can watch either the 100K or 300K version. You can't damage your computer by choosing the wrong version; the video will just play with some skipping.

✔ Media Player's Recorded TV area lists TV shows recorded by Windows 7's *Media Center,* which I cover in the "Working with Media Center" section, later in this chapter. You can watch those recorded shows in both Windows Media Center and Windows Media Player.

Playing Music Files (MP3s and WMAs)

Media Player plays several types of digital music files, but they all have one thing in common: When you tell Media Player to play a song or an album, Media Player immediately places that item on your *Now Playing list* — a list of items queued up for playing one after the other.

You can start playing music through Media Player in a number of ways, even if Media Player isn't currently running:

✔ Double-click the Library icon on your taskbar, right-click an album or a music-filled folder, and choose Play with Windows Media Player. The player jumps to the screen to begin playing your choice.

✔ While you're still in your own Music library, right-click items and choose Add to Windows Media Player list. Your PC queues them up in Media Player, ready to be played after you've heard your currently playing music.

✔ Double-click a song file, whether it's sitting on your desktop or in any folder. Media Player begins playing it immediately.

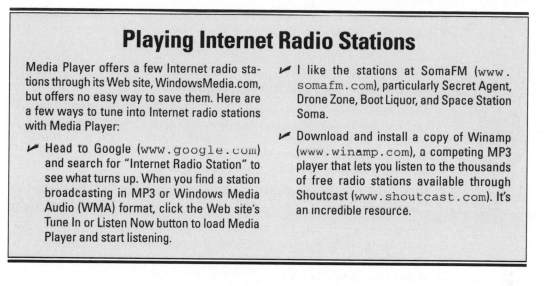

Playing Internet Radio Stations

Media Player offers a few Internet radio stations through its Web site, WindowsMedia.com, but offers no easy way to save them. Here are a few ways to tune into Internet radio stations with Media Player:

✔ Head to Google (www.google.com) and search for "Internet Radio Station" to see what turns up. When you find a station broadcasting in MP3 or Windows Media Audio (WMA) format, click the Web site's Tune In or Listen Now button to load Media Player and start listening.

✔ I like the stations at SomaFM (www.somafm.com), particularly Secret Agent, Drone Zone, Boot Liquor, and Space Station Soma.

✔ Download and install a copy of Winamp (www.winamp.com), a competing MP3 player that lets you listen to the thousands of free radio stations available through Shoutcast (www.shoutcast.com). It's an incredible resource.

To play songs listed within Media Player's own library, right-click the song's name and choose Play. Media Player begins playing it immediately, and the song appears in the Now Playing list.

Here are other ways to play songs within Media Player:

✔ To play an entire album in Media Player's library, right-click the album from the library's Album category and choose Play.

✔ Want to hear several files or albums, one after the other? Right-click the first one and choose Play. Right-click the next one and choose Add to Now Playing list. Repeat until you're done. Media Player queues them all up in the Now Playing list.

✔ To return to a recently played item, right-click Media Player's icon in the taskbar. When the list of recently played items appears, click your item's name.

✔ No decent music in your music library? Then start copying your favorite CDs to your PC — a process called *ripping,* which I explain in the "Ripping (Copying) CDs to Your PC" section, later in this chapter.

Creating, Saving, and Editing Playlists

A *playlist* is simply a list of songs (and/or videos) that play in a certain order. So what? Well, the beauty of a playlist comes with what you can *do* with it. Save a playlist of your favorite songs, for example, and they're always available for playback with a single click.

You can create specially themed playlists to liven up long-distance drives, parties, special dinners, workouts, and other events.

To create a playlist, follow these steps:

1. **Open Media Player and find the playlist.**

   Don't see the playlist hugging Media Player's right edge? Click the Play tab near the top-right corner. Or, when the player is in Now Playing mode, right-click a blank part of the Media Player window and choose Show List from the pop-up menu: The list of currently playing items appears along Media Center's right edge.

2. **Right-click the album or songs you want, choose Add To, and select Play List.**

   Alternatively, you can drag and drop albums and songs onto the Playlist pane along Media Player's right edge, as shown in Figure 15-6. Either way, Media Player begins playing your playlist as soon as you add the first song. Your song choices appear in the right pane in the order you've selected them.

Figure 15-6: Choose items from the middle pane and then drag and drop them into the rightmost pane.

3. **Fine-tune your playlist to change the order or remove songs.**

   Added something by mistake? Right-click that item from the playlist and choose Remove from List. Feel free to rearrange your playlist by dragging and dropping items farther up or down the list.

Check the line at the bottom of the playlist to see how many items you've added to the playlist, as well as your playlist's length in minutes.

4. **When you're happy with your playlist, click the Save List button at the list's top, type a name in the highlighted box, and press Enter.**

Media Player lists your new playlist in the library's Playlists section, ready to be heard when you double-click it.

After you save a playlist, you can burn it to a CD with one click, as described in the next tip.

 Make your own Desert Island Disc or Greatest Hits playlists; you can then burn them to a CD to play in your car or on your stereo. After you create a playlist of less than 80 minutes, insert a blank CD into your CD burner and click the Burn tab. Take up the player's offer to import your current playlist and then click the Start Burn button.

To edit a previously created playlist, double-click the playlist's name in the Library's Playlists area. Rearrange, add, or delete items in the playlist and then click the Save List button.

Ripping (Copying) CDs to Your PC

In a process known as *ripping*, Windows 7's Media Player can copy your CDs to your PC as MP3 files, the industry standard for digital music. But until you tell the player that you want MP3 files, it creates *WMA* files — a format that won't play on iPods.

To make Media Player create songs with the more versatile MP3 format instead of WMA, click the Organize button, choose Options, and click the Rip Music tab. Choose MP3 instead of WMA from the Format pull-down menu and nudge the audio quality over a tad from 128 to 256, or even 320 for better sound.

To copy CDs to your PC's hard drive, follow these instructions:

1. **Open Media Player, insert a music CD, and click the Rip CD button.**

You may need to push a button on the front of the drive before the tray ejects.

Media Player connects to the Internet, identifies your CD, and fills in the album's name, artist, and song titles. Then the program begins copying the CD's songs to your PC and listing their titles in the Media Player Library. You're through.

If Media Player can't find the songs' titles automatically, however, move ahead to Step 2.

Media Player's ripping quality settings

Musical CDs contain a *huge* amount of information — so much, in fact, that the Rolling Stones catalog probably wouldn't fit on your hard drive. To keep music files manageably small, ripping programs, such as Media Player, *compress* songs to about one-tenth of their normal size. Compressing the songs lessens their quality, so the big question becomes, how much quality loss is acceptable?

The answer is "when you can hear the difference," a much-debated point among listeners. When listening through a portable player's headphones, many people can't tell the difference between a CD and a song ripped at 128

Kbps (kilobits per second), so Media Player defaults to that standard.

If you'll be playing your music through larger speakers, or a home stereo, kick up the quality a notch: Click the Organize button, choose Options, and click the Rip Music tab. Slide the bar to the right (Best Quality) to rip at a higher quality. To create music files that don't lose *any* fidelity, choose Windows Media Audio Lossless from the Format drop-down list, and prepare for huge files. (So much for the entire Rolling Stones catalog....)

---

2. **Right-click the first track and choose Find Album Info, if necessary.**

   If Media Player comes up empty-handed, right-click the first track and choose Find Album Info.

   If you're connected to the Internet, type the album's name into the Search box and then click Search. If the Search box finds your album, click its name, choose Next, and click Finish.

   If you're not connected to the Internet, or if the Search box comes up empty, right-click the first song, click Edit, and manually fill in the song title. Repeat for the other titles, as well as the album, artist, genre, and year tags.

Here are some tips for ripping CDs to your computer:

✔ Normally Media Player copies every song on the CD. To leave Tiny Tim off your ukulele music compilation, however, remove the check mark from Tiny Tim's name. If Media Player has already copied the song to your PC, feel free to delete it from within Media Player. Click the Library button, right-click the song sung by the offending yodeler, and choose Delete.

✔ Some record companies add copy protection to their CDs to keep you from copying them to your computer. If you buy a copy-protected CD, try holding down the Shift key for a few seconds just before and after pushing the CD into the CD tray. That sometimes keeps the copy-protection software from working.

✔ Don't work your computer too hard while it's ripping songs — just let it sit there and churn away. Running large programs in the background may distract it, potentially interfering with the music.

✔ Media Player automatically places your ripped CDs into your Music library. You'll also find your newly ripped music there as well as in the Media Player Library.

Burning (Creating) Music CDs

To create a music CD with your favorite songs, create a playlist containing the CD's songs, listed in the order you want to play them; then burn the playlist to a CD. I explain how to do that in the "Creating, Saving, and Editing Playlists" section, earlier in this chapter.

But what if you want to duplicate a CD, perhaps to create a disposable copy of your favorite CD to play in your car? No sense scratching up your original. You'll want to make copies of your kids' CDs, too, before they create pizzas out of them.

Unfortunately, neither Media Player nor Windows 7 offers a Duplicate CD option. Instead, you must jump through the following five hoops to create a new CD with the same songs as the original CD:

1. **Rip (copy) the music to your hard drive.**

   Before ripping your CD, change your burning quality to the highest quality: Click Organize, choose Options, click the Rip Music tab, and change the Format box to WAVE (Lossless). Click OK.

2. **Insert a blank CD into your writable CD drive.**

3. **In Media Player's Navigation Pane, click the Music category and choose Album to see your saved CDs.**

4. **Right-click the album in your library, choose Add To, and choose Burn List.**

   If your Burn List already had some listed music, click the Clear List button to clear it; then add your CD's music to the Burn List.

5. **Click the Start Burn button.**

Now, for the fine print. Unless you change the quality to WAV (Lossless) when copying the CD to your PC, Media Player compresses your songs as it saves them on your hard drive, throwing out some audio quality in the process. Burning them back to CD won't replace that lost quality. If you want *true* duplicates of your CDs, change the Ripping Format to WAV (Lossless).

If you do change the format to WAV (Lossless) in order to duplicate a CD, remember to change it back to MP3 afterward, or your hard drive will run out of room when you begin ripping a lot of CDs.

A simpler solution might be to buy CD-burning software from your local office supply or computer store. Unlike Windows Media Player, most CD-burning programs have a Duplicate CD button for one-click convenience.

Copying Songs to Your Portable Player

Media Player 12 works with only a handful of portable music players. It can't connect with Apple's iPod, for example. It won't even work with Microsoft's own Zune. And it's clearly optimized for transferring WMA files — not the MP3 files favored by most portable players.

In fact, most people don't bother with Media Player, instead opting for the transfer software that came with their portable player: iTunes for iPods (www.apple.com/itunes) and Zune software for the Zune (www.zune.com). But if you own one of the few gadgets that Media Player likes, follow these steps:

1. **Connect your player to your computer.**

   This step usually involves connecting a USB cord between your device and your computer. The cord's small end pushes into a hole on your player; the large end fits into a rectangular-shaped port in the front or back of your PC.

   The plugs only fit one way — the right way — on each end.

2. **Start Media Player.**

   Several things may happen at this point, depending on your particular music player and the way its manufacturer set it up. (Try looking for some of these options on your player's setup menus.)

   If Media Player recognizes your player, a Sync List pane appears along Media Player's right edge.

   If your player is set up to *Sync Automatically,* Media Player dutifully copies all the music (and video, if your player supports it) from Media Player's library to your player. It's a fairly quick process for a few hundred songs, but if your player holds thousands, you may be twiddling your thumbs for several minutes.

   If your player is set up to *Sync Manually,* click Finish. You need to tell Media Player what music to copy, covered in the next step.

   If your player does nothing, or Media Player's library holds more music than will fit on your player, you're forced to go to Step 3.

The wrong player keeps opening my files!

You'd never hear Microsoft say it, but Media Player isn't the only Windows program for playing songs or viewing movies. Many people use iTunes for managing their songs and movies, because it conveniently drops items into their iPods for on-the-road enjoyment. Many Internet sounds and videos come stored in Real's (www.real.com) competing RealAudio or RealVideo format, which Media Player can't handle, either.

And some people use Winamp (www.winamp.com) for playing their music, videos, and a wide variety of Internet radio stations. With all the competing formats available, many people install several different media players — one for each format. Unfortunately, these multiple installations lead to bickering among each player because they all fight to become your default player.

Windows 7 attempts to settle these arguments with its new Default Programs area. To choose the player that should open each format, click the Start button, choose Default Programs, and click Set Your Default Programs. A window appears where you can choose which program plays your CDs, DVDs, pictures, video, audio, and other media.

3. **Choose what music to stuff onto your player.**

   You can choose what music goes onto your player in a couple of ways:

   - **Shuffle Music:** Found in the Sync List pane, this quick and easy option tells Media Player to copy a random mix of songs to the Sync List. It's great for an on-the-fly refresher, but you give up control over exactly what music will live on your player.

   - **Playlist:** Create a *playlist* — a list of music — that you want to appear on your player. Already created a playlist or two that you like? Right-click them and choose Add to Sync List, and Media Player will toss those songs onto the Sync List that's aimed at your player.

4. **Click the Start Sync button.**

   After you've chosen the music to transfer — and it's all sitting in the Sync List pane along the player's right side — copy it all to your player by clicking the Start Sync button at the bottom of Media Player's right pane.

   Media Player sends your music to your player, taking anywhere from several seconds to a few minutes.

   - If Media Player can't seem to find your portable player, click the Sync button along Media Player's top and choose Refresh Devices. That tells Media Player to take another look before giving up.

   - To change how Media Player sends files to your particular media player, click the Organize button, choose Options, and click the

Devices tab. Double-click your player's name to see its current options. Some players offer zillions of options; others only offer a few.

- Some players may require *firmware upgrades* — special pieces of software — before they'll work with Media Player 12. Downloadable from the manufacturer's Web site, firmware upgrades run on your PC like any software installation program. But instead of installing software on your PC, they install software onto your portable player to bring it up to date.

Working with Media Center

The Windows Media Center began its life as a special version of Windows designed to be viewed on a TV screen and manipulated with a remote control. Its big screen history makes its odd menus and large-button controls look awkward on your computer monitor. The program plays CDs, DVDs, music, and video — the same things that Windows Media Player can do much better.

But Media Center does *one* big thing that Media Player can't: Media Center turns your PC into a digital video recorder (DVR) that automatically records your favorite TV shows and movies in the background, letting you watch them on your own time (and fast-forward through the commercials).

All this free TV-recording fun requires a few things from your PC, though:

- ✔ **The right version of Windows 7:** Luckily, Microsoft tosses the Media Center into all of the Windows 7 versions except for the cheapo Starter and Home Basic versions that rarely appear in the stores. (Microsoft stripped Media Center from most versions of Windows Vista, by contrast.)

- ✔ **TV tuner:** Your PC doesn't need a TV set to view or record TV shows. Instead, your PC needs its own *TV tuner:* special circuitry that lets you receive TV signals and switch channels on your PC's monitor. Big bonus points go to TV tuners that come with remote controls, but Media Center also works well with a mouse and/or keyboard.

- ✔ **TV signal:** Like a TV set, a PC's TV tuner needs a TV signal that carries channels. So, you can unplug the cable from your TV set and plug it into your PC's TV tuner. (Better yet, buy a splitter to give that cable two ends: one for your TV set, the other for your tuner.) If you're desperate, you can attach an antenna (rabbit ears) to the tuner, but the picture won't look nearly as good.

Running Media Center for the first time

Don't start Media Center for the first time unless you have a good 15 or 20 minutes to kill. It takes that long to set things up. Choosing the Express option only bypasses your reading and approving the 50-some page privacy statement.

Media Center leaves you at the Recorded TV option. Since you don't have anything recorded yet, you must click the adjacent option, Live TV Setup, to set everything up. Media Center begins by poking and prodding your PC to look for an Internet connection and home network and then gives you a fairly lengthy interview, asking you to type in your zip code, select the provider supplying your TV signal, and download copy-protection software.

When it finally finishes, Media Center displays a *TV Guide*-type of listing on the screen, which

lets you browse shows and choose the ones to watch or record for later viewing. Although you may watch live TV immediately, you can't search for upcoming shows until the program finishes downloading and indexing the Guide Listings for your area, a task that takes anywhere from 15 minutes to an hour.

If Media Center didn't guess your settings correctly, choose the Tasks category from the main menu, and choose Settings. (If you don't see the Tasks category on-screen, press the Up or Down arrows on your keyboard until Tasks appears.) There, look for the Windows Media Center Setup option, which lets you tweak settings regarding your Internet connection, TV signal, speakers, and TV and monitor.

✔ **Video with TV-Out port:** TV looks great on your computer monitor. But to watch those shows on a *real* TV, your PC's tuner needs a place to plug into your TV set. Most tuners offer a combination of S Video, composite, and occasionally coax connectors, the three connectors used by most TV sets.

When run on a PC with a tuner and a TV signal, Media Center is ready for action. To give the program a test run, click Start, choose All Programs, and choose Windows Media Center.

If Media Center *doesn't* find those things, you probably need a new Windows 7–compatible driver for your tuner card. Depending on the tuner's age, you may find a driver downloadable for free from the tuner manufacturer's Web site.

Pressing F8 mutes the sound in Media Center, a difficult thing to remember because *Media Player* mutes when you press F7. (Thanks, Microsoft.)

Browsing Media Center's menus

Media Center offers a *lot* of options. And because Microsoft designed Media Center as a way to control your PC through your television, you'll see some duplication of things found elsewhere in Windows 7. For example, Media Center contains menus for things like playing Windows 7's built-in games, as well as playing your music and burning CDs — options that already appear in Windows Media Player.

Everything starts from Media Center's main menu, shown in Figure 15-7. To explore a particular menu's offerings, click its name with your mouse. To return to the previous menu, click the arrow button in the upper-left corner. (Move the mouse to make the arrow reappear.) To return to the main menu, click the adjacent green button.

Figure 15-7: Media Center lets you watch and record TV shows, play your music, and view your videos.

Having been designed for a remote control, Media Center may be difficult to manipulate entirely with a mouse. When it seems awkward, poke the keyboard's arrow keys, instead.

The main menu offers these categories (press the Up or Down arrows to scroll through them all):

✔ **Extras:** This hodgepodge category lets you play Windows 7's games, as well as access Internet video and radio.

✔ **Pictures + Videos:** Just as you'd expect, this setting displays pictures from your Pictures folder and videos from your Videos folder.

✔ **Music:** Media Center can play music, a perk if you've connected your PC to your home entertainment center and its glorious speakers. But if you're still listening to music on your PC's speakers, Media Player works just as well. This category's Radio option doesn't tune in to Internet stations, but to FM stations that may piggyback on your TV signal. (You may find live music concerts that have sneaked in here from the Internet, as well.)

✔ **Now Playing:** Head here to scoot away from all the menus and return to whatever's playing, be it TV, music, or video.

✔ **Movies:** This category lets you watch recordings stored in your movie library, view the movie guide to schedule upcoming recordings, play a DVD, or watch movie trailers from the Internet. (Nope, you won't find YouTube videos here.)

✔ **TV:** Echoing the choices from the Movies category, this lets you watch recorded TV shows and live TV, view a guide to schedule recordings, and search for shows by titles, keywords, categories, actors, or directors.

✔ **Sports:** Two main categories live here: games on now and games on later that you may want to record. The other categories let you search the Internet for game scores, player information, and league updates.

✔ **Tasks:** Enter here for settings that tweak everything from your TV reception to how Media Center displays your album art. This section also lets you burn CDs from your digital music collection and DVDs from recorded TV shows — without editing out the commercials, unfortunately.

To move from one menu to another, use the remote control that came with your TV tuner. No remote? Then point your mouse where you want to go, and tap your keyboard's arrow keys for more controlled menu hopping.

To return to a previous menu, use the remote's Back button, use the mouse to click the Back arrow in the screen's upper-left corner, or press the keyboard's Backspace key.

Getting the most out of Media Center

Because Media Center duplicates Media Player's functions, you probably won't find yourself using it much. It comes in handy only in these particular circumstances:

✔ **Xbox hooked up to TV:** Microsoft's game box, the Xbox 360, hooks up to a TV for playing games. But when hooked up to a network, the Xbox 360 can connect to Media Center, sharing its libraries of music, photos, and movies.

✔ **Your PC has a TV tuner:** If you've never recorded shows to watch later, you're in for a surprise. You can finally watch shows on your *own* time, not when the networks say you should watch them. Plus, you can fast-forward through commercials.

✔ **PC hooked up to TV:** Few people want a large, noisy PC sitting next to their TV. But if your PC serves exclusively as part of your home theater, Media Center provides an admirable command center.

✔ **Ease of access:** Media Center's large and simple menus won't satisfy control freaks. But if you're looking for easy-to-read menus for handling simple chores, you may prefer Media Center to Media Player.

If you're interested in more information about Windows Media Center, drop by The Green Button (www.thegreenbutton.com). Supported by people who enjoy Media Center on a daily basis, it's a great place to find answers.

Chapter 16

Fiddling with Photos and Movies

. . . .

In This Chapter

▶ Copying digital camera photos into your computer

▶ Viewing photos in your Pictures library

▶ Saving digital photos to a CD

▶ E-mailing and printing photos

▶ Editing photos with Windows Live Photo Gallery

▶ Copying camcorder footage into your computer

▶ Creating a slide show with DVD Maker

▶ Editing your video into a movie and saving it to a DVD

. . . .

This chapter introduces you to the ever-growing relationship between Windows, digital cameras, and camcorders — both the new digital and older analog models. This chapter explains how to move your digital photos and movies onto your computer, edit out the bad parts, display them to friends and family, e-mail them to distant relatives, and save them in easy-to-find locations on your computer.

One final note: After you've begun creating a family album on your computer, please take steps to back it up properly, as I describe in Chapter 12. (This chapter explains how to copy them to a CD or DVD, as well.) Your family memories can't be replaced.

Using Your Computer as a Digital Shoebox

The following sections help you turn your PC into a digital shoebox. I explain how to move your camera's photos onto your PC, browse through them, and save them to a CD or DVD. I also explain how to manage your collection, letting you solve the biggest problem among photographers: finding that quintessential shot you took a few weeks back.

Windows 7 doesn't recognize my camera!

Although Windows 7 usually greets cameras as soon as you connect them to your PC, sometimes the two don't become friends immediately: Windows 7 may not display its Import Photos menu, or another program may intervene. If those problems occur, unplug your camera, and wait ten seconds before plugging it back in.

If that doesn't do the job, follow these steps:

1. **Click Start, choose Default Programs, and select Change AutoPlay Settings.**

2. **Scroll down to the Devices area.**

The Devices area lives near the window's bottom.

3. **Choose your camera, select Import Using Windows from the drop-down list, and click Save.**

If Windows 7 *still* doesn't greet your camera when you plug it in, Windows 7 needs a translator to understand your camera's language. Unfortunately, that translator will have to be the camera's bundled software. If you no longer have the software, you can usually download it from your camera manufacturer's Web site.

For more hands-on editing, I explain how to download Microsoft's free Windows Live Essentials program to fix those mistakes you didn't notice when snapping the picture.

Dumping the camera's photos into your computer

Most digital cameras come with software that grabs your camera's photos and places them into your computer. But you needn't install it, or even bother trying to figure it out, thank goodness. Windows 7's built-in software easily fetches photos from nearly any make and model of digital camera when you follow these steps:

1. **Plug the camera's cable into your computer.**

   Most cameras come with two cables: One that plugs into your TV set for viewing, and another that plugs into your PC. You need to find the one that plugs into your PC for transferring photos.

    Plug the transfer cable's small end into your camera, and the larger end (shown in the margin) into your computer's *USB port,* a rectangular-looking hole about ½-inch long and ¼-inch high. (Most USB ports live on the back of the computer; newer computers offer them up front, and laptops place them along the sides.)

2. **Turn on your camera (if it's not already turned on) and wait for Windows 7 to recognize it.**

If you're plugging in the camera for the first time, Windows 7 sometimes heralds the camera's presence by listing its model number in a pop-up window above your taskbar by the clock.

If Windows 7 doesn't recognize your camera, make sure that the camera is set to *display mode* — the mode where you can see your photos on the camera's viewfinder — rather than the mode you use for snapping photos. If you still have problems, unplug the cable from your PC, wait a few seconds, then plug it back in.

When Windows 7 recognizes your camera, the AutoPlay window appears, as shown in Figure 16-1.

Don't see the AutoPlay window? Try opening Computer from the Start menu and double-clicking your camera icon, shown in the margin.

Figure 16-1:
Click the
Import
Pictures and
Videos Using
Windows
option
so that
Windows
7 auto-
matically
extracts
your cam-
era's photos.

3. **In the AutoPlay window, select the check box called Always Do This for This device and then click the Import Pictures and Videos Using Windows option.**

   Selecting the Always Do This for This Device check box is a timesaver that tells Windows 7 to automatically grab your camera's pictures whenever you connect it to your PC.

   After you click the Import Pictures and Videos Using Windows option, the Import Pictures and Videos dialog box appears, as shown in Figure 16-2.

4. **Type a *tag* or name for your photos and click the Import button.**

   Type a word or two to describe the photos, as shown in Figure 16-2. If you type the word **Cat**, for example, Windows 7 names the incoming photos as Cat 001, Cat 002, Cat 003, and so on. Later, you can find these pictures by searching for the word **Cat** in your Start menu's Search box.

Grabbing your camera's photos with a card reader

Windows 7 grabs photos from your camera fairly easily. But a *memory card reader* not only speeds up the job, it's your only option when you've lost your camera's transfer cable. A memory card reader is a little box with a cable that plugs into your computer's USB port — the same spot used by your camera.

To move your camera's pictures into your computer, remove the camera's memory card and slide the card into the slot in the card reader. Windows 7 notices that you've inserted the card and treats it much like your camera, offering similar menus.

Or, choose Computer from the Start menu and double-click the card reader's drive letter to see all the photos. From there, you can select the photos you want and cut and paste them to a folder in your Pictures library.

Memory card readers are cheap (less than $20), easy to set up, fast at copying images, and much more convenient. Plus, you can leave your camera turned off while dumping the vacation photos, saving battery life. When buying a card reader, make sure that it can read the type of memory cards used by your camera — as well as several other types of memory cards. (That ensures it will work with any new computer-related gadgets you might acquire around the holidays.)

Tagging works best when all your photos come from *one* session — that rainy afternoon spent with the cat, for example.

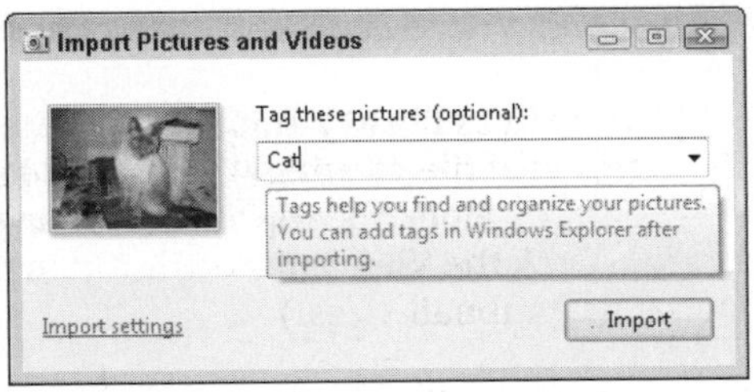

Figure 16-2:
Type a tag
or name that
describes
your photo
session.

Clicking the Import button brings your camera's photos into your PC and automatically renames them.

Clicking the words Import Settings, shown in the bottom left of Figure 16-2, lets you change how Windows 7 imports your photos. It's worth a look-see because it lets you undo any options you've mistakenly chosen when importing your first batch of photos.

5. **Select the Erase After Importing check box.**

   If you don't delete your camera's photos after Windows 7 copies them into your PC, you won't have room to take more photos. As Windows 7 grabs your photos, click Erase After Importing, shown in Figure 16-3, and

Windows 7 erases the camera's photos, saving you the trouble of rummaging through your camera's menus.

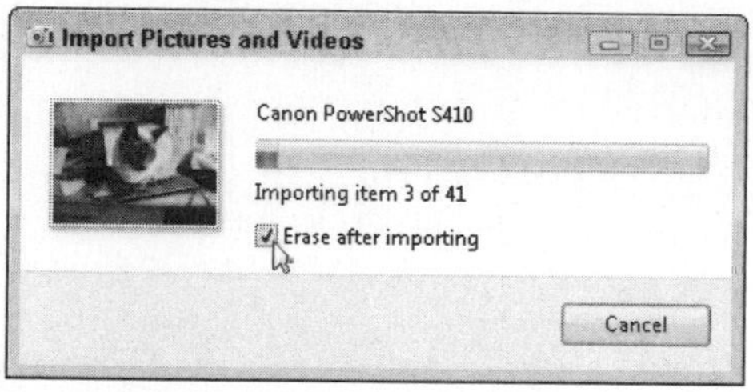

Figure 16-3:
Select the
Erase After
Importing
check box
to free up
your camera
for more
photos.

When Windows finishes importing your photos, it displays the folder containing your new pictures.

Browsing your photos in the Pictures library

Your Pictures library, located one click away on the Start menu's right side, easily earns kudos as Windows 7's best place to store your digital photos. When Windows 7 imports your digital camera's photos, it automatically stuffs them there to take advantage of that folder's built-in viewing tools.

 To peek inside any folder in your Pictures library, double-click the folder's icon. Inside, each folder offers the usual file-viewing tools found in every folder, plus a convenient row of buttons along the top for displaying, e-mailing, or printing your selected photos. (Click the View button, shown in the margin, to cycle quickly through different thumbnail sizes.)

Shown in Figure 16-4, the Pictures library offers oodles of ways to sort quickly through thousands of photos by clicking different words, dates, and ratings listed on the Arrange By drop-down list. Double-click any photo to see a larger view in Photo Viewer; return to the Pictures library by closing the Photo Viewer with a click on the red X in the Photo Viewer's upper-right corner.

The options in the Arrange By drop-down list let you sort your photos in a variety of ways:

✔ **Folder:** The most common view, this shows your Pictures library, complete with all the folders inside it. Double-click any folder to see inside; click the blue back arrow in the top-left corner to return.

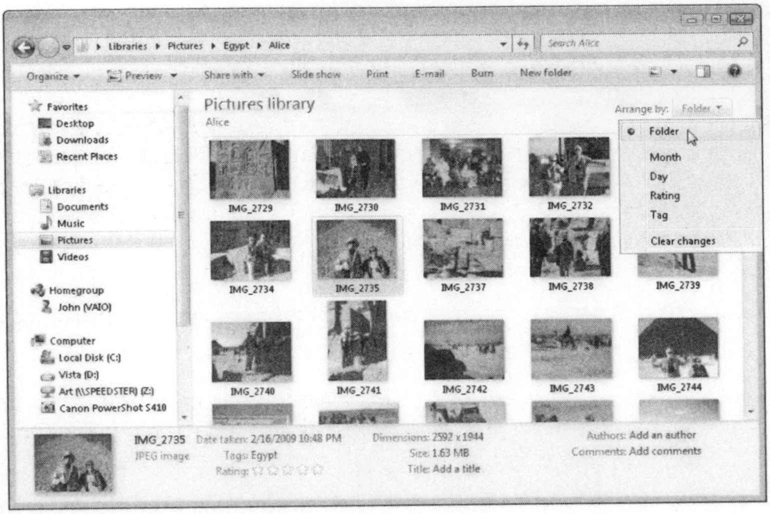

Figure 16-4:
The Pictures library lets you sort through your pictures by folder, chronologically, by tag, or by your personal rating.

✔ **Month:** Handy for viewing photos taken over the long term, this option stacks your photos into piles organized by the month and year you shot them. Double-click the July 2008 stack, for example, to see all the photos you snapped in that particular month.

✔ **Day:** Click this when you want to see all the photos snapped on a particular day. The Pictures library groups them by day, with your most recent photos in the topmost group.

✔ **Rating:** Spot a photo that's a real keeper? Or perhaps a stinker? Rate your currently selected photo or photos by clicking any of the rating stars on the Details Pane, as shown along the bottom of Figure 16-4.

✔ **Tag:** Remember the tag you assigned to your photos when importing them from your digital camera in Figure 16-2? The Pictures library stacks your photos according to their tags, letting you retrieve your tagged photos with a click. Feel free to add tags on the fly: Select your photos of Uncle Frank (select several photos by holding down Ctrl as you click each one), click the Tag area in the Details Pane along the window's bottom, and type **Uncle Frank** to add that name as a tag.

By sorting dates, tags, and ratings, you can ferret out the particular photos you're after. The following tips also increase your chances of locating a particular photo:

✔ Spot a blurred or ugly photo? Right-click it and choose Delete. Taking out the garbage with the Delete key makes the good photos easier to find.

✔ You can assign several different tags to one photo, adding a tag for each person in a group picture, for example: **Barack; Michelle; Sasha; Malia**. (The semicolon separates each tag.) Adding several tags makes that photo appear in searches for *any* of its tags.

Fixing rotated pictures

In the old days, it never mattered how you tilted your camera when taking the photo; you simply turned the printed photo to view it. Most of today's computer monitors don't swivel, so Windows 7 rotates the photo for you — if you figure out how.

The trick is to right-click any photo that shows up sideways. Choose Rotate Clockwise or Rotate Counter Clockwise to turn your green cliffs back into grassy meadows.

✔ Windows 7 dropped Vista's Preview Pane from the library's right edge. To replace it with Windows 7's more limited Preview Pane, click the Organize button, choose Layout, and select Preview Pane.

✔ Don't see enough details about a photo along the folder's bottom edge? Drag the Details Pane's top edge upward with your mouse, and the pane expands to show oodles of information.

✔ Type any photo's tag into the Pictures library's Search box, located in its top-right corner, and Windows 7 quickly displays photos assigned with that particular tag.

✔ Want to cover your entire desktop with a photo? Right-click the picture and choose Set As Background. Windows immediately splashes that photo across your desktop.

✔ Hover your mouse pointer over any photo to see the date it was taken, its rating, size, and dimensions. (That information also appears in the Details Pane along the window's bottom.)

Viewing a slide show

Windows 7 offers a simple slide slow that displays one photo after another. It's not fancy, but it's a built-in way to show photos to friends crowding around your monitor. Start the photos flowing across the screen either of these two ways:

✔ When in your Pictures library or folder, click the Slide Show button (shown in the margin) from along the folder's top.

✔ When viewing a single photo in Windows Photo Viewer, click the large, round Play Slide Show button (shown in the margin) from along the folder's bottom center.

Windows immediately darkens the monitor, fills the screen with the first picture, and then cycles through each picture in the folder.

The Slide Show button creates quick, on-the-fly slide shows, but if you're looking for slide shows to save to a DVD and give to friends, check out this chapter's last section. There, I explain how to create and save slide shows with Windows 7's built-in Windows DVD Maker program.

Here are more tips for successful on-the-fly slide shows:

- ✔ Before starting the slide show, rotate any sideways pictures, if necessary, so that they all appear right-side up: Right-click the problem photo, and choose Rotate Clockwise or Rotate Counterclockwise.

- ✔ The slide show only includes photos in your current folder; it won't dip into folders *inside* that folder, and show their photos, too.

- ✔ Select just a few of a folder's pictures and click the Slide Show button to limit the show to just those pictures. (Hold down Ctrl while clicking pictures to select more than one.)

- ✔ Feel free to add music to your slide show by playing a song in Media Player, described in Chapter 15, before starting your show. Or, if you picked up a Hawaiian CD while vacationing on the islands, insert that in your CD player to play a soundtrack during your vacation slide show.

Copying digital photos to a CD or DVD

To back up all your digital photos, fire up Windows 7's backup program, covered in Chapter 12. But if you just want to copy some photos to a CD or DVD, stick around.

Head to the computer or office-supply store and pick up a stack of blank CDs or DVDs to match your PC's drive. (I explain how to tell what type of disc drive lives inside your PC in Chapter 4.)

Then follow these steps to copy files in your Pictures library to a blank CD or DVD:

Burn

1. **Open your Pictures library from the Start menu, select your desired photos, and click the Burn button.**

   Open the Pictures library, and open the folder containing the photos you want to copy to disc. Select the photos and folders you want to copy by holding down the Ctrl key and clicking their icons. Or, to select them *all*, hold down Ctrl and press the letter A. When you click the Burn button, Windows 7 asks you to insert a blank disc into your drive.

2. **Insert a blank CD or DVD into your writable disc drive.**

   If you're copying a lot of files, insert a DVD into your DVD burner, as DVDs can store five times as much information as a CD. If you're giving away the disc to a friend, insert a blank CD, instead, as blank CDs cost less at the store.

Keeping digital photos organized

It's tempting to create a folder called New Photos in your Pictures library and start dumping new pictures into it. But when it comes time to finding a particular photo days later, that system breaks down quickly. The Windows 7 importing tools do a fairly good job of naming each photo session after the date and the tag. These tips also help keep your pictures organized and easy to retrieve:

✔ Assign a few key tags, such as *Home, Travel, Relatives,* or *Holidays,* to photos. Searching for those tags makes it easy to see all the pictures taken at your own house, while traveling, when visiting relatives, or during holiday events.

✔ Windows assigns your chosen tag to each batch of photos you import. Spend a little time immediately afterward to assign more tags to each photo. (You can assign several tags to one photo by placing a semicolon between each tag.)

✔ If digital photography turns into a hobby, consider one of many free third-party photo programs like Windows Live Photo Gallery (http://explore.live.com), which I describe in this chapter, or Google's Picasa (www.picasa.google.com). They provide more photo-management and editing features, improving upon Windows 7's basic tools.

3. **Decide how you want to use the disc.**

   Windows offers two options when creating the disc:

   • **Like a USB flash drive:** Choose this option when you intend for other PCs to read the disc. Windows 7 treats the disc much like a folder, letting you copy additional photos to the disc later. It's a good choice when you're backing up only a few pictures, because you can add more to the disc later.

   • **With a CD/DVD player:** Choose this option to create discs that play on CD and DVD players attached to TVs. After you write to the disc, it's sealed off so you can't write to it again. Don't choose this unless you plan to view the disc on a TV.

4. **Type a name for your backup disc and click Next.**

   Type today's date and the words **Photo Backup,** or something similarly descriptive. Windows 7 begins backing up all of that folder's photos to the disc.

5. **Click the Burn or Burn to Disc button again, if necessary.**

   If you selected With a CD/DVD Player in Step 3, click Burn to Disc to start copying your photos to the disc.

   If you didn't select any photos or folders in Step 1, Windows 7 opens an empty window showing the newly inserted disc's contents: nothing. Drag and drop the photos you want to burn into that window. Or, to copy them all, go back to the Pictures library and click Burn.

Don't have enough space on the CD or DVD to hold all your files? Unfortunately, Windows 7 isn't smart enough to tell you when to insert the second disc. Instead, it whines about not having enough room and doesn't burn *any* discs. In that case, head for Windows 7's much smarter backup program (see Chapter 12), which has the smarts to split your backup between several discs.

E-mailing photos

Unlike Windows XP and Windows Vista, Windows 7 no longer includes an e-mail program. So, how do you send e-mail? Well, many people end up turning to an online program like Google's Gmail (www.gmail.com).

Microsoft prefers that you download its own Windows Live Mail program as a replacement, so I cover that program — and how to make it e-mail your photographs — in Chapter 9.

Printing pictures

Windows 7's Photo Printing Wizard offers nearly as many options as the drugstore's photo counter, printing full-page glossies, wallet prints, and nearly anything in between.

The key to printing nice photos is buying nice (and expensive) photo paper and using a photo-quality printer. Ask to see printed samples before buying a printer and then buy that printer's recommended photo-quality paper.

Before printing your photos, feel free to crop and adjust their colors in a photo-editing program like Windows Live Photo Gallery, which I describe later in this chapter's "Fixing Photos with Windows Live Photo Gallery" section.

Here's how to move photos from your screen to the printed page:

1. **Open Pictures from the Start menu and select the photos you'd like to print.**

   Want to print one photo? Then click it. To select more than one photo, hold down the Ctrl key as you click each one.

2. **Tell Windows 7 to print the selected photos.**

   You can tell Windows 7 to print your selection either of these ways:

   Print

   - Click the Print button from the folder's toolbar. You'll spot a handy Print button atop every folder in your Pictures library.

   - Right-click any of the selected photos and choose Print from the pop-up menu.

   No matter which method you choose, the Print Pictures window appears, shown in Figure 16-5.

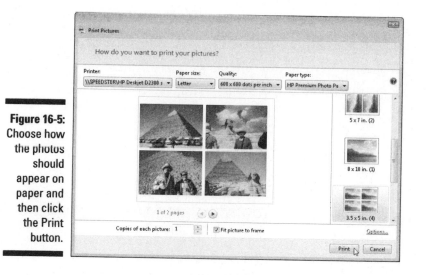

Figure 16-5:
Choose how
the photos
should
appear on
paper and
then click
the Print
button.

3. **Choose your printer, paper size, quality, paper type, photo layout, and the number of times to print each picture.**

   The Print Pictures window lets you tweak several settings. (If you don't tweak *anything*, Windows 7 prints one copy of each photo across an expensive sheet of 8½-x-11-inch photo paper.)

   - **Printer:** Windows 7 lists your default printer — your only printer, if you only have one — in the top-left drop-down list. If you own a second printer that you use only for photos, select that printer from the drop-down list.

   - **Paper size:** Windows 7 lists different paper sizes in this drop-down list in case you'll be printing on something besides normal 8½-x-11-inch photo paper.

   - **Quality:** Leave this at 600 x 600 dots per inch for most photo printers. If you're printing on a regular printer, switch to 300 x 300 dots per inch.

   - **Paper Type:** Choose the type of paper you've placed in your printer, usually Photo Paper.

   - **Layout:** On the Print Picture Windows' right edge, choose how Windows 7 should arrange the photos on the page. For example, you can print each photo to fill an entire page, print nine wallet photos, or print something in between. Each time you choose an option, the wizard displays a preview of the printed page, as shown in Figure 16-5.

   - **Copies of each picture:** Choose anywhere from 1 to 99 copies of each picture.

- **Fit Picture to Frame:** Leave this check box selected so Windows 7 fills the paper with the photo. (This option may slightly crop your photo's edge a tad for a better fit.)

4. **Insert photo paper into your printer and click Print.**

   Follow the instructions for inserting your photo paper into your printer. It must face the correct direction and print on the correct side. Some paper requires a stiff paper backing sheet, as well.

   Click Print, and Windows 7 shuttles your photo off to the printer.

 Most photo developers print digital photos with *much* better quality paper and ink than your own printer can accomplish. And with the cost of expensive printer paper and ink cartridges, photo developers often cost less than printing photos yourself. Check their pricing and ask the photo developer how you should submit your photos — by CD, memory card, or over the Internet.

Fixing photos with Windows Live Photo Gallery

Windows 7's built-in photo tools work fine for basic browsing, viewing, e-mailing, and printing. But you may yearn for a simple photo editor as you begin to spot common mistakes in your photos: tilted horizons, red eyes from flash photos, washed out colors, or photos that need some cropping to bring out details.

Microsoft hopes its free Live Photo Gallery will fulfill your photo-editing needs. The program's photo fixes aren't permanent. If you make a mistake, click the Revert to Original button at the screen's top, right corner. If you decide several days later you've made a mistake, double click that problematic figure, click Revert to Original button, and Windows 7 can *still* revert to the original photo.

Live Photo Gallery can also import videos from a digital camcorder, so it's a must for camcorder owners.

The following sections explain how to download and install the program, as well as perform a few quick fixes on your photos.

Installing Windows Live Photo Gallery

I describe downloading a Live Essentials program more fully in Chapter 9, where I describe how to download Windows Live Mail. If you don't want to turn to that page, these basics should do the trick:

1. **Visit the Windows Live Web site (http://explore.live.com) and download the Windows Live Essentials installation program to your Downloads folder.**

2. **Double-click the installation program in your Downloads folder.**

3. **Place a check box next to the Photo Gallery and Movie Maker program and then click the Install button.**

   You don't need to download *all* of the Windows Live programs. I describe the others in Chapter 6

4. **Make sure the installation program doesn't change your Web browser's home page and search provider, and click Continue.**

5. **If you need an e-mail address, create a Windows Live account and then click OK; otherwise, click Close.**

6. **Load the program.**

   Click the Start button, choose All Programs and click Windows Live Photo Gallery.

7. **Log in with a Windows Live ID, if you want. If you don't want to sign in, just click Cancel.**

   When started for the first time, the program asks you to sign in with a Windows Live ID. (That gives you access to an online photo sharing area.) Don't feel you have to sign up for Yet Another E-Mail Address unless you need one. Just click Cancel to begin using the program.

   If you want to sign in later with a Windows Live ID, click the Sign In button, which you'll always find in the program's upper-right corner.

The program also asks whether you want Windows Live Photo Gallery to open JPG, TIF, PNG, WDP, BMP, and ICO files. If you want your new Windows Live Photo Gallery to handle the chores, click Yes. (I click No because Window's plain ol' photo viewer runs more quickly.)

After a few moments, the program appears on your screen with your photos already arranged by the date you snapped them, shown in Figure 16-6.

The next few sections explain how to fix your photos with the gallery's easy-to-use fix-it tools.

Be sure to fix your photos *before* printing them or sending them to be printed. A little bit of cropping and adjustment helps make your photos look their best before you commit them to paper.

Most of the program's editing tools rely on sliding a bar to the left or right. Instead of timidly nudging the bar to edit a photo, first move it all the way to one side, and then the other. That lets you see the results of over-correcting and under-correcting, letting you make more subtle corrections.

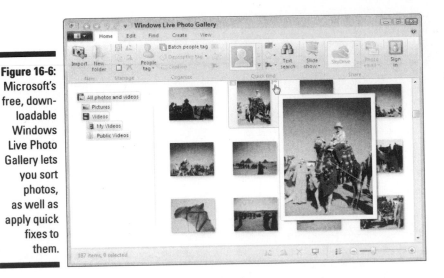

Figure 16-6: Microsoft's free, down-loadable Windows Live Photo Gallery lets you sort photos, as well as apply quick fixes to them.

Adjusting photos automatically

Photographs capture the light entering the camera's lens, and that light rarely looks the same as the light beaming back at you from your computer monitor. To adjust for the difference, Windows Live Photo Gallery lets you adjust a photo's color, as well as correct for photos that are *over-exposed* or *under-exposed* — a problem when your camera picks up too much or too little light. Here's the quickest and easiest way to adjust a particular photo's lighting:

1. **Open the Windows Live Photo Gallery, double-click the awful photo, and click the Edit tab on the menu.**

   When downloaded and installed, the Windows Live Photo Gallery lives in the Start menu's All Programs area.

2. **Click Auto Adjust from the Edit menu, then click the Fine Tune button.**

   The Fine Tune repair tools appear along the window's right edge, as shown in Figure 16-7.

   Surprisingly enough, simply clicking Auto Adjust usually makes the photo look much better. If you think the photo now looks perfect, you're through; click the Close File button to save your changes and return to the rest of your images. But if the photo looks worse or isn't quite fixed yet, move to Step 3.

3. **Click Adjust Exposure from the right pane and then adjust the Brightness, Contrast, Shadows, and Highlights settings.**

   The program's Auto Adjust tool almost always changes a photo's exposure settings slightly. The slider bars are normally centered, but after Auto Adjust does its work, one or both will be off-center. If necessary, slide one or more of the bars to further tweak Auto Adjust's changes. If the photo *still* doesn't look right, move to Step 4.

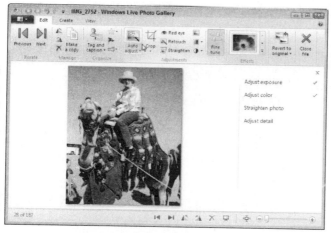

Figure 16-7:
Windows
Live Photo
Gallery
offers its
photo-fixing
tools along
its right
side.

After using a tool like Adjust Exposure, click its name to hide its tools. That makes it easier to find and adjust the other category settings.

4. **Click Adjust Color from the right pane and then adjust the Tint, Color Temperature, and Saturation settings.**

   Just as before, slide the bars to the center or edge to either enhance or remove Auto Adjust's settings.

5. **Save or discard your changes.**

   If you're pleased with the outcome, save your changes by clicking the Close File button in the top-left corner.

   But if the photo looks worse than ever, discard your changes: Click the Revert to Original button next to the Close File button.

Straightening photos

When focusing on a squirrel scurrying up the pine tree, few people remember mundane tasks like keeping the horizon exactly straight in the viewfinder. Photographed buildings also tend to tilt. The Straighten tool fixes slanted horizons and tilted buildings quite easily.

Edit

1. **Open the Windows Live Photo Gallery, double-click the tilting photo, and click the Edit tab on the toolbar.**

   Windows Live Photo Gallery opens your photo and displays its toolbar of one-click fixes.

2. **Click Straighten from the toolbar.**

   The program immediately guesses what's wrong and takes a shot at straightening your photo. If everything's straight, click Close file. If it needs more tweaking, click Fine Tune.

3. **If needed, click Straighten Photo along the right pane; then, drag the sliding bar to adjust the tilt.**

   Slide to the right for a clockwise tilt; slide to the left to tilt the photo counterclockwise. As you slide, line up the overlaid grid with the horizon, a building edge, or a standing person.

4. **Click Close File to save your changes.**

Don't click Auto Adjust after straightening your image. When Auto Adjust guesses at correcting exposure and color, the tool also guesses at how straight your photo should be, wiping out your carefully adjusted changes in the process. If you want to Auto Adjust a photo, use that command *before* using the Straighten Photo tool.

Cropping photos

You crop a photo every time you take a picture: You look through the camera's viewfinder or at its color screen, aiming the camera and zooming in or pulling back until the subject appears nicely framed.

But when you go home, you may notice your quick framing wasn't as nice as you'd thought. A telephone pole protrudes from a person's head, for example, or that little tree frog disappears in the leafy background.

Cropping can solve both of those problems, letting you remove a photo's bad parts and enhance the good. These steps show how to crop a photo taken from indoors to remove the window framing and make a distant object appear closer.

1. **Open the Windows Live Photo Gallery, double-click the problem photo, and click Edit from the toolbar.**

   When downloaded and installed, the Windows Live Photo Gallery lives in the Start menu's All Programs area.

2. **Click the Crop tool and choose your proportion.**

   The Crop Picture tool places a rectangle in your photo, shown in Figure 16-8. The rectangle shows the cropped area — everything outside the rectangle will be cropped out.

   From the Crop tool's drop-down menu, choose a proportion that matches how you'll be viewing the photo — as a 5-x-7-inch print, for example. Feel free to click Rotate Frame if that frames your subject better.

   Planning on making a slide show DVD with Windows DVD Maker? Cropping photos horizontally to a Widescreen (16 x 9) proportion makes them appear full-screen on a widescreen TV.

Figure 16-8:
Adjust the rectangle to fit the area you want to crop.

3. **Adjust the cropped area around your subject.**

Windows 7 places the rectangle in the center of your photo, which is rarely the best place to crop. Reposition the rectangle by pointing at it, and while holding down the mouse button, move the mouse to drag the cropping area to a new position. Then adjust the rectangle's size by dragging the corners in or out.

For more interesting crops and shots, follow the *rule of thirds*. Imagine two vertical and horizontal lines dividing your photo into equal thirds. Then position the photo's subject anyplace where those lines intersect.

4. **Click the Crop button again to crop the image.**

Windows Live Photo Gallery crops away the photo portions outside your frame. (Notice how the waterline and castle in Figure 16-8 follow the rule of thirds.)

5. **Click Revert to Original if you're unhappy with the crop; if you're happy with it, click the Close File button.**

Cropping comes in handy for creating pictures for your user account photo — the square photo that appears atop your Start menu. Choose Square from the Crop button's Proportion menu, crop out everything but your head, save the shot, and then visit the Control Panel's User Accounts area to use your new head shot for your account picture. (I explain user accounts in Chapter 13.)

Removing red-eye

Flash photos work so quickly that the pupil doesn't have time to contract. Instead of seeing a black pupil, the camera catches the blood-red retina in the back of the eye, a problem commonly known as *red-eye*.

Adjusting detail and adding black and white effects

Two of the least-used fixes offered by Windows Live Photo Gallery are Adjust Detail and black and white Effects. Here's why you'll rarely use them:

✔ **Adjust Detail:** This sliding control takes your smooth photo and sharpens it, which fools the eye into thinking it has more texture. Unless used with a light touch, though, it also adds noise, giving your photo a grainy look. Barely touch this control, or don't bother.

✔ **Black and White Effects:** These let you choose an era for your photos by giving them the sepia tones of early photography, a '60s Kodak moment, or an Ansel Adams black and white look. Scrapbookers might enjoy these for a few shots, but the novelty wears off quickly.

Windows 7's Red Eye tool replaces the red with the more natural black, fixing a problem that's plagued party photographers around the world.

Edit

1. **Open the Windows Live Photo Gallery, double-click your red-eye photo, and click Edit from the toolbar.**

   When downloaded and installed, the Windows Live Photo Gallery lives in the Start menu's All Programs area.

   Zoom in on the red-eye area by sliding the Navigation Pane's bar to the right along the window's bottom right. Then drag the photo with your mouse pointer until the red-eye comes into view.

2. **Click the Red Eye button from the toolbar, drag a rectangle around the red part of the pupil, and then release the mouse button.**

   Click just above and to the side of the red portion of the pupil, hold down your mouse button, and drag down and to the side to surround the red portion with a square.

   Releasing the mouse button turns the red into black.

Creating a DVD Movie or Slide Show with Windows DVD Maker

Windows DVD Maker does something Windows XP never could: Create DVDs that play back on a DVD player. In Windows XP, people had to buy a DVD-burning program from another company or hope that their new computer came with one pre-installed.

Note: If you want to copy or back up files to a blank DVD, don't use DVD Maker. Instead, copy the files to the DVD the same way you copy files to a CD or any folder, a process I cover in Chapter 4.

Follow these steps to create a DVD movie or slide show for playing back on a DVD player and watching on your TV:

1. **Load Windows DVD Maker, if necessary.**

   Click the Start button, click All Programs, and click Windows DVD Maker.

2. **Click Add Items, add your photos or videos, and click Next.**

   Click the Add Items button and choose the movie file, perhaps something you've created in Windows Live Movie Maker.

   To create a photo slide show, choose photos you'd like to add to your DVD. If you're creating a slide show, here's your chance to arrange the photos' display order by dragging and dropping them in different places.

   To add *all* the photos in a folder, hold down the Ctrl key and press A.

3. **Customize the opening menu, if desired.**

   Spend some time here to craft your DVD's *opening menu* — the screen you watch until the last person's settled around the TV set and you can push Play on your remote. DVD Maker offers these menu options:

   • **Menu Text:** Click this button to choose the title of your movie or slide show, as well as what options should appear on the menu. Or, stick with the default options found on every DVD: Play and Scenes.

   • **Customize Menu:** Here you can change the opening menu's font and photo, choose a video to repeat in the background, choose music to play, and even change the shape of the *scenes menu* — that screen where you can jump quickly to different parts of your movie. Click the Preview button to make sure that it's just what you want.

   • **Slide Show:** Meant specifically for slide shows, this option lets you choose the background music, the amount of time the photos should display, and their transitions.

   • **Menu Styles:** The drop-down list here lets you dump DVD Maker's stock background for these spruced up graphics. (I like the Video Wall style for movies and the Photographs or Travel style for photo slide shows.)

4. **Click Burn.**

   Then walk away from your computer for a few hours. DVD Maker's a certified slowpoke.

   When DVD Maker finishes, it spits out a DVD, ready for you to label with a magic marker and pop into your DVD player to watch on TV.

Creating, Editing, and Viewing Digital Movies

The shelves of most camcorder owners weigh heavy with tapes filled with vacation footage, sporting events, and mud-bathing children. Unfortunately, Windows 7 dumped the handy movie-editing program that came with Windows XP and Windows Vista.

So, if you want to turn that pile of tapes into complete, edited movies, Microsoft wants you to download its diluted substitute, Windows Live Movie Maker. The new stripped-down version works best for creating short videos.

Windows Live Movie Maker comes bundled with Windows Live Photo Gallery, described in the previous section.

The rest of this section explains the three steps involved in movie making:

1. Import.

   For some reason, Windows Live Movie Maker can't import your video from your digital video camera. You must import it through Windows Live Photo Gallery, instead.

2. Edit.

   This step combines your video clips, music, and pictures into a structured movie. Edit each clip down to its best moments and add *transitions* — the way one clip fades into the next — between the clips. Toss in a soundtrack, as well.

3. Publish.

   When you finish editing, Movie Maker combines your batch of clips or photos into a complete movie, ready to be played back on your computer or saved to a DVD.

Creating movies requires a *lot* of free hard drive space. A 15-minute movie can consume 2.5GB. If Movie Maker complains about space, you have two choices: Create smaller videos or upgrade your computer with a second hard drive, a job I describe in *Upgrading and Fixing PCs For Dummies: Do It Yourself.*

Step 1: Import video, pictures, and music

If you've already imported footage from a digital camera or camcorder, jump ahead to Step 4 in this section and begin there. You're several steps ahead of the pack.

But if you're importing video from a digital camcorder, you must work a little harder. Before Movie Maker can edit your digital camcorder's video, you must copy the footage onto your computer through a cable. Most digital camcorders connect to a computer's FireWire or USB 2.0 port.

When importing video, you need only connect a single cable between the camcorder and USB or FireWire port. With that one cable, Windows 7 grabs the sound and video, *and* controls the camera.

To copy digital video into your computer, follow these steps:

1. **Download and install Windows Live Photo Gallery, described earlier in this chapter. Connect your digital camera or camcorder to your computer, open Windows Live Photo Gallery, click the Home tab, and choose Import.**

   If this is your first time plugging in the digital camera or camcorder, Windows 7 should recognize it immediately. To catch Windows 7's attention, switch your camcorder to the setting where it plays back — not records — video. (Some camcorders label that setting as VCR.)

2. **Choose the icon for your camera in the Import Photos and Videos window. Then click Import.**

3. **If using a digital camcorder, enter a name for your video, choose how to import the footage, and click Next.**

   First, name your incoming video after the event you've filmed, be it a vacation, a wedding, or a visit to a skateboard park.

   Next, choose one of the three ways Windows 7 offers to import the video into your Videos folder:

   • **Import the Entire Video:** This option imports *all* the video on your tape, breaking each shot into a separate segment. The best choice, this lets you grab the good shots for your finished product and leave the rest on the cutting room floor.

   • **Choose Parts of the Video to Import:** Choose this laborious option for importing only a few portions of the tape. Windows 7 displays a playback window with on-screen controls. Fast forward to the section you want, click the Import button to record your desired snippet, and then click Stop. Repeat until you've gathered any other shots you want, and then click Finish.

- **Burn the Entire Video to DVD:** Choose this to copy your entire video, unedited, to a DVD. Although convenient, this forces your audience to see *everything* you've shot, even the excruciatingly boring portions.

Let your computer work uninterrupted while it's grabbing video, because it needs lots of processing power for smooth captures. Don't work with other programs or browse the Web.

Windows 7 saves your video in your Videos library, visible when you click the taskbar's Windows Explorer icon.

4. **Open Windows Movie Maker Live if it's not already running.**

   To summon Movie Maker Live, click the Start menu, choose All Programs and select Windows Live Movie Maker.

5. **Gather the videos, pictures, and music you want to include in your video.**

   Shown in Figure 16-9, the menu in Movie Maker Live lets you add a few things:

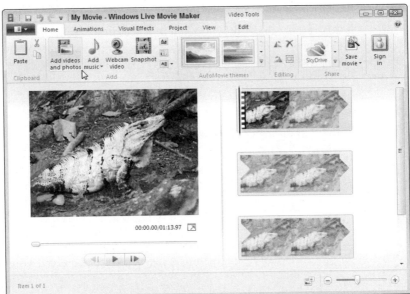

Figure 16-9: Click the Add buttons to add items to your movie.

- **Add videos and photos:** Click this button, select the videos you want from your Videos library, and then click Open: Your selected videos appear in Windows Live Movie Maker's right pane. Repeat the process to add photos from your Pictures library.

- **Add music:** Click this button to add any music files from your Music library.

- **Webcam video:** This records live video from your PC's camera.

- **Snapshot:** This saves the current frame from your displayed video.

- **Add title, captions, and credits:** These three small buttons to the right of the Snapshot icon add a blank screen for you to type in words, making your movies look more professional.

Every item you add immediately appears in the right pane. If you add any items by mistake, click them and click the Remove button. (That just removes the items from the list, it doesn't delete the originals.)

At the end of this step, Movie Maker Live's right side will be stocked with all the video, photos, and music you need to assemble your movie. In the next step, described in the next section, you begin combining them all into a finished work.

Step 2: Edit your movie

At this step, you're finished, if you want to be. The program splices together the clips, photos, and songs in the order you've added them, and creates a movie. Click the Play button — the blue triangle along the bottom — to watch it.

If you're feeling creative and have some time, however, edit your movie in any of the following ways:

- ✔ **Change the playback order:** Drag clips and photos to different positions on the right pane, changing when they'll play back.

- ✔ **Remove bad shots or photos:** Spot a shaky camera angle or blurry photo? Right-click the item and choose Remove.

- ✔ **Add text:** Your title, captions, and credits appear as black squares. Click one and start typing to add information you want to see on-screen.

- ✔ **Trim clips:** To trim a specific clip, right-click where you want it to begin and choose Set Start Point. Right-click where you want it to end, and choose Set End Point. The program trims anything before or after those points, leaving your edited clip. Satisfied? Click Save and Close. Unsatisfied? Hold down Ctrl and press Z to undo your latest action.

- ✔ **Add animations:** Animations, also known as transitions, dictate how shots flow into each other. To add one, click Animations. Rest your mouse pointer over a transition to see a preview of how the current clip will flow into the next. When you spot one you like, click it to add it to your movie.

- ✔ **Add visual effects:** These change the colors of your video or photos. Use them sparingly.

Don't worry that your edits will harm your original video. You're only working with a copy, and you still have the master copies in your Videos library.

As you work, feel free to play back your movie at any time. Just click the Play button on the preview window. Also, hover your mouse pointer over any confusing buttons or icons; Windows quickly explains the button's purpose or shows you how the effect alters your movie.

Step 3: Save your edited movie

When you've finished editing your clips into a movie, click the down arrow beneath the Save Movie icon. The program can save or upload your movie in any of these formats:

- ✔ **Recommended for this project:** Windows gauges your video's size and quality, the saves it in appropriate format.

- ✔ **High-Definition (1080p):** Choose this if you intend to watch the movie only on high-definition TVs.

- ✔ **Burn a DVD:** This option saves your movie as a WMV file and then loads the file into the Windows DVD Maker program for you to finish the DVD-creation process. (I cover the Windows DVD Maker program in the previous section.)

- ✔ **For Compuuter:** This saves the movie so it looks best when played on your computer.

- ✔ **For e-mail:** Choose this to create small movies suitable for e-mailing.

- ✔ **Zune HD:** This creates a small file for playback on Microsoft's iPod clone, the Zune. (The program can't save videos in a format for playing back on an iPod.) Choose the Zune 720p Display option only if you'll be playing from the Zune to a HDTV.

- ✔ **Windows Phone (large/small:** These choices save movies suitable for viewing on Microsoft's Windows 7 phone. Choose Large only for phones with plenty of storage space, otherwise choose Small.

After you choose an option, type in a name, and click Save, Windows creates your movie, choosing the appropriate file size and quality for the destination you choose.

Publishing movies can take a *long* time. Windows needs to arrange all your clips, create the transitions and soundtracks, and compress everything into a single file.

Part VI
Help!

The 5th Wave

By Rich Tennant

"You know, I'll never get used to that 'exploding bomb' error message icon!"

In this part . . .

Windows 7 can do hundreds of tasks in dozens of ways, which means that several thousand things can fail at any given time.

Some problems are easy to fix — if you know how to fix them, that is. For example, one misplaced click on the desktop makes all your icons suddenly vanish. Yet, one more click in the right place puts them all back.

Other problems are far more complex, requiring teams of computer surgeons to diagnose, remedy, and bill accordingly.

This part of the book helps you separate the big problems from the little ones. You'll know whether you can fix a mistake yourself with a few clicks and a kick. You also discover how to solve one of the biggest computing problems of all: how to copy your old PC's information to your *new* PC.

Chapter 17

The Case of the Broken Window

Sometimes you just have a sense that something's wrong. The computer makes quiet grumbling noises, or Windows 7 starts running more slowly than Congress. Other times, something's obviously gone haywire. Programs freeze, menus keep shooting at you, or Windows 7 greets you with a cheery error message when you turn on your computer.

Many of the biggest-looking problems are solved by the smallest-looking solutions. This chapter may be able to point you to the right one.

Windows 7 Keeps Asking Me for Permission

When it came to security, Windows XP was fairly easy to figure out. If you owned an Administrator account — and most people did — Windows XP mostly stayed out of your face. Owners of the less powerful Limited and Guest accounts, however, frequently faced screens telling them that their actions were restricted to Administrator accounts.

Windows Vista took a more strident path, sending nag screens even to Administrator accounts, often for seemingly innocuous actions. Although Windows 7 improves markedly on Windows Vista, you'll occasionally brush up against Windows 7's barbed wire fence. When another program tries to change something on your PC, Windows 7 pokes you with a message like the one shown in Figure 17-1.

Figure 17-1:
The
Windows 7
permission
screens pop
up when
a program
tries to
change
something
on your PC.

Figure 17-1: The Windows 7 permission screens pop up when a program tries to change something on your PC.

Standard account holders see a slightly different message that commands them to fetch an Administrator account holder to type in a password.

Of course, when screens like this one pop up too often, most people simply ignore them and give their approval — even if that means they've just allowed a piece of spyware to latch onto their PC.

So, when Windows 7 sends you a permission screen, ask yourself this question:

Is Windows 7 asking permission for something *I* did or requested? If your answer is yes, then give your approval so Windows 7 can carry out your bidding. But if Windows 7 sends you a permission screen out of the blue, when you haven't done anything, click No or Cancel. That keeps potential nasties from invading your PC.

If you don't have time for this bothersome security layer and your PC is well protected with a firewall and an up-to-date antivirus program, you can find out how to turn off Windows 7's user account permissions by reading Chapter 10.

I Need System Restore to Fix My PC

When your computer is a disaster, wouldn't you love to go back in time to when Windows worked *right?* Just as with Windows XP and Windows Vista, Windows 7's built-in time-traveling program, System Restore, lets you turn back the clock with a few clicks.

System Restore works like this: Every so often, Windows takes a snapshot, known as a *restore point,* of its most important settings and saves them by time and date. When your computer begins acting up, tell System Restore to return to a restore point created when everything worked fine.

System Restore won't erase any of your files or e-mail, but programs installed after a restore point's creation date may need to be reinstalled. System Restore is also reversible; you can undo your last restore point or try a different one.

To send your computer back to a restore point, when it was working much better, follow these steps:

1. **Save any open files, close any loaded programs, and load System Restore.**

   Choose Start, click All Programs, and begin weaving your way through the menus: Choose Accessories, select System Tools, and click System Restore. The System Restore window appears.

   Don't like wading through menus? Load the program more quickly by typing **System Restore** into the Start menu's search box along the bottom and pressing Enter.

2. **Select either the first listed restore point, Undo System Restore, or Choose a Different Restore Point. Then click Next.**

   System Restore behaves slightly differently under different conditions. Nevertheless, you'll always spot at least one of these options:

   • **First Listed Restore Point:** System Restore places your most recent restore point atop the list of available restore points. Choosing this restore point uninstalls your PC's most recent update, driver, or software installation, as that's usually the culprit that made things suddenly go wacky.

   • **Undo System Restore:** Choose this option only if using System Restore made things *worse,* heaven forbid. This option rolls back your most recently applied restore point, returning your PC to its former state. You're then free to try a different restore point.

   • **Choose a Different Restore Point:** This lets you choose any restore point from a list. If your previously chosen restore point didn't fix your PC, try choosing one farther down the list. (The restore points are listed by date, with the newest at the top.)

   Wondering exactly how any of these options affect your PC? Click Scan For Affected Programs. System Restore examines your PC and lists exactly which programs will be impacted by your current choice.

3. **Make *sure* that you've saved any open files, click Next, if needed, and then click Finish.**

   Your computer grumbles a bit and then restarts, using those earlier settings that (hopefully) worked fine.

If your system is *already* working fine, feel free to create your own restore point, as I describe at the beginning of Chapter 12. Name the restore point something descriptive, such as Before Letting the Babysitter Use the PC. (That way, you know which restore point to use if things go awry.)

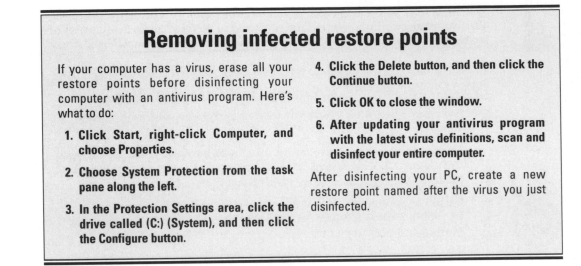

Removing infected restore points

If your computer has a virus, erase all your restore points before disinfecting your computer with an antivirus program. Here's what to do:

1. **Click Start, right-click Computer, and choose Properties.**

2. **Choose System Protection from the task pane along the left.**

3. **In the Protection Settings area, click the drive called (C:) (System), and then click the Configure button.**

4. **Click the Delete button, and then click the Continue button.**

5. **Click OK to close the window.**

6. **After updating your antivirus program with the latest virus definitions, scan and disinfect your entire computer.**

After disinfecting your PC, create a new restore point named after the virus you just disinfected.

These tips help wring the most fix-it power from System Restore:

✔ Before installing a program or any new computer toys, create a restore point in case the installation is a disaster. Create a restore point *after* successfully installing something, too. Returning to that restore point will keep your successful installation intact. (I describe how to create restore points in Chapter 12.)

✔ You can save quite a few restore points, depending on your hard drive's size. You'll likely have room for a dozen or more. Windows 7 deletes the oldest restore points to make room for the newer ones, so make your own Restore Points as often as you like.

✔ If you restore your computer to a time *before* you installed some new hardware or software, those items may not work correctly. If they're not working correctly, reinstall them.

I Need to Retrieve Deleted or Damaged Files

Everybody who's worked on a computer knows the agony of seeing hours of work go down the drain. You'll mistakenly delete a file by accident, for example, or try to change one for the better only to realize that you've messed it up rather than improved it.

System Restore won't help here — it memorizes your PC's settings, not your files. But Windows 7 offers ways not only to retrieve deleted files, but also to dig up their earlier versions, the two tasks described in the following sections.

Undeleting accidentally deleted files

Windows 7 doesn't really delete files, even if you tell it to delete them. Instead, Windows 7 slips those files into your Recycle Bin (shown in the margin), which lives on your desktop. Open the Recycle Bin with a double-click, and you'll find every file or folder you've deleted in the past few weeks. Click the file you want back and click the Restore This Item button on the Recycle Bin's menu bar. The Recycle Bin places the file back in the place where you deleted it.

I cover the Recycle Bin in Chapter 2.

Retrieving previous versions of files and folders

Have you ever changed a file and saved it, only to realize that the original was much better? Or have you ever wanted to start from scratch from a document you began changing last week? Windows 7 lets you send a grappling hook into the past to retrieve old versions of files.

To find and retrieve an older version of an existing file, right-click the file and choose Restore Previous Versions. In the dialog box that appears, Windows 7 lists all the previous versions available for that particular file, as shown in Figure 17-2.

Windows 7 lists all the previous versions available in chronological order, leading to the big question: Which version is the one you want? To take a quick peek at a previous version, click its name and click Open. Windows 7 opens the file, letting you see whether you've struck pay dirt.

If you're positive that the older version is better than your current version, click the Restore button. Windows 7 warns you that restoring the old file will delete your existing file; when you approve the deletion, Windows 7 puts the restored version in its place.

If you're not quite sure whether the older version is better, a safer alternative is to click the Copy button, instead. Windows 7 lets you copy the previous version to a different folder, letting you manually compare the old and new files before deciding which one to save.

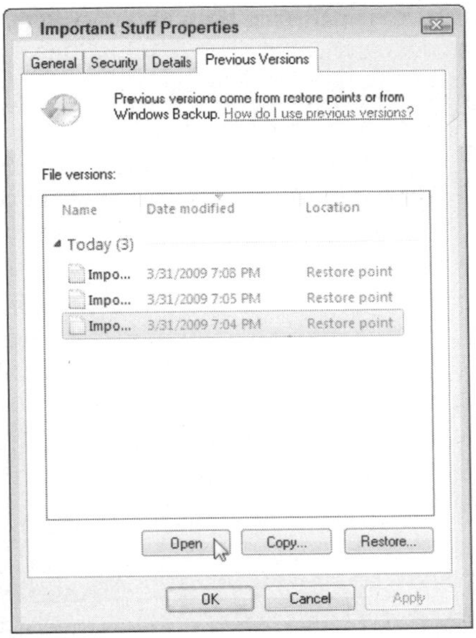

Figure 17-2:
Windows 7
tracks
previous
versions of
your files,
letting you
return to
older
versions in
case of a
mishap.

Important Stuff Properties

General | Security | Details | Previous Versions

Previous versions come from restore points or from Windows Backup. How do I use previous versions?

File versions:

Name	Date modified	Location
▲ Today (3)		
Impo...	3/31/2009 7:08 PM	Restore point
Impo...	3/31/2009 7:05 PM	Restore point
Impo...	3/31/2009 7:04 PM	Restore point

Open | Copy... | Restore...

OK | Cancel | Apply

Windows 7's Restore Previous Versions feature even works for folders, letting you see older versions of items no longer living inside the folder.

My Settings Are Messed Up

Sometimes you want to return to the way things were *before* you started messing around with them. Your savior lies in the Restore Default button, which awaits your command in strategically placed areas throughout Windows 7. A click of that button returns the settings to the way Windows 7 set them up originally.

Here are a few Restore Default buttons you may find useful:

- **Libraries:** Every folder's Navigation Pane lists your *libraries* — collections of your files and folders that I cover in Chapter 4. But if one of your libraries is missing, say the Music library, you can put it back. Right-click the word Libraries in the Navigation Pane and choose Restore Default Libraries. Your Documents, Music, Pictures, and Videos libraries all reappear.

- **Start menu:** You can customize your Start menu by dragging icons onto and off of it. But if you've messed up the menu something awful, return to the original Start menu: Right-click the Start button, choose Properties, click the Customize button, and click Use Default Settings. Your Start menu returns to its original settings.

✔ **Taskbar:** Right-click a blank part of the taskbar and choose Properties. Click the Customize button and choose Restore Default Icon Behaviors at the bottom of the window.

✔ **Internet Explorer:** When Internet Explorer seems clogged with unwanted toolbars, spyware, or just plain weirdness, take the last resort of bringing back its original settings: In IE, click Tools and choose Internet Options from the drop-down menu. Click the Advanced tab and click the Reset button.

This action wipes out nearly *everything*, including your toolbars, add-ons, and search engine preference. If you also select the Delete Personal Settings check box, clicking the Reset button even kills your browser history and saved passwords, so that you must start from scratch. Only your favorites, feeds, and a few other items remain. (For a complete list, click that page's How Does Resetting Affect My Computer option.)

✔ **Firewall:** If you suspect foul play within Windows Firewall, bring back its original settings and start over. (Some of your programs may need to be reinstalled.) Click the Start menu, choose Control Panel, choose System and Security, and open Windows Firewall. Click Restore Defaults in the left column.

✔ **Media Player:** When Media Player's library contains mistakes, tell it to delete its index and start over. In Media Player, press the Alt key, click Tools, choose Advanced from the pop-out menu, and choose Restore Media Library. (Choose Restore Deleted Library Items instead if you've accidentally removed items from Media Player's library.)

✔ **Folders:** Windows 7 hides a slew of switches relating to folders, their Navigation Panes, the items they show, how they behave, and how they search for items. To mull over the options or return them to normal, open any folder, click the Organize button, and choose Folder and Search Options. You can find a Restore Defaults button on each tab: General, View, and Search.

I Forgot My Password

When Windows 7 won't accept your password at the logon screen, you may not be hopelessly locked out of your own PC. Check all these things before letting loose with a scream:

✔ **Check your Caps Lock key.** Windows 7 passwords are *case-sensitive*, meaning that Windows 7 considers **OpenSesame** and **opensesame** to be different passwords. If your keyboard's Caps Lock light is on, press your Caps Lock key again to turn it off. Then try entering your password again.

✔ **Use your Password Reset Disk.** I explain how to create a Password Reset Disk in Chapter 13. When you've forgotten your password, insert that disk to use as a key. Windows 7 lets you back into your account, where you can promptly create an easier-to-remember password. (Flip to Chapter 13 and create a Password Reset Disk now if you haven't yet.)

✔ **Let another user reset your password.** Anybody with an Administrator account on your PC can reset your password. Have that person choose Control Panel from the Start menu, choose User Accounts and Family Safety, and click User Accounts. There, they can choose Manage Another Account, click your account name, and choose Remove Password, letting you log in.

If none of these options work, then you're in sad shape, unfortunately. Compare the value of your password-protected data against the cost of hiring a password recovery specialist. You'll find a specialist by searching for "recover windows password" on Google (www.google.com) or another search engine.

My Folder (Or Desktop) Doesn't Show All My Files

When you open a folder — or even look at your desktop — you expect to see everything it contains. But when something's missing or there's nothing inside at all, check these things before panicking:

✔ **Check the Search box.** Whenever you type something into a folder's Search box — that little box in the folder's top-right corner — Windows 7 begins looking for it by hiding everything that doesn't match your search. If a folder isn't showing everything it should, delete any words you see in the Search box.

✔ **Make sure that the desktop isn't hiding things.** To make sure that your desktop isn't cloaking your icons, right-click an empty part of your desktop, choose View, and select the Show Desktop Icons check box.

If everything's really gone, check out the previous versions of that folder, as described in the "Retrieving previous versions of files and folders" section, earlier in this chapter. Windows 7 not only tracks previous versions of files, but it keeps track of a folder's past life, as well.

My Mouse Doesn't Work Right

Sometimes, the mouse doesn't work at all; other times, the mouse pointer hops across the screen like a flea. Here are a few fixes to try:

- ✔ If no mouse arrow is on the screen after you start Windows, make sure that the mouse's tail is plugged snugly into the computer's USB port. (If you have an older mouse with a round PS/2 port instead of a rectangular USB port, you need to restart your PC to bring the newly plugged-in mouse back to life.)

- ✔ To restart your PC when the mouse doesn't work, hold down the Ctrl, Alt, and Del keys simultaneously. Press Tab until the tiny arrow next to the red button is surrounded by the lines, and then press Enter to reveal the Restart menu. Press your up arrow to choose Restart and then press Enter to restart your PC.

- ✔ If the mouse arrow is on-screen but won't move, Windows may be mistaking your brand of mouse for a different brand. You can make sure that Windows 7 recognizes the correct type of mouse by following the steps on adding new hardware in Chapter 11. If you own a cordless mouse, the little guy probably needs new batteries.

- ✔ A mouse pointer can jump around on-screen erratically when the mouse's innards become dirty. Follow the cleaning instructions I give in Chapter 12.

- ✔ If the mouse was working fine but the buttons seem to be reversed, you've probably changed the right- or left-handed button configuration setting in the Control Panel. Open the Control Panel's Mouse settings area and take a look at the setting for Switch Primary and Secondary Buttons. Lefties want it turned on; righties don't. (I cover this setting in Chapter 11.)

My Double-Clicks Are Now Single Clicks

In an effort to make things easier, Windows 7 lets people choose whether a single click or a double-click should open a file or folder.

But if you're not satisfied with the click method Windows 7 uses, here's how to change it:

1. **Open any folder — the Start menu's Documents folder will do.**

2. **Click the Organize button and choose Folder and Search Options.**

3. **Choose your click preference in the Click Items As Follows section.**

4. **Click OK to save your preferences.**

Don't like to follow steps? Just click the Restore Defaults button in Folder and Search Options, and Windows brings back double-clicking and other standard Windows 7 folder behaviors.

My program is frozen!

Eventually one of your programs will freeze up solid, leaving no way to reach its normal Close command. These four steps will extricate the frozen program from your computer's memory (and the screen, as well):

1. **Hold down the Ctrl, Alt, and Delete keys simultaneously.**

   Known as the "three finger salute," this combination always catches Windows 7's attention, even when it's sailing o'er rough seas. In fact, if Windows 7 doesn't respond, press your PC's power button until your PC shuts down. After a few seconds, push the power button again to restart your PC

and see whether Windows 7 is in a better mood.

2. **Choose the Start Task Manager option.**

   The Task Manager program appears.

3. **Click the Task Manager's Applications tab, if necessary, and then click the frozen program's name.**

4. **Click the End Task button, and Windows 7 whisks away the frozen program.**

   If your computer seems a bit groggy afterward, play it safe by restarting your computer from the Start menu.

I Can't Run Older Programs under Windows 7

Many programmers design their software to run on a specific version of Windows. When a new Windows version appears a few years later, some older programs feel threatened by their new environment and refuse to work.

If an older game or other program refuses to run under Windows 7, there's still hope because of Windows 7's secret *Compatibility mode.* This mode tricks programs into thinking that they're running under their favorite older version of Windows, letting them run in comfort.

If your old program has problems with Windows 7, follow these steps:

1. **Right-click the program's icon and choose Properties.**

2. **When the Properties dialog box appears, click the Compatibility tab.**

3. **In the Compatibility Mode section, select the Run This Program in Compatibility Mode For check box and select the program's desired Windows version from the drop-down list, as shown in Figure 17-3.**

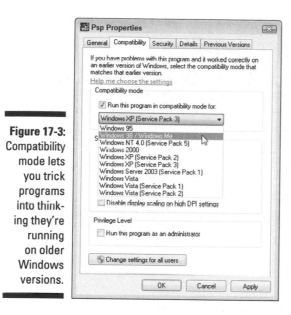

Figure 17-3:
Compatibility
mode lets
you trick
programs
into think-
ing they're
running
on older
Windows
versions.

Check your program's box or look at its manual to see what version of
Windows it expects.

**4. Click OK and then try running your program again to see whether it
works better.**

Microsoft's free Virtual Windows XP program lets you run Windows XP
programs in their own XP-compatible window. Although it's the most
compatible way to run older programs, the program won't run on every PC,
and it's difficult to use. For more information, visit www.microsoft.com/
windows/virtual-pc.

I Can't Find the Folder Menus

To keep things alarming, both Windows 7 and Windows Vista hide the folder
menus that users have come to depend on for the last decade. To make them
reappear atop a folder, press the Alt key. To make Windows 7 glue them back
atop every window where they belong, click the Organize button, choose
Folder and Search Options, click the View tab, and click the Always Show
Menus option. Click OK to save your changes.

My Computer Is Frozen Up Solid

Every once in a while, Windows just drops the ball and wanders off somewhere to sit under a tree. You're left looking at a computer that just looks back. None of the computer's lights blink. Panicked clicks don't do anything. Pressing every key on the keyboard doesn't do anything, or worse yet, the computer starts to beep at every key press.

When nothing on-screen moves (except sometimes the mouse pointer), the computer is frozen up solid. Try the following approaches, in the following order, to correct the problem:

✔ **Approach 1:** Press Esc twice.

This action rarely works, but give it a shot anyway.

✔ **Approach 2:** Press Ctrl, Alt, and Delete simultaneously and choose Start Task Manager.

If you're lucky, the Task Manager appears with the message that it discovered an unresponsive application. The Task Manager lists the names of currently running programs, including the one that's not responding. Click the name of the program on the Application tab that's causing the mess and then click the End Task button. You lose any unsaved work in that program, of course, but you should be used to that. (If you somehow stumbled onto the Ctrl+Alt+Delete combination by accident, press Esc to quit Task Manager and return to Windows.)

If that still doesn't do the trick, press Ctrl+Alt+Delete again and look for the little red button in the bottom-right corner of the screen. Click the little arrow next to that button's circle, shown in the margin. Choose Restart from the menu that pops up. Your computer should shut down and restart, hopefully returning in a better mood.

✔ **Approach 3:** If the preceding approaches don't work, push the computer's reset button. If the Turn Off Computer box appears, choose Restart.

✔ **Approach 4:** If not even the reset button works (and some computers don't even have reset buttons anymore), turn off the computer by pushing its power button. (If that merely brings up the Turn Off the Computer menu, choose Restart, and your computer should restart.)

✔ **Approach 5:** If you keep pressing the computer's power button long enough (usually about 4 to 5 seconds), it eventually stops resisting and turns off.

Chapter 18

Strange Messages: What You Did Does Not Compute

*E*rror messages in *real* life are fairly easy to understand. A VCR's flashing clock means that you haven't set its clock yet. A car's beeping tone means that you've left your keys in the ignition. A spouse's stern glance means that you've forgotten something important.

But Windows 7's error messages may have been written by a Senate subcommittee, if only the messages weren't so brief. The error messages rarely describe what you did to cause the event or, even worse, what to do about it.

In this chapter, I've collected some of Windows 7's most common messages. Match up an error message's subject or picture with the ones here and then read your appropriate response and the chapter covering that particular problem.

Activate Windows Now

Meaning: If you don't activate Windows, Windows darkens the screen and nags you with the message shown in Figure 18-1.

Probable cause: Microsoft's copy-protection scheme requires every person to activate his or her Windows 7 copy within 30 days after installing or upgrading to Windows 7. Once activated, your copy of Windows 7 is linked to your particular PC so that you can't install it onto another computer, including a laptop.

Solutions: Click the message and let Windows connect to the Internet to activate itself. No Internet connection? Then dial the activation phone number and talk to the Microsoft people personally. *Note:* If you never see this message, your copy of Windows has already been activated by the PC's manufacturer. Don't worry about it.

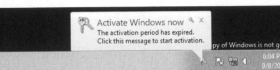

Could Not Perform This Operation Because the Default Mail Client Is Not Properly Installed

Meaning: The particularly cryptic message in Figure 18-2 means you're trying to send e-mail on your PC, but you haven't installed an e-mail program.

Probable cause: Windows 7 doesn't come with a built-in program to send or receive e-mail. If you click any program's Send This or E-mail This option, this message appears until you choose and install an e-mail program.

Solutions: You can download and install an e-mail program or set up an e-mail program at one of many Web sites. I describe choosing and setting up e-mail in Chapter 9.

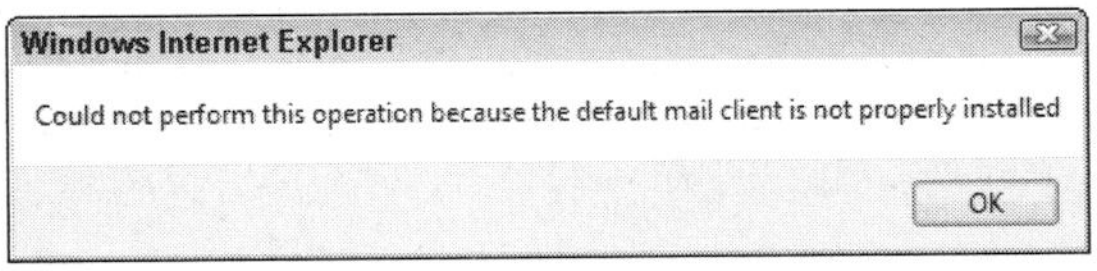

Figure 18-2:
You need
to install an
e-mail
program.

Windows Internet Explorer

Could not perform this operation because the default mail client is not properly installed

OK

Device Driver Software Was Not Successfully Installed

Meaning: Figure 18-3 appears when you're trying to plug in or add a new part to your PC, but that part's software didn't install correctly.

Probable cause: The software isn't compatible with Windows 7, or it simply hit a glitch.

Solutions: If you've plugged a cable or device into one of your PC's connectors, unplug it. Wait 30 seconds and then plug it back in. If it still doesn't work, leave it plugged in, but restart your PC. If it still doesn't work, you need to contact the part's manufacturer and ask for a Windows 7–compatible driver.

I cover tracking down and installing drivers in Chapter 12.

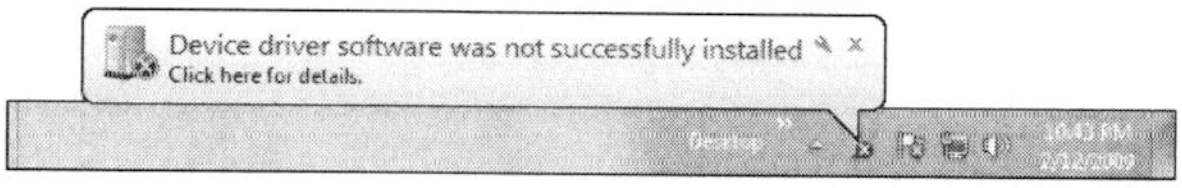

Figure 18-3:
Your new
part won't
work.

Device driver software was not successfully installed
Click here for details.

Do You Trust This Printer?

Meaning: Figure 18-4 appears when a printer on your network is trying to install its software onto your PC.

Probable cause: You're trying to install a printer that's attached to another PC on your network.

Solutions: If you really *are* trying to add a printer that's connected to another PC through a network, click Yes. That allows the other PC to send your PC that printer's software. If this message appears unexpectedly, however, click No.

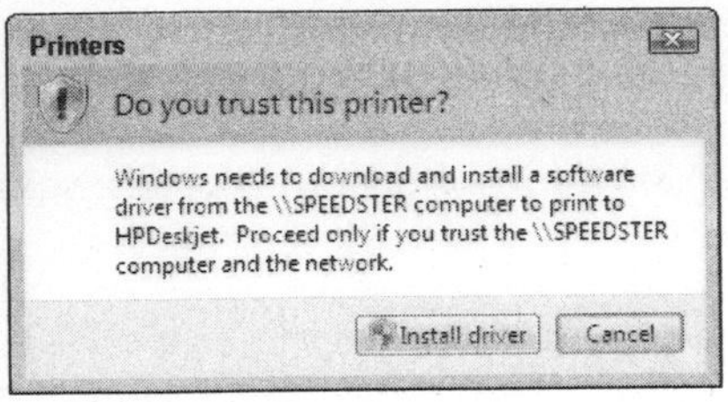

Figure 18-4:
Windows
thinks
you're
trying to
install a
printer's
software
over a
network.

Do You Want to Allow the Following Program to Make Changes to This Computer?

Meaning: A program is trying to change settings, files, or programs on your PC.

Probable cause: When Figure 18-5 appears, Windows darkens the screen to get your attention and then sends this message as a security measure, asking you to approve the change or nip it in the bud. Although this looks ominous, there's no harm done . . . yet.

Solutions: If you're trying to install a program or change a setting, click Yes. But if you see this message appear unexpectedly, click No to stop what could be a harmful program.

If the message requests a password, summon an Administrator account holder to type in his or her password, as I describe in Chapter 10, before clicking the Yes button.

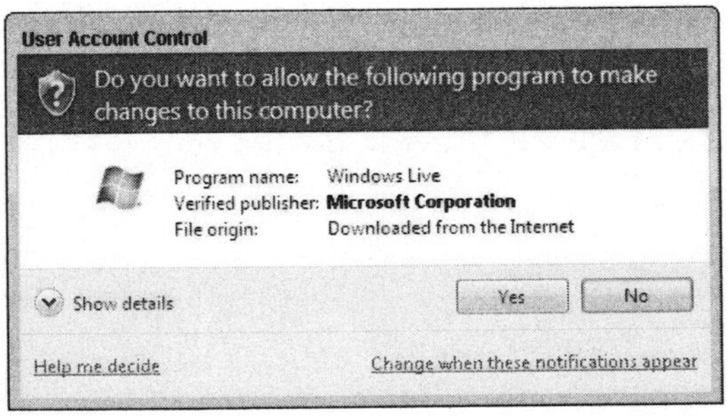

Figure 18-5:
A program
is trying
to make
changes to
your com-
puter.

Do You Want to Install (Or Run) This Software?

Meaning: Are you sure that this software is free from viruses, spyware, and other harmful things?

Probable cause: A window similar to the one shown in Figure 18-6 appears when you try to run or install a program you've downloaded from the Internet.

Solutions: If you're sure the file is safe, click the Run or Install button. But if this message appears unexpectedly, or you think it may not be safe, click the Cancel or Don't Run button. To be on the safe side, scan everything you download with an antivirus program. I cover safe computing in Chapter 10.

Figure 18-6:
Do you think this software is safe?

> **Internet Explorer - Security Warning**
>
> **Do you want to run this software?**
>
> Name: epson12242.exe
>
> Publisher: Epson America, Inc.
>
> ☒ More options   [Run]   [Don't Run]
>
> While files from the Internet can be useful, this file type can potentially harm your computer. Only run software from publishers you trust. What's the risk?

Do You Want to Save Changes?

Meaning: Figure 18-7 means you haven't saved your work in a program, and your work is about to be lost.

Probable cause: You're trying to close an application, log off, or restart your PC before telling a program to save the work you've accomplished.

Solutions: Look in the window's title bar for the program's name — Paint, in this case. Find that program on your desktop (or click its name on the taskbar to bring it to the forefront). Then save your work by choosing Save from the File menu or clicking the program's Save icon. I cover saving files in Chapter 5. Don't want to save the file? Then click Don't Save to discard your work and move on.

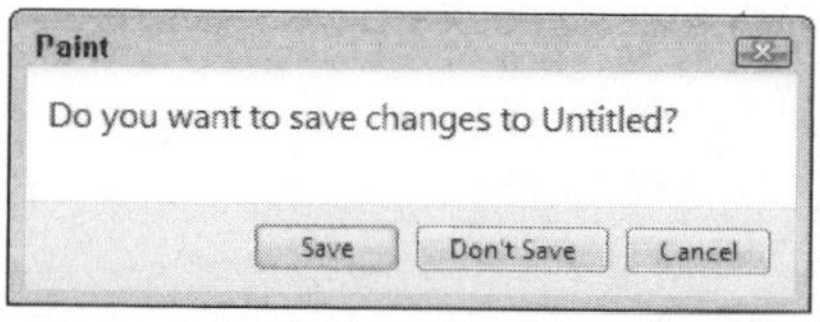

Figure 18-7:
Do you want to save your work?

> **Paint**
>
> Do you want to save changes to Untitled?
>
> [Save]   [Don't Save]   [Cancel]

Do You Want to Turn AutoComplete On?

Meaning: Internet Explorer's AutoComplete feature, shown in the left side of Figure 18-8, guesses what you're about to type into a form and tries to fill it in for you.

Probable cause: Every Windows user is eventually asked whether to turn on AutoComplete or leave it turned off.

Solutions: AutoComplete handily fills in some online forms with words you've used previously. Although a timesaver, AutoComplete poses a potential security problem for some people: It lets other people know what words you've previously typed into forms. To see or change its settings, open Internet Explorer, open the Tools menu, choose Internet Options, and click the Content tab. In the AutoComplete section, click Settings and deselect every check box that shouldn't enlist AutoComplete.

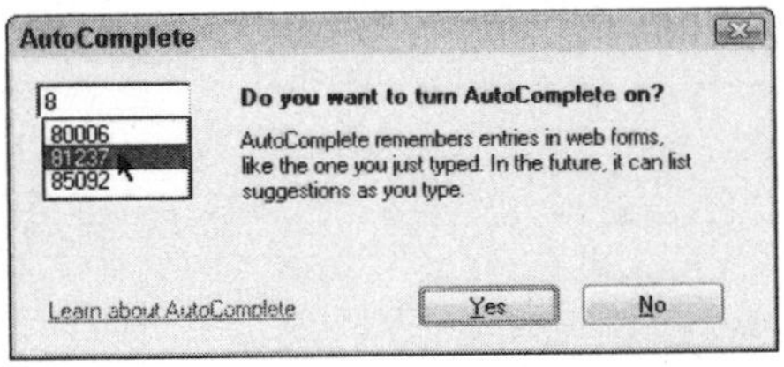

Figure 18-8:
Auto-
Complete
helps by fill-
ing in words
as you begin
to type
them.

Find an Antivirus Program Online

Meaning: The message in Figure 18-9 appears when your PC has security problems.

Probable cause: Your antivirus program isn't working. A similar message can also appear if Windows Firewall isn't turned on, Windows Defender isn't running, Windows Update isn't working, Internet Explorer's security settings are too low, or User Account Control (the perpetrator of all those permission screens) isn't turned on.

Solutions: Click the balloon to see the exact problem. If the balloon disappears before you have a chance to click it, click the white flag icon (shown in the margin) in the taskbar. Windows points out the problem and offers a solution, which I cover in Chapter 10.

Figure 18-9:
Windows
can't find
an antivirus
program.

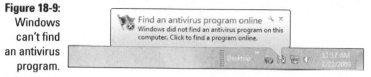

Installing Device Driver Software

Meaning: Windows recognizes a newly installed computer part and is trying to make it work automatically.

Probable cause: The message in Figure 18-10 usually appears after you plug something new into your computer's USB port.

Solutions: Relax. Windows knows what's going on and will take charge. If Windows can't find a driver, however, you need to find one on your own. I describe that tiresome process in Chapter 12.

Figure 18-10:
Windows
finds a new
device.

Set Up Windows Internet Explorer 8

Meaning: Windows 7 comes with a new version of Internet Explorer, the Web browser. The dialog box in Figure 18-11 appears when Internet Explorer asks you to turn on its new features.

Probable cause: When Internet Explorer loads the first time, it asks every Windows user to choose options.

Solutions: If you're in a hurry, click the Ask Me Later button, and Microsoft begins using its own services, like its Bing search engine. If you prefer to search the Web with Google, I explain how to switch in Chapter 8.

If you're not rushed, click Next and approve or decline each option. (You can always change your mind later by clicking the Tools menu, choosing Internet Options, and clicking the Search area's Setting button.)

Figure 18-11:
Internet
Explorer
wants you
to set up
its new
options.

View Important Messages

Meaning: Instead of nagging you whenever something in Windows or your PC needs attention, Windows sends the message in Figure 18-12.

Probable cause: You need to perform maintenance chores on your PC, which could be anything from setting up an antivirus program, creating a backup, or changing your security settings.

 Solutions: Click the pop-up message or click the taskbar's icon of a little white flag with an adjacent red X. The Action Center appears, showing a list of tasks for you to perform.

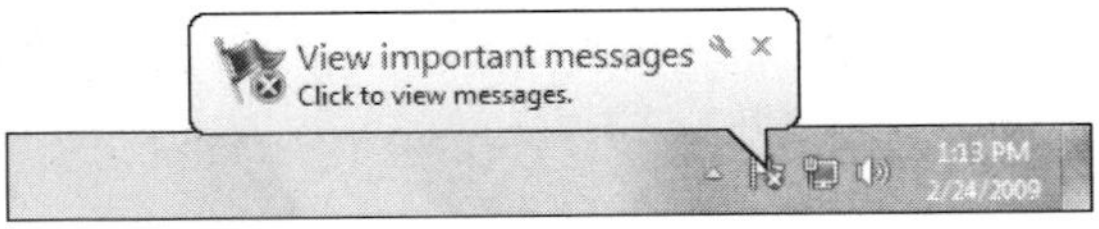

Figure 18-12:
Windows
has
messages
for you.

Windows Can't Open This File

Meaning: The dialog box in Figure 18-13 appears when Windows doesn't know which program created the file that you double-clicked.

Probable cause: Windows 7 programs add hidden secret codes, known as *file extensions,* onto the ends of filenames. When you double-click a Notepad file, for example, Windows 7 spots the file's secret, hidden file extension and uses Notepad to open the file. But if Windows doesn't recognize the file's secret code letters, this error message appears.

Solutions: If *you* know what program created the mysterious file, choose the Select a Program from a List of Installed Programs option, click OK, and select that program from Windows 7's list. Then select the check box for Always Use the Selected Program to Open This Kind of File.

If you're stumped, however, choose Use the Web Service to Find the Correct Program. Windows examines the file, consults the Internet, and offers suggestions and links for downloading the right program for the job. (I cover this problem in Chapter 5.)

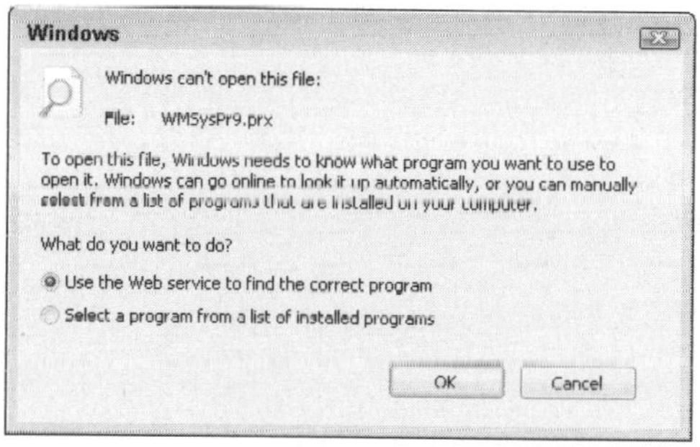

Figure 18-13:
Windows
doesn't
know what
program
should open
this file.

You Don't Currently Have Permission to Access This Folder

Meaning: If you see the dialog box in Figure 18-14, that means Windows 7 won't let you peek inside the folder you're trying to open. (The folder's name appears in the message's title bar.)

Probable cause: The computer's owner hasn't given you permission.

Solutions: Only a person with an Administrator account — usually the computer's owner — can grant permission to open certain folders, so you need to track down that person. (If you're the administrator, you may grant access to others by copying or moving the folder or its contents into the Public folder, described in Chapter 14.)

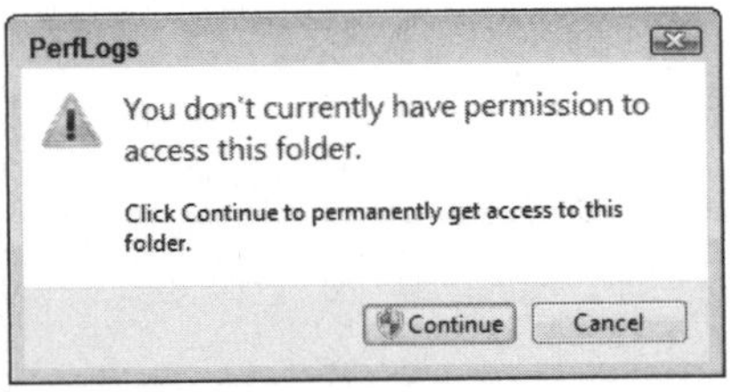

Figure 18-14:
Find somebody with an Administrator account to open the folder or file.

PerfLogs

You don't currently have permission to access this folder.

Click Continue to permanently get access to this folder.

[Continue] [Cancel]

Chapter 19

Moving from an Old Computer to a New Windows 7 PC

In This Chapter

▶ Copying your old PC's files and settings into your new PC

▶ Using Windows Easy Transfer

▶ Transferring files through an easy transfer cable, network, or portable hard drive

▶ Getting rid of your old computer

*W*hen you bring home an exciting new Windows 7 computer, it lacks the most important thing of all: your *old* computer's files. How do you copy your files from that drab old Windows XP or Vista PC to that exciting new Windows 7 PC? How do you even *find* everything you want to move? To solve the problem, Microsoft stocked Windows 7 with a virtual moving van called Windows Easy Transfer. Windows Easy Transfer grabs not only your old computer's data but also settings from some of your programs: your browser's list of favorite Web sites, for example.

Not everybody needs Windows Easy Transfer. If you're upgrading a Windows Vista PC to Windows 7, for example, Windows 7 keeps your files and most settings in place. Windows Vista upgraders don't need the transfer program — or this chapter.

But should you need to copy information from a Windows XP or Windows Vista PC to a Windows 7 PC, this chapter introduces the program and walks you down the path.

Note: Windows Easy Transfer doesn't work with older Windows versions like Windows Me or Windows 98.

Preparing to Move into Your New PC

Like any other moving day, the event's success depends on your preparation. Instead of rummaging for boxes and duct tape, you must do these two things to prepare your PCs for Windows Easy Transfer:

✔ Choose the method for copying the information to your new PC

✔ Install your *old* PC's programs onto your *new* PC

The next two sections explain each topic in more detail.

Choosing how to transfer your old information

PCs are very good at copying things, much to the dismay of the entertainment industry. They're so good, in fact, that they offer a zillion different ways to copy the same thing.

For example, Windows Easy Transfer offers *four* different ways to copy your old PC's information into your new PC. Each method works at a different level of speed and difficulty. Here are the contenders:

✔ **Easy Transfer cable:** Because every modern PC includes a USB port, an Easy Transfer cable is your least expensive solution. This special cable often looks like a normal USB cable that has swallowed a mouse: The cable usually bulges in the middle, as shown in Figure 19-1. These cables cost less than $30 at most electronics stores or online. Plug one end into each PC's USB port, and you're ready to copy. (No, a normal USB cable won't work.)

Older Easy Transfer cables made for Windows Vista work fine with Windows 7, but don't try to use Windows Vista's version of the Easy Transfer program. Fire up the Windows 7 version, instead.

✔ **External hard drive:** Costing between $100 and $200, a portable hard drive makes copying your information quick and easy. Most portable drives plug into both a wall outlet and your PC's USB port; others draw their power right from the USB port.

✔ **Flash drive:** These little memory sticks, often spotted sprouting from nerds' key chains, plug into a computer's USB port. They're handy for transferring small batches of files or settings, but they lack enough storage space to hold much else. They work great, however, for copying the Windows 7 Easy Transfer program to your old PC.

✔ **Network:** If you've linked your two PCs through a *network* (a chore I cover in Chapter 14), the Easy Transfer program can transfer your old PC's information that way.

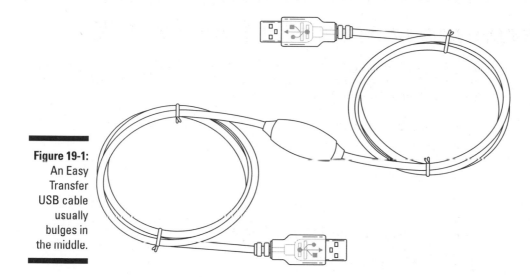

Figure 19-1:
An Easy
Transfer
USB cable
usually
bulges in
the middle.

If your PCs aren't connected through a network, and they live more than a cable's reach apart, a portable hard drive is your best option. Choose one with as much capacity as the hard drive inside your new PC. After transferring the files, put the hard drive to work backing up your files each night, an extremely prudent task I describe in Chapter 12.

Installing your old PC's programs onto your new PC

The Easy Transfer program can transfer your PC's *data* — your e-mail, digital photos, letters, and other things you've created — as well as your programs' *settings:* your Web browser's list of favorite Web sites, for example.

But the Easy Transfer program can't copy the *programs* themselves. That's right: Your old PC's programs must be reinstalled onto your new PC. And you need to install those programs *before* running the Easy Transfer program to ensure that the programs will be ready to accept their incoming settings.

To install the old programs, dig out their installation CDs and any copy protection codes you may need to reenter. The codes are usually printed on either the CD itself, the CD's packaging, or a sticker on the program's manual. (If you purchased a program online, you may be able to retrieve the copy-protection code from the manufacturer's Web site.)

Unfortunately, not all your old programs will run on Windows 7. Most antivirus programs, for example, require versions built specifically for Windows 7.

Transferring Information Between Two PCs with Windows Easy Transfer

Windows Easy Transfer works in just a few short steps or a lengthy series of leaps, depending on the method you choose to pipe your old PC's information into your new PC: cable, network, or portable drive. The next three sections provide step-by-step walkthroughs of how to transfer all of your old PC's information using each of the three methods. The optional fourth section aims at fine-tuners who want to pick and choose the type of information they want transferred from their old PC.

Be sure to log on to your old and new PCs with an Administrator account; Standard, Limited, and Guest accounts don't have the authority to copy files. And take your time: You can always return to a previous screen by clicking the blue arrow in the window's top-left corner.

Transferring through an Easy Transfer cable

If you're transferring from a Windows XP PC with an Easy Transfer cable, shown earlier in Figure 19-1, be sure to install the Easy Transfer cable's bundled drivers. (You needn't worry about drivers in Windows Vista or Windows 7, because they automatically recognize the cable as soon as you plug it into a USB port.)

To test the cable, plug it into your Windows XP PC; when your PC recognizes the cable with a little pop-up message in the screen's bottom-right corner, you're set: Unplug the cable and wait until a step tells you to plug it back in.

To transfer files with an Easy Transfer cable, follow these steps on your new Windows 7 PC:

1. **Close all currently running programs on your new Windows 7 PC.**

2. **Open the Start menu, choose All Programs, click Accessories, click System Tools, and then click Windows Easy Transfer.**

   The Windows Easy Transfer window opens.

3. **Click Next at the opening screen.**

4. **Choose the An Easy Transfer Cable option.**

   The program asks whether you're working from your new PC or old PC.

5. **Choose the This Is My New Computer option.**

The program asks whether you need to install the Windows Easy Transfer program on your old PC.

6. **Choose the I Need To Install It Now option.**

The program offers to install itself on your old PC in one of two ways:

External Hard Disk or Shared Network Folder: Plug in your portable hard disk if you want to store the program there.

USB Flash Drive: Insert your flash drive, if you want to store it there.

When you choose one of the options, the Browse For Folder dialog box appears, as shown in Figure 19-2.

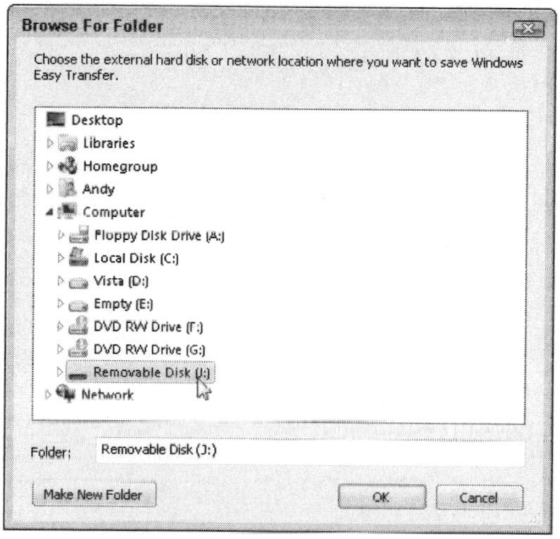

Figure 19-2:
Choose
where to
store the
program,
usually a
removable
drive.

Browse For Folder
Choose the external hard disk or network location where you want to save Windows Easy Transfer.
🖥 Desktop
▷ 📚 Libraries
▷ 👥 Homegroup
▷ 👤 Andy
⊿ 💻 Computer
▷ 💾 Floppy Disk Drive (A:)
▷ 💽 Local Disk (C:)
▷ 💽 Vista (D:)
▷ 💽 Empty (E:)
▷ 💿 DVD RW Drive (F:)
▷ 💿 DVD RW Drive (G:)
▷ 💾 Removable Disk (J:)
▷ 🖧 Network
Folder: Removable Disk (J:)
Make New Folder   OK   Cancel

Don't have a portable hard drive, flash drive, or network? Then find your solution in the sidebar, "I can't copy Windows Easy Transfer to my old PC!" After installing the program, jump ahead to Step 8.

7. **Navigate to the place you want to store the Windows Easy Transfer program and then click OK.**

To store the program on your newly plugged-in drive, click Computer in the Browse For Folder dialog box, choose the letter of your removable drive, and click OK.

The Easy Transfer program places a copy of itself onto the drive so you can run it on your old PC.

8. **Unplug the drive from your new PC and plug it into a USB port of your old PC to start the Easy Transfer program.**

The Windows Easy Transfer program should leap to life automatically on your old PC. (You may need to click OK to let it run.)

If it doesn't run automatically, you might need to look for the drive: Open the Start menu, choose Computer or My Computer, and look for the drive's icon. (Your old PC might assign your drive a different letter than your new PC did.)

9. **On your old PC, click Next to move past the opening screen. Then choose the An Easy Transfer Cable option.**

10. **On your old PC, choose the This Is My Old Computer option.**

   Connect the Easy Transfer cables between your two PCs' USB ports.

11. **Click Next on both PCs.**

   At this point, both PCs are open to a similar page in the Easy Transfer program. When you click Next on either or both PCs, they search for each other and connect.

   Your new Windows 7 PC begins searching your old PC to see what it can transfer.

12. **Choose what to transfer.**

   The program normally copies everything from everybody's user account. To pick and choose exactly what to copy, read the "Picking and choosing the files, folders, and accounts to transfer" section, later in this chapter.

13. **Click the Transfer button on your new PC to begin copying the information.**

   Don't touch either PC during the transfer process.

14. **Finish up.**

   The program leaves you with these two options:

   - **See What Was Transferred.** This rather technical report shows exactly what was transferred.

   - **See a List of Programs You Might Want to Install on Your New Computer.** Another overly technical report tells you what programs you may want to install in order to open some of your transferred files.

Unplug your Easy Transfer cable from both PCs, save it for later, and you're through.

Transferring through a network

Setting up a network, a chore I describe in Chapter 14, isn't for the fainthearted. You must buy networking equipment, set it up, and then tweak the settings on each PC until they can chatter amongst themselves. But once your network begins working, it's a fast and easy way to transfer files between two or more PCs.

I can't copy Windows Easy Transfer to my old PC!

Windows 7 can pack a copy of Windows Easy Transfer onto a flash drive, portable hard drive, or network location, so you can grab that program with your Windows XP or Windows Vista PC. But what if you have a cheap Easy Transfer cable, but you don't *have* a network, portable hard drive, or flash drive? Fortunately, you can still run the program on your old PC with either of these methods:

✔ **Download the program.** Microsoft lets you download the Easy Transfer program from its Windows 7 Web site at (www. microsoft.com/windows7). After downloading and installing the program on your old PC, launch it with a double-click, and head for Step 8 of the "Transferring through an Easy Transfer Cable" section.

✔ **Use the Windows 7 DVD.** The Easy Transfer program comes on the Windows 7 retail DVD. If your PC came with Windows 7 pre-installed, you probably didn't receive a Windows 7 retail DVD.

But if you bought a Windows 7 DVD at the store, insert that DVD into your old PC's DVD drive. If the installation program jumps to the screen, cancel the installation by clicking the X in the Install Windows program's upper-right corner. Then follow these steps:

1. **Open the Start menu and choose either My Computer (in Windows XP) or Computer (in Windows Vista).**

2. **Right-click the DVD drive's icon and choose Explore.**

3. **Open the Support folder.**

The Easy Transfer program lives inside a folder named MigWiz (short for Migration Wizard). To run the program on your old PC, open the MigWiz folder and start the Easy Transfer program by double-clicking the program's cryptic name: MigSetup or MigSetup.exe.

If you've already set up a network, follow these steps on your new Windows 7 PC to begin siphoning your older PC's files:

1. **Close all currently running programs on your new Windows 7 PC.**

2. **Start Windows Easy Transfer on your Windows 7 PC. Click Start, click All Programs, click Accessories, click System Tools, and then click Windows Easy Transfer.**

    The Windows Easy Transfer window opens.

3. **Click Next at the opening screen.**

4. **Choose the A Network option.**

5. **Choose the This Is My New Computer option.**

6. **Click the I Need To Install It Now option.**

    Already have a copy of the Windows 7 Easy Transfer program on your old PC? You can jump to Step 9.

7. **Choose the External Hard Disk or Shared Network Folder option.**

The Browse For Folder dialog box appears, as shown in Figure 19-3.

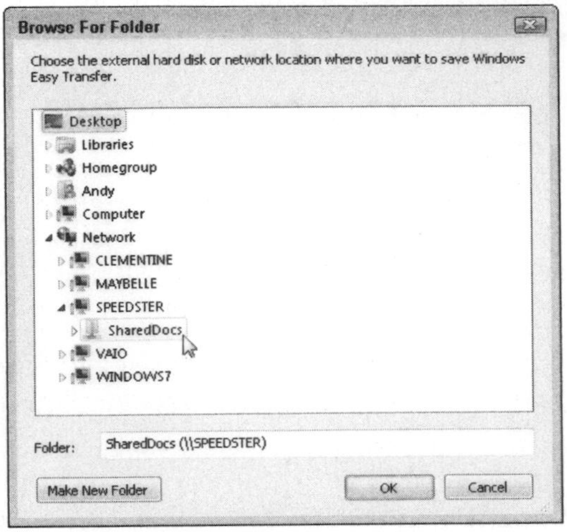

Figure 19-3:
Click
Network
and then
choose
a shared
folder on
your old PC.

8. **Navigate to the place you want to store the Windows Easy Transfer program and then click OK.**

   Because your network is already set up, copy the Easy Transfer program to a shared folder on your old PC: Click Network, click the name of your old PC, and choose a shared folder on that PC.

   When you click OK, the Easy Transfer program places a copy of itself in a shared folder on your old PC.

9. **On your old PC, run your newly copied version of Easy Transfer.**

   Open the shared folder on your old networked PC and then double-click the Windows Easy Transfer icon, shown in the margin. The Windows Easy Transfer program leaps to life on your old PC.

   Can't find where you stashed the program on your network? Head back to the Windows 7 PC and look at the Easy Transfer program's still-open window. Click Open the Folder Where You Saved Windows Easy Transfer to see a window showing the network folder containing the program. (Look along that window's top to see the networked PC's *name* and its *shared folder.*)

10. **On your old PC, click Next to move past the opening screen. Then choose the A Network option.**

11. **On your old PC, choose the This Is My Old Computer option.**

    Windows Easy Transfer on your old PC displays a six-digit password called an Easy Transfer Key. Write it down because you need to enter those numbers on your new PC in order to grab the files.

12. **Click Next on your new PC. Then, on your new PC, enter the six-digit password and click Next.**

    At this point, both PCs are open to a similar page in the Easy Transfer program. When you enter the password and click Next on your new PC, the two PCs search for each other.

    The two PCs connect, and your new PC begins sniffing the files on your old PC to see what it can transfer.

13. **On your new PC, choose what to transfer from your old PC.**

    The program normally copies everything from everybody's user account. To pick and choose exactly what to copy, read the "Picking and choosing the files, folders, and accounts to transfer" section, later in this chapter.

14. **Click Transfer on your new PC to begin copying the information.**

    Don't touch either PC during the transfer process.

15. **On your old PC, click Close to shut down Easy Transfer.**

16. **Finish up.**

    On your new PC, the Easy Transfer program leaves you with these two options:

    - **See What Was Transferred.** This rather technical report shows exactly what was transferred.

    - **See a List of Programs you Might Want to Install on Your New Computer.** Another overly technical report tells you what programs you may want to install in order to open some of your transferred files.

Transferring through a portable hard drive or flash drive

Unless you're grabbing only a tiny amount of information from your old PC, don't bother trying to transfer information with a flash drive. Those tiny sticks barely hold the information scattered across a person's desktop, much less an entire PC. No, you need a *portable hard drive* that's at least as large as your old PC's hard drive.

Don't plug in your drive just yet, though. Instead, follow these steps on your new Windows 7 PC to run Windows Easy Transfer. You'll plug in the drive while following these steps:

1. **Close all currently running programs on your new Windows 7 PC.**

2. **Open the Start menu, choose All Programs, click Accessories, click System Tools, and then click Windows Easy Transfer.**

The Windows Easy Transfer window opens.

3. **Click Next at the opening screen.**

4. **Choose the An External Hard Disk or USB Flash Drive option.**

   External hard disk is Microsoft's term for what everybody else calls a *portable hard drive.*

5. **Choose the This Is My New Computer option.**

6. **Choose No.**

   This tells the program you haven't yet collected the information from your old PC.

7. **Choose the I Need to Install It Now option and then plug your portable drive into one of your new Windows 7 PC's USB ports.**

   If you've never plugged in the drive before, Windows 7 automatically installs the hard drive's drivers.

8. **Choose the External Hard Disk or Shared Network Folder option.**

   The Browse For Folder dialog box appears, shown earlier in Figure 19-2.

9. **Navigate to the place you want to store the Windows Easy Transfer program and then click OK.**

   To store the program on your newly plugged-in portable hard drive, for example, click Computer in the Browse For Folder dialog box, choose the letter of your removable drive, and click OK.

   When you click OK, Windows Easy Transfer places a copy of itself onto the drive so you can run it on your old PC.

10. **When the program finishes copying itself to your drive, unplug the drive from your new PC and plug it into a USB port on your old PC.**

    Windows Easy Transfer leaps to life on your old PC. (You may need to click OK to let it install itself and run.)

11. **On your old PC, click Next to move past the opening screen, then choose the An External Hard Disk or USB Flash Drive option.**

12. **On your old PC, choose the This Is My Old Computer option.**

13. **Choose what to transfer and click Next.**

    The program normally copies everything from everybody's user account. To pick and choose exactly what's copied, read the "Picking and choosing the files, folders, and accounts to transfer" section, right after this section.

14. **Enter a password, if you want, to protect the information, and then click Save.**

    This optional but prudent step keeps others from grabbing your information. (To be even more prudent, reformat your portable hard drive when you've finished transferring the information.)

15. **Choose a place to save the information, click Open, and click Save.**

    When the Save Your Easy Transfer File window appears, click the letter of your portable hard drive, click Open to see its contents, and then click Save. The program names your file "Windows Easy Transfer – Items From Old Computer."

16. **Click Next, and then unplug the drive from your old PC.**

    After the program saves your file, click Next and set the drive next to your new Windows 7 PC.

17. **Click Next on your new PC, then click Yes to say you've grabbed the information.**

18. **Plug your portable hard drive into your new PC and open the drive's transferred file.**

    When the Open an Easy Transfer window appears, double-click your portable hard drive's name, then double-click the file called "Windows Easy Transfer – Items From Old Computer."

    Enter the password you gave it earlier, if necessary, and click Next.

19. **Click the Transfer button on your new PC to begin copying the information.**

    Don't touch either PC during the transfer process. If you've grabbed more information than your new PC can hold, you'll encounter the Choose What to Transfer window from Step 13. There, you must whittle down the information you want to transfer. (I cover that window and its whittling process in this chapter's next section.)

20. **Finish up.**

    The program leaves you with these two options:

    - **See What Was Transferred.** This rather technical report shows exactly what was transferred.

    - **See a List of Programs You Might Want to Install on Your New Computer.** Another overly technical report tells you what programs you may want to install in order to open some of your transferred files.

Picking and choosing the files, folders, and accounts to transfer

No matter what route you choose to transfer your files, you'll eventually face the window shown in Figure 19-4, along with the program's stern demand: Choose What to Transfer.

Figure 19-4:
Click
Transfer
to transfer
everything
possible
to your
new PC.

This window appears on your *old* PC if you're transferring by portable drive; the window appears on your *new* PC if you're transferring by cable or network.

To transfer *everything* from *all* your old PC's user accounts to accounts on your new PC, simply click the Transfer button. If your new PC has enough space, the program copies everything from your old PC to your new PC. You can always delete unwanted items later from your new PC if you want.

But if your new PC doesn't have enough storage space or you don't want everything copied, here's how to choose which items to transfer:

- ✔ **User Accounts:** Want to transfer your own account to your new PC, but leave the other accounts behind on the family's PC? Here's your chance: Windows Easy Transfer puts a check mark next to each user account it will transfer, as shown in Figure 19-4. Click to remove the check mark from the user accounts you *don't* want transferred.

- ✔ **Advanced Options:** Haven't set up accounts for everybody on your new PC? The Advanced Options area, just above the Transfer button, lets you create new accounts on your new PC, then fill them with the appropriate incoming files. This area also comes in handy for old PCs with two or more drives, as it lets you map which drive's contents go to which drive on your new PC.

- ✔ **Customize:** Sometimes you don't need it all. To pick and choose what categories of items should be transferred from each account, click the Customize button under each account's name, shown back in Figure 19-4. A window pops up, as shown in Figure 19-5, letting you exclude certain categories. Remove the check mark from My Videos, for example, to grab everything but your videos from your old PC.

✔ **Advanced:** The Advanced button, shown at the bottom of the pop-up list in Figure 19-5, works for techies who enjoy micromanaging. By weeding through the tree of folder and file names, this area lets you pick and choose individual files and folders to copy. It's overkill for most people, but it's an option, nevertheless.

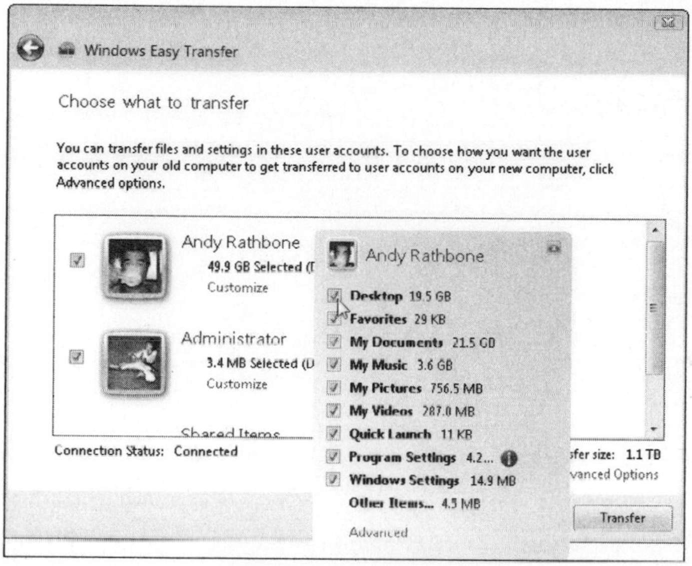

Figure 19-5: Click Customize to whittle down what's transferred from each account.

If you've customized your transfer, click the Save button to return to the Choose What to Transfer window. Then click Transfer to begin transferring your carefully selected files and settings to your new Windows 7 PC.

Disposing of Your Old Computer

After you've transferred everything of value from the old computer to the new, what do you do with the old computer? You're left with several options:

✔ **Hand me down:** Many people simply pass their old computers down to the kids. Kids don't need powerhouse computers for typing term papers.

✔ **Charities:** Charities have grown pickier about what they'll accept. Make sure that the computer and its monitor still work. (Some charities take only flat-panel monitors.)

- ✔ **Salvage:** Take the green route and salvage your old PC's parts. For example, you can usually put your old PC's hard drives into your new PC for backup storage. Most new PCs can handle a second monitor for extra-wide desktops. I cover what and how to salvage items from your old PC in my other book, *Upgrading & Fixing PCs For Dummies*, 8th Edition (Wiley Publishing, Inc.).

- ✔ **Recycle it:** Dell will recycle your old Dell computer for free. Dell even recycles competitors' PCs when you buy a new Dell computer. Even if you're not buying Dell, visit the recycling page (www.dell.com/recycling) at Dell's Web site for lots of general recycling information. Ask your IBM dealer about its recycling plan as well.

- ✔ **Freecycle:** When your old PC is no longer loved by either you or your friends, visit the Freecycle Network (www.freecycle.org). With chapters in many cities worldwide, the Freecycle Web site lets you list unwanted items; other people swing by and take them off your hands. A starving student may still find some value in your old PC, perhaps even for parts.

- ✔ **Trash:** An increasing number of cities and states ban this option in order to keep hazardous waste out of the landfills. It's illegal to throw away PCs or monitors in California, Texas, and several other states. Call your local landfill to see if it offers special "electronic device drop off" days where you can bring your electronic discards for disposal.

Keep your old computer around for a few weeks while you break in your new computer. You might remember an important file or setting on the old computer that hasn't yet been transferred.

Erasing the old computer's hard drive

A freshly donated hard drive can be a thief's delight. If it's like most hard drives, it contains passwords to Web sites, e-mail accounts, and programs; credit-card numbers; identifying information; and possibly financial records. None of this information should fall into the wrong hands.

If your hard drive contains particularly sensitive information, purchase a data-destruction program, available in the Utilities section of most computer stores. These specially designed programs completely erase the hard drive and then fill it up again with random characters. (Many programs repeat that process several times to reach the required government privacy specification.)

If you have a tech-savvy friend or child, have him or her download Darik's Boot And Nuke program (www.dban.org). The freebie program creates a bootable CD that wipes your hard drive clean.

Alternatively, take it out to the street and hit it with a sledgehammer until it's beyond repair.

Chapter 20

Help on the Windows 7 Help System

Don't bother plowing through this whole chapter for the nitty gritty: Here are the quickest ways to make Windows 7 dish out helpful information when you're stumped:

- ✔ **Press F1:** Press the F1 key from within Windows or any program.

- ✔ **Start menu:** Click the Start menu and choose Help and Support.

- ✔ **Question Mark:** If you spot a little blue question mark icon near a window's top-right corner, pounce on it with a quick click.

In each case, Windows 7 fetches its Help and Support program, beefed up with tables, charts, updated information from the Web, and step-by-step instructions for you to follow.

This chapter explains how to wring the most help from Windows Help and Support.

Consulting a Program's Built-In Computer Guru

Almost every Windows program includes its own Help system. To summon a program's built-in computer guru, press F1, choose Help from the menu, or click the little blue question mark icon shown in the margin. To find help in Windows Media Player and start asking pointed questions, for example, follow these steps:

1. **Choose Help from the program's menu and choose View Help. (Alternatively, press F1, or click the blue question mark icon.)**

   The Windows Help and Support program opens to its page dedicated to Windows Media Player (see Figure 20-1). There, the program lists the topics that give people the most headaches.

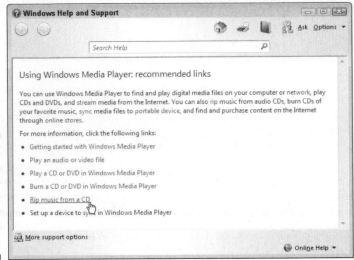

Figure 20-1: Choose the topic confusing you in Windows Media Player.

   The Search Help box at the top of the screen lets you search the Help program's index. Typing a few words describing your question often fetches the exact page you need, saving you a few steps.

2. **Click the topic where you need help.**

   For example, clicking the Rip Music From a CD link tells Windows 7 to explain more about copying a CD's music files to your PC.

3. **Choose the subtopic that interests you.**

   After a brief explanation about the topic, the Help page offers several subtopics: You can see how to find songs copied to Media Player's library, for example, or how to edit media information like the titles of your copied songs. Don't miss the topics listed at the page's bottom; they can fetch related information you may find helpful.

4. **Follow the listed steps to complete your task.**

   Windows 7 lists the steps needed to complete your task or fix your problem, sparing you from searching through the menus of your problematic program. As you scan the steps, feel free to look at the area below them; you often can find tips for making the job easier next time.

Confused about an odd term used in the Help window? If the term appears in a different color and sprouts an underline when you point at it with the mouse, click it. A new window pops up, defining the word.

Try to keep the Help window and your problematic program open in adjacent windows. That lets you read each step in the Help window and apply the steps in your program without the distraction of the two windows covering each other up.

The Windows 7 Help system is sometimes a lot of work, forcing you to wade through increasingly detailed menus to find specific information. Still, using Help offers a last resort when you can't find the information elsewhere. And it's often much less embarrassing than tracking down the neighbor's teenagers.

If you're impressed with a particularly helpful page, send it to the printer: Click the Printer icon (shown in the margin) at the page's top. Windows 7 shoots that page to the printer so that you can keep it handy until you lose it.

Finding the Information You Need in Windows Help and Support Center

When you don't know where else to start, fire up Windows Help and Support center and begin digging at the top.

To summon the program, choose Help and Support Center from the Start menu. The Help and Support Center rises to the screen, as shown in Figure 20-2.

The program offers three sections:

- ✔ **Find an Answer Quickly:** This section simply reminds you to type your troublesome subject into the Search Help box along the window's top. Instead of phrasing a complete question, type just a word or two about your trouble: Type **Printer**, for example, rather than **My printer isn't working**.

- ✔ **Not Sure Where to Start:** If the Search Help box comes up empty, turn here. Click the How to Get Started with Your Computer link to get advice on setting up a new PC for the first time. The Learn about Windows Basics link takes you to overviews about your PC and basic Windows 7 tasks. Or, click the Browse Help Topics link to see large categories which let you click through to more detailed information.

Figure 20-2:
The
Windows
Help and
Support
Center
offers
assistance
with
Windows
and your
computer.

✔ **More on the New Windows Website:** Don't click here unless you're connected to the Internet, because this link tells the Help program to display Windows 7's online Help page at Microsoft's Web site. That site is sometimes more up-to-date than Windows 7's built-in Help program, but it uses more technical language.

The Windows Help and Support program works much like a Web site or folder. To move back one page, click the little blue Back arrow in the upper-left corner. That arrow helps you out if you've backed into a corner.

Summoning the Windows 7 Troubleshooters

When something's not working as it should, the Troubleshooting section of the Windows Help and Support program may sleuth out a fix. Sometimes it works like an index, narrowing down the scope of your problems to the one button that fixes it. Then it displays the button on the Help page for your one-click cure.

Sometimes it interviews you about the problem, narrowing down the list of suspects until it finds the culprit — and your magic button to fix the situation.

Other times, a magic button isn't enough. If your wireless Internet signal isn't strong enough, for example, the Troubleshooter tells you to stand up and move your laptop closer to the transmitter.

To summon the troubleshooters, follow these steps:

1. **Right-click the Activity Center icon in your taskbar and choose Troubleshoot a Problem.**

   The Troubleshoot Computer Problems window, shown in Figure 20-3, is ready to tackle a wide variety of problems, from general to specific.

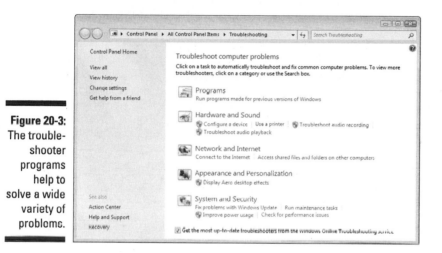

Figure 20-3: The trouble-shooter programs help to solve a wide variety of problems.

2. **Click the subject that troubles you.**

   The Troubleshooting section offers these five topics that mimic their counterparts in Control Panel, which I cover in Chapter 11:

   - **Programs:** This guides you through running older programs that initially balked at running under Windows 7. It also takes a look at your Web browser, and tries to fix any problems it finds.

   - **Hardware and Sound:** This area shows how to diagnose driver problems, the biggest cause of bickering between Windows 7 and things plugged into or inside your PC. It also helps diagnose problems with your printer, speakers, and microphone.

   - **Network and Internet:** Head here for help with Internet connections, as well as common problems encountered when connecting two or more PCs in your home.

- **Appearance and Personalization:** Can't see Windows 7's famous translucent windows? This troubleshooter checks your PC's video settings to make sure you're seeing Windows 7 in its full glory.

- **System and Security:** A catch-all section for everything else, this helps out with security and improving your PC's performance.

Click a topic, and Windows 7 whisks you to the page dealing with that subject's most common problems. Keep clicking the subtopics until you find the one dealing with your particular problem.

3. **Follow the recommended steps.**

Occasionally, you'll stumble onto numbered steps that solve your problem. Follow those steps one at a time to finish the job.

When you right-click on a misbehaving icon, you may see Troubleshoot Problems listed on the pop-up menu. Click it to fetch the troubleshooter for that particular item, saving you some time.

At the window's bottom, be sure to select the check box called Get the Most Up-To-Date Troubleshooters From the Windows Online Troubleshooting Service. That lets Microsoft add any newly developed troubleshooters to your arsenal through the Internet.

Part VII
The Part of Tens

The 5th Wave   By Rich Tennant

"Don't laugh. It's faster than our current system."

In this part . . .

No *For Dummies* book is complete without a Part of Tens section: lists of ten easy-to-read informational nuggets. Of course, the lists don't always contain exactly ten, but you get the general idea.

The first list explains ten things you'll absolutely hate about Windows 7 (followed by ways to fix those problems).

The second list contains tips exclusively for laptoppers. It explains how to change how your laptop reacts when you close its lid, for example, as well as quick ways to adjust screen brightness, volume, and turn on that built-in wireless adapter.

I also throw in step-by-step instructions for tasks laptoppers repeat constantly: logging onto the Internet in different ways, changing your current area code, and setting the clock for a new time zone.

Chapter 21

Ten or So Things You'll Hate about Windows 7 (And How to Fix Them)

In This Chapter

▶ Stopping the permission screens

▶ Finding the Windows 7 menus

▶ Turning off Aero Glass to speed up your PC

*W*indows 7 certainly outshines its ungainly predecessor, Windows Vista. Still, you may find yourself thinking Windows 7 would be perfect if only . . . *(insert your pet peeve here)*. If you find yourself thinking (or saying) those words frequently, read this chapter. Here, you find not only a list of ten or so of the most aggravating things about Windows 7, but also ways you can fix them.

I Can't Stand Those Nagging Permission Screens

You can take either of two approaches to Windows 7's nagging permission screens:

- ✔ **Microsoft's preferred approach:** Before automatically clicking the Yes or Continue button, ask yourself this question: Did *I* initiate this action? If you deliberately asked your PC to do something, click Yes or Continue for the PC to carry out your command. But if the permission screen pops up unexpectedly, click Cancel, because something's wrong.

- ✔ **The easy way out:** Turn off the permission screens, as I explain in Chapter 17. Unfortunately, that leaves your PC more susceptible to viruses, worms, spyware, and other evil things tossed at your PC during the course of the day.

Neither option is perfect, but that's the choice that Microsoft has given you with Windows 7: Listen to your PC's occasional nags or turn off the nags and instead trust your own antivirus and antispyware programs.

I recommend Microsoft's preferred approach — it's much like wearing a seatbelt when driving: It's not as comfortable, but it's safer. Ultimately, though, the choice lies with your own balance between comfort and safety.

I Can't Copy Music to My iPod

You won't find the word *iPod* mentioned in the Windows 7 menus, help screens, or even in the Help areas of Microsoft's Web site. That's because Microsoft's competitor, Apple, makes the tremendously popular iPod. Microsoft's strategy is to ignore the little gizmo in the hope that it will go away.

What won't go away, though, are the problems you'll face if you ever try to copy songs onto an iPod with Media Player. You face two hurdles:

- Windows Media Player won't recognize your iPod, much less send it any songs or videos.

- When you plug in your iPod, Windows might recognize the slick gadget as a portable hard drive. It may even let you copy songs to it. But your iPod won't be able to find or play them.

The easiest solution is to download and install iTunes software from Apple's Web site (www.apple.com/itunes). Because iTunes and Media Player will bicker over which program can play your files, you'll probably end up choosing iTunes. (To settle the song-playing-rights battle, click the Start button, choose Default Programs, click iTunes in the Programs column, and choose Set This Program as Default.)

The Menus All Disappeared

In Microsoft's zeal for giving Windows 7 a clean look, the programmers swept away the folder menus used for the past decade. To reveal a folder's missing menus, press Alt. The menus appear, letting you choose the option you're after.

Organize ▾ To keep the menus from disappearing again, click the Organize button (shown in the margin), choose Layout, and choose Menu Bar from the pop-up menu.

The "Glass" Effects Slow Down My PC or Laptop

One of Windows 7's much touted special effects, Aero, may be too much for some PCs to handle. Aero makes your windows' frames translucent, letting bits and pieces of your desktop shine through them. The effects also let some programs, like Windows 7's chess game, "float" in the air, allowing you to watch the game from all angles.

But the calculations required for those visual gymnastics slow down PCs that don't have high-powered graphics — and that includes many of today's tiny laptops called *netbooks*.

Even worse, the fancy graphics may drain your batteries to a fraction of their battery life, and they can overheat your PC. If you don't like the extra burden Aero dumps on your PC, dump Aero by following these steps:

1. **Right-click a blank part of your desktop and choose Personalize to summon the Control Panel.**

2. **In the Basic and High Contrast Themes area, choose Windows 7 Basic.**

   That theme lives near the Personalization window's bottom. Your desktop's appearance changes as soon you select the theme's name.

If your computer is *still too slow*, try choosing Windows Classic in Step 2.

To turn Aero Glass back on for impressing your friends, follow the first step in the preceding list, but choose Windows 7 in the Aero Themes area.

 If Windows 7 *still* isn't snappy enough, right-click Computer on the Start menu, choose Properties, and select Advanced System Settings from the task pane on the left. Click the Settings button in the Performance section, choose Adjust for Best Performance, and click OK.

My Quick Launch Toolbar Is Gone!

Many people didn't know what it was called, but the *Quick Launch toolbar* — that handy little strip of icons resting near the Start button — served as a single-click launching pad for favorite programs in both Windows XP and Vista.

Windows 7 strips the Quick Launch toolbar from its new, revamped taskbar. In the toolbar's place, the taskbar now shows three icons next to your Start button: Internet Explorer, Libraries, and Media Player. Don't like those icons? Right-click any offender and choose Unpin This Program from Taskbar from the pop-up menu.

You can also treat that portion of your taskbar as a makeshift Quick Launch toolbar by adding your own icons there. Follow these steps to copy icons from your Start menu to the taskbar:

1. **Click the Start menu and locate your cherished program.**

2. **Right-click the program's icon and choose Pin to Taskbar.**

   Feel free to rearrange icons on the taskbar by dragging them with the mouse to the right or left.

By pinning your favorite program's icons to the taskbar's *left* side, you can keep them separate from the taskbar's icons of *running* programs, which stay on the right side.

Windows Makes Me Log On All the Time

Windows offers two ways to return to life from its swirling and churning screen saver. Windows can return you to the opening screen, where you must log back on to your user account. Alternatively, Windows 7 can simply return you to the program you were using when the screen saver kicked in.

Some people prefer the security of the opening screen. If the screen saver kicks in when they're spending too much time at the water cooler, they're protected: Nobody can walk over and snoop through their e-mail.

Other people don't need that extra security, and they simply want to return to work quickly. Here's how to accommodate both camps:

If you don't *ever* want to see the opening screen, then use a single user account without a password, which I describe in Chapter 13. That defeats all the security offered by the user account system, but it's more convenient if you live alone.

1. **Right-click a blank part of your desktop and choose Personalize.**

2. **Click Screen Saver in the bottom-right corner.**

   Windows 7 shows the screen saver options, including whether or not Windows should wake up or resume at the logon screen.

3. **Depending on your preference, select or deselect the On Resume, Display Logon Screen check box.**

   If the check box *is selected,* Windows 7 is more secure. The screen saver wakes up at Windows 7's opening screen, and people must log on to their user accounts before using the computer. If the check box *isn't selected,* Windows 7 is more easygoing, waking up from the screen saver in the same place where you stopped working.

4. **Click OK to save your changes.**

The Taskbar Keeps Disappearing

The taskbar is a handy Windows 7 feature that usually squats along the bottom of your screen. Sometimes, unfortunately, it up and wanders off into the woods. Here are a few ways to track it down and bring it home.

If your taskbar suddenly clings to an edge of your desktop — or even the ceiling — try dragging it back in place: Instead of dragging an edge, drag the taskbar from its middle. As your mouse pointer reaches your desktop's bottom edge, the taskbar suddenly snaps back into place. Let go of the mouse, and you've recaptured it.

Follow these tips to prevent your taskbar from wandering:

✔ To keep the taskbar locked into place so that it won't float away, right-click a blank part of the taskbar and select Lock the Taskbar. Remember, though, that before you can make any future changes to the taskbar, you must first unlock it.

✔ If your taskbar drops from sight whenever the mouse pointer doesn't hover nearby, turn off the taskbar's Auto Hide feature: Right-click a blank part of the taskbar and choose Properties from the pop-up menu. When the Taskbar and Start Menu Properties dialog box appears, deselect the Auto-Hide the Taskbar check box. (Or, to turn on the Auto Hide feature, select the check box.)

1 Can't Keep Track of Open Windows

You don't *have* to keep track of all those open windows. Windows 7 does it for you with a secret key combination: Hold the Alt key and press the Tab key, and a little bar appears, displaying the icons for all your open windows. Keep pressing Tab; when Windows highlights the icon of the window you're after, release the keys. The window pops up.

Or visit the taskbar, that long strip along the bottom of your screen. Covered in Chapter 2, the taskbar lists the name of every open window. Click the name of the window you want, and that window hops to the top of the pile.

If a program icon on the taskbar contains several open windows — you're simultaneously editing several documents in Microsoft Word, for example — right-click the Microsoft Word icon. A pop-up menu appears, letting you click the document you want to access.

In Chapter 6, you find more soldiers to enlist in the battle against misplaced windows, files, and programs.

I Can't Line Up Two Windows on the Screen

With its arsenal of dragging-and-dropping tools, Windows 7 simplifies grabbing information from one window and copying it to another. You can drag an address from an address book and drop it atop a letter in your word processor, for example.

 However, the hardest part of dragging and dropping comes when you're lining up two windows on the screen, side by side, for dragging. *That's* when you need to call in the taskbar. First, open the two windows and place them anywhere on the screen. Then shrink all the other windows into taskbar icons by clicking their Minimize buttons (shown in the margin).

Now, right-click a blank area of the taskbar and then choose either Show Windows Stacked or Show Windows Side By Side. The two windows line up on the screen perfectly. Try both to see which meets your current needs.

 Windows 7 introduces another way to align windows for easy dragging and dropping: Drag one window *violently* against a left or right edge; the window reforms itself to fill the screen's side. Quickly drag another window against the opposite edge, and they align themselves side by side.

It Won't Let Me Do Something Unless I'm an Administrator!

Windows 7 gets really picky about who gets to do what on your computer. The computer's owner gets the Administrator account. And the administrator usually gives everybody else a Standard account. What does that mean? Well, only the administrator can do the following things on the computer:

- Install programs and hardware.
- Create or change accounts for other people.
- Dial the Internet through a dial-up modem.
- Install some hardware, like some digital cameras and MP3 players.
- Perform actions affecting other people on the PC.

People with Standard accounts, by nature, are limited to fairly basic activities. They can do these things:

- Run previously installed programs.
- Change their account's picture and password.

Guest accounts are meant for the babysitter or visitors who don't permanently use the computer. If you have a broadband or other "always on" Internet account, guests can browse the Internet, run programs, or check their e-mail. (As I describe in Chapter 13, Guest accounts aren't allowed to *start* an Internet session, but they can use an existing one.)

If Windows says only an administrator may do something on your PC, you have two choices: Find an administrator to type his or her password and authorize the action; or convince an administrator to upgrade your account to an Administrator account, covered in Chapter 13.

I Don't Know What Version of Windows I Have

Windows has been sold in more than a dozen flavors since its debut in November 1985. How can you tell what version is really installed on your computer?

Open the Start menu, right-click Computer, and choose Properties. Look in the Windows Edition section at the top to see which version of Windows 7 you own: Starter, Home Basic, Home Premium, Professional, Enterprise, or Ultimate.

In older versions of Windows, the version type appears on that same window, but beneath the word *System*.

My Print Screen Key Doesn't Work

Windows 7 takes over the Print Screen key (labeled PrtSc, PrtScr, or something even more supernatural on some keyboards). Instead of sending the stuff on the screen to the printer, the Print Screen key sends it to Windows 7's memory, where you can paste it into other windows.

If you hold the Alt key while pressing the Print Screen key, Windows 7 sends a picture of the current *window* — not the entire screen — to the Clipboard for pasting.

If you *really* want a printout of the screen, press the Print Screen button to send a picture of the screen to its memory. (It won't look like anything has happened.) Then click Start, choose All Programs, select Accessories, open Paint, and click the Paste icon from the top menu. When your image appears, choose Print from the main menu to send it to the printer.

I Can't Upgrade to Windows 7 from Windows XP!

The biggest delight enjoyed by Windows Vista owners could be sticking in an inexpensive Windows 7 Upgrade disc and transforming their PC into Windows 7: Their files and programs remain in place, and Windows Vista goes away forever.

Windows XP owners can also buy the upgrade disc. Unfortunately for them, upgrading to Windows 7 means wiping their hard drive clean and starting from scratch.

I explain how to make this process as painless as possible in this book's Appendix.

Chapter 22

Ten or So Tips for Laptop Owners

For the most part, everything in this book applies both to PCs and laptops. Windows 7 offers a few settings exclusively for laptops, however, and I cover those items here. I also throw in a few tips and quick references to make this chapter especially suited for laptop owners who need information in a hurry.

Adjusting Your Laptop's Settings Quickly

Windows 7 offers a quick way for laptop owners to see the things that most affect their little PC's on-the-go lifestyle. Called the Mobility Center, it's a one-stop shop for tweaking your laptop's main settings. To open the Mobility Center, follow these steps:

1. **Click Start and choose Control Panel.**

2. **Hold down the Windows key and press the X key.**

   Windows Mobility Center, shown in Figure 22-1, rises to the screen.

3. **Make your adjustments.**

   As shown in Figure 22-1, Mobility Center lets you make quick adjustments to your laptop's main settings, as described in the following list. (Don't worry that something's wrong if your laptop's options differ slightly from these, because Microsoft customizes the options to match your particular laptop's features.)

   - **Volume:** Tired of your laptop's annoying audio blast every time you turn it on? Slide down the volume level here. (Or select the Mute check box to turn it off completely, saving batteries and letting you turn it on only when needed.)

Figure 22-1:
Windows
Mobility
Center
puts a
laptop's
most
common
adjustments
in one
window.

- **Battery Status:** Choose Power Saver when long battery life is essential (you'll work at a snail's pace), and switch to High Performance only when you're plugged in and need maximum speed for hoggy programs. For the best of both worlds, leave the setting at Balanced.

- **Wireless Network:** If your laptop offers it, here's an easy-to-find On/Off switch for your laptop's wireless network adapter, whether built-in or plugged in through a USB port.

- **Brightness:** (Not shown in Figure 22-1.) If your laptop model offers it, a simple sliding control lets you dim your laptop in low-light situations (or simply to save battery power) or increase the brightness when working outdoors.

- **External Display:** Ever plug your laptop into a larger monitor or projector for giving presentations? Head here to set it up.

- **Sync Center:** Windows 7 lets you keep your laptop or Windows 7 PC in synchronization with a network server found in some offices. This switch brings you to the Sync Center, where you can set up a partnership with sync-compatible places and click the Sync All button for them to exchange information.

- **Screen Rotation:** (Not shown in Figure 22-1.) Found on some tablet PCs and netbooks, this feature lets you rotate the screen for easier viewing on an odd-sized display.

- **Presentation Settings:** This option lets you control what appears on the projector when you hook up your laptop. With the click of one button, you can turn your desktop's wallpaper into something business-safe, turn off your screen saver, adjust the PC's volume, and squelch any other distractions.

Although some buttons take you to yet more areas full of settings, the Mobility Center works well as a launching pad. It's your first stop to customize your laptop to match its latest surroundings.

Choosing What Happens When You Close Your Laptop's Lid

Closing the laptop's lid means that you're through working, but for how long? For the night? Until you get off the subway? For a long lunch hour? Windows 7 lets you tailor exactly how your laptop should behave when you latch your laptop's lid.

To start tweaking, follow these steps:

1. **Click Start, choose Control Panel, and then choose System and Security.**

2. **Choose Power Options and then select Choose What Closing the Lid Does from the left pane.**

   Shown in Figure 22-2, Windows 7 offers three lid-closing options for whether your laptop is plugged in or running on its batteries: Do Nothing, Hibernate, or Shut Down.

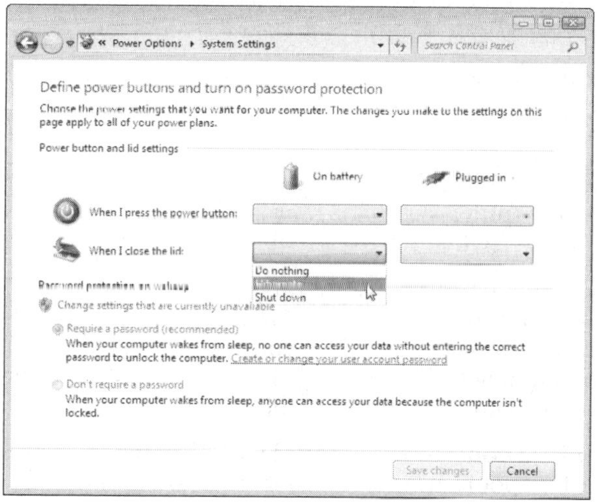

Figure 22-2: Change your laptop's reactions when plugged in or on batteries.

Generally, choose Hibernate, because it lets your laptop slumber in a low-power state, letting it wake up quickly so that you can begin working without delay. But if you'll be shutting down your laptop for the evening, turning it off is often a better idea. That option lets the laptop conserve its battery power and, if plugged in overnight, wake up with fully charged batteries.

Also, you can choose whether your computer should require you to enter a password when it's turned back on. (Passwords are always a good idea.)

3. Click Save Changes to make your changes permanent.

Adjusting to Different Locations

PCs don't move from a desktop, making some things pretty easy to set up. You need only enter your location once, for example, and Windows 7 automatically sets up your time zone, currency symbols, and similar things that change over the globe.

But the joy of a laptop's mobility is tempered with the agony of telling the thing exactly where it's currently located. These sections supply the steps you need to change when traveling to a different area.

Changing your time zone

Follow these steps to let your laptop know you've entered a new time zone:

1. Click the clock in the taskbar's bottom-right corner.

A calendar and clock appear in a small window.

2. Choose Change Date and Time settings.

The Date and Time dialog box appears.

3. Choose Change Time Zone, enter your current time zone in the Time Zone pull-down menu, and click OK twice.

If you frequently travel between time zones, take advantage of the Additional Clocks tab in Step 3. There, you can add a second clock; to check the time quickly in Caracas, just hover your mouse pointer over the taskbar's clock. A pop-up menu appears, listing your local time as well as the time in the additional location you've entered.

Connecting to a wireless Internet hotspot

Every time you connect to a wireless network, Windows 7 stashes its settings for connecting again the next time you visit. I explain wireless connections more thoroughly in Chapter 14, but here are the steps for quick reference:

1. **Turn on your laptop's wireless adapter, if necessary.**

   You can often turn it on with a click in the Mobility Center, shown in Figure 22-1. Some laptops offer a manual switch somewhere on the case. If your laptop lacks built-in wireless, plug a wireless adapter into its USB port.

2. **Click your taskbar's network icon, shown in the margin.**

   Windows 7 lists every way it can connect with the Internet — including any wireless networks it currently finds within range.

3. **Connect to the wireless network by clicking its name and clicking Connect.**

   At many places, clicking Connect may connect your laptop to the Internet immediately. But if your laptop asks for more information, move to Step 4.

4. **Enter the wireless network's name and security key/passphrase, if asked.**

   Some secretive wireless networks don't broadcast their names, so Windows lists them as Unnamed Network. If you spot that name, track down the network's owner and ask for the network's name and security key or passphrase to enter here.

   When you click Connect, Windows 7 announces its success. Be sure to select the two check boxes, Save This Network and Start This Connection Automatically, to make it easier to connect the next time you come within range.

When you're through online, turn off or unplug your laptop's wireless adapter to save your laptop's batteries.

Dialing a modem from a new location

I give a detailed explanation of how to connect with a dialup modem in Chapter 8. Here, I assume that you're setting up a connection in a *different* city, where you must enter a different phone number, area code, calling card, or something similar. Follow these steps to connect to a dialup Internet connection in a new location:

1. **Click your taskbar's Network icon (shown in the margin).**

   Windows 7 lists all Internet connections you've used in the past, including wireless locations and dialup numbers — including the first dialup location you set up.

2. **Right-click your existing dialup location and choose Properties.**

   Windows 7 lists the settings for your current dialup connection.

3. **Select the Use Dialing Rules check box and click Dialing Rules.**

   The Dialing Rules dialog box appears, listing the names of locations you've entered when setting up different dialup connections. The setting called My Location is the one Windows 7 created when you set up your first dialup connection.

4. **Click New and enter the changed settings for your new location.**

   When the New Location dialog box appears, enter the name of your new location, as well as the changes required for dialing in that location: a different area code or access number, a hotel that makes you dial 9 for an outside line, or perhaps a code to disable call waiting.

   As you enter your changes, the bottom of the New Location dialog box lists the number Windows 7 will dial to make the connection.

5. **Click OK when you finish, click OK to exit the Phone and Modem Options dialog box, and click OK to exit the Properties dialog box.**

   Windows 7 leaves you back at the Connect to a Network dialog box that names your dialup connection.

6. **Click Connect.**

   Windows 7 dials the Internet number using the new settings you've entered. If you need to dial a completely different phone number rather than tweak the existing settings, head to Chapter 8 for instructions on setting up a dialup account. Your newly entered region settings will be waiting for you there.

Backing Up Your Laptop Before Traveling

I explain how to back up a PC in Chapter 12, and backing up a laptop works just like backing up a desktop PC. Please, please remember to back up your laptop before leaving your home or office. Thieves grab laptops much more often than desktop PCs. Your laptop can be replaced, but the data inside it can't.

Keep the backed up information at home — not in your laptop's bag.

Appendix A

Upgrading to Windows 7

* *

In This Appendix

▶ Preparing for Windows 7

▶ Upgrading Windows Vista to Windows 7

▶ Installing Windows 7 over Windows XP

* *

*N*ew computers today come with Windows 7 preinstalled — it's practically unavoidable. If you're reading this chapter, then your computer is probably still running Windows XP or Windows Vista. If it's running Windows 98 or Windows Me, don't bother trying to install Windows 7. You need a more modern PC.

Windows Vista owners have it easy: Upgrading to Windows 7 is a snap. Just insert the DVD, and Windows 7 replaces Windows Vista, leaving all your files and programs intact.

Windows XP owners must sail through more treacherous seas: Windows 7 won't upgrade your PC, forcing you through a multistep process I describe here.

Moving to Windows 7 from either Windows Vista or XP is a one-way street. Once you've switched, you can't return to your old version of Windows. Don't follow these instructions unless you're sure you're ready for Windows 7.

Preparing for Windows 7

Windows 7 usually runs well on computers purchased within the past three or four years. Before upgrading, make sure that you've run through the following checklist:

✔ **Computer power:** Make sure that your computer is strong enough to run Windows 7. I cover Windows 7's requirements in Chapter 1.

✔ **Compatibility:** Before upgrading or installing, insert the Windows 7 DVD and choose Check Compatibility Online. When Windows 7 takes you to Microsoft's Web site, download and run Microsoft's Windows 7 Upgrade Advisor. The program alerts you beforehand what parts of your computer may not run well under Windows 7. You can find the Upgrade Advisor on Microsoft's Web site at www.microsoft.com/Windows7/.

✔ **Security:** Before upgrading to Windows 7, turn off your antivirus software and other security programs. They may innocently try to protect you from Windows 7's upgrade process.

✔ **Upgrade path:** Because Vista and Windows come in so many different versions, Table A-1 explains which versions are eligible for which upgrades.

Table A-1	Vista Upgrade Compatibility
This Version of Vista . . .	*. . . May Upgrade to This Version of Windows 7*
Windows Vista Home Premium, Windows Vista Home Basic	Windows 7 Home Premium
Windows Vista Business	Windows 7 Professional
Windows Vista Ultimate	Windows 7 Ultimate

After you upgrade, you can pay extra to unlock the features of a fancier version, a strategic Microsoft marketing move.

✔ **Backup:** Back up all of your PC's important data in case something goes wrong.

Upgrading from Windows Vista to Windows 7

Follow these steps to upgrade your copy of Windows Vista to Windows 7:

1. **Insert the Windows 7 DVD into your DVD drive and click the Install Now button, as shown in Figure A-1.**

   Windows 7 churns away, preparing to install itself.

Figure A-1:
Click the
Install Now
button
on the
Windows 7
installation
screen.

2. **Choose Go Online to Get the Latest Updates for Installation (Recommended).**

   This step tells Windows 7 to visit Microsoft's Web site and download the latest updates for your particular PC — drivers, patches, and assorted fixes — to help make your installation run as smoothly as possible.

3. **Read the License Agreement, select the I Accept the License Terms check box, and click Next.**

   Read Microsoft's 25-page License Agreement. You must select the I Accept the License Terms check box before Microsoft allows you to install the software.

4. **Choose Upgrade and click Next.**

   Upgrading preserves your PC's old files, settings, and programs. If this option doesn't work, any of these things could be wrong:

   - You're trying to upgrade a Windows XP PC, which isn't allowed.

   - You're trying to upgrade a Windows Vista version that doesn't allow upgrades. (Refer to Table A-1.)

   - Your copy of Windows Vista doesn't have Service Pack 1. To fix this, visit Windows Update (www.windowsupdate.com) and download and install Service Pack 1. If the site refuses, you may not have a genuine copy of Windows Vista installed. Call your PC's vendor, be it a store or the kid down the street who built it for you.

   - Your hard drive isn't big enough. Your hard drive needs up to 16GB of free space to install Windows 7.

5. **Read the Compatibility Report, if offered, and click Next.**

   If you told Windows 7 to go online in Step 2, Windows 7 explains any compatibility problems it finds with your PC's programs. When you click Next, it begins the upgrade, a process that could take several hours.

6. **Type your product key and click Next.**

   The *product key* usually lives on a little sticker affixed to the CD's packaging. (If you're reinstalling a version of Windows 7 that came pre-installed on your PC, look for the product key printed on a sticker affixed to the side or back of your PC.)

   Don't select the Automatically Activate Windows When I'm Online check box. You can do that later when you know Windows 7 works on your PC. (You must enter the product key and activate Windows 7 within 30 days of installation; Windows 7 nags you incessantly as the deadline approaches.)

   Write your product key on top of your Windows 7 DVD with a felt-tip pen. (Write on the side of the disc that's *printed.*) That way, you'll always have your valid product key with your disc.

   Windows 7's Activation feature takes a snapshot of your computer's parts and links it with Windows 7's serial number, which prevents you from installing that same copy onto another computer. Unfortunately, the Activation feature may also hassle you if you change a lot of parts in your computer, forcing you to call Microsoft and explain the situation.

7. **Choose Use Recommended Settings.**

   This allows Windows to visit the Internet to update itself with security patches, warn you of suspicious Web sites, check for troubleshooting information, and send technical information to Microsoft to fine-tune Windows' performance.

8. **Confirm the time and date settings and then click Next.**

   Windows 7 usually guesses these correctly.

9. **If you're connected to a network, choose your PC's location.**

   Windows 7 gives you options: Home, Work, or Public.

   If you choose Home or Work, Windows 7 eases up on the security a bit, letting the PCs on the network see each other. If you're in a public setting, though, choose Public. Windows 7 keeps your PC more secure by not letting other PCs share any of its files.

   After rummaging around inside your PC for a few more minutes, Windows 7 appears on the screen, leaving you at the logon screen. But don't rest yet. Run through the following steps to complete the process:

   • **Use Windows Update.** Visit Windows Update, described in Chapter 10, and download any security patches and updated drivers issued by Microsoft.

- **Make sure that Windows 7 recognizes your software.** Run all your old programs to make sure that they still work. You may need to replace them with newer versions. Windows XP upgraders must reinstall all their programs from their original disks.

- **Check the user accounts.** Make sure that your PC's user accounts work correctly.

Welcome to Windows 7!

Installing Windows 7 Over Windows XP

Windows 7 can't directly upgrade a PC running Windows XP. That means if you want to run Windows 7 on your Windows XP PC, you need to follow these series of steps. They're not for the faint-hearted.

1. **Run Windows Easy Transfer on your Windows XP PC.**

   I cover Windows Easy Transfer in Chapter 19. For best results, transfer your files and settings to a portable hard drive that's at least as large as the drive in your Windows XP PC. Then unplug the portable drive and set it aside for later.

2. **Rename your Windows XP drive.**

   This step isn't necessary, but it helps you identify the correct drive a few steps later. Open the Start menu, choose My Computer, and right-click your C drive. Choose Rename, type in **XP**, and press Enter.

   This step helps you recognize your drive later.

3. **Insert the Windows 7 DVD into your DVD drive and restart your PC.**

   Your PC restarts, but loads from the Windows 7 DVD. (You may have to press a key to tell your PC to load from the DVD drive rather than the hard drive.)

4. **Click Next.**

   This tells the program to install everything in English, including menu language, keyboard layout, and currency symbols.

5. **Click the Install Now button.**

6. **Read the License Agreement, select the I Accept the License Terms check box, and click Next.**

7. **Choose Custom (Advanced).**

   If you try the Upgrade option, the program says to load Windows XP and then run the Installation DVD. (And then, when you return to this screen and click Upgrade, it says you can't upgrade directly to Windows 7 from Windows XP.)

The Custom option shows you a window listing your PC's partitions and/or drives.

8. **Click your Windows XP drive, click Drive Options (Advanced), click Format, and click OK to approve the format process. Then click Next.**

   Your Windows XP drive will have the letters XP in its name from Step 2.

   Clicking Format completely erases your copy of Windows XP and all of your information on that partition. There's no going back after you finish this step, so make *sure* you've backed up your Windows XP files in Step 1. After you click Next, Windows 7 begins installing itself on your old Windows XP drive, a process that takes about 10 to 30 minutes on most PCs.

9. **Enter your user name and a name for your PC, and click Next.**

   Feel free to type in the same user name and computer name as you did on your Windows XP PC. Or make up new names, if you prefer.

10. **Type and retype a password, then type a password hint, then click Next.**

    The password hint should be a phrase that reminds you of your password, but doesn't give it away. For example, if your password is the name of your elementary school, the password hint could be, "My first elementary school."

11. **Jump to Step 6 in the previous section, Upgrading from Windows Vista to Windows 7.**

    From here onward, the installation steps are identical to the steps in that section. Except, unfortunately, Windows XP owners must end their Windows 7 installation by reinstalling all their programs from scratch.

A safer way to install Windows 7 over XP

If your Windows XP hard drive is less than half full, take these few extra steps for a safer switch to Windows 7.

In Step 3, insert your Windows 7 DVD but don't restart your PC. Instead, double-click the DVD's Setup file to start the installation process. Choose Go Online to Get the Latest Updates (Recommended), accept the license terms, and click Next.

Then, in Step 8, select your Windows XP partition but don't choose Format. Just click Next. As Windows 7 installs itself, it saves your PC's old XP files in a folder called windows.old, which can be retrieved by a repair shop should something go horribly awry. If the installation goes fine, however, delete the windows.old folder to give Windows 7 more room.

Index